LATIN AMERICAN POLITICAL ECONOMY
Financial Crisis and Political Change

About the Book and Editors

Faced with an explosion of foreign debt, falling export prices, and rising real interest rates, Latin American countries have experienced in recent years a dramatic worsening in their economic prospects and policy options. This volume of original essays considers the major historical and contemporary determinants of the development crisis facing Latin America from a political economy perspective and compares the effects of and responses to the crisis in a number of countries. Contributors examine the importance of external and internal factors in the debt crisis, discuss the internal policy errors that led to recent financial "blowups" in Mexico, Brazil, Argentina, and Chile, and relate earlier experiences of populist and postpopulist politics to general patterns of economic policymaking in Latin America. The next part is devoted to individual country studies. The "spectacular failures" of Peru and the bureaucratic-authoritarian regimes of the Southern Cone are contrasted to the moderate successes of Mexico and Colombia, and the cases of socialist Cuba and Nicaragua are examined. Each of the country studies discusses the economic and policy record that has led to the current crisis and describes the political and economic context in which policy choices were made.

At the end of the book comments by eminent scholars are included to provide a broader context in which to consider the issues raised. Alternative, or even opposing, points of view expressed in the commentaries encourage discussion of the often difficult questions and problems posed by the contributors. Taken together, the essays and the commentaries offer an unusually current and comprehensive view of what is happening in Latin America. They allow the student and scholar to compare policy responses in different countries, understand the political and economic constraints facing policymakers, and evaluate prospects for the future.

Jonathan Hartlyn is assistant professor of political science, and **Samuel A. Morley** is professor of economics at Vanderbilt University. Both have written extensively on economic and political problems in Latin America.

LATIN AMERICAN
POLITICAL ECONOMY
Financial Crisis and Political Change

edited by Jonathan Hartlyn
and Samuel A. Morley

Westview Press / Boulder and London

Chapter 6 by Marcelo Diamand has been previously published in Spanish.

Published in 1986 in the United States of America by Westview Press, Inc.; Frederick A. Praeger, Publisher; 5500 Central Avenue, Boulder, Colorado 80301

Library of Congress Cataloging-in-Publication Data
Latin American political economy.
  Includes index.
  1. Latin America—Economic policy. 2. Debts, External
—Latin America. 3. Latin America—Politics and
government—1948–   I. Hartlyn, Jonathan.
II. Morley, Samuel A.
HC125.L3525 1986   338.98   86-7733
ISBN 0-8133-0329-X (alk. paper)
ISBN 0-8133-0330-3 (pbk.: alk. paper)

Printed and bound in the United States of America

∞ The paper used in this publication meets the requirements of the American National Standard for Permanence of Paper for Printed Library Materials Z39.48-1984.

10   9   8   7   6   5   4   3   2   1

Contents

Part 3
Commentaries 351

A

B

C

D

Tables

Acknowledgments

Many of the papers in this book were first presented at the International Conference on Models of Political and Economic Change in Latin America held at Vanderbilt University in November 1983 under the sponsorship of the Center for Latin American and Iberian Studies (CLAIS) at Vanderbilt, the Universidad de los Andes (Bogotá, Colombia), and the Fundação Instituto de Pesquisas Econômicas, Universidade de São Paulo (Brazil). A generous grant from the Tinker Foundation; additional assistance from the Rockefeller Foundation, the Exxon Foundation, the Inter-American Foundation, and the Vanderbilt University Research Council; and the able support and encouragement of Professor Enrique Pupo-Walker, director of CLAIS, are gratefully acknowledged.

In addition to the authors and commentators whose papers appear in this book, a number of other scholars also participated in the conference sessions and made valuable comments. These were Bruce Bagley, Fernando Cepeda Ulloa, David Collier, James Lang, Roberto Macedo, Kevin Middlebrook, John Sheahan, Alfred Stepan, and J. Samuel Valenzuela. We also thank Eliseo Da Rosa, Roberto González Echevarría, and Marshall Eakin. The conference was facilitated by the administrative wizardry of Caroline Naifeh. The research assistance of Andy Morrison and Ken Ellinger and the expert typing of Nancy Latham under difficult conditions helped bring this volume to print.

Jonathan Hartlyn
Samuel A. Morley

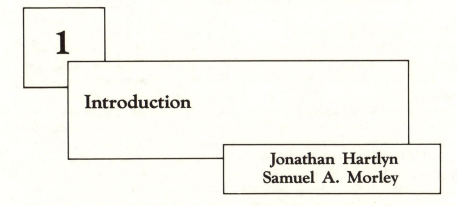

1

Introduction

Jonathan Hartlyn
Samuel A. Morley

Latin America is currently confronting its worst financial and economic crisis since the Great Depression. Despite a wide variety of policies and economic conditions, every country on the continent has a balance-of-payments problem and a crippling level of external indebtedness, and each has been forced into recession as it struggles to meet the interest payments on its debt. This grim economic picture is a new phenomenon. Prior to the 1980s, the post–World War II period had been a prosperous one for Latin America. On average, from 1950 to 1980, per capita income on the continent grew by 2.4 percent per year, and from 1960 to 1980, life expectancy increased by ten years, in a context of very rapid population growth. Not surprisingly, Latin America was considered by many economists to be an example of successful long-run development.

If the 1980s have been devastating to Latin America in an economic sense, they have at the same time witnessed a retreat from military authoritarianism. Since 1980, military regimes have relinquished power in Argentina, Uruguay, Brazil, Peru, Ecuador, El Salvador, Panama, Honduras, and Bolivia. In a way, this situation is ironic. Social scientists used to think that economic growth would lead to improved social conditions that would be conducive to democracy. But during the 1960s and 1970s, many civilian regimes, including those in the most advanced countries, were overthrown by military coups. The growth-democracy view was replaced by the conviction that the conditions required for economic growth—particularly wage restraint, profit incentives, and high levels of saving and investment—could not be guaranteed in a democracy but would require instead a long period of institutionalized military rule. Yet recent events have demonstrated that the military regimes in Argentina, Brazil, Chile, and Uruguay have shown themselves to be no better, and in most cases worse, than the civilian regimes they replaced in generating satisfactory and noninflationary long-run growth rates. Their poor economic performance is one of the main factors why the military has stepped down from power in so many countries. It is, of course, too early to tell whether the successor civilian regimes will be able to resolve the severe economic problems that the military regimes left behind, or whether the civilian regimes will be able to consolidate themselves politically.

A natural and common theme of the chapters in this book is the question of what went wrong. How did so many countries, employing such a variety of economic strategies, end up in a similar mess? What mistakes did they make, and why did they make them? Was economic theory deficient or poorly implemented? What role did external events— largely beyond the control of Latin policymakers—play in causing the current crisis? Did political pressures force governments knowingly to adopt unwise economic policies? Did certain kinds of regimes, notably those less subject to populist pressures or those less linked to the international financial system, perform better?

These issues are important ones. Practically all the countries in Latin America are aligned with the West and have bet their economic futures on its capitalist market economy and its international trading and financial system. Prior to 1980, that decision looked like a wise one. Latin America and Asian countries such as Taiwan and Korea were economic success stories. In the current crisis conditions, there will inevitably and appropriately be many people in Latin America who will question the wisdom of the development choices that were made and the advisability of continuing unchanged along the same course. We in the United States would be wise to try to understand the grave difficulties of our southern neighbors and their thoughts about how the crisis happened and what they should do about it. We hope these pages will help develop such awareness and comprehension.

In the chapters that follow, the authors (all but one of whom are from the country about which they write) review their country's economic and political history and look for answers to current problems in the policies and politics of the past. In addition, the four overview essays in Part 1 compare different country experiences and draw some important policy conclusions, and the commentaries in Part 3 give additional perspective on the issues raised in the essays. A short summary of each chapter follows.

Part 1

The four chapters in Part 1 provide comparative perspectives. In the first, Jonathan Hartlyn and Samuel Morley give an overview of different political regimes and their economic performances, and in the second, they analyze the performance of the bureaucratic-authoritarian (B-A) regimes in Argentina, Chile, and Brazil. They argue that the poor economic performance of these regimes was no better than the performance of the civilian regimes they replaced or of the other Latin American civilian regimes of the 1970s. They present three major factors whose interaction helps explain this phenomenon. First, even disregarding the social cost to vast population sectors in these countries, the version of international monetarism applied by the regimes—especially their decisions to prefix the exchange rate and drive up internal interest rates—had disastrous results. Inflation did not decline as predicted, and the increasingly overvalued currency hurt industry particularly. The difficulties of the policies were hidden by a massive influx of foreign funds until world interest rates increased suddenly and sharply. The second factor that helps explain the disastrous performance of these regimes was the absence of any international constraints to their policies as, until the dramatic change in 1981–1982, foreign commercial banks were eagerly lending to a variety of countries and were particularly attracted to these political regimes.

The third factor, of particular relevance for Chile and Argentina, was the total absence of a domestic political constraint, which almost certainly allowed the regimes to apply their radical free-market policies far longer than they would otherwise have been able to do. In Chile and Argentina, the presumed "benefits" of the invulnerability of military regimes to political pressures were far more disastrous economically than the vulnerability of civilian regimes. The Brazilian B-A regime, no longer able to justify its existence on the basis of a populist "threat," sought foreign loans in an attempt to continue strong growth and thus legitimacy during its uncertain process of political liberalization. Chapter 3 ends with a brief consideration of the relationship of these B-A regimes to broader historical processes that suggest these regimes have appeared in Latin American countries with "pendular" economic and political patterns. In contrast, governments in other countries have pursued more "moderate" patterns.

In Chapter 4, Albert Fishlow compares the adjustments of various countries to the oil shocks of 1973 and 1979. For 1973, two broad patterns stand out. One was a reliance on external finance and import substitution or export promotion to sustain relatively high rates of growth; the other was acceptance of lower income growth rates to curb imports along with efforts to increase exports. Brazil, Korea, and Mexico—each relatively large and with a history of successful import substitution and/or export promotion—followed the first broad pattern. Chile, Taiwan, and Singapore—being smaller and having more open economies—followed the second.

Albert Fishlow then turns to an analysis of the current crisis and its roots in the 1979 oil shock. Up to 1980, the adjustment to the shock appeared to be satisfactory. However, conditions swiftly deteriorated as a worldwide recession drove down the demand for Latin exports and cut off the supply of credit as sharply higher interest rates raised the cost of foreign debt. The result was a balance-of-payments crisis that forced every economy on the continent into a severe contraction.

Although the results were similar across countries, Albert Fishlow shows that the causes of the crisis were quite different in each country. In Mexico, excess aggregate demand, fed by rapid expansion of the public sector and the oil bonanza, was the key culprit. In Brazil, rising oil prices and the "scissors effect" of high interest costs and a falling export demand explain nearly all of that country's subsequent balance-of-payments problems. In contrast Chile's domestic policy errors, which encouraged a rapid accumulation of foreign debt without a comparable increase in total saving, were responsible for its balance-of-payments crisis of 1982 and beyond.

Austerity programs are being applied just as many countries are seeking redemocratization. Despite the appeal of populist solutions, Fishlow argues that there is a widespread realization in Latin America that export promotion and greater internal sacrifice will be necessary to improve the situation. These measures can be accepted, but only if there is an equal sense of flexibility on the part of the external lenders, particularly a willingness to extend debt repayment schedules, allow increases in imports to developed countries, and explore ways to lower the interest burden.

In Chapter 5, David Felix analyzes the financial "blowups" that resulted from the neoliberal policies followed by the bureaucratic-authoritarian regimes in Argentina, Chile, and Uruguay and the state-directed policies adopted in Brazil and Mexico. Despite their promise and early success, all of these five economies have been overwhelmed by economic crisis since 1982. David Felix seeks to explain why. He asserts that in the neoliberal economies, the main cause was the prefixed exchange rate and excessive capital inflows in the 1979–1981 period. Basically, the capital inflows permitted an increasingly serious overvaluation of the exchange rate, which caused large current account deficits and a shift away from the domestic production of tradable goods. Firms were confronted by a killing combination of high real interest rates and low-priced foreign goods, and many went deeply into debt, much of which was denominated in dollars and was unserviceable when the exchange rate overvaluation was finally corrected. The result was a downward spiral of bankruptcies, falling output, and reduced employment. A full-fledged financial collapse was averted only by belated government intervention.

Financial difficulties were also central in Mexico's road to crisis. The shift to "shared development" under Luis Echeverría Alvarez in 1970 and the oil bonanza under José López Portillo dramatically increased public sector deficits and borrowing requirements. Inflation increased, and there were massive current account deficits and large increases in public foreign borrowing, much of which was offset by private capital flight. When oil prices began to decline in 1981, foreign credit dried up, and Mexico was forced to accept a severe stabilization policy.

Brazil's story is different. Like Fishlow, Felix does not believe financial crisis and capital flight are the main culprits in this case. In the 1970s, Brazil followed a capital-intensive growth strategy that was largely financed by external borrowing, not internal saving. After the second oil shock hit, large balance-of-payments deficits resulted from the scissors effect of high interest rates, lower export receipts, and high oil prices. When further international credit was shut off in 1982, Brazil was forced to accept a stringent International Monetary Fund (IMF) stabilization plan.

Part 2

Part 2 examines "spectacular failures" and "moderate successes" in a number of country case studies, the first of which is the tragic case of Argentina. Marcelo Diamand argues that for decades, Argentine economic performance has been harmed by government economic policies that have swung like a pendulum between the orthodox and the populist, neither of which is capable of generating sustained growth in an economy that has an unbalanced productive structure. Argentine industry is intrinsically neither more nor less efficient than industry in other countries. Its problem is that it coexists with the most productive agricultural sector in the world and cannot compete internationally at the exchange rate determined by the agricultural sector.

In the past, populist, Keynesian-type policymakers took office after a bout of orthodox stabilization left the country with a high level of foreign reserves. The populists expanded demand, and the country enjoyed a period of rapid economic growth. But there was little effort to increase exports—indeed, agricultural prices were generally held below production costs because of the political importance of food prices—and the country soon exhausted its foreign exchange reserves. The government then turned to foreign exchange controls, which caused capital flight, shortages of essential imports, and finally a balance-of-payments crisis with rising inflation.

The crisis brought to power an orthodox-minded government whose program typically consisted of a contractionary monetary and fiscal policy coupled with an abrupt devaluation. The balance of payments improved temporarily simply because of the recession, but there was little resource switching into traded goods because industrial products were not even close to the margin of competitiveness. Meanwhile, the rising relative price of traded goods and declining real wages caused workers and the industrial sector to fight back, leading to a period of rising inflation that eroded the initial change in relative prices. In recent years, the orthodox governments have also relied on high interest rates and foreign borrowing to compensate for the failure to improve the balance of trade. Capital inflows have permitted devaluations to lag behind internal inflation, but the cost has been a widening of the current account deficit, mounting foreign debt, and widespread bankruptcy of domestic industry due to the overvalued exchange rate.

Diamand argues that the new Alfonsín government should design a new program based on the following principles: (1) the promotion of industrial exports through a system that amounts essentially to multiple exchange rates; (2) the promotion of agricultural exports by a devaluation accompanied by a tax on land; (3) selective import substitution; and (4) the avoidance of excessive dependence on short-term financial capital to solve foreign exchange problems.

The Bolivar Lamounier and Alkimar R. Moura chapter is an account of the relationship between the way in which Brazil confronted its principal economic challenges, the two oil shocks of 1973 and 1979, and its main political problem of how to move from the highly repressive structure inherited from the Medici administration to a more representative and open political system. In partial contrast to Albert Fishlow and David Felix, the authors of this chapter argue that the country should have accepted an economic slowdown and a real adjustment to less favorable conditions well before 1980.

They decisively reject the hypothesis that the delay in adjustment was dictated by populist political pressures. Despite the political liberalization that occurred under Ernesto Geisel (1974–1979), opposition leaders posed no effective threat to the technocrats directing policy. Rather, government leaders underestimated the seriousness of the external constraints in part because they were sensitive to the political importance of maintaining high rates of economic growth, their principal source of continuing legitimacy.

Politically, the process of liberalization was too gradual and hesitant. Never willing or able to create a viable political party of the center, the Geisel government failed to form a solid basis of support for a more realistic policy of adjustment to external shocks. In 1979, an amnesty for political prisoners, the return of political exiles, and other liberalizing measures created the impression that the country was in a clear transition to democracy. But in the following year municipal elections were postponed, and a period of political turmoil and paralysis ensued. The transition to a civilian government was finally managed by means of a broad alliance of the main opposition party and the Liberal Front, a new political movement made up of dissidents of the former government party. The question now is whether the process of liberalization can continue in the context of orthodox stabilization under the unfavorable external conditions now facing Brazil.

Manuel Antonio Garretón explores the likelihood of a possible transition to democracy in Chile by analyzing the central characteristics of that country's prior democracy, the causes of its collapse, and the major sociopolitical transformations that have taken place under the military regime. Prior to 1973, the political party system served as the "backbone" of Chilean society and as the main arena for integrating social groups and mediating their demands. The state played a central role in the development process and successfully integrated the middle class and the organized working class into the political system. The political exclusion of the peasantry and the urban poor and the continued foreign ownership of the country's basic resource, copper, were the central unresolved issues of the 1960s when the system began to break down.

The right began to lose legitimacy after the Alessandri regime was defeated. The Radicals, the main party of the center, lost ground to the Christian Democrats, who tended to polarize the political system because of their messianic rhetoric and their emphasis on agrarian reform and changes in the capitalist system to make it more beneficial to workers and society. Finally, economic chaos and the extreme polarization of society, which was characterized by a mobilization of the masses on the one side and the ruling and middle classes on the other during the Allende years, provoked the military to intervene.

The Pinochet regime that came to power in 1973 sought to transform the social, economic, and political systems by means of brutal repression and radical free-market economics. Yet the facts that elements of the preceding political system remained—particularly the political parties—and the church began to replace the lost political forums made it difficult for the regime to realize its designs. These disintegrated with the final collapse of the economic model in 1981–1982. This defeat left the military regime with no program other than to fight for its own survival within the restrictive framework imposed by the constitution of 1980.

Regardless of the economic problems of Chile and the latent opposition to the military, Garretón feels that a forced overthrow of the regime is unlikely. Rather, the problem is how to induce the military to step aside voluntarily. To accomplish this change, a way must be found to unite the center and the left into a broad political force in favor of redemocratization. Unfortunately, even should a democratic regime reappear, its long-run prospects are precarious, because of the economic crisis, which leaves little room to satisfy repressed economic demands, and because of a cautious acceptance of democracy by the urban masses and middle-sector groups and limited support for it within the armed forces. Ultimately, any future political democracy will be defeated by conservative forces unless a sociopolitical majority of the center and of the left, combining political democracy and social change, can be formed.

Since 1980, the economic performance of Peru has been one of the worst in Latin America. Daniel M. Schydlowsky's basic hypothesis is that to a significant extent, Peru's current problems are the result of a series of avoidable policy errors, many involving an unwillingness to nurture nontraditional industrial exports. Like other Latin American countries, Peru's basic development policy has been based on import-substituting industrialization (ISI). The fundamental error has been that Peru has developed an industrial sector much of which can survive only with high levels of protection, even though experience at the end of the 1970s demonstrated that with supportive government policy, it could have become more internationally competitive and export oriented. Peru's problem has been compounded by the same sort of unbalanced productive structure that Diamond describes for Argentina. Peru's industry generally cannot compete with low-cost copper, oil, and other raw material exports without a supportive government policy. The result, as in Argentina, has been a "pendular" series of balance-of-payments crises, each of which has been followed by orthodox stabilization.

The situation since 1979 has been particularly unfortunate. In 1975, there was a balance-of-payments crisis that led to an orthodox stabilization and an unorthodox and successful effort to promote nontraditional industrial exports. However, in 1979 the government, convinced that the raw materials boom was permanent, gave up the effort of supporting nontraditional exports.

There was also a complementary policy error. The authorities, particularly the technocrats of the new Belaúnde administration installed in 1980, were convinced that Peru's inflation problem was one of excess demand, controllable by limiting the growth rate of money. Since international reserves add to the domestic money supply, the authorities were determined to "burn up" those reserves by increasing imports. The result was widespread destruction of both industrial production and export capacity. Subsequently, when the export boom collapsed in 1982, Peru was confronted with a new foreign exchange crisis that was more virulent than any that had preceded it, and the country went into the crisis with an industrial sector severely weakened by the anti-industrial policy of the previous years.

José Ayala and Clemente Ruiz Durán argue that throughout the postwar period, Mexico has failed to find an internal self-generating growth strategy. Plagued by a backward agricultural sector, an underdeveloped capital goods industry, and a very unequal distribution of income and wealth, Mexico's development tends to be driven primarily by external forces such as oil exports. As a result, development since 1970 has been characterized by a series of stop-and-go cycles, each of which has corresponded to a six-year presidential term. The Echeverría cycle (1970–1976) was based on the idea of shared or equitable development. Public welfare expenditures and the government deficit were both sharply increased, which led to higher growth and inflation and then to a balance-of-payments crisis in 1976. López Portillo (1976–1982) was forced to impose an IMF-approved stabilization program.

During the first years of the López government, there was a debate about the appropriate way to develop the oil industry. Nationalists wanted a gradual expansion of oil exports because they were worried that Mexican industry could never compete with imports at the exchange rate that would result from the implied rapid growth of oil exports. Their opponents, who won the debate, wanted to expand oil production as fast as possible and use the proceeds to eliminate the balance-of-payments deficit. Nationalist fears turned out to be well founded. There was an oil-financed spending spree in 1978–1981. The public sector deficit rose from 6.7 percent of the gross national product (GNP) in 1977 to 17.6 percent in 1982, which triggered a boom in the economy, but the situation was dangerously dependent on external events. Much of the rise in oil revenues was dissipated by a binge of importing, which both exacerbated the balance-of-payments deficit and limited the stimulus to domestic manufacturing. When the world went into recession in 1981, oil prices fell and foreign credit suddenly dried up. In 1982, Mexico was forced into a stabilization-induced recession under the watchful eye of the IMF that was far more severe than the one in 1976. José Ayala and Clemente Ruiz Durán conclude with a call for a longer-range development strategy in which the government would assume the role of "developer of last resort," directing investment resources toward the development of articles of mass consumption and encouraging a shift in the Mexican economy toward rapid and self-sustaining growth rather than a continuation of stop-and-go cycles.

Although noting that Colombia is currently undergoing a serious economic and political crisis, Edgar Revéiz and María José Pérez believe that the central elements of Colombian development in the past several decades have been continuity and moderation. Colombia has obtained better results in reaching economic, social, and political goals than many Latin American countries, without sacrificing economic growth. They discuss three background factors that helped establish this pattern. The first is the importance of the country's major export product, coffee, and the fact that the coffee sector has unparalleled access to the state. The second is the country's two-party system. With the establishment of the coalition National Front in 1958, party conflict over control of the state apparatus was eliminated, which, though at the cost of political exclusion of new economic and social forces, provided for stability. The third has been the country's relatively balanced regional development.

The authors consider the trends of economic diversification and modernization of the state in the period from 1950 to 1970, during which time international financial agencies as well as the coffee sector had the most influence over economic policy. Under Carlos Lleras (1966–1970), a framework was created that facilitated a partial shift to a model of export promotion, diversified the economy, and strengthened the political system by making it more difficult for any one group to assume a hegemonic role. However, problems such as the Congress's loss of power, the failure of agrarian reform, the lack of redistribution of income to poorer groups, and the emergence of new political groups have meant that the more recent period has been one of less political stability.

The changing development emphases during the 1970s and early 1980s have focused on urban construction and the public sector itself as "leading sectors." The unexpected coffee and drug bonanza of the 1970s led the López government (1974–1978) to cut back on progressive public investments in order to seek to stabilize the economy. Prudent management of the country's reserves during this period was a key factor in the country's relatively good current debt situation. However, a sharp industrial recession has recently engulfed the financial sector in a serious crisis. The Betancur government (1982–1986) confronts the challenge of managing the country's most serious economic situation in decades even as it strives to create a new political consensus in the country to fortify Colombia's political democracy and improve its economic prospects.

Carmelo Mesa Lago's chapter focuses on Cuba's poor economic performance as measured by the country's growth rate, labor productivity, and ability to generate savings and investment or the growth and diversity of exports. The author argues that these problems have been largely due to domestic policy choices. These poor results have been counterbalanced by the country's best indicators of income equality and social development in Latin America, including reductions in unemployment and improvements in health and literacy. Revolutionary Cuba has consciously traded growth for greater equity.

In spite of an enormous effort to diversify the economy and exports and to industrialize, Cuba remains basically a monoculture economy. Sugar continues to generate about one-fourth of the country's global social product (GSP) and over 80 percent of export revenues, more than before the revolution. Cuba's cycles of rapid and slow growth are closely related to the price of sugar. Unlike any other Latin American country, the share of industry has actually shrunk since the revolution.

The failure to significantly expand and diversify production and exports, combined with ambitious social programs and population growth, has provoked an economic disequilibrium, which is most clearly evident in foreign trade. Cuba has run a negative trade balance every year except two since the revolution, and this deficit is rising in absolute value, despite the fact that a great deal of Cuba's trade is subsidized by the Soviet Union. To complicate matters, Mesa Lago argues there are indications that the Soviets may be increasingly less willing to continue to subsidize the Cuban economy.

Elizabeth Dore's chapter examines the record of Nicaragua's economy since the Sandinistas came to power in 1979. A central argument is that three background factors are fundamental to an understanding of the country's economy in the contemporary period. One is the history of U.S. intervention and the nature of the Somoza family dynasty that ruled Nicaragua for more than forty years with U.S. support. The second is the nature and extent of domestic opposition to the Somoza regime— spanning business, middle, labor, peasant, urban, and church sectors. The last is the magnitude of the economic destruction and social dislocation that occurred during the insurrection against Somoza. When the Sandinistas came to power in 1979, over one-fourth of the country's industrial capacity and about one year of the country's GNP had been lost. Over 2.5 percent of the population over fifteen had been killed, and Somoza and his cronies had fled the country with most of its foreign exchange reserves.

In examining the record of the Sandinistas as they attempted economic reconstruction (1979–1982) and then as they dealt with war and external aggression (1983–1985), Dore notes that their economic strategy followed no set model but emerged from certain basic commitments and day-to-day management of economic problems. Although there was agreement on the confiscation of Somoza's properties, on a greater role for the state in the economy, and that special priority should be given to social and economic equity, there were internal discussions regarding the appropriate type of land reform, how much of industry to nationalize, and how to induce the private sector to invest and produce. The economic system that emerged was far more moderate than that in Cuba. By the end of 1982, about 40 percent of GNP was being generated by the public sector, which is estimated to own no more than one-third of industrial and agricultural assets, shares not much higher than those in other Latin countries.

During the first two years of the current regime (1979–1981), the economy was recovering well from the civil war. However in 1982, the expansion came to a halt, and Nicaragua faced a very severe balance-of-payments problem. Remarkably though, its growth record since 1981 has been better than that of most other Latin American countries. Furthermore, Dore argues, its problems are not largely attributable to the choice of economic policies by the government or to the efficiency with which they were implemented, although both could be faulted. In addition to low prices, reduced international demand for the country's primary products, and problems related to debt payments, trade imbalances, and fiscal deficits common to most Latin American countries, Nicaragua has also had to confront the U.S. economic boycott and to finance a defense effort against U.S.-backed contras. Past U.S. actions have polarized the views of business people and leaders of the Sandinista National Liberation Front (FSLN) alike, making internal accommodation increasingly more difficult.

Part 1
Historical and Comparative Perspectives

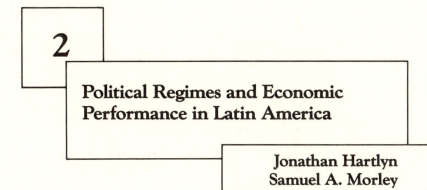

2

Political Regimes and Economic Performance in Latin America

Jonathan Hartlyn
Samuel A. Morley

Political Regimes

A country's political regime refers to the structures of a government's roles and processes, including such issues as the basis for legitimacy of rule, patterns of leadership recruitment, mechanisms of representation, and particular forms of domination and control (see Collier 1979:402–403; Cardoso 1979:38). A complementary way of conceptualizing a regime is to view it as a pattern of policymaking (see Chalmers and Robinson 1982:11). A lack of agreement on the most appropriate way to classify political regimes in Latin America stems, in part, from the facts that many political institutions in Latin America are fragile and that there is often a large gap between formally stated regime procedures, or citizen rights, and actual implementation by political regimes. It would also appear that among the most important political and social actors, there is acceptance of a wide variety of political regimes; thus, support for an existing regime or for a new one is often conditional on regime performance in economic and control issues (Chalmers and Robinson 1982:7–8).

Some analysts have drawn a distinction between the political regime and the state, though there are significant differences among authors regarding their specific usages of the terms. For our purposes, the term *state* will refer to the administrative, legal, coercive, and other institutions and systems that encompass the public sector. As such, to employ Cardoso's terminology, it encompasses a basic alliance or "pact of domination" of certain social classes or parts of social classes (Cardoso 1979:38). At this level of abstraction, there appear to be some basic similarities among Latin American countries, particularly those at similar levels of development, in regard to the major social groups that form part of the dominant coalition supporting the state and to the general patterns of international and domestic actors that influence state policy. For all the countries discussed in this book except Cuba and in certain respects Nicaragua, state rule involves issues of altering or transforming

15

Table 2.1

POLITICAL REGIME TYPES AND HEADS OF GOVERNMENT[1]

Political Regime	Power Transfer[2]	Head of Government
		ARGENTINA
Military moderator	c	Eduardo Lonardi (Sept.-Nov. 1955)
	c	Pedro Eugenio Aramburu (1955-1958)
Semicompetitive	e	Arturo Frondizi (1958-1962)
Military-civilian moderator	c	José María Guido (1962-1963)
Semicompetitive	e	Arturo Illia (1963-1966)
Bureaucratic-authoritarian	c	Juan Carlos Onganía (1966-1970)
	c	Roberto Levingston (1970-1971)
Military-transitional	c	Alejandro Lanusse (1971-1973)
Competitive	e	Héctor Cámpora (May-July 1973)
Semicompetitive	e	Juan Perón (1973-1974)
	s	Isabel Perón (1974-1976)
Bureaucratic-authoritarian	c	Jorge Videla (1976-1981)
	c	Roberto Viola (March-Dec. 1981)
	c	Leopoldo Galtieri (1981-1982)
	c	Reynaldo Bignone (1982-1983)
Competitive	e	Raul Alfonsín (1983-)
		BRAZIL
Semicompetitive	e	Juscelino Kubitschek (1956-1961)
	e	Jânio Quadros (Jan-Aug. 1961)
Transitional	s	Ranieri Mazzilli (Aug.-Sept. 1961)
Semicompetitive	s	João Goulart (1961-1964)
Transitional	c	Ranieri Mazzilli (Aug.-Sept. 1964)
Bureaucratic-authoritarian	c	Humberto Castello Branco (1964-1967)
	s	Artur da Costa e Silva (1967-1969)
	s	Military junta (Aug.-Oct. 1969)
	s	Emilio Garrastazu Medici (1969-1974)
	s	Ernesto Geisel (1974-1979)
	s	João Baptista Figueiredo (1979-1985)
Semicompetitive	s	José Sarney (1985-)
		CHILE
Competitive	e	Carlos Ibáñez del Campo (1952-1958)
	e	Jorge Alessandri Rodriguez (1958-1964)
	e	Eduardo Frei Montalva (1964-1970)
	e	Salvador Allende Gossens (1970-1973)
Bureaucratic-authoritarian	c	Augusto Pinochet Ugarte (1973-)

COLOMBIA

Military moderator-populist	c	Gustavo Rojas Pinilla (1953-1957)
Military transitional	c	Military junta (1957-1958)
Semicompetitive	e	Alberto Lleras Camargo (1958-1962)
	e	Guillermo León Valencia (1962-1966)
	e	Carlos Lleras Restrepo (1966-1970)
	e	Misael Pastrana (1970-1974)
	e	Alfonso López Michelsen (1974-1978)
	e	Julio César Turbay Ayala (1978-1982)
	e	Belisario Betancur Cuartas (1982-)

CUBA

Traditional	c	Fulgencio Batista (1952-1959)
Socialist mobilizational	r	Fidel Castro (de facto, 1959-)

MEXICO

Semicompetitive	e	Adolfo López Mateos (1958-1964)
	e	Gustavo Díaz Ordaz (1964-1970)
	e	Luis Echeverría Alvarez (1970-1976)
	e	José López Portillo (1976-1982)
	e	Miguel de la Madrid Hurtado (1982-)

NICARAGUA

Traditional	e	Luis Somoza Debayle (1956-1963)
	e	René Schick Gutiérrez (1963-1966)
	s	Lorenzo Guerrero Gutiérrez (1966-1967)
	s	Anastasio Somoza Debayle (1967-1972)
	s	Triumvirate for Somozas (1972-1974)
	s	Anastasio Somoza Debayle (1974-1979)
Socialist mobilizational	r	FSLN Joint National Directorate (1979-1985)
Socialist mobilizational	e	Daniel Ortega Saavedra (1985-)

PERU

Military moderator-populist	c	Manual A. Odría (1950-1956)
Semicompetitive	e	Manuel Prado y Ugarteche (1956-1962)
Military moderator	c	Military junta (1962-1963)
	s	Nicolás Lindley López (March-July 1963)
Semicompetitive	e	Fernando Belaúnde Terry (1963-1968)
Military populist	c	Juan Velasco Alvarado (1968-1975)
	c	Francisco Morales Bermudez (1975-1980)
Semicompetitive	e	Fernando Belaúnde Terry (1980-1985)
	e	Alan García (1985-)

---

[1]Current as of August 1985.

[2]Change in head of government: e, national election; c, coup; s, other scheduled change; r, revolutionary change.

Sources: Thomas E. Skidmore and Peter A. Smith, Modern Latin America (New York and Oxford: Oxford University Press, 1984), esp. pp. 388-394, and Martin C. Needler, An Introduction to Latin American Politics (Englewood Cliffs, N.J.:   Prentice-Hall, 1983).

capitalism domestically while still essentially maintaining it. States may also be compared with regard to their autonomy from domestic social groups and from specific international actors such as other states, international financial institutions, or major firms. Similarly, their capacity to influence world market forces may vary, although most Latin American states are rather limited in their capacity to affect this factor, which is so crucial to their own development efforts.

A variety of political regimes are possible for similar kinds of states. Since changes in political regimes lead to modifications in political structures, they often can have significant consequences in terms of political liberties and respect for human rights. Regime changes also lead to changes in the ways policies are determined, which may or may not in turn lead to changes in the substance of the policies themselves. Thus, regime changes can be but are not inevitably associated with changes in economic and social policy and with the resultant distributional consequences. Indeed, similar kinds of political regimes, or the same regime through time, may pursue very different economic and social policies.

Table 2.1 lists the political regimes of a number of Latin American countries, providing information on the heads of government and the means by which they came to office. The table builds upon a basic distinction between democratic, or competitive, and authoritarian regimes. To paraphrase one of the generally accepted procedural definitions of democratic rule by Juan J. Linz, three criteria are important: (1) the right to free association, free speech, and associated rights; (2) the requirement that a country's leaders compete in elections for periodic validation of their claim to govern; and (3) the ability of all citizens in the country to effectively participate.[1] Authoritarian regimes can be viewed as those that fail to meet these basic criteria.[2]

Another way of distinguishing the two basic kinds of regimes is to contrast their different impacts on patterns of policymaking. Thus, competitive regimes tend to be more pluralistic and to encourage more points of view and greater and more diverse information in the policy process than authoritarian ones. Democratic regimes control political dissidence more by the use of generally accepted legal procedures than by repression, and decisions are generally made through institutions formally assigned such responsibility by means of recognized procedures rather than simply by the top leader or leaders (see Chalmers and Robinson 1982:15).

To some extent, democratic and authoritarian regimes may be viewed as forming part of a continuum, with each of the two types containing one or more subtypes of particular relevance to Latin America and to the country cases discussed in this book. The goal here is not to attempt a fully comprehensive typology of political regimes but to present an initial classi- fication of regimes and governments that will be helpful to readers. Thus, Table 2.1 categorizes regimes as competitive, semicompetitive, or one of six different kinds of authoritarian regimes: traditional, military moderator, bureaucratic-authoritarian, military populist, transitional (a caretaker regime between military and civilian regimes), and socialist mobilizational.

Competitive or semicompetitive regimes have often alternated with authoritarian regimes in Latin America, and democratic norms continue to retain ideological strength and legitimacy on the continent. As Table 2.1 suggests, regime oscillations have been especially apparent in Argentina, Brazil, and Peru. Chile (and Uruguay) had been governed by institutionalized democratic regimes for many decades. That these regimes eventually succumbed to brutal military rule has certainly been one of the most dramatic and tragic transformations on the continent, forcing scholars to rethink the interrelationships among economic growth, democratic rule, and development. Regime changes in these countries have often been associated with abrupt, pendular shifts in economic policies.

Of the countries analyzed in Part 2 of this book, only one, Colombia, might be said to have retained a form of competitive rule for most of the contemporary period under consideration. Yet, because the country has been governed by a coalition rule of the two major parties, Liberal and Conservative, initially under the very restrictive conditions of the National Front (1958–1974), the regime is best considered semicompetitive, a limited democratic consociational regime (see Dix 1980; Hartlyn 1985). The nature of Colombia's political regime appears to be a significant factor in explaining the fact that changes in the country's economic policies have been moderate through time rather than abrupt. Other countries, such as Argentina, have been ruled at times by civilian regimes that can also be labeled semicompetitive because the rights of certain groups in society were forcibly limited as the military played a powerful role behind the visible arena of politics.

For our purposes, particularly as we later will contrast the economic performance of civilian and military regimes, we also consider Mexico to be a semicompetitive regime, though it might more accurately be labeled a liberal authoritarian one. In Mexico, the regime and the ruling party, Institutional Revolutionary Party (Partido Revolucionario Institucional, PRI), have a basis of legitimacy stemming from the experience of the Mexican revolution. The PRI has been able to resolve the issue of leadership succession, and the scope of political control has been fairly extensive, employing a mixture of co-optation (often by corporatist mechanisms of state penetration and control over major interest groups, especially organized labor) and occasionally repression. Opposition parties and groups regularly compete in elections, but the PRI is a hegemonic party. Certain upper-class and middle-class groups experience considerably more autonomy and freedom than popular sector groups.[3]

Authoritarian regimes have historically been among the most common on the continent. Traditional authoritarian regimes have been personalistic, with the leader often possessing a base within the military, as was the case with Fulgencio Batista in Cuba. Sometimes, these regimes have transformed themselves into family dynasties, as occurred with Nicaragua under the Somozas. Throughout the twentieth century, several countries in Latin America—including Argentina, Brazil, and Peru—have had military coups d'etat in which the military assumed power briefly to depose the head of government, often in anticipation of or as a result of an electoral victory by a threatening political movement. These "moderator" or "guardian" coups,[4] however, were replaced by a very different kind of military government, first in Brazil in 1964 and then in Argentina in 1966. Because these political regimes were characterized by the military's ruling as an institution, rather than as individual military leaders, and because of the apparent technocratic, bureaucratic approach to policy of these regimes, they are characterized as bureaucratic-authoritarian.[5] Then, in 1973, two of what had appeared to be among the continent's most institutionalized democratic polities, Chile and Uruguay, were replaced by bureaucratic-authoritarian regimes; in 1976, another bureaucratic-authoritarian regime reappeared in Argentina.

The bureaucratic-authoritarian regimes have employed the state apparatus to depoliticize and thus scale back the demands of organized labor, and they have based their claim to legitimacy on the need to address the "threat" of leftist mobilization from below and to impose economic stabilization and efficiency to ensure renewed and more vigorous growth. Intrinsic to their nature, then, is the elimination of most channels of representation and communication with society, such as political parties. In some cases, weak surrogates have been created, but the clear intent of these regimes has been to demobilize and if possible depoliticize the country's population. Because the perceived threat from below was greater, the scope and extent of repression of the regimes of the 1970s were greater than those of the 1960s.[6]

Bureaucratic-authoritarian regimes have been justified politically by the threat of communism or demagogic populism and linked to the economic goals of stabilization, efficiency, and growth regardless of the distributional consequences. Given the perception that organized labor and other lower-class groups represent a threat to the state, such regimes have utilized both political and economic rationales for drastically reducing workers' wages as they implemented stabilization packages. At the same time, particularly in the 1970s, inefficient and oversubsidized industrialists were also perceived by the military and the economic policymakers as being part of the economic problem and, indirectly, the political problem. Thus, although many of these industrialists initially supported the military coups, they soon found themselves negatively affected by new regime policies.

These outwardly "strong" regimes have not been able to legitimize their rule. The bureaucratic-authoritarian regimes in Argentina have twice been replaced by civilian regimes. Brazil and Uruguay are now ruled by civilian regimes, and in Chile, issues of redemocratization are central concerns of numerous social actors and key topics of national debate.

The nationalist, populist-reformist military regime established in Peru in 1968 was unusual. It attempted to implement a series of reforms to favor labor, the peasantry, and other lower-class and middle-sector groups and to channel popular sector support through a variety of government-created organizations. Its development and foreign policies were statist and nationalist. Politically, the regime's major failing was its inability to gain support even from groups that were the major beneficiaries of its initial reform efforts. In contrast, the civilian government of Fernando Belaúnde that replaced it pursued economic policies that were much more similar to those of bureaucratic-authoritarian regimes.

The current socialist-mobilizational regimes in Cuba and Nicaragua both emerged as a result of revolutionary movements in countries with a long history of U.S. intervention and frustrated nationalism. Each regime has demonstrated a commitment to a dramatic restructuring of its country's social structure. Once in power, both regimes increased the sphere of state activity and sought to actively mobilize the population in support of the regime, by mass movements such as literary crusades and by political organizations such as neighborhood committees and women's, youth, peasant, and other associations.

Still, there are crucial differences between the regimes in Cuba and Nicaragua. The Sandinistas came to power in Nicaragua in 1979 after a prolonged and bitter struggle that caused much more extensive economic destruction and social dislocation than occurred in Cuba. The plurality of the domestic and foreign actors involved in the initial struggle in Nicaragua was also greater than in Cuba, and their role since 1979 has also been greater. Although the situation in Nicaragua has polarized considerably since 1981, there was still in 1985 a degree of tolerance for domestic critics and a role for the private sector that were clearly absent in Cuba six years after Fidel Castro assumed power in 1959. Both the extent and the nature of the external threat to the Sandinista regime, as well as its possible sources of external support, are also considerably different than those that affected Castro's regime in its early years.

Economic Growth and Social Equity

Of the key macroeconomic indicators of economic performance for Latin American countries in the period since World War II, Table 2.2 shows the growth in per capita income, private consumption, and the rate of inflation. The first thing that should be apparent from the table is that the postwar period has been a prosperous one. On average, over the thirty-some years

Table 2.2

ECONOMIC PERFORMANCE INDICATORS

	1984 Income/ Capita (in 1982 $)	Growth in Income/Capita[1] annual (%)					Growth in Consumption[2] per capita in %			
		1950-60	60-65	65-70	70-81	80-84	1955-60	60-65	65-70	70-80
Argentina	$1,929	0.9	2.1	3.2	0.4	-3.5	-0.8	3.1	2.4	-0.7
Brazil	1,625	3.6	1.0	5.4	5.5	-2.8	3.8	0.8	5.7	6.6
Chile	1,674	1.8	1.6	2.4	0.3	-2.9	3.8	0.4	2.8	1.2
Colombia	1,041	1.5	1.3	3.0	3.6	-0.3	0.3	2.1	3.7	4.2
Costa Rica	1,565	n.a.	1.5	3.6	2.4	-2.9	n.a.	2.3	2.5	1.9
Mexico	2,086	2.5	4.0	4.4	3.4	-1.6	2.3	3.1	4.9	3.2
Nicaragua	873	2.7	7.2	1.5	-3.0	-1.9	1.8	6.5	0.6	-1.3
Peru	978	2.9	3.2	0.5	0.5	-3.8	0.7	5.5	3.1	1.2
Venezuela	2,339	8.0	7.4	5.1	4.5	-4.6	3.9	1.7	1.9	5.3
Latin America	1,618	1.9	2.0	3.4	2.7	-2.4	n.a.	n.a.	n.a.	n.a.

23

	Growth in Private Consumption per capita in %				Inflation[3] (yearly rate)		
	1950-60	60-65	65-70	70-81	1950-60	60-70	70-81
Argentina	-0.9[5]	2.5	2.8	-0.5	27.5	21.4	134.2
Brazil	3.3	0.9	5.7	6.6	18.8	46.1	42.1
Chile	2.9	0.4	2.5	-0.9	36.1	33.0	164.6
Colombia	1.1	2.7	3.2	3.7	8.1	11.9	22.4
Costa Rica	n.a.	1.9	2.3	1.4	1.8[4]	1.9	16.2
Mexico	1.5	3.0	4.6	2.8	7.1	3.5	19.2
Nicaragua	2.7	7.2	-0.1	-2.0	4.9	1.8	13.8
Peru	1.4	5.8	2.9	0.5	7.8	10.4	34.3
Venezuela	3.4	1.4	0.9	6.4	0.0	1.3	12.4
Latin America	n.a.	1.9	3.5	2.0	n.a.	n.a.	n.a.

(1) based on regression, not end points
(2) private plus government
(3) GDP deflator
(4) consumer price index
(5) for 1955-1960
n.a. not available

Sources: World Bank, World Tables, 3rd ed. (Baltimore: Johns Hopkins University Press, 1983) and World Bank, World Development Report 1985 (New York: Oxford University Press, 1985). For 1984 income and income growth rates, Inter-American Development Bank, Economic and Social Progress in Latin America (Washington, D.C., 1985).

	Gross National Saving as Percentage of Gross Investment		
	1950-60	1960-70	1970-81
Argentina	100.0	99.0	93.7
Brazil	93.9	96.4	80.1
Chile	66.7	88.3	54.3
Colombia	93.1	84.2	94.9
Costa Rica	68.2	61.5	50.7
Mexico	92.0	90.7	86.0
Nicaragua	87.8	70.3	39.5
Peru	93.3	92.2	73.8
Latin America	110.3	113.9	109.6

(1) Gross national saving excludes transfers from abroad. All ratios are calculated from current prices.

Sources: The World Bank, World Tables, 3rd ed. (Baltimore: Johns Hopkins University Press, 1983) and World Bank, World Development Report 1985 (New York: Oxford University Press, 1985).

Table 2.3

SAVING AND INVESTMENT

	Average National Saving Rate(1)					Investment/GNP					
	1960	1965	1970	1980	1981	1955	1960	1965	1970	1980	1981
Argentina	20.8	20.4	20.5	22.7	22.7	17.6	21.8	19.2	21.1	25.7	20.5
Brazil	20.5	23.4	21.6	16.4	16.3	14.9	22.1	22.0	22.7	21.1	19.5
Chile	9.5	13.9	15.0	13.4	7.5	15.1	14.0	14.7	16.5	20.7	22.0
Colombia	19.6	16.7	17.8	24.8	23.0	18.0	20.5	17.7	22.0	25.7	27.7
Costa Rica	12.0	7.4	12.6	11.0	15.3	n.a.	17.5	19.5	20.5	26.6	28.1
Mexico	17.0	17.1	19.9	25.1	24.8	18.1	19.7	21.7	22.7	28.1	28.9
Nicaragua	11.9	16.2	13.3	7.1	1.2	15.7	15.0	20.9	18.6	15.4	23.6
Peru	25.5	18.0	15.4	15.1	9.9	23.1	25.4	20.7	13.3	18.4	19.0
Venezuela	28.6	27.9	30.7	33.0	30.7	29.1	20.6	23.6	29.5	24.5	24.5
Latin America	19.4	20.4	20.4	n.a.	19.5	18.0	20.4	20.4	21.9	n.a.	26.0

covered by the table, per capita income increased by 2.4 percent per year, which implies that the gross domestic product increased by 5.1 percent per year. There are few periods as long anywhere else in the world in any time period that can match so sustained an advance in economic growth.

Several further features of the table merit comment. First, with the exception of Colombia and possibly Brazil, economic performance peaked in the 1960s. Growth rates of income fell in the 1970s, and the rate of inflation increased in every country but Brazil, largely but not entirely because of the oil shocks of 1973 and 1979.

Second, economic performance was strongly influenced by whether or not a country was forced to stabilize, that is, to endure a contraction in output in order to reduce balance-of-payments deficits and growing inflation. Brazil's performance, for example, was relatively bad in the early 1960s because there was just such a stabilization recession in the period 1963–1967.

If the period up to 1980 was a prosperous one, the years since have been an economic disaster. By 1984, GDP per capita had fallen in every one of the Latin American republics, and at the same time, inflation has accelerated, the balance of payments has moved sharply into deficit, and external debt has risen to the highest levels ever recorded for the continent. Regimes of all kinds have been forced to push their economies into recession, with strong pressure from international creditors seeking to ensure repayment. Thus, regimes have curtailed monetary expansion and cut back on government spending in order to reduce the level of imports, and they have sought to promote their countries' exports more vigorously.

In some countries, the ensuing recession may be thought of as a delayed reaction to the oil shocks of the 1970s. During that decade, other countries were forced by rising oil costs to reduce their rates of growth, but many Latin American nations, encouraged by foreign bankers eager to recycle petrodollars, elected for a variety of political and economic purposes to borrow in order to finance their higher import bills. As a result, they continued to grow fairly rapidly up to around 1980. At that point, the unwillingness of international lenders to extend further credit forced them into recession. If these countries had borrowed less during the 1970s, that decade would have been less prosperous, but there would not have been as severe a decline after 1980.

The table also illustrates the sharp disparities in economic growth across the continent. Brazil, Mexico, Colombia, Costa Rica, and Venezuela have been far more successful than Chile, Argentina, Nicaragua, and Peru. In some cases, such as Venezuela and to a lesser extent Mexico, one can point to the advantage of having oil. Yet, other countries have also been at least partially successful in overcoming bottlenecks and achieving growth.

Two key bottlenecks that must be overcome for an economy to grow are the shortages of physical capital (machines, factories, and infrastructure) and foreign exchange, which is needed to buy essential imports. In order to acquire physical capital, a society must set aside from its total national product an amount to be used either to build or to import that capital. The amount of capital so acquired is called investment, and the amount of national product set aside to pay for it is called domestic saving. The rate of domestic saving is the best indicator we have of the internal effort a society is making to raise its rate of economic growth.

There are two sources of domestic saving, the private sector and the government. In the private sector, saving comes from corporate retained earnings and from the saving of households. Government saving is simply the difference between tax revenues and noninvestment government expenditures. When governments operate at a deficit, as many did in Latin America in the 1970s, government saving is negative.

Typically, countries invest more during the course of their development than they are able to save. This fact is reflected in total expenditure being greater than domestic production, the difference being made up by an excess of imports over exports, that is, a current account balance-of-payments deficit. This deficit is foreign saving and can be financed by foreign direct investment, loans from foreign banks, or aid from foreign governments and international agencies. Whatever form the financing takes, the total amount of foreign saving is measured by the current account deficit.

To recapitulate, physical capital is required to produce output. Therefore, if a society wants to grow, it must invest. If it wishes to invest, either its citizens must save, or the country must be able to attract foreign saving. Table 2.3 shows the investment and domestic saving ratios for a number of Latin American countries for several different years and indicates how much of their savings these countries invested.

According to the table, there has been a significant upward trend in the rate of investment. By 1980, only Peru and Nicaragua had investment rates less than 23 percent, which is a high figure. In relation to other developing countries, the Latin American countries invested a good deal. That does not necessarily guarantee higher growth rates of course, because the investment may have been highly capital intensive or mismanaged. Nonetheless, to the extent that investment is a prerequisite for growth, most Latin American countries appear to have been laying a solid foundation for higher growth rates in the future.

They have not, however, paid for all of that investment out of their own saving or their own resources. Even though investment has increased over the last thirty years, the national saving needed to finance it has not always done so. Indeed, as Table 2.3 shows, in many countries the national saving rate fell at the same time that the investment rate was rising. What that fact implies is that the Latin American countries have been turning to an increasing extent to foreign saving to finance their investment. One can see that with the exception of Colombia, there has been a decline in the share of investment financed by national saving, which is the main cause of the rising level of Latin American debt since the mid seventies.

There is nothing inherently wrong with borrowing to finance investment. Whether or not doing so is a good idea depends on the interest costs of the foreign loan and the payoff or benefit of the project that the loan finances. However, the fact that a larger and larger share of Latin American investment has been financed by foreign loans does mean that the national development effort has been a good deal smaller than the investment ratio makes it appear to be. It also means that much of that investment carries a very serious liability for future generations of Latin Americans because they will have to earn the foreign exchange needed to pay back those loans.

Unfortunately, the majority of the loans made to finance investment projects in the 1970s were commercial bank loans at variable interest rates. Before 1980, the rates were generally quite low, and the benefits of borrowing appeared to exceed the costs. However, the rise in interest rates since 1980 has drastically increased the cost of most outstanding loans because their interest rates were variable. This situation has left virtually every country on the continent with a crippling load of high-cost foreign debt. The mechanisms by which each country slipped into the debt morass are different, but the end result is more or less the same. National saving rates went down, investment rates went up, and a huge future foreign exchange liability was built up. That liability casts a large shadow on the favorable growth implications of high investment rates and threatens the future growth prospects of every country on the continent.

We turn now to the balance-of-payments record of our sample of Latin countries since 1950. It will be remembered that developing economies face two major constraints on growth, capital and foreign exchange. Shortages of either limit a country's growth prospects. We have already discussed how the capital constraint has been resolved through investment. How has the balance-of-payments constraint been dealt with?

The clear message from Tables 2.4 and 2.5 is that the balance-of-payments constraints have been met primarily through external borrowing. Since 1970, there has been an increasing imbalance between exports and imports in every major country in Latin America, which has resulted in growing current accounts deficits that have been financed by borrowing from both public and private sources. External foreign debt grew by almost nine times between 1970 and 1981, and total foreign debt grew an additional $50 billion in the succeeding two years. But the special conditions that made that borrowing possible, particularly the large supply of recycled petrodollars and the relatively low level of previous debt, no longer exist. However one chooses to measure debt burden, it is clear from Table 2.5 that the Latin American countries have too much debt. Because of the debt explosion of the 1970s, their debt service ratios are among the highest in the world, so foreign saving is not likely to be an important source of resources for growth in the future.

Looking back, it is clear that the availability of foreign loans in the 1970s was a one-time opportunity for Latin American countries to import far in excess of what they could pay for by their sales abroad. Given the current load of debt, such an opportunity is very unlikely to come again. From now on, if Latin America wants more imports, it will have to find some way to increase exports to pay for them.

As most students of Latin American know, the period up to around 1965 was a period of import substitution. In most countries, the import ratio fell, and exports, which tended to be ignored by policymakers, also declined. The Latin American growth strategy was inward looking, and those industries undergoing import substitution tended to be the leading sectors in every country. By the mid sixties, it became clear to many people that further economic progress through import substitution was likely to be expensive and inefficient, and policymakers, particularly those in the military regimes in Argentina and Brazil, began to think again about export promotion. In many countries, tariff barriers were cautiously reduced, export subsidies were adopted, and exchange rates were kept at more realistic levels. The result was that the import share actually declined in three of the countries in the table and was constant in a fourth.

The trend toward a more open economy accelerated in the 1970s. In every country except Mexico, there was an increase in the import ratio, and most of the countries show an increase in the export share as well. To some extent this trend is misleading, because it was caused by the rising cost of oil. That increase tended to force up the import share of oil importers like Brazil or Chile, and those countries were then forced to increase exports to pay for the higher priced oil. Thus, a fairly severe process of import substitution in capital goods actually took place in Brazil in the mid seventies after the first oil shock, but that is disguised in the data by the rise in the cost of oil imports. Notwithstanding these points, there is little doubt that Latin America has become more export oriented since 1965. The small economies, as one would expect, are extraordinarily open, with some—such as Chile, Panama, Costa Rica, and Nicaragua—selling one-fourth or more of their GNP abroad.

A key question is the extent to which the economic growth experienced by Latin American countries was employed to improve the standard of living of the poorest groups in those countries, and a current concern is the extent to which the present economic retrenchment falls dispro-

Table 2.4

TRADE DATA

	Exports/GDP in %						Imports/GDP in %					
	1955	1960	1965	1970	1975	1980	1955	1960	1965	1970	1975	1980
Argentina	5.9	9.9	7.7	9.2	7.8	6.9	5.9	10.9	6.3	9.0	8.0	9.1
Brazil	6.7	5.1	7.4	6.5	7.1	8.6	6.2	6.2	5.2	6.9	10.9	10.7
Chile	9.2	14.0	14.1	15.0	25.5	22.7	8.0	16.3	13.0	14.4	27.4	27.1
Colombia	12.4	15.6	11.4	14.1	15.5	16.2	14.3	15.6	10.4	16.2	14.6	17.0
Costa Rica	n.a.	21.4	23.5	28.2	30.1	26.5	n.a.	26.2	33.5	35.0	38.5	36.8
Mexico	16.7	10.3	9.3	7.7	6.9	12.6	15.7	12.6	10.3	13.6	9.6	13.5
Nicaragua	27.4	23.6	29.3	26.7	28.0	23.0	24.3	26.1	32.4	29.2	36.9	41.1
Peru	17.7	20.2	15.5	17.6	10.8	15.8	19.9	18.1	16.8	14.0	19.2	15.0
Venezuela	32.5	32.0	30.6	23.7	33.7	33.4	21.1	19.1	20.1	19.1	25.7	25.2
Latin America	12.2	14.5	13.5	12.5	n.a.	16.9[1]	11.3	14.8	12.9	13.5	n.a.	18.9[1]

| | Current Account Balance (millions of U.S. dollars) | | | |
	1960	1965	1970	1981
Argentina	-204	218	-163	-3,974
Brazil	-517	284	-837	-11,762
Chile	-130	-43	-91	-4,813
Colombia	-94	-21	-293	-1,943
Costa Rica	-16	-68	-74	-372
Mexico	-324	-403	-1,068	-12,933
Nicaragua	-8	-23	-40	180
Peru	8	-148	202	-1,511
Venezuela	394	35	-104	3,996
Latin America	-1,113	-246	-3,453	-37,473

(1) - 1981 data
n.a. not available

Source: The World Bank, World Tables, 3rd ed. (Baltimore: Johns Hopkins Press, 1983).

Table 2.5

DEBT AND DEBT SERVICE

	Foreign Debt GNP percent		Total Debt Service Exports percent		Current Acct. Deficit GDP percent		External Public Debt (in billions)			Total External Debt (in billions)	
	1970	1981	1970	1981	1970	1981	1970	1975	1981	1981	1983
Argentina	8.2	8.7	21.5	18.2	0.7	3.7	$2.5	$5.2	$14.5	$35.7	$42.0
Brazil	7.1	16.0	12.5	31.9	1.8	4.1	4.7	17.7	58.1	65.0	83.0
Chile	25.8	14.1	18.9	27.2	1.1	15.8	2.5	4.4	4.9	15.5	17.6
Colombia	18.8	14.0	11.9	13.3	4.1	5.1	1.9	3.0	7.6	8.2	10.3
Costa Rica	13.8	92.6	10.0	15.9	7.5	15.5	0.2	0.7	2.6	2.3	3.1
Mexico	9.1	18.5	23.6	28.2	3.0	5.4	3.8	13.8	47.5	72.0	85.0
Nicaragua	20.7	80.2	11.1	n.a.	5.1	n.a.	0.2	0.8	2.5	2.2	3.4
Peru	12.6	28.6	11.6	44.5	-2.9	7.1	1.1	4.0	8.5	8.2	10.6
Venezuela	6.0	16.9	2.9	12.4	-0.9	5.9	0.9	1.4	11.5	28.4	30.0
Latin America	n.a.	n.a.	13.0	21.9	n.a.	n.a.	20.4	57.9	178.2	257.9	309.8

Sources: World Bank, World Tables, 3d ed. (Baltimore: Johns Hopkins University Press, 1983). For total external debt, source is Economic Commission for Latin America, Notas sobre la Economia y el Desarrollo de America Latina (Santiago, 1984).

Table 2.6

SOCIAL INDICATORS

	Life Expectancy at birth (in years)			Adjusted School Enrollment Rates (1) (in percent)								Income Dist. Variable	
				Primary			Secondary			Higher Education		Share of bottom 40%	Share of top 20%
	1960	1970	1981	1960	1970	1980	1960	1970	1980	1960	1980		
Argentina	65	67	71	98	106	116	32	37	56	11	23	17.3	52
Brazil	57	61	64	95	83	93	11	27	32	2	12	10.0	62
Chile	57	62	68	109	107	117	24	39	55	4	12	13.0	57
Colombia	53	59	63	77	100	128	12	23	46	2	11	9.4	59
Costa Rica	62	67	73	96	110	108	21	28	48	5	26	14.7	51
Mexico	58	62	66	80	104	120	11	22	37	3	15	10.5	64
Nicaragua	47	50	57	66	83	100	7	18	43	1	9	n.a.	n.a.
Peru	48	53	58	83	107	112	15	30	56	4	16	6.5	60
Venezuela	59	66	68	100	94	104	21	37	39	4	21	n.a.	n.a.
Latin America	55	60	64	88	95	105	14	27	39	n.a.	n.a.	n.a.	n.a.

(1) Number in school as percent of school age population.
n.a. not available

Sources: World Bank, World Tables, 3d ed. (Baltimore: Johns Hopkins University Press, 1983); for income shares, M. A. Ahluwalia, "Inequality, Poverty, and Development," Journal of Development Economics 3 (December 1976).

portionally on the people least able to afford it. A good deal of the income growth that occurred was used to upgrade both the health and education levels of the people. Table 2.6 shows two areas in which substantial progress was made, life expectancy and education. Since 1960, average life expectancy has increased by ten years, and countries such as Argentina and Costa Rica now approach the level of the developed nations (seventy-five).

Over the same years, there has been a truly phenomenal investment in education throughout the continent. Most countries already had a relatively high primary school enrollment ratio in 1960, but the number of children going on to secondary school was very small, around one in five. Over the next twenty years, a great deal of progress was made in extending high school and college education to a much wider segment of the population.

This change has two implications for the labor force. On the one hand, it has meant that to a larger and larger extent, teenagers have been in school, not in the labor market, which has eased the problem of labor absorption. But on the other hand, the problem of finding adequate jobs for the better-educated workers when they finish school has begun to cause real problems. Typically, unemployment is concentrated in the group of young, relatively well-educated workers who are just entering the labor market for the first time. Although their higher education levels represent an opportunity for Latin societies, they also represent a serious potential for social unrest if these people cannot find work suitable for their higher level of aspirations.

A darker side of the economic performance of Latin American countries is the virtually total lack of progress toward ameliorating the distribution of income. Most countries on the continent have always had a highly skewed distribution of income, and one indicator on Table 2.6 shows that distribution—the income shares of the bottom 40 percent and top 20 percent of the population. By and large, the rapid growth in the postwar period did nothing to improve the situation. On the contrary, the highly capital- and skill-intensive growth strategy practiced in countries like Brazil and Mexico made the distribution even less equal than it had been. Most of the gains went to the people who were comparatively far up the income pyramid for they had the skills and the capital that were paid a premium during the growth process. To some extent, the picture one gets is a biased one because it ignores upward mobility, but there is no avoiding the general impression that economic growth under capitalism for most Latin Americans has been highly inequitable. This situation is particularly true when the Latin American countries are compared with East Asian countries like Korea and Taiwan, which managed to grow even faster than Brazil or Mexico but in which the bottom 40 percent earned around 20 percent of the total income in 1977, a figure double that in Brazil (Bergsman 1979).

Cuba's performance presents a marked contrast. Although that country's figures are not reported on a comparable basis to international agencies, there is little doubt that one of the main effects of the revolution has been a massive redistribution of income and an increase in both education and life expectancy. According to one source quoted in Mesa Lago's chapter, the personal income share of the bottom 40 percent rose from 6.5 percent in 1953 to 20.2 percent by 1978. At the same time, the share of the top 20 percent fell from 57.9 percent to 33.4 percent. According to Mesa Lago, illiteracy dropped from about 24 percent before the revolution to 4 percent in 1980. Life expectancy has risen from sixty-one years to a projected seventy-one, which, if achieved, will be one of the highest rates in Latin America. These are impressive accomplishments, and they must be borne in mind when evaluating Cuba's relatively low per capita income growth.

Notes

1. Linz 1978:5. An earlier procedural definition can be found in Schumpeter 1975:250–302; see also Dahl 1971.

2. Linz, in a seminal article (1964), defined authoritarian regimes as possessing limited political pluralism, neither intensive nor extensive political mobilization, no distinctive ideology, and a leader or a small group of leaders that rules within generally predictable, if not formally defined, limits (see also Linz 1975:esp. 264). The problem with this definition is that it includes in its specification what is perhaps best left to empirical study, including the relationship between different kinds of political regimes and the nature and extent of pluralism and mobilization in society (cf. Collier 1982:5–12).

3. For another view of Mexico's authoritarian and pluralist features, see Levy and Székely 1983; for analyses of Mexico as an authoritarian regime, see Reyna and Weinert 1977.

4. Alfred Stepan contrasts the earlier moderator coups in Brazil of 1930, 1945, 1954, and 1955—which "removed a chief executive"—with the 1964 coup in which the military "assumed political power" (Stepan 1971:123; see also 62–66, 123–133). Nordlinger 1977:21–29 distinguishes guardian coups from "ruler" coups such as the bureaucratic-authoritarian coups discussed in the text.

5. Collier 1979:4–5. An essential reference is O'Donnell 1973.

6. For a critique of the "threat" hypothesis, see Remmer and Merckx 1982; see also the reply by O'Donnell, 1982.

References

Ahluwalia, M. S. 1976. "Inequality, Poverty, and Development." *Journal of Development Economics* 3 (December):307–342.

Bergsman, Joel. 1979. "Growth and Equity in Semi-industrialized Countries." Working Paper No. 351. Washington, D.C.: World Bank.

Cardoso, Fernando Henrique. 1979. "On the Characterization of Authoritarian Regimes in Latin America." In David Collier, ed., *The New Authoritarianism in Latin America*. Princeton: Princeton University Press.

Chalmers, Douglas A., and Robinson, Craig H. 1982. "Why Power Contenders Choose Liberalization." *International Studies Quarterly* 26 (March):3–36.

Collier, David, ed. 1979. *The New Authoritarianism in Latin America*. Princeton: Princeton University Press.

Collier, Ruth. 1982. *Regimes in Tropical Africa: Changing Forms of Supremacy, 1945–1975*. Berkeley: University of California Press.

Dahl, Robert A. 1971. *Polyarchy*. New Haven: Yale University Press.

Dix, Robert H. 1980. "Consociational Democracy: The Case of Colombia." *Comparative Politics* 12 (April):303–321.

Hartlyn, Jonathan. 1985. "Producer Associations, the Political Regime, and Policy Processes in Contemporary Colombia." *Latin American Research Review* 20, no. 3:111–138.

Levy, Daniel, and Székely, Gabriel. 1983. *Mexico: Paradoxes of Stability and Change.* Boulder, Colo.: Westview Press.

Linz, Juan J. 1964. "An Authoritarian Regime: Spain." In E. Allardt and Y. Littunen, eds., *Cleavages, Ideologies, and Party Systems: Contributions to Comparative Political Sociology*. Helsinki: Academic Bookstore.

———. 1975. "Totalitarian and Authoritarian Regimes." In Fred I. Greenstein and Nelson Polsby, eds., *Handbook of Political Science*, Vol. 3, *Macropolitical Theory*. Reading, Mass.: Addison-Wesley.

———. 1978. "Crisis, Breakdown, and Reequilibriation." In Juan J. Linz and Alfred Stepan, eds., *The Breakdown of Democratic Regimes*. Baltimore: Johns Hopkins University.

Needler, Martin C. 1983. *An Introduction to Latin American Politics.* Englewood Cliffs, N.J.: Prentice-Hall.

Nordlinger, Eric. 1977. *Soldiers in Politics.* Englewood Cliffs, N.J.: Prentice-Hall.

O'Donnell, Guillermo. 1973. *Modernization and Bureaucratic-Authoritarianism: Studies in South American Politics.* Institute of International Studies, Politics of Modernization Series no. 9. Berkeley: University of California.

———. 1982. "Reply to Remmer and Merckx." *Latin American Research Review* 17, no. 2:41–50.

Perlmutter, Amos. 1981. *Modern Authoritarianism.* New Haven: Yale University Press.

Remmer, Karen L., and Merckx, Gilbert W. 1982. "Bureaucratic-Authoritarianism Revisited." *Latin American Research Review* 17, no. 2:3–40.

Reyna, José Luis, and Weinert, Richard, eds. 1977. *Authoritarianism in Mexico.* Philadelphia: Institute for the Study of Human Issues.

Schumpeter, Joseph A. 1975. *Capitalism, Socialism, and Democracy.* 3d ed. New York: Harper and Row, Harper Colophon.

Skidmore, Thomas E., and Smith, Peter A. 1984. *Modern Latin America.* New York and Oxford: Oxford University Press.

Stepan, Alfred. 1971. *The Military in Politics.* Princeton: Princeton University Press.

World Bank. 1983. *World Tables.* 3d ed. Baltimore: Johns Hopkins University Press.

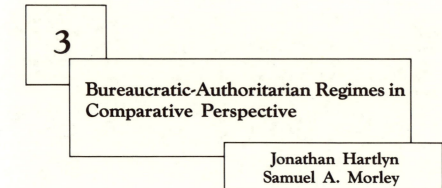

3

Bureaucratic-Authoritarian Regimes in Comparative Perspective

Jonathan Hartlyn
Samuel A. Morley

For Latin America, the emergence of bureaucratic-authoritarian (B-A) regimes in some of the most industrialized and democratic countries on the continent was one of the tragic events of the 1970s. In the 1980s, the B-A regimes (as well as many other military regimes in Latin America) have given way to civilian regimes, except in Chile. The repressive and harsh economic measures of the B-A regimes were justified as necessary to establish the political and economic foundations for stable economic growth in their countries. Given the serious economic situation confronting current civilian political regimes, it is therefore important to analyze the economic record of those B-A regimes, and the economic and political factors that most affected that record, in comparison with the records of other civilian regimes on the continent.

In this chapter, we will lay the basis for the comparative analysis of military and civilian regimes to be carried further in succeeding chapters. First, we will seek to establish that the B-A regimes were not better economic managers than the civilian competitive or semicompetitive regimes by comparing the B-A regimes with the civilian regimes they replaced as well as with other Latin American civilian regimes of the 1970s. Second, we will present what we believe are the principal reasons for the economic failure of the B-A regimes. In a concluding section, we expand the time horizon both backward into history and forward into the future. Some people have argued that historical patterns, particularly regarding the timing and phasing of industrialization and the manner in which a popular sector is incorporated into the political life of a country, have an important impact on a country's economic and political structures. How do current regime outcomes and prospects fit into the patterns identified, and what implications do they have for future developments in the region?

Civilian and Bureaucratic-Authoritarian Regimes: Economic Comparisons

Bureaucratic-authoritarian regimes were established in Argentina in 1966 and again in 1976, in Brazil in 1964, and in Chile and Uruguay in 1973. These regimes, particularly those initiated in the 1970s, pursued a common set of economic policies. First, they all believed in price mechanisms and a free market, which was expressed in a desire to let profit incentives and prices, rather than government planners, determine the allocation of resources in the economy. The Chileans were far more orthodox and rigid in this regard than the Brazilians, whose B-A regime created a host of large state enterprises at the same time that the Chileans were selling state enterprises inherited from the Allende regime.

Second, each of the B-A regimes was dedicated to controlling inflation and correcting the balance of payments. In large measure, these regimes came into power because of economic crises, reflected by rising or repressed inflation and foreign exchange shortages, that civilian governments had been unable to control. The military response to these two problems was to cut government deficits by such measures as raising taxes, reducing the expansion of the money supply, suppressing wage demands in order to reduce cost-push pressures on prices, and devaluing the currency to make exports more competitive and to correct the balance-of-payments deficit. In short, what these B-A regimes did was to impose a classic, orthodox stabilization program of the sort generally demanded by the International Monetary Fund.

Subsequently, when the immediate balance-of-payments and inflation crises were overcome, the long-run economic characteristics of the regimes became clearer. The two most important were a greater orientation toward both exports and agriculture. The regimes tended to reverse the more extreme import substitution policies—domestic industrial promotion at the expense of agriculture—that had been followed by their predecessors. They lowered tariffs and established the crawling-peg exchange rate so that exporters would not have to worry about overvaluation. They also established a variety of subsidies for exports, both industrial and agricultural. Finally, they all held out a welcome mat for foreign direct investment, which they hoped would join in a constructive partnership to develop their countries and, not incidentally, help shore up the kind of political and social order they were hoping to establish.

Within-Country Comparisons

Were the B-A regimes able to produce a higher-growth, lower-inflation economy than the governments they had replaced? Do their claims of better economic management hold up under scrutiny? One way to answer these questions is to compare the growth, inflation, and balance-of-payments records of the military regimes with those of the civilian regimes they replaced. Such a comparison can be partially misleading because external conditions are different over time. In the post-oil-shock period of the 1970s, it was more difficult to produce good results. Put another way, we cannot be sure how civilian regimes would have performed over the years the military were in power. In addition, an earlier regime may appear to have done well, but it could have left underlying problems in the balance of payments, inflation rate, or foreign indebtedness that its successor had to deal with. Nevertheless, this is a useful initial comparison, and it can serve as a backdrop to the more complex discussions in subsequent chapters.

Examined in broad terms, the economic record of the four military regimes was not better than that of the civilian regimes they replaced. The basic data for our comparison are given in Tables 3.1 and 3.2.[1] It is clear that only the first Argentine military regime outperformed its civilian counterpart in terms of economic growth.[2] The balance-of-payments record of the military was certainly worse than the civilian regimes whichever way we choose to measure. In Chile, the Allende government left a debt service ratio of almost 11 percent (at least partially a result of the U.S. economic blockade). Seven years later the ratio was 29 percent, and the same pattern can be seen in the other two countries as well. It is clear that the increase in foreign debt liabilities accelerated during the Latin American debt crisis after 1980, but one can see indications of the problem earlier, particularly in Chile and Brazil. The fact is that all four military regimes believed in foreign borrowing and went out of their way to encourage it, both by keeping internal interest rates high and by prefixing the exchange rate.[3] All the regimes were attractive to lenders who were awash with funds after the second oil shock. The result was an explosion of foreign liabilities that has left all three countries with an overwhelming interest burden, which will surely hold down growth rates in the future.

The record of the military is somewhat better on inflation than it is on the other measures. However, given the determination to stop inflation that all of the military regimes claimed, it is somewhat surprising that their records are not better.

In all three countries, the military took over in the midst of very serious outbreaks of inflationary pressure, which they promised to eliminate. In this endeavor, they were generally quite successful although the cost in terms of recession was also generally high, particularly in Chile. There, the reported inflation at the end of the Allende period was over 300 percent, and there is general agreement that because of

Table 3.1

PERFORMANCE INDICATORS
FOR ARGENTINA, BRAZIL, AND CHILE (IN PERCENT)

	Military				Civilian	
	1966-73	1976-80	1976-82	1976-82[3]	1955-66	1973-76
Argentina						
Growth (GDP)	5	2.6	-0.2	0.3	3.3	
Inflation[1]	28	141	145		31	173
Debt Service/Export	18		34			19
Interest/Exports[2]	0.4	6	19		3.1	
		1964-80	1964-82	1964-82	1948-63	
Brazil						
Growth (GDP)		7.7	6.9	6.6	6.6	
Inflation[1]		39	45		24	
Debt Service/Exports		36.7	33.7[4]			
Interest/Exports[2]		21.4	49.5		8.7	
	1974-82	1973-80	1973-82	1973-82	1950-73	
Chile						
Growth (GDP)		1.4	1.4	2	3.7	
Inflation[1]	83	158	116		43	
Debt Service/Exports		29.2	30.2[4]		10.9	
Interest/Exports[2]		11.8	42.9		10	

(1) Annual average GDP deflator
(2) Interest charge on accumulated current account deficit divided by final year exports
(3) 1982 is a weighted average of 1981-1983.
(4) For 1981

Source: International Monetary Fund, International Financial Statistics (Washington, D.C., various years).

price controls, the true rate was far higher than that. Yet after four years of very tough stabilization, the Pinochet government had brought the inflation rate down to less than 40 percent. Indeed, in 1982, the consumer price index increased only 10 percent. In Argentina, the Videla regime brought the Perón inflation down from over 400 percent to 150 percent from 1976 to 1979. In Brazil, as in the other two countries, the military took over during a period of rapidly accelerating inflation, which reached an annual rate of 125 percent in the first quarter of 1964. Within three years, the Castello Branco government had reduced that rate to 20

Table 3.2

SAVING AND INVESTMENT RATES
FOR ARGENTINA, BRAZIL, AND CHILE (IN PERCENT)

	Military		Civilian	
	1966-73	1976-80	1955-66	1973-76
Argentina				
I/Y	19.8	26.1	18.0	25.4
S/Y	19.7	26.0	18.2	25.7
	1964-80		1950-63	
Brazil				
I/Y	21.6		20.5	
S/Y	19.0		19.2	
	1973-80		1950-73	
Chile				
I/Y	17.5		15.5	
S/Y	11.9		12.7	

Note: I/Y and S/Y are the ratios of investment and saving to GDP.

Source: International Monetary Fund, International Financial Statistics (Washington, D.C., various years).

percent. Subsequently, particularly after the second oil shock, the Brazilian government let inflation get out of hand again, and the rate rose to over 200 percent in 1983. That is why the Brazilian military's inflation record appears to be the worst of the three countries, even though it too had substantial early success and at a much lower cost in terms of lost output than was true in either Chile or Argentina.

As noted in Chapter 2, two ways to measure the effort that a society is devoting to economic growth are the ratio of investment and domestic saving to GNP. The first tells how much capital is being built up, and the second tells how much a society is forgoing consumption to pay for that capital. Let us now compare these two key ratios for the civilian and military regimes under consideration (see Table 3.2). This comparison has the added advantage that these measures are more or less under the control of the society, whereas growth and inflation could well be strongly affected by external events.

One can see from the table that all four military regimes did increase the investment ratio. Indeed, there appears to have been a rising trend in all three countries. However, we have already shown that growth under the military was lower in all but the first Argentine military regime. That fact implies that even though the other societies were investing more, they were getting less for their investment. Rising capital intensity, mismanagement, corruption, and waste—among other factors—are likely to have constrained the growth process, but what is clear is that the extra investment effort did not pay extra growth dividends, at least not through 1983.

When we turn to the saving ratios, we find that only in Argentina were the rates higher under a B-A regime. What happened in both Chile and Brazil is that the investment ratio increased but the saving rate declined, which means that a far larger share of the investment was financed by foreign savings rather than by domestic saving. As we have already seen, the military governments were all attractive to foreign lenders. Each country took advantage of this fact to increase investment without asking its own citizens to pay for it through a higher saving rate. Of course, the other side of this picture is that each military government left a huge burden of foreign indebtedness that future generations will have to repay.

It is surprising that the saving ratios were not higher under the B-A regimes. The military regimes demonstrated their willingness to repress wages and allow a substantial shift in income distribution toward profits. Deficit-producing government subsidies to middle- and lower-income groups were scaled back or eliminated. These facts suggest a significant increase in income inequality. Yet, in spite of the fact that most non-government saving occurs on the part of high-income individuals and corporations, the domestic saving rates did not climb substantially. Instead, the consumption of luxury goods dramatically increased in the years immediately after the military came to power.

These comparisons provide little evidence to support the notion that either the growth performance or the growth effort was greater under the B-A military regimes than they had been under the popularly elected governments that those regimes replaced. In addition, there were societal costs generated by increased inequality and by state-directed and state-sponsored terrorism against each country's citizens.

Across-Country Comparisons

If the B-A regimes did not outperform civilian governments in the same country, how did these same regimes compare with civilian regimes

Table 3.3

PERFORMANCE INDICATORS FOR SELECTED LATIN AMERICAN COUNTRIES

(in percent)

	Growth GDP/capita	Inflation 1976-1982	Debt Service Exports 1981	Current Acct. Def. GDP 1981	Average I/GDP 1970-1981	Average S/Y 1970-1981
B-A regimes						
Argentina	-1.3[(1)]	133.4[(4)]	18.2	3.7	25.8[(5)]	26.6
Brazil	4.5[(2)]	42.1	31.9	4.1	21.8	17.5
Chile	0.3[(3)]	132.6	27.2	15.8	17.5	11.9
Civilian regimes	1976-1982					
Colombia	3.1	22.4	13.3	5.1	23.9	22.7
Costa Rica	0.9	16.2	15.9	15.5	25.2	12.8
Mexico	2.8	19.2	28.2	5.4	25.7	22.1
Venezuela	0.1	12.4	12.4	5.9	30.8	33.6

(1)   1976-1982

(2)   1970-1982

(3)   1973-1982

(4)   1976-1981

(5)   1976-1980

in other countries during the 1970s? The answer is, not particularly well (see Table 3.3).[4] On the whole, they did not grow faster, save more, or have lower inflation rates. Only in the balance of payments does their performance appear better, and even there the decision would depend on which measure of external imbalance one choses to use.

Looking first at growth, we see from the table that Brazil had the highest rate of per capita income growth of any of the countries in the sample. But in three of the four civilian regimes (Colombia, Costa Rica, and Mexico), that growth rate was greater than in either Chile or Argentina. When we look at either the saving or the investment effort, we see the same picture. On average, both ratios were lower in the B-A regimes. Chile had the lowest ratio in both cases, and Venezuela, the highest. Thus, the evidence suggests that by and large, the B-A regimes had greater trouble generating saving, investment, and growth than did the more open political regimes.[5]

Looking now at the other performance indicators, inflation and balance of payments, again we see no obvious pattern favoring the military regimes. Inflation was clearly worse in the Southern Cone dictatorships than elsewhere, and the balance-of-payments comparison is a standoff. On average, the debt service ratios in the B-A regimes in 1981 were higher, but the current account deficits were a bit lower. Both the B-A and the open political regimes went on a binge of external borrowing during the late seventies to cover current account deficits and rising investment. Chile and Costa Rica were relatively the worst offenders in this regard, but no country escaped the external imbalance problem altogether.

We conclude that the evidence both within and across countries does not support the proposition that the B-A regimes were better economic managers than the competitive regimes. Some observers of B-A regimes have explained or justified their emergence in terms of the requirements of continued capitalist growth, and the regimes themselves based a substantial part of their claim to rule on their ability to generate rapid, noninflationary growth. Yet, the experience of the years reviewed here suggests that the B-A regimes outperformed neither the civilian regimes in their own countries nor the competitive regimes elsewhere on the continent.

The expectation that a major difference between B-A and civilian regimes would be that the former would have a better economic record does not appear to be supported by the evidence. The economic performance of the military regimes was disappointing, even according to the indicators they themselves considered important, such as growth, inflation, and balance of payments. The fact that civilian regimes in countries of equivalent or only slightly lower levels of development had better economic results suggests that the views of some analysts that the economic requirements for growth were too demanding for civilian political regimes may have been overdrawn. However, two qualifications are in order. To some extent, the record of the civilian regimes appears so good only because that of the military regimes was so much worse. In addition, though the political differences between the bureaucratic-authoritarian and the civilian regimes are indisputable, some civilian regimes, such as those in Mexico and Colombia, place limits on domestic political expression so that we have labeled them semicompetitive rather than fully competitive.

The one area of dramatic contrast between B-A and civilian regimes is in terms of levels of repression. The widespread use of a variety of repressive techniques—including torture, "disappearance," and other extrajudicial executions, exile, and censorship and the banning of unions, political parties, and public demonstrations—on the part of the B-A regimes has been well documented. The military governments, particularly when the perceived degree of threat by mobilization from below has been great, have been more likely to employ repression that is broader in scope, more severe, and of a longer duration than under civilian regimes.[6]

The B-A Failures: Economic Theory, International Finance, and Repression

The bureaucratic-authoritarian regimes we have been discussing came to power with clear and coherent economic programs, good technical advisers, and virtually complete freedom from political constraints. Why didn't they do better? Was their theory inappropriate, was it implemented badly, or were they particularly unlucky in facing external constraints?

At the outset, one should distinguish between the short-run stabilization program, which each of these regimes imposed to reduce inflation and correct the trade deficit, and the longer-run growth strategies. The record shows that the tough stabilization programs of Videla in Argentina, Pinochet in Chile, and Castello Branco in Brazil were all successful in the short-run goals of reducing inflation and eliminating trade deficits. These orthodox stabilizations worked as their designers said they would, though one can certainly wonder whether a less draconian strategy could have been designed, particularly in Chile. There was a fairly sharp recession in all three countries, but by the late 1970s, each had resumed rapid growth at a far lower rate of inflation than under the preceding civilian regime.

When one looks at the macroeconomic performance of these B-A regimes, the record is particularly poor after 1980. Superficially, one might attribute this situation to the oil shock, but as Albert Fishlow shows in Chapter 4, that argument can really be made only for Brazil, not Argentina or Chile. We would argue that the poor economic performance since 1980 stems from the interaction of various factors. The B-A regimes had an economic theory that encouraged an excessive integration of their economies into the international financial system and prompted them to borrow too much abroad just before a major exogenous shift in real interest rates. This factor was combined with the active promotion of borrowing by foreign commercial banks and the inability of any of the negatively affected domestic groups to express their opposition to regime policies. The economic theory underlying the programs of these regimes was a form of international monetarism that argued that in the long run inflation rates are determined by international prices and movements in the exchange rate and that monetary policy primarily affects the balance of payments. This theory was taken to imply that one could reduce the amount of inflation by prefixing the exchange rate and that one could cure a balance-of-payments deficit by a contractionary monetary policy, which would drive up internal interest rates and attract foreign capital if barriers to capital movements could be reduced.

This theory proved to be fairly disastrous in practice, primarily because in all three countries, it led to a tremendous increase in foreign indebtedness just before the worldwide rise in real interest rates. Each country went through a period of prefixing the exchange rate while raising internal interest rates—generally through a contractionary monetary policy. Contrary to the predictions of the theory, inflation rates did not decline. Indeed, they generally increased. The result was an increasingly serious overvaluation of the domestic currency, which created havoc for all industries producing traded goods, whether exportable or import substitutes. But the potential difficulty was glossed over by a large inflow of foreign funds and the political inability of the negatively affected groups to express their opposition. This description applies particularly in the cases of Argentina and Chile. In Brazil, the capital inflow simply delayed adjustment to the second oil shock, which made the adjustment far more costly when it came in 1982.

In any case, all three countries dramatically increased their foreign debts during the period 1978–1981, which was an exceedingly unwise policy choice because conditions in the international capital market changed dramatically in 1981. Banks became reluctant to advance more capital, and real interest rates rose, drastically increasing the cost of the past policy decisions to link up internal and external capital markets. Each of the three countries was belatedly forced into a new stabilization to correct the current account deficit, though now under far less auspicious circumstances than had prevailed in the late 1970s. The result was a new round of virulent inflation, particularly in Argentina and Brazil, and severe recession in all three countries.

All governments run the risk of choosing economic policies that are inappropriate to the conditions faced by their countries. Democratic and populist governments in Latin America in the past have often erred on the side of being too expansionary and relying too much on high protection of the domestic industrial sector. Such policies discriminate against the export sector, and they have generally led to a balance-of-payments crisis coupled with inflation. Industrialists have sometimes turned against such regimes because of regime policies that favor the working class and other popular sector groups and because of concern about the balance-of-payments problem. Such governments eventually exhaust their ability to borrow to finance trade deficits because of a combination of external and domestic pressure (suspension of loans, capital flight, etc.), and thus they are forced to change their policies. This process results in the stop-

and-go cycles described in Marcelo Diamand's chapter on Argentina. In these instances, external and domestic constraints act to reverse failed policy, though often in a sharply pendular fashion. In the more successful cases, the reversal happens fast enough to prevent widespread damage to any important sector.

In the case of the B-A regimes, both external and political constraints were absent for a relatively long period of time. Rather than acting as a brake on unwise policy, the external sector positively encouraged it. The B-A regimes were attractive to foreign lenders, and their monetarist policies made them more so. At a time when they should have been doing everything in their power to push exports, they were instead holding down exchange rates and generating large inflows of foreign capital. Despite the complaints of bankrupted business people, there was nothing to stop these regimes from continuing their policies until the foreign sources of finance dried up in 1982. By that time, an unprecedented amount of damage had been done to the private sector, the sector the B-A regimes had intended to encourage. Although the B-A regimes were not the only ones to borrow too much in the 1970s, it is unlikely that the policy of opening up an economy to international competition could have been followed to the extreme that it was, particularly in Chile, under anything but a repressive regime.

It is also especially clear in the Chilean case that the radical economic theory was linked with a vision of a totally different political and social order. As Garretón indicates in Chapter 8, the Pinochet regime's monetarist economic orthodoxy was associated with an effort to restructure the social and political bases of the country by extending the logic of the market to areas such as health, public welfare, and education. These economic and social policies, it was thought, would attract the country's citizens because the changes would increase the people's freedom of choice as the scope of state intervention was rolled back. Linked to the regime's efforts to destroy party, labor, and other organizations, these policies were intended to destroy old allegiances and create new loyalties. However, even as the economic model failed, it became clear that the notion that the entrenched party system and other allegiances could be simply eliminated or replaced was simplistic.[7]

In addition, B-A regimes could not remain completely impervious to societal demands indefinitely. Especially as their justification for existence against a threat from below diminished through time, the B-A regimes began to feel the necessity of responding to general societal demands in a quest for continued legitimacy. That fact was especially evident in the case of Brazil where the regime committed itself to maintaining growth after the first oil shock of 1973. Fishlow notes that Brazil used the debt less to finance adjustment than as a substitute for it. And, as Lamounier and Moura argue, this policy was the result not of explicit demands upon the state by industrial or labor groups but of a co-optive effort on the part of the military government, which was beginning to concern itself with seeking broader political support domestically in the context of an ill-defined project of political liberalization. Thus, the Brazilian military leaders, in spite of their dictatorial powers, found themselves unwilling to avoid a slowdown of growth in the 1970s. This situation made Brazil particularly vulnerable to the scissors effect of increasing interest rates and declining exports following the second oil shock.[8]

Civilian regimes are considered to be far more vulnerable to domestic political pressure. What is sometimes overlooked is that they may also possess wider legitimacy and thus greater political space in which to carry out their policies. The civilian regimes considered in this volume are characterized by the fact that a new government often enters office with greater room for maneuverability than an examination of the potential power of social actors would suggest and that business groups generally have had greater access to policymaking than popular sector groups. However, regime legitimacy has rested in part on responding to popular sector groups. In the case of Mexico, for example, the state has maintained relatively strong corporatist control over the popular sectors even as it has sought to channel some resources toward them. Mexico borrowed extensively after the first oil shock to maintain public subsidies on fuel, food, and other items of popular consumption (5.3 percent of GNP in 1973–1976). It then imposed a brief stabilization program and repeated the experience of the period 1979–1981. At that point, the expectation of additional state revenues because of the oil boom was an important factor leading to the country's current devastating financial crisis. Mexico was unable to shift expectations quickly enough as oil prices flattened. Thus, some of Mexico's extensive foreign debt resulted from government desires to channel additional resources toward the popular sector in a context of an expected continuation of high state revenues from oil. Underscoring regime control over the popular sector, though, the Mexican government under Miguel de la Madrid has been implementing a relatively rigorous stabilization program in spite of that program's negative impact on the same groups that were favored with loan-supported subsidies in the 1970s.

The Colombian political regime, more open to powerful societal interests, managed its bonanza of the 1970s in a very different manner. The country's export boom generated by coffee and illegal drugs differed from Mexico's oil boom in two key respects: The export receipts were not channeled through the state, and there were low expectations that they would continue. Indeed, as Edgar Revéiz and María José Pérez note in Chapter 11, the political strength of the coffee sector meant that most of the benefits during the period of the bonanza flowed to it. The popular sector was negatively affected because the government was forced to cut back on progressive public investment. Nevertheless, the government's decision not to accept additional foreign commercial loans at that time is a key factor in explaining why Colombia avoided the financial crisis that devastated most of its continental neighbors in the early 1980s.

Conclusion

The difficult period Latin Americans are now suffering through would be more acceptable if they at least had a greater understanding of why they entered it and how they could emerge from it. In this chapter, we have argued that the economic performance of the B-A regimes was generally unsatisfactory both in comparison to the earlier civilian regimes in their own countries and in comparison to civilian regimes in other Latin American countries during equivalent time periods. In considering their policy failures in contrast to civilian regimes, we have stressed various recent factors, including their choice of economic theory and the lack of any international constraint until 1981. In addition, in reflecting on the unexpected intensity with which some of the B-A regimes chose radical policies and were able to stay with them for long periods of time, we have emphasized the importance of their repressive capacities as military regimes. However, for many of these countries, we believe there were also important historical antecedents for the kind of policy approach the B-A regimes pursued.

Earlier historical processes shaped these countries and made certain political responses and economic outcomes more likely. The authors of several chapters and commentaries in this book speak of countries with "pendular" economic and political patterns as opposed to "moderate" ones. A historical review suggests that prior to the current period of crisis, some countries—such as Colombia, Mexico, and Venezuela— pursued moderate and relatively continuous economic policies in contrast to others—such as Argentina, Chile, and Peru—that followed more pendular ones. The latter three countries had a similar historical pattern of regime orientation, beginning with authoritarian populists, followed by civilian reformers, "radicals," and then monetarist economic orthodoxy (and bureaucratic-authoritarian regimes in the two more-industrialized countries).[9]

In contrast, the countries that followed a moderate policy had experienced populism and reform differently and had avoided the extreme orientations of the "radical" or "monetarist" phases. Thus, they have generally eschewed radical populist policies—with high inflation, extreme protection, dramatic wage increases, and extensive fiscal deficits—or extreme neoliberal ones—brusquely eliminating state subsidies and fiscal deficits, imposing massive devaluations, sharply curtailing wage increases, controlling the money supply, and reducing tariffs. The moderate countries generally shifted at an earlier stage of their industrialization and in a more gradual fashion from import-substituting industrialization to one that also focused on export promotion. In this way, their problems of foreign exchange scarcity and employment generation associated with the more advanced stages of import substitution were not as severe. In turn, this moderation was partially aided by the fact that the popular sector was integrated into the political life of the country in a more gradual, controlled, and less contested fashion, largely preventing the intensely conflictual periods of "inclusion" and then "exclusion" associated with pendular shifts in economic policy.

Consideration of historical moderate and pendular patterns challenges us to consider two basic issues. In regard to the moderate countries, to what extent has their success come at a cost of slow progress toward social equity, which, if not addressed, could eventually challenge the countries' political structures? For many people this will be a price worth paying if they believe the alternative is the experience of the pendular cases. Others might turn to the socialist cases for inspiration.

The question in the pendular countries is not simply how to improve their performances. It is more how to transform them to slow down or eliminate the brusque policy shifts with the goal of avoiding future bureaucratic-authoritarian or other more repressive regimes. Diamand and Fishlow both note how such countries currently confront a pattern that is different from that associated with earlier pendulum swings. In the past, the bulk of these countries' debt was accumulated by the populist civilian governments, and austerity was imposed by the military governments. Recently, the military governments in these countries began by imposing austerity and then accumulated debts far in excess of any ever accumulated by the populist governments. Thus, civilian governments have taken power with the need to impose austerity programs of their own. We must ask if international economic actors will be more flexible in their response to Latin America's debt situation. And we can hope that the painful history of polarization and repression in these countries will lead to "political learning" that can break their tragic historical pattern.

Notes

Comments on an earlier version of this paper by Daniel Levy, Carmelo Mesa-Lago, Kevin Middlebrook, Guillermo O'Donnell, and John Sheahan are gratefully acknowledged.

1. Our comparisons are very sensitive to the choice of ending year because of the violent fluctuations in output, prices, and balance-of-payments pressures since 1980. To minimize that problem, we have used three alternative endpoints where possible: 1980, 1982, and a weighted average of 1981–1983. We have presented several indicators of balance-of-payments performance. The standard measure of debt service as a fraction of exports excludes private commercial debt, which was very large in both Chile and Argentina, and includes amortizations, which should be treated separately. As an alternative measure, we have estimated the interest charge on the change in the total debt over a regime's period in office and compared that figure with exports in the final year. In this way, we can contrast the increase in interest liabilities incurred by a regime with the export receipts during its years in power.

2. Any regime in office at the end of the 1970s is likely to look bad in comparison to a regime in the 1940s or 1960s. If the record of the Brazilian military regime were taken only from 1964 to the end of the so-called miracle in 1973, the average growth rate was 9 percent, far higher than the record of the civilian governments in Brazil in the 1950s.

3. For more detail, see the next section and Chapter 5.

4. The results of this comparison need to be considered with some caution since the historical economic performance of the different countries is not considered.

5. Costa Rica is an exception to this general statement. It had a high investment rate, but, because of substantial government deficits, it had a very low saving rate. In the 1970s, the difference was covered by foreign borrowing. However, by 1981 the debt-to-GNP ratio had reached 92 percent, the highest of any of the countries in the sample. When and if Costa Rica is forced to pay back those loans, its growth rate will probably suffer. It had a high rate of growth in the 1970s, but that had changed by 1981.

6. See O'Donnell 1982. It needs to be pointed out, however, that in some countries recent civilian rulers appear to have had worse records than military ones. The repression and state terrorism in Argentina during the time Juan Perón and then his wife Isabel were in office (1973–1976) were worse than under General Juan Carlos Onganía (1966–1970). The conflicts with guerrillas in the Peruvian southern highlands led the Belaúnde government to institute repressive measures that may have been more severe than those of the military when it held office.

7. An analysis of the transition from B-A regimes to civilian ones is outside the scope of this chapter. The Chilean case underscores, however, that economic failure by itself is insufficient to bring down a B-A regime, except perhaps in the very long term. Other factors such as the nature and unity of the ruling coalition and of the opposition must be considered.

8. Fishlow (Chapter 4) is less condemnatory of Brazil's strategy of adjustment to the increased oil prices than are Lamounier and Moura (Chapter 7), and thus he places more of the blame on the scissors effect following the second oil shock than on the earlier policy choices.

9. For an analysis of the redistributive efforts of the populists, reformers, and radicals in these three countries, see Ascher 1984. Brazil could be considered an intermediate case, in which the reformist and radical episodes were compressed and terminated by the 1964 military coup.

References

Ascher, William. 1984. *Scheming for the Poor: The Politics of Redistribution in Latin America.* Cambridge: Harvard University Press.

O'Donnell, Guillermo. 1982. "Reply to Remmer and Merkx." *Latin American Research Review* 17, no. 2:41–50.

4

Latin American Adjustment to the Oil Shocks of 1973 and 1979

Albert Fishlow

Three developments have dominated the political economy of Latin America over the last decade. The first was the broad regional commitment to debt-financed adjustment to the oil price shock of 1973-1974 and its aftermath. Even Latin American countries favorably influenced by the higher price of oil chose to take advantage of expanding international credit markets. The consequence was a level of debt in the region that was 40 percent of the developing country total of $830 billion at the end of 1984, strikingly disproportionate to Latin America's 28 percent share of developing country income and its 16 percent share of exports of goods and services.[1]

Second, there was the widespread failure of such a debt-dependent strategy by the beginning of the 1980s. From 1981 to 1983, average income per capita in the region declined absolutely, a result without precedent since the availability of national accounts for the region in the post–World War II period. Equally noteworthy, the decline affected virtually every Latin American country. For a region so heterogeneous, the uniformity of the contraction makes it clear that this was no run-of-the-mill adjustment. Only at the end of 1984 were there some signals of recovery, and even they were tempered by the poorer performance of the industrial countries and of world trade in 1985. For almost all countries, the dismal recent record is worse than that of the Great Depression of the 1930s.

Yet, in the midst of such difficulties, a third trend is perceptible: a retreat from military rule in favor of popularly chosen civilian governments. In South America, only Paraguay and Chile remain under dictatorial regimes. Elsewhere, transitions have been successfully managed. Even in Brazil, the indirect election was won by the opposition candidate, Tancredo Neves, despite an electoral college controlled by the government. In Pinochet's Chile, the constitutional term of military control until 1989

54

is accepted, but a new, and unified, opposition of political parties (excluding the Communists) is seeking to implement a transition to follow. Not since the early 1960s, before the coup in Brazil in 1964 and during the heyday of the reformism embodied in the Alliance for Progress, has the region exhibited such a civilian complexion.

The purpose of this chapter is to examine the factors responsible for these pronounced tendencies of the last several years and, in particular, to explore some aspects of the complex and subtle interrelationship between political forms and economic policies and performance. The first section focuses on the period 1974–1978 and the style of Latin America's adjustment to the oil price shock. It does so in a comparative perspective, drawing upon different national experiences within the region as well as upon the East Asian pattern exemplified by Korea, Singapore, and Taiwan. The second section analyzes the regional response to the second oil price shock of 1979 and the accompanying world recession, differentiating between the relative force of external and internal factors in the deterioration of the regional balance-of-payments and commenting upon the archetypical Mexican, Brazilian, and Chilean responses. The third section takes as a starting point the near ubiquity of International Monetary Fund (IMF) stabilization programs in the region and poses the question of the compatibility of evolving popular political participation in many countries and the design of economic policies to curb inflation and to improve the balance of payments.

Patterns of Economic Adjustment to the Oil Shock

When the quadrupling of oil prices struck the world economy in the fall of 1973, developing countries were in the midst of a phase of accelerating growth. Improving terms of trade from the early 1960s on and continuing rapid expansion of world trade offered increasing incentives to outward-oriented development strategies. The countries that so opted, most prominently Korea and Taiwan but also some in Latin America— like Brazil and Colombia—that gave increasing weight to export promotion, were rewarded with higher rates of growth. Integration into the international economy was not exclusively via exports. Even in the late 1960s, an expanding Eurocurrency market had begun to discover the profitability of commercial loans to what would soon be baptized "the newly industrialized countries." Their import capacity and their access to needed capital goods and intermediate inputs thereby outstripped export earnings. The foreign exchange constraint that had been so prominent a structuralist explanation of lagging developing country growth in the mid-1960s no longer seemed to apply.

The abrupt rise in oil prices in 1973 threatened such optimism. Its direct consequence was to increase the cost of petroleum imports, but the indirect effects also hampered the prospects of developing countries. There was a sharp recession in the industrialized countries as they responded with restrictive aggregate policies to the inflationary impulse of the higher oil prices. That recession translated into reduced export demand just when export receipts were even more essential for Latin American countries. The second impact was the stimulus given to the prices of other tradables as the oil price shock ramified through the economic structure. Although prices of both imports and exports rose, developing countries tended to experience a deterioration of their nonoil terms of trade in the face of diminished demand for their primary exports. They also were subject to a strong surge of imported inflation and potential exchange rate appreciation.

The resulting balance-of-payments deterioration could be offset by compensating adjustments in imports and exports, by an inflow of new capital, or in the short term, by variation in the level of reserves. Countries pursued a variety of policies as they sought to adapt to the shock. Those fully committed to an export-led growth strategy emphasized an increasing participation in the more slowly expanding, and sometimes shrinking, industrialized-country markets. Others turned to relief on the import side, either by substituting domestic production for imports or by slowing growth to reduce import demand. Still others supplemented such real adjustment mechanisms by relying on external finance to gain time and reduce the short-term costs of the more immediate response.

Bela Balassa has shown how it is possible to decompose the balance-of-payments effects of higher import and export prices and reduced external demand into export promotion, import substitution, lower growth, and additional net finance.[2] I apply that framework, modifying it to measure the extent of the shock on the basis of expected, rather than realized, trade. Such a revision not only gauges the shock more accurately, prior to the adjustment of imports and exports, but also distributes the various policy responses more comparably in current prices.

Table 4.1 presents the results of the decomposition of the effects of higher tradable prices in 1974–1978 relative to 1971–1973 and of slower export growth relative to a 1963–1973 trend—if countries had maintained constant market shares. The first captures the direct and indirect terms-of-trade impacts of the rise in oil prices; the second, the reduction in export volume as a result of changes in world trade. The rise in exports resulting from an increase in a country's market share is measured by the difference between its actual and its 1971–1973 share. Reduced imports through substitution of domestic production are calculated as the difference between actual and projected imports on the assumption of actual growth rates and 1963–1973 import demand elasticities. In turn, the difference between such a projection and the 1963–1973 import growth trend reflects the effect of reduced income growth in 1974–1978 relative to the previous decade. Increased finance is measured relative to the net requirements implicit in the 1963–1973 import and export trends. Such capital requirements exclude borrowing to cover interest and dividend payments, or acquisition of reserves.

Eight countries, five Latin American and three East Asian, are included in Table 4.1. The magnitude of the shock relative to GNP was clearly greater for each of the East Asian countries than for any of the Latin American ones. Measured as a proportion to trade, only Chile and Brazil compare with Korea, Singapore, and Taiwan. Colombia actually gained from terms-of-trade tendencies during the period, after the coffee price rose in 1975–1976, and neither Argentina nor Mexico was very affected—a situation that corresponded to the energy balance of the former and the increasing net export position of the latter.

Only the countries that were significantly affected needed to devise aggressive export responses, and they were the only ones to show an increase in market shares during the period. In the case of Korea, the gain in export receipts was sufficient to meet more than half of the initial balance-of-payments loss. For the others, the contribution of export promotion was smaller and forced reliance on other measures. For Chile, Taiwan, and Singapore, the principal answer was found in a reduction of imports through reduced income growth. For Brazil, the dominant form of adjustment was import substitution, which permitted the attainment of a growth rate in 1974–1978 above the 1963–1973 trend (although below the "miracle" years of 1968–1973). Note, moreover, that Korea systematically reduced import requirements as well and thereby obtained an additional basis for accelerating product growth.

Of all the countries represented, only three visibly resorted to significant borrowing in excess of trend requirements: Brazil, Mexico, and Singapore. But the methodology obscures a fourth and important case, Korea. Because both import substitution and additional finance requirements are measured with reference to the historical level of import demand, Korea's uncommonly high import propensity translates into presumptive high and continuing capital inflows and a low value for *additional* finance requirements. The counterpart is a larger scope for import substitution effects. In fact, Korea's highly unbalanced trade during the 1960s had been financed by official aid on generous terms, but that amount of aid was no longer available. Hence, Korea's reliance on new, commercial indebtedness in the aftermath of the shock is understated.

Table 4.2, with its specific information on the sources of external funds and their applications and on the external debt, usefully supplements

Table 4.1

EXTERNAL SHOCKS AND POLICY RESPONSES, 1974-1978

A.
(million current $)

	Argentina	Brazil	Chile	Colombia	Mexico	Korea	Singapore	Taiwan
Shocks								
Price effects	319	4,026	1,338	-479	-343	3,898	747	1,324
Export volume effects	52	966	105	273	522	791	577	884
Total	371	4,992	1,443	-206	179	4,689	1,324	2,208
Policies								
Added net finance	-195	791	-43	62	1,442	-1,630	682	-673
Increase in export shares	-140	817	547	-36	-402	2,761	461	158
Import substitution	677	3,951	379	-221	-1,148	4,663	-784	574
Import effects of slower growth	28	-566	559	-10	284	-1,106	963	2,151

B.
(%)

	Argentina	Brazil	Chile	Colombia	Mexico	Korea	Singapore	Taiwan
Total shock as Proportion of:								
Average trade	8.9	41.1	68.0	-10.4	3.4	53.0	15.5	27.2
GNP	0.6	3.5	11.2	-1.1	0.2	13.5	22.8	12.2
Increase in export shares as proportion of exports	-3.0	7.9	25.5	-1.8	-18.2	34.6	6.4	1.9
Import substitution as proportion of imports	18.2	28.3	18.1	-11.4	-17.5	47.9	-8.0	7.1
Import effects of slower growth as proportion of imports	0.7	-4.0	26.7	0.5	4.4	-11.4	9.8	26.7

Notes:

Calculation of $(P_{M_1} - P_{M_0})M_1^t - (P_{X_1} - P_{X_0})X_1^t + P_{X_1}(X^t - X^h) \equiv (R_X - R_1^t) + P_{X_1}(X_1 - X_1^h)$

           Price Effect   Export Volume   Additional   Increase in
                           Effect   Net Finance   Export Shares

$$+ P_{M_1}(M_1^h - M_1) + P_{M_1}(M_1^t - M_1^h)$$

           Import   Import Effects
           Substitution   of Slower Growth

where: P_{M_1} and P_{X_1} are prices of imports and exports in 1974-78 and 1971 and 1973

      M_1^t and X_1^t are 1974-78 imports and exports extrapolated from 1963-73 trend

      M_1^h is 1974-78 imports predicted by constant 1963-73 import income elasticity

      X_1^h is 1974-78 exports predicted by constant 1971-73 market share of trade

      M_1 and X_1 are actual 1974-78 imports and exports

      R_1 is the 1974-78 resource gap, $P_{M_1}M_1 - P_{X_1}X_1$

      R_1^t is the 1974-78 resource gap extrapolated from $P_{M_0}M_1^t - P_{X_0}X_1^t$

For original data and a variant decomposition see Bela Balassa, "The Newly Industrializing Developing Countries after the Oil Crisis," Weltwirtschaftliches Archiv, vol. 117, no. 1 (1981).

Table 4.2

EXTERNAL FINANCE, 1974-1978

	Argentina	Brazil	Chile	Colombia	Mexico	Korea	Singapore	Taiwan
A. Sources and Uses, Average (millions current $)								
Sources:								
Direct investment	73	1,426	49	-61	601	88	542	67
Portfolio capital[a]	134	6,388	235	654	2,453	1,750	580	-281
Uses								
Resource gap	-1,156	3,880	-341	44	1,098	854	660	-390
Factor payments	558	2,771	272	369	1,864	265	67	131
Increase in reserves	803	1,164	353	179	93	720	396	45
B. External Debt (millions current $ and %)								
Gross medium and Long-term debt								
1973	3,323	12,572	2,102	4,048	8,310	3,556	459	1,281
1978	7,290	43,500	3,361	6,911	32,622	11,992	1,120	3,903
Net medium and Long-term debt								
1973	2,215	6,156	1,568	3,964	6,955	2,667	-1,827	158
1978	2,143	31,606	905	6,109	30,675	9,461	-4,183	2,394
Gross debt service ratio (relative to exports of goods and services)								
1963	19.9	37.7	22.4	36.3	28.7	12.9	6.2	4.8
1978	40.3	59.1	13.2	44.5	60.3	13.7	5.2	6.0

[a]Includes errors and omissions and official transfers

Sources: For original data and a variant decomposition see Bela Balassa, "The Newly Industrializing Developing Countries after the Oil Crisis," Weltwirstschaftliches Archiv, vol. 117, no. 1 (1981); World Bank, World Debt Tables: External Debt of Developing Countries (Washington, D.C., 1984).

the decomposition of Table 4.1. In the case of Singapore, the latter table confirms that the additional finance mainly took the form of direct investment rather than indebtedness. Over the period of 1974–1978 as a whole, Singapore's average annual inflow of $542 million in equity was more than four times as large as the portfolio investment of $123 million. Even including the latter with the sizable errors and omissions category, the equity form remains about as large as all other possible sources. The recorded gross debt rose quite modestly in relation to GNP between 1973 and 1978, while debt service declined as a percentage of exports from 6 percent to only 5 percent. In 1978, as a result of continuing reserve acquisition, Singapore became a net creditor.

Both Colombia and Taiwan, in accordance with the decomposition analysis, show a very modest dependence upon increased indebtedness. Instead, each had a surplus of merchandise exports over imports. For Colombia, unaffected for the most part by the rise in oil prices, there was no reason to borrow. For Taiwan, where the shock was considerable, such an explanation does not serve. In fact, the annual data do show an initial acceptance of foreign borrowing to meet the balance-of-payments deficit, but this acceptance was not part of a strategy of debt-financed adjustment. Instead, deflationary polices were applied as early as 1974, in response to the domestic inflation and external trade imbalance caused by the higher oil prices. The real money supply fell by 24 percent, and there was an immediate effect on reduced economic growth. As this reduction began to influence imports and a more aggressive exchange rate policy stimulated exports, borrowing ceased to play a role. Indeed, the balance-of-payments entry for net capital inflow, inclusive of errors and omissions, is negative. The positive change in debt, although small, reveals a larger gross inflow compensated for by outflows.

Adjustment in Argentina, Chile, and Mexico

More surprisingly, in view of their later prominence as victims of the debt crisis in the early 1980s, neither Argentina nor Chile were considered to be among the countries dependent upon foreign credit. Argentina did not need capital inflows to rectify its balance of payments in 1974 because of its own energy balance and favorable export prices; in 1975, more-adverse terms of trade and increasingly chaotic internal conditions led to some net borrowing, and to even larger gross flows to offset capital flight. Over the period as a whole, exports exceeded imports, and thus, a substantial part of the factor payments and increases in reserves were covered. The recorded debt increase therefore was not applied for productive purposes, nor did the money even apparently stay in the country. It officially entered only to leave under private auspices as the large divergence between net capital entry and change in the debt indicate. After 1978, the difference became even more striking as capital flight accelerated.

Like Argentina, Chile felt the brunt of changing terms of trade only in 1975 when there was a very sharp reduction in copper prices. Indeed, in 1974, Chile had benefited from a resumption of capital inflow—much of it bilateral—as part of the rescheduling of obligations undertaken by the new military government. When the shock did occur, Chile met the adverse circumstances by a massive decline of income per capita, on the order of 15 percent. Already under the strictures of the IMF in 1975 and committed to internal stabilization rather than to adjustment to new external conditions, extensive borrowing in the capital market was never a realistic possibility. Argentina could not borrow amid the signs of the weakness of its economy and of the diminishing authority of its Peronist government, although it sought greater access to capital markets. Chile voluntarily forwent a debt-financed adjustment strategy in favor of more radical and immediate reform, although it might very well have encountered difficulty in borrowing had it chosen otherwise. Private sources of funds were not attracted by economic orthodoxy in lieu of performance.

The three countries with good credit ratings could all point to a record of prior performance and successful commercial borrowing. That seems to have been the common factor. Mexico borrowed well beyond the requirements imposed by adverse external circumstances. Instead, the realized balance-of-payments deficit was the result of expansive internal policies under the auspices of a larger public sector role. Ironically, such new policies, involving a significant modification of the previous model of stabilizing development, were initially intended to reduce the fiscal deficit and to encourage exports. Thus, dependence on external resources might be reduced, and a growth that was more oriented toward employment and income distribution could be implemented. Such intentions, extending to import liberalization and lesser subsidies for national industrialization, were implemented more effectively on the public expenditure than on the revenue side. As the share of the public sector increased in capital formation and the industrial sector, so did the deficit. Higher domestic inflation and a larger balance-of-payments shortfall followed.

The governmental and balance-of-payments deficits could not be financed from abroad indefinitely. Mexico was forced to devalue its currency and to accept an IMF-administered stabilization program in 1976 with the advent of a new presidential administration. Restrictive policies in 1977 reduced borrowing requirements, but the country gave way to more expansive tendencies once more in 1978. By that time, Mexican oil was a reality rather than a prospect, and financial markets were eager to share the fruits of the country's prosperity.

Mexico's adjustment to the new international economy prevailing after 1973 was thus increasingly favored by the oil price rise that had ushered it in.[3] A rising share of petroleum exports—by 1978, they were almost a third of the merchandise exported—meant progressively more favorable terms-of-trade effects relative to the early 1970s. As a marginal producer, there were no quantity limitations of market demand, only supply constraints that borrowing partially helped overcome. The resumed reliance upon debt and the dramatic deterioration of the debt service ratio by 1978 were only modestly worrisome. Mexico's export growth seemed automatic because of oil.

Such optimism ignored two negative aspects of the aggressive use of debt. First, the borrowing was increasingly going to finance remittances of interest and dividends on past capital inflows rather than to support new merchandise imports for investment. Second, debt was being contracted in order to satisfy demands for capital outflows. The reported debt increased by $24 billion in 1974–1978; net capital entries increased by only $10 billion or so. Capital flight in anticipation of devaluation in 1975-1976 is a prominent part of the explanation.

Adjustment in Brazil and Korea

In Brazil, a country caught by the oil price rise in the midst of a period of very rapid growth, the adverse balance-of-payments effects were real enough.[4] They provoked a delayed response, met in the first instance by massive borrowing to offset the unprecedented import surplus of 1974. That initial decision was a decisive one. It increased subsequent capital requirements to meet service payments on the debt, and more important, it demonstrated the feasibility of sustaining high rates of growth despite changes in external circumstances. The Brazilian determination to maintain high growth was subsequently reinforced by the favorable upturn of coffee prices in late 1975 and 1976 as well as by a demonstrated capacity to increase export shares modestly.

Although the volume of borrowing thus undertaken was considerable, the underlying adjustment strategy was dominated by import substitution: Capital goods and intermediate imports were reduced to a minimum, and domestic investment provided incentives to produce local alternatives. Even oil requirements would be tackled by aggressive efforts to use alcohol in place of gasoline. Public sector enterprises, themselves more easily able to borrow abroad, were a favored instrument in the implementation of the substitution strategy.

By 1978, the debt had more than trebled from its 1973 level. The continuing favorable reception of Brazil in financial markets, and Brazil's willingness and eagerness to borrow, are signaled by how much of the capital inflow was superfluous, serving, as Table 4.2 shows, for the acquisition of reserves rather than to finance a current account deficit. Still, over the period as a whole, the principal application of borrowing was to permit a large excess of imports over exports. Unlike the Mexican case, there was neither a problem of capital flight nor an excessive absorption of resources to service past capital flow.

Brazil's adjustment to the oil shock remained partial, however, and export promotion never was an important source of relief, as Table 4.1 makes clear. Import substitution had lowered foreign inputs to a minimum, leaving little additional flexibility in the balance of payments. The costs of servicing the debt were at an uncomfortably high level in 1978 and already dominated the current account deficit. There was the danger that debt was substituted for adjustment rather than financing it.

In Korea, external borrowing was again a central component of adjustment strategy.[5] It could hardly fail to be in view of the magnitude of the balance-of-payments shock: 53 percent of the average value of trade and 13.5 percent of GNP. Unlike Taiwan, however, the use of external credit was more than a temporary expedient. Korean policy was aimed at actively enhancing traditional export participation while relying upon extensive investment in heavy and intermediate industry to establish the basis for both import substitution and subsequent export penetration. Continued rapid growth, not deflation, was pursued, and external finance was required to make the policy objectives compatible. Far from concentrating their borrowing in the aftermath of the oil price shock, the Koreans continuously used external finance to finance the resource gap between imports and exports and reserve acquisition.

As a consequence, the Korean debt increased in percentage terms between 1973 and 1978 only a little less rapidly than the Mexican or Brazilian, but two circumstances made it far less worrisome. First, there was a large official component to the debt that made its average, and marginal, cost cheaper. In 1978, variable interest rate loans were only 21 percent and concessional loans 23 percent of the total debt, the marginal interest rate was less than 9 percent, and maturity of new commitments was more than fourteen years. In Brazil, variable interest loans were about two-thirds of the total debt and concessional loans less than 5 percent, the marginal interest rate exceeded 10 percent, and maturity was less than ten years. Mexico's terms were even more unfavorable, reflecting a greater reliance on commercial sources of credit and a willingness to finance on a shorter-term basis.[6]

Second, debt service was therefore cheaper for Korea, and its capacity to meet those obligations was also greater. Because export receipts quadrupled between 1973 and 1978, the debt service ratio remained stable, and because they were a large percentage of the total gross product, the ratio remained low (see Table 4.2). Although there was later to be criticism of the Korean strategy because of its excessive emphasis upon capital-intensive intermediate industry at the expense of exports and its pursuit of rapid growth at the expense of inflationary pressures, foreign borrowing never got out of hand or later posed a significant threat to domestic objectives.

Two Patterns of Adjustment

This brief comparative analysis confirms distinctive styles of economic adaptation to the oil price shock of 1973-1974 with its attendant effects on the international economy. Two broad patterns stand out. One is a reliance on finance, cum import substitution and export promotion in varying degrees, to sustain relatively high rates of growth. The other is an acceptance of lower initial growth to curb imports accompanied by efforts to increase export proceeds to permit economic recovery. Brazil and Mexico fall into the first group; Chile, Singapore, and Taiwan in the latter. Korea is intermediate, relying on debt for industrial development directed toward exports. Argentina and Colombia, relatively unaffected by the changes in prices and the international recession, followed policies of limited debt accumulation that were dictated by internal circumstances rather than by external necessities.

These two patterns correspond roughly to what might be expected of the ideal models of the passive small economy and the active large economy. For a small economy engaged significantly in trade, the effect of changing international relative prices and world demand will provoke relatively large income and output effects. Deterioration of the terms of trade reduces real income, and if properly reflected in real exchange rates, should induce more domestic production of exports and import substitutes. Such a substitution cannot avert the real income decline, but it can maintain output and employment. For countries faced with an elastic external demand, the accompanying lower real wages mean greater competitiveness, larger market shares, and an opportunity for resumed growth. If resources are relatively flexible, so that the costs of adjustment are small, there is little reason to debt finance and to postpone the inevitable initial decline in domestic income and the subsequent realignment of production and relative prices.

The story for a large economy is different. It too cannot avert the income and output implications of worsened terms of trade, but because these are relatively smaller for a large economy and economic activity is more oriented to the domestic market, reallocation is biased toward import substitution and increased investment. Furthermore, there is likely to be more resistance to real income declines emanating from external shocks in large economies: Trade is not so pervasive, and competitiveness is not so central an objective. Debt is therefore attractive as a means of financing the new activities as well as averting an unnecessarily large drop in income in order to restore an immediate balance-of-payments equilibrium through the reduction of imports. Debt thus has a strategic as well as a tactical significance.

These considerations of economic size do not fully explain actual policy choice, however. Structural inflexibilities reflect not only technical characteristics but also responses of private economic agents and government policymakers. It is wrong therefore to presume that the decisions taken were ordained simply by size. In the first place, the decision makers relied upon their perception of opportunities in the external market, not necessarily the reality. In the second, they depended upon an evaluation of the political feasibility of immediate income declines versus more gradual accommodation. In the third, they incorporated different assessments of the permanence of the shock. Finally, they reflected attitudes to uncertainty inherent in a debt-financed strategy that postpones costs until the future.

The choice for debt was a natural one for the Latin American economies, which were long accustomed to an active and interventionist tradition. Presiding over an automatic reduction of real income equivalent to the petroleum tax was not a relevant policy option. In neither Brazil nor Mexico was there confidence in the possibility of increasing exports— Mexico had already felt the pinch of a foreign exchange constraint prior to 1973—and the prospect of large income declines to reduce import demand was an unattractive confession of futility in the face of external circumstances. Moreover, such a recession would come at an especially inopportune time as the issue of income inequality was coming to the fore.

The Echeverría administration in Mexico sought to incorporate distributionist concerns in its correction of the previous model of development that was beginning to show signs of deterioration. New import substitution under state guidance and employment creation without adverse import effects were important aspects of the new strategy. Larger public sector deficits and the need for external finance were its consequences. To fail to take advantage of the new resources that were so readily available in the capital markets was to reject an opportunity that seemed tailor-made. Those resources would allow Mexico to pursue its distribution objectives without yielding to either foreign exchange limitations or constraints on public sector finance.

In Brazil, the pressures to distribute the absolute gains of the rapid growth more equitably were no fewer. To sustain growth in order to accommodate social pressures, and thereby to manage a controlled extrication from military rule, was only one motive. The military view of national security had increasingly linked Brazil's preeminence with economic performance, and the challenge of adjusting to the oil shock was a welcome opportunity to display the new maturity of the technocratic state and the virtues of central, planned direction. National enterprise was a third element in the equation. The new surge of import substitution was a source of potential profits and a reinforcement of the virtues of national solutions. It is easy to see how the program to use alcohol instead of gasoline epitomized all of these tendencies and won broad support—except from the hard-pressed finance ministry, which had to find the resources for the project.

The role of economic growth as a legitimizing factor in the Korean case was no smaller. Although the pattern of growth was not income concentrating, nor did the issue have the same emerging importance as in the Latin American countries, its strategic significance was greater. Even before the oil shock, the most recent plan had given greater attention to a deepening of industry via domestic production of intermediate and capital goods. It had done so in response to the potential vulnerability of the country because of diminished U.S. support. Security was proximately, rather than potentially, linked to economic success.

Indeed, the puzzle is not so much to explain the option for debt as to explain why it was not followed. Market conditions made it attractive indeed: Through 1974 and 1975, interest rates were negative in real terms when measured in terms of export prices, and barely positive in terms of a general deflator. Interest rate differentials, after widening, narrowed. The small country model did not rule out capital flows but made them an integral part of the adjustment to external shocks. Excessively deflationary policies and high domestic interest rates would attract the capital that would permit more expansion of imports.

Colombia was not tempted to pursue an extravagant course. It took advantage of its improved circumstances to sustain its historical rate of growth but responded to the inflationary shock by seeking to dampen price rises. Policymakers seemed to concern themselves with not allowing government expenditure to get out of hand. In addition, rising coffee prices soon after the oil shock improved the country's balance of payments. Caution could be afforded, moreover, because economic growth had never been converted into a fetish, or a basis for political legitimacy.

Singapore and Taiwan also desisted and rejected market solutions in favor of much more conservative responses. Each placed more emphasis upon the restoration of competitiveness than upon immediate growth performance. Competitiveness was central to the success of economic models in which exports were the principal form of production. In Singapore, they actually exceeded the value of gross product; in Taiwan, they were almost half. Better to err in the direction of containing domestic disequilibrium to accomplish the necessary realignment quickly and directly. Fixed exchange rates, high domestic inflation rates, and limited capital inflow made a reduction in income the only instrument available. The fact that both countries could undertake such a policy was a tribute to the security of each governing party, and the public's appreciation of the imperatives facing a small country. Taiwan at this point was not without security concerns after Nixon's surprise visit to China in 1972, but it saw fit to deal with them by ensuring that its international position would not be compromised by dependence on capital rather than trade.

The Chilean reluctance was not similarly based. The acceptance of a dramatic drop in income was related to the new model of privatization and internationalization, and government interference was eschewed in favor of a market realignment of real wages. But Chile did not correspond to the East Asian countries in the extent of responsiveness of exports, nor in their importance to total production. The consequence was a larger decline in income to bring about a precarious equilibrium in the balance of payments. Of equal importance, the objective was, not growth, but stabilization. The further burden of confronting unfavorable terms of trade, the most unfavorable of all the countries considered, was as welcome to the Chilean military leaders as it was unwelcome to the Brazilian. The former could make their point by showing their willingness to pay the price of adjustment imposed by technical requirements. The latter could prove that an intelligent, technocratic domestic response could insulate Brazil from the consequences. In Korea, a military government emphasized diversification of national output and expansion of exports, which minimized the risk of increased indebtedness. Each course of action, however different in appearance, was similar in motivation, to reinforce authoritarian rule.

There is thus no simple relationship to which one can turn in assessing the interaction between politics and critical economic policy decisions. National circumstances dominate civilian/military distinctions. What is essential is the significance attached to uninterrupted economic growth as a basis for legitimacy, and the importance of centrality becomes even clearer in the response of the Latin American countries to the deterioration of economic conditions after the second oil price shock of 1979.

Internal and External Causes of the Crisis: The Region

The initial balance-of-payments consequences of the first 1973 oil shock were negative in Latin America. Despite an immediate gain for Venezuela, the increased deficits in the other countries of the region more than offset that gain. Although the rise in the price of oil produced a favorable change in the aggregate trade accounts of the region, the higher costs of other imports and their greater volume added up to a deterioration in the payments position.

A stronger import demand resulted from the decision to continue to pursue high growth targets despite the newly adverse terms of trade. This option of gradual adjustment without lowering income was financed by resorting to debt, a special characteristic of the region. Other developing countries chose to expand exports more rapidly or to cut back on income and imports. In Latin America, responding to favorable terms and quantities of loans, there was a distinct preference for sustaining growth *and* domestic expenditure.

For the next several years, the countries of the region had to respond to the new structure of relative prices and to the increased debt burden. On the whole, most seemed to be succeeding. The current account deficit of Latin America (excluding Venezuela) went from $13.5 billion in 1974 to $8.5 billion in 1977 and up again to $13.3 billion in 1978. Even at the last level, the ratio with respect to regional output was 3 percent compared to a 1973 preoil shock ratio of 2.1 percent and a bloated 1975 ratio of 5.2 percent.[7] Control over the balance of payments had been reasserted after the immediate postoil shock excesses.

To be sure, the intervening accumulation of capital inflows to sustain the adjustment had led to more than a proportional growth of indebtedness: In 1978, outstanding debt was more than twice the value of exports and about a third of the gross product, much higher levels than five years earlier. But so long as real interest rates were low (and negative with respect to the price of exports) and grace periods postponed repayment of principal, there seemed to be no debt service problem. And projections of a continuing decline in current account deficits and an expansion of export growth were persuasive in assuring that the future would be no more worrisome. As late as its 1979 annual report (written in 1980), the Inter-American Development Bank concluded, "At the end of the 1970s, the overall balance of economic results achieved by Latin America appears to be highly satisfactory, especially if we bear in mind the extraordinarily unfavorable conditions prevailing in the world economy in the last five years."[8]

The optimism of the late 1970s soon proved quite misplaced. The current account deficit climbed progressively after 1978, reaching $45.4 billion in 1981 despite radically reduced economic growth in that year. The deficit declined in 1982, but only because of a more than 20 percent reduction in imports, which was enforced by a lack of continuing access to credit. Of the cumulative and increasing shortfall of foreign exchange relative to the 1978 level, about 10 percent was contributed by a larger trade gap; the principal source of the rest was increased interest payments on the outstanding debt.

The special feature of the world recession that began with slower U.S. growth in 1979 was the conscious effort to attack high inflation in the industrialized countries. This effort translated into a decision not to validate the rise in oil prices that began with the Iran-Iraq war in that year. Despite the supply shock, continued tight money polices were pursued to force declines in demand growth. The consequence was an increase in interest rates, which was reinforced in 1981 by declining oil-exporting-country surpluses and the record fiscal deficits in the United States that accompanied the new Reaganomics. In contrast to the recession following the first oil price shock, which was brief and featured high inflation rates, the recession set in motion at the beginning of the 1980s was longer and explicitly targeted to disinflation via monetary restraint.

Whereas developing countries suffered from diminished demand for their exports during the first episode, there was at least the compensation of cheap credit to make up the deficiency. This equilibrating mechanism, in which trade and debt accounts offset each other, failed in the later period. Starting from much higher levels of debt in 1978, there was an adverse interest rate effect that came on top of the trade effect. Although initially, capital flows were available to avert dramatic adjustment efforts, by 1981 Latin America's growth could no longer be sustained. Despite a valiant reversal in trade, the inertia caused by debt service made the effort futile. It is the latter point that is critical.

Components of the Balance-of-Payments Crisis

Table 4.3 examines this later experience in more detail by disaggregating the components of changes in the current account of the region (excluding Venezuela) between 1979 and 1982. It is evident that debt interest payments played a dominant role. The trade deficit of $10 billion in 1981 was overwhelmed by the gross interest payments, which were almost three times greater. I have estimated the effect of the oil price changes after 1978 upon the trade balance. Note that for this regional aggregate, excluding Venezuela, the net impact was minimal because of the close balance between oil imports and exports. Whatever the indirect implications of the oil price shock, one cannot appeal to its direct effect to explain the regional deterioration in the balance of payments.

Nor can one simplistically invoke the recession as the explanation. I have reconstructed the regional balance of payments under the alternative scenario of a constant 3.2 percent growth rate for the industrialized countries from 1979 through 1982, an average attained in the 1973–1979 period. This recession effect is captured by combining estimates of the

Table 4.3

SOURCES OF DETERIORATION IN THE
CURRENT ACCOUNT OF LATIN AMERICA,[a] 1979-1982
(billions of dollars)

	1978	1979	1980	1981	1982	Cumulative 1979-1982
Actual trade balance	-1.2	-4.1	-8.9	-10.0	5.5	
Adjusted trade balance		-3.2	-8.3	-1.3	13.3	
Oil effect		0.9	0.6	-1.1	-3.6	
Recession effect				9.8	11.4	21.2
Export volume						
Terms of trade				9.8	11.4	21.2
Import policy effect		5.7	10.4	11.3	-8.3	19.1
Interest payments on debt						
Service (gross)	7.9	12.4	19.5	28.7	35.3	
Interest rate						
Effect (gross)		-1.1	1.5	12.8	21.0	34.2
Interest rate						
Effect (net)		-0.6	0.5	8.6	15.9	24.4
Actual current account	-13.3	-21.4	-33.4	-45.4	-34.9	
Adjusted current account		-21.1	-32.2	-28.1	-11.2	

[a]Excluding Venezuela

Adjusted Trade Balance: Actual trade balance minus sum of oil, and recession effects.
Oil Effect: Cost of net imports of oil minus hypothetical cost estimated on basis of variation in post-1978 oil price equivalent to nonoil export prices.
Recession Effect: Composite of terms-of-trade and volume effects.
Export Volume: Nonoil export value times cumulative negative percentage deviation between actual export volume and volume predicted from statistical regression substituting 3.2 percent industrialized-country growth in 1980-1982.
Terms of Trade: Cumulative negative percentage deviation between actual terms of trade (export prices of Latin American nonoil exporters, import prices of Latin American oil exporters) and terms of trade from statistical regression substituting 3.2 percent industrialized-country growth in 1980-1982.
Import Policy Effect: Actual import value adjusted by rates of hypothetical import volume to actual volume.
Interest Rate Effect: Based on difference between 1975-1978 average real interest rate and actual real rates. For short-term interest payments, the U.S. prime was used; for long- and medium-term, a weighted average of 0.7 for the prime rate and 0.3 for the OECD multilateral nonconcessional loan rate. Averages of year end debts were used. Net interest rate effect subtracts actual interest earnings adjusted by ratio of hypothetical real prime to actual from gross payments.
Adjusted Current Account: Actual current account minus sum of oil, recession, and net interest effects.
Sources: International Monetary Fund, World Economic Outlook 1983 (Washington, D.C., 1983); International Monetary Fund, Balance of Payments Statistics: Yearbook 1983 (Washington, D.C., 1983); Economic Commission for Latin America, Economic Survey of Latin America 1982 (New York: United Nations, 1983).

effect of variations in industrialized-country growth upon both the volume of Latin American exports and the terms of trade. Statistically significant relationships for both variables have been calculated for the period 1973–1982. They reveal a change of 1.3 percentage points of export growth for every percentage point change in the rate of growth of industrialized-country gross national product and a 2.4 percentage point improvement in the terms of trade with every percentage point change in the growth of gross product. The reported effects are the changes in trade deficits that would have occurred assuming constant growth and actual import values and prices.

The striking result is the absence of an export volume effect for the region as a whole. The reason is that actual volume in the period 1980–1982 outperformed the predicted level for even the higher growth rate. Under the pressure of the balance-of-payments necessity, there was already, before 1982, a concerted effort to increase the level of exports. There was a terms-of-trade deterioration, however, relative to what might have been expected with higher industrialized-country growth. That situation cost the region more than $21 billion in 1981 and 1982, offsetting the export volume response and complicating adjustment in those years.

Table 4.3 also shows the even larger effect of fixing real interest rates at their 1975–1978 level in comparison with actual real rates. In both 1979 and 1980, the impact was minimal—actually positive in the former year. The reason is that the continuing high rates of inflation in those years offset the high nominal interest rates. With subsequent disinflation, and real rates that approximated 10 percent in 1982, the constant real financial costs are much more significant. In the latter year, they clearly exceeded the estimated recession effect, which is what differentiates the Latin American situation, with its disproportionate debt at commercial rates, from the situation of developing countries as a whole.

Such calculations show that if the terms of trade had not deteriorated in an international setting of continuing growth or the real interest rates had remained at low levels, the crisis might have been avoided. In the former case, Latin America could have afforded a large fraction of the higher interest payments, although still not avoiding the adverse real income consequences. In the latter circumstance, favorable financial conditions would have made it possible to postpone the consequences of the adverse trade experience until the future. Despite the magnitude of the debt actually contracted, reductions in imports and economic activity could then have been avoided.

In fact, the countries of the region confronted both a declining demand for exports and rising real interest rates simultaneously. In response to such adversity, they could of course seek to stimulate more rapid export growth. Such a policy contributed to sustaining export volume but could not avert the ensuing terms-of-trade deterioration. Table 4.3 demonstrates the consequences of another option: more limited, and hence more prudent, import growth beginning in 1979. For this projection I assumed a pattern of real import increases of only 4 percent in 1979 and 1980, 2 percent in 1981, and none in 1982 versus an actual profile of 14, 8, 2, and −22 percent.

Such self-denial has an impact that is almost comparable to the recession or interest rate effects. Four years of such slower expansion would have saved $19 billion. In 1979 and 1980, such a policy would have meant small positive balances on merchandise account, and in 1981, it would have counterbalanced the deterioration in the terms of trade. But it still could not have averted the crisis in 1982. In that year, the policy would have required $8.3 billion more imports than were actually registered, and even the interim economies would have had an implied debt that was only a little more than 10 percent smaller than actually realized. Under the circumstances of an early commitment to a debt strategy, it was not easy to avoid the later problems by internal actions. But it is wrong to ignore that avenue completely in favor of placing exclusive blame on the trends in the international economy.

These estimates usefully delineate the nature of the external limitations the hemisphere was facing. By having embarked on a policy of growth-led debt in adjusting to the oil shock, some countries became vulnerable to debt-led debt when interest rates later rose. Then they could do little about the situation. Other countries that might have been able to do so instead increased their debt to finance larger imports. Even though the debt policy financed increases in investment, some foreign resources also underwrote domestic consumption. There was a partial substitution of potential national saving by cheap external capital. Statistical analysis suggests that each percentage point of additional real foreign resources reduced domestic savings by 0.3 percentage points.[9] Reliance on debt finance was at the expense of the harder task of domestic capital market reforms to assure the resources for the larger volume of investment that was required to sustain continuing growth. The problem was not that investment did not occur at all, and thus that the debt was wholly unproductive, as the investment ratio in the region did rise after 1973. Rather, the problem was that more was borrowed to accomplish that task than was desirable.

Although initially apparently inexpensive, the ultimate real cost of the loans was unknown because interest rates were variable, export demand was subject to external circumstances, and the supply of capital could not be taken for granted. What seemed to be highly favorable cost-benefit ratios proved progressively more illusory after 1979. As the current account deficit became dominated by interest payments, it contributed proportionally less to the real import surplus that influenced domestic growth capacity. Put another way, the debt increasingly became a vehicle for financing itself. Larger loans were required to meet the debt service obligations rather than to buy needed inputs for domestic investment.

The deterioration in the balance of payments after 1979 was abetted by policies in many countries that overvalued their exchange rates, reducing the incentive to export and increasing the attractiveness of imports. Overvaluation was the natural concomitant of access to foreign capital markets on disequilibrium terms. Neither the quantity nor the price of credit was accurately reflective of future conditions. For the time being, there seemed to be no shortage of foreign exchange, and cheaper imports were an advantage. Indeed, for some countries in the Southern Cone, such a strategy of overvaluation became a centerpiece of anti-inflation policy by encouraging potential competition from imports to alter inflationary expectations.

This further distortion had side effects of its own. The most serious was capital flight. An overvalued rate stimulated cumulative expectations of devaluation; dollars were better to have than pesos, and it was better to have the dollars outside the country than to have dollar-designated accounts within it. Soaring debt totals that exceeded net capital entry in Argentina and Mexico reflected a simple transfer of assets and liabilities: Argentine and Mexican citizens acquired dollar deposits and investments abroad while their governments borrowed on credit the dollars that they needed. Under these conditions, there was no real domestic investment counterpart to the debt at all. Between 1979 and 1982, Latin America, excluding Venezuela, lost approximately a third of the resources borrowed through offsetting capital flight.[10]

The combination of much more adverse external conditions and earlier domestic policies that increased vulnerability brought the countries of the region to their knees by 1982. It is clearly wrong to absolve Latin America of any complicity, but it is equally erroneous to ignore the new international environment after 1979 and the limited degrees of freedom at that time for borrowers who had chosen wrong and relied so extensively on external capital markets.

Mexico, Brazil, and Chile

This discussion in the aggregate has significant national variations. Although the broad hemispheric perspective is useful in characterizing the outlines of the problem, in the last analysis it is an artificial construct. There is no Latin American debt or foreign exchange earnings to service it, only national obligations and policies.

It is therefore useful to comment briefly upon the different experiences of Mexico, Brazil, and Chile to illustrate the diversity of the challenge and the source of the inadequacy of the responses to it. Mexico, as an expanding oil exporter, benefited from the second oil shock; Brazil, as the largest developing-country oil importer, was quite adversely affected; Chile pursued a special free-market strategy of international economic integration that was designed to improve economic performance.

Brazil conformed most characteristically to the regional aggregate, except for some adverse large oil effects that were neutralized for the region as a whole. By 1979, Brazil's prior debt accumulation had left that country so vulnerable to adverse international trends that only good fortune could have averted a major restructuring of the economy. Instead, the news was all bad, and that fact led to an ineffective policy of unrealism that made matters worse. The ministers of planning and finance, earlier the objects of acclaim for their technocratic managerial capacity, regularly reassured the financial community of Brazil's ability to adjust even after it became clear that Brazil could not do so. The country's leaders delayed in going to the IMF until late 1982, a decision that was rationalized as a fallout of Mexico's debt and lack of capital availability. Even then, Brazil received less than it might have, and the country set ambitious balance-of-payments targets that could be achieved only at the expense of slowing the economy.

Politics played a role in this Brazilian response. The guided transition to civilian governance demanded an apparent control over economic conditions to reassure a military leadership that only a few years earlier had been given reason to expect continuing economic growth. To avoid later unrest, the government unwisely modified the wage law in the midst of accelerating inflation and thus complicated its efforts at stabilization. To obscure the seriousness of the situation, the full extent of the indebtedness was understated, lest it provoke even more criticism of the government and the loss of its residual authority.

In the end, however, there was a severe debt burden and a sharp rise in interest rates. Imports had already been limited severely and were not a potential source of relief. More sensible exchange rate policies in 1980 would not have much increased export receipts in that year any more than rapid devaluation would have averted the progressively worsening terms of trade. Brazil lost as a result of its strategy primarily because post-1979 conditions were not like those of post-1973.

On the contrary, Mexico was favored by a massive injection of oil revenues that only later was partially offset by recession and interest rate effects. When those effects did occur, the government was unable to reverse the massive expenditure policies that many people had considered imprudent even before 1982. The country's debt doubled between 1978 and 1981, as a consequence, not of dire need, but of favorable opportunity as lenders sought out oil-rich Mexico.

In contrast to the regional picture, internal decisions in Mexico rather than exogenous circumstances governed the evolution of the balance of payments. An illustration is the effect more effective limits on imports would have had. Even presuming a high import elasticity of two through 1981, the debt at the end of that year would have been 33 percent smaller than the amount actually contracted, with favorable consequences for interest costs as well as capital flight. Domestic policies are very much the villain of the piece. Excess aggregate demand, generated by a rapid rise in the deficit of the public sector, was reflected in the external accounts. Between 1980 and 1982, the deficit rose from 7 to 17.6 percent of the gross domestic product.[11] Devaluation in early 1982 was poorly managed because since it was unaccompanied by needed complementary monetary and fiscal measures, it failed to discourage speculative capital outflow and only reinforced the expectation of a further currency re-alignment and made capital flight more attractive. Mexico reacted badly to the decline in oil prices and attempted, unsuccessfully, to sustain its prices.

Because the eventual collapse was primarily the result of domestic policies, the country's politics were critical. The principal factor was López Portillo's insistence upon unbridled expansion. Oil was a resource to be exploited to the hilt in satisfying all demands placed upon the state, without regard to the value of the particular projects that were undertaken. López Portillo's *sexenio* ("six-year term") was to be a historic time. That belief, rather than populist pressures and popular demands, fed the exaggerated boom. At its height, with the gift of doubled oil prices, Mexico's prosperity seemed able to afford waste and corruption. But domestic expenditures went too far, fueled by large infusions of debt. When interest rates rose and real oil prices declined, the stage was set for a crisis that need never have occurred. López Portillo wanted both massive investment and high rates of consumption. Lesser, but still high, levels of both variables could have been met on a sustained basis, or domestic consumption and imports might have been restrained. Only at the very end of his term, when it was much too late, did he implement restrictive exchange rate policies that were more consistent with the increase in the size of the public sector over which he had presided.

Chile's response to the second oil shock was conditioned by three sets of circumstances that differentiated it from the other two cases. First was Chile's adjustment to the first shock through declining income rather than increasing debt, which left the country with much lower service obligations in 1979. Second was its commitment to private market signals and an eager effort to promote an automatic adjustment of domestic economic activity to the international economy. Third was the country's conservative fiscal policy, which assured that the private sector, not the public one, would receive the external loans.

These responses did not avert a debt crisis, belying the claim that excessive public sector expansion is the universal cause of post-1979 problems in the region. The magic of the market failed for two reasons: International market signals were valid only for the short term and inadequate guides for the future, and domestic signals discouraged investment in the primary and secondary sectors in favor of an expansion of services and investment in construction.

Unlike Brazil, Chile's large borrowing in 1980 and 1981 was not motivated by balance-of-payments problems, nor was it motivated by an expansion of public investment as in Mexico. Oil imports remained at only 15 percent of total imports in Chile compared to about 50 percent in Brazil. The current account adjusted to the capital account rather than the other way around. External savings were encouraged as a way of equalizing Chile's high interest rates with much lower world levels. Because it was private firms that were doing the borrowing, it was argued that even though capital inflows were rapidly accelerating, the debt could not be excessive. Not only did the firms obviously understand what they were doing, but also the obligation was commercial rather than sovereign.

More generally, free capital markets went hand in hand with the implementation of international monetarism and the establishment of a fixed exchange rate in June 1979 that was intended to force the country's inflation rate down to the international level. In fact, the domestic inflation rate remained higher until 1981, provoking a cumulative overvaluation of the exchange rate. It could remain fixed, however, because the capital inflow more than compensated for the large trade deficits. Still, overvaluation distorted the production structure against the very exports and import substitutes necessary to permit a rapid adjustment of the balance of payments to changed international conditions.

Inside the country there occurred financial and real estate speculation in which foreign resources were directly applied. Large economic conglomerates used foreign capital obtained by subsidiary banks to finance at a favored cost the groups' nonbank enterprises. In 1982, the bubble burst, with corresponding sharp declines in construction and employment, but instead of an automatic domestic price adjustment to the fall in copper prices and export earnings, the shock resulted in a dramatic fall in production levels. Debt had become proportionally larger in relation to income than in Mexico or Brazil, and resulting interest costs, as in the other cases, made it necessary to turn to the IMF for assistance.

As in the other countries we have discussed, political considerations underlay the economic strategy followed in the wake of the oil shock. There was little appeal in restraining the economic recovery that was giving Pinochet's government new legitimacy and vindicating the free-market philosophy espoused by his economic advisers, and it was unnecessary to do so. On the contrary, the volume of borrowing showed the new confidence with which lenders viewed the prospects of the Chilean economy. If Brazil viewed the evolution of its international situation with alarm, and Mexico exploited its newfound source of real wealth, Chile's leaders indulged in premature self-congratulation that the country could manage well by passively disregarding what was happening around it. Such complacence came to an end in 1982. Pinochet was forced to dismiss his free-market ideologues, devalue, and rely on a public deficit to sustain limited domestic demand. Practical politics, even in Chile, dominated economic ideology.

The Political Economy of Austerity and Adjustment

Since 1982, virtually all the countries in the region—Colombia and Venezuela being the prominent exceptions—have been pursuing adjustment under the aegis of IMF stabilization programs. Their ubiquity derives neither from the attractiveness of the plans nor from the direct resources made available through IMF standby or even extended facility loans. Rather, it was only after agreement had been reached with the IMF that commercial banks became willing to reschedule their much larger loans and to make limited amounts of new money available.

Now, several years later, even the people who initially believed that a combination of internal adjustment efforts and a favorable external environment would establish the basis for a sustained economic recovery in the region are beginning to have second and third thoughts.[12] There is talk in the highest circles of the Reagan administration about bringing the World Bank and structural readjustment loans to the fore and allowing stabilization objectives and the IMF to recede somewhat. Such concern can hardly be surprising in view of the growth experience of the region. Per capita income, after declining 3.4 percent in 1982 and 5.6 percent in 1983, managed to increase only 0.6 percent in 1984, despite a buoyant international economic environment.

What has gone wrong? Certainly external conditions have been part of the problem. Industrialized-country growth did not recover strongly until 1984, and when it slid again in 1985, there was also increasing protectionist pressure. And while nominal interest rates have fallen sharply, real interest costs to developing countries still are something like 5 percent a year and thus considerably above the 3 percent that is usually taken as the long-term norm. The unfavorable evolution of the terms of trade of developing countries is another feature of the region's economy, and one not reversed in the anticipated fashion by the cyclical upturn that began in 1983.

But a large part of the difficulty also stems from the inadequacy of the stabilization policies that have been followed. Even when external conditions have been conducive to export growth, as in 1984, there has been a significant dichotomy between the improved trade accounts and internal measures like investment rates, inflation, and public sector deficits.

Central to the IMF model, and its conditionality requirements and performance targets, is a direct relationship between internal and external success. The former is necessary to the latter; the latter then increases output and employment—the best any country can do to offset the inevitable real income declines deriving from deterioration of the terms of trade and higher interest rates.

The IMF model, rather than its implementation, seems to be at fault. Countries have engaged in real devaluations and managed to enforce reductions in real wages. They have cut back on public expenditures, largely investment. They have sought to impose limitations on credit, pushing real interest rates to record levels—sometimes as high as 30 percent for private sector borrowing.[13] Although countries have regularly missed their credit and deficit targets, it is wrong to say that it is because they have not tried or not tried hard enough.

Mexico, especially, has been held in favor as a result of its serious commitment to the IMF prescription and its significant reduction of the public sector deficit. Not surprisingly, the country's commitment is explicable in terms of the much greater applicability of an IMF excess demand diagnosis to the Mexican situation, and hence a greater consensus among Mexican economists on the need for a strong response. As a result, Mexico has frequently been held up to other Latin American countries as proof of what political resolve might yield. Yet evidence has been mounting that results in Mexico have fallen badly short; even before its tragic earthquake, the country had failed to comply with its performance targets and had been forced to restrain a recovery that had begun at the end of 1984. Inflation stubbornly remained close to 60 percent, the public sector deficit was not easily compressible, and there was a threat of capital flight despite realistic exchange rates.

The limitations of the stabilization model for Latin America derive to a considerable extent from the sheer magnitude of the external and internal transfers required to service the region's debt. Latin American interest costs alone are on the order of 5 percent of the regional gross product and represent some 30 percent of foreign exchange earnings, or two-thirds of merchandise imports. For non–Western Hemisphere developing country debtors, the comparable ratios are 2 percent and 8 percent.[14] In the post-1982 circumstances of sharply reduced commercial bank lending to Latin America, these much higher costs are unmatched by capital inflows and represent not only gross but also net transfers of resources out of the continent.

The large trade surpluses required as a consequence have been accompanied by restrictions on imports. Indeed, despite the export gains experienced by some countries in 1984, there is no question but that the bulk of the improved balance-of-payments situation in the region stems from the more than $40-billion reduction in imports compared to their 1981 level. These declines in imports have had significant deleterious effects on production efficiency and investment capability. They have also exacerbated the inflationary problem by forcing aggressive devaluations and limiting the reliance on marginal foreign supply to restrain markups on the part of domestic producers.

The internal counterpart of the export surplus is an excess of national saving over domestic investment, to the extent of the net transfer of interest abroad. This excess has been obtained at the expense of reductions in investment rather than increases in saving. High interest rates have not evoked the expected supply response. Instead, they have discouraged virtually all private capital formation in favor of holding financial assets, much of which are public. Since the largest portion of the external debt is a public responsibility, the payment of interest abroad requires larger flows of funds to the government at the expense of private credit. And because the interest rates are much higher than the rate of growth of public revenues, the costs of servicing the internal debt are rising rapidly as a proportion of government outlays and are an important source of the public sector deficit.

These effects are superimposed on an economic structure already characterized by rigidity and inflexibility. Indexing, formal or informal, makes it difficult to reduce inflation. Markets are not competitive, and reductions in demand are translated predominantly into recessions rather than price reactions. Stabilization would not be easy under any circumstances; in conjunction with the large transfers, it becomes virtually impossible.

Nor are the short-term successes on the external account a good omen for medium-term adjustment. On a continuing basis, exports cannot be dependent upon excess capacity but require new investment and technology. But with capital formation at record low levels and foreign investment discouraged by the absence of growth more than by regulations, such prospects seem bleak. Pressure on the public sector has led to significant reductions of expenditure, but frequently in the very areas that are important for continuing economic development: education, nutrition, health, complementary infrastructure, etc. Reductions in real wages and rises in real interest rates to record levels have exacerbated inequality in the distribution of income and forced families into poverty status.

In the face of these results, there is a mounting political resistance in the region. It has come less from an unwillingness to accept austerity or to acknowledge the obligation to service and repay the debt than from frustration with more of the same. Countries are being advised to continue what they are doing even when the program does not seem to work and yet results in costs that are unprecedentedly high. In the 1920s, German reparations were set at about 2.5 percent of national income and were paid from new borrowing rather than internal resources.[15] That transfer of resources was not easily sustainable during the difficult years of the early 1930s and was soon canceled, although not in time to avert the continuing international economic slide. In Latin America's case, the proportional reduction of national income is twice as great, and the economies are much poorer.

Difficult economic circumstances hastened the exit of authoritarian military governments in the early 1980s. By showing themselves unable to manage, they had thereby lost an important basis for legitimacy. Just as during the Great Depression, regimes in power were weakened, and substitutes have been put in place. Now, however, it is the civilians who are saddled with the burden, and it is their governments that will be held responsible for continuing poor performance. That is why President Alan García of Peru, searching for relief, starkly framed the issue as one of debt or democracy in a speech before the United Nations in September 1985.

It is wrong to translate García's appeal into an excuse for not paying and not adjusting. On the contrary, one must admire the courage of an Alfonsín, for example, who has accepted the full burden of a debt contracted by a predecessor military government, and Fidel Castro's attempt to foment a unilateral moratorium has met with rejection. The new leaders are not demagogues, nor are they populists unprepared to face economic realities.

Rather, they take another position, one that reflects three propositions. First, the inevitable rising and sometimes inconsistent demands of society can be more readily reconciled in a climate of renewed growth rather than in one of continuing decline. What is essential is to convert stabilization from a zero-sum game to one in which there are positive-sum opportunities. Second, an important basis for fueling a transition to sustained growth is a reduction in the sizable resource transfer abroad: Imports can be substituted for interest payments, and domestic stabilization can be facilitated. Third, stabilization and adjustment are not mere technical exercises but processes that require continuity and, hence, broad political support. The policies that have so prominently failed in Latin America are those that have been based upon radical changes in expectations within an authoritarian political setting.

Increasing consensus can be found in the region on the kinds of economic policies necessary to achieve an adequate adjustment. There is broad acceptance of the need to continue export promotion: Countries erred before in the asymmetry of their international integration and acceptance of large capital inflows in the absence of vigorous export capacity. There is recognition that external savings will not be available in the excess proportions of the 1970s and that a strong effort to increase and effectively channel internal resources will be necessary. There is appreciation that sheer expansion and nurturing of the public sector do not form an adequate development strategy any more than simple and complete reliance upon market signals.

These are important advances. They do not signal absolute agreement, nor need they. The virtue of democracy is that a range of positions can be aired. But with the larger differences of the past narrowed, the prospects for an effective and a sustained economic policy are enhanced. What should be fixed is, not a particular measure of one kind or another, but the policy framework. Such a framework is what helps make the impact of individual actions more readily predictable and reinforcing.

Rather than interpreting Latin American efforts to elevate the question of the debt to a political level as an abdication of economic responsibility, bankers and officials in the industrialized countries ought to see them for what they are. Elected leaders are seeking to reconcile external obligations with renewed and sound economic growth as well as with a lively and open society. They are not preaching something for nothing, or economic heterodoxy for its own sake. Quite the contrary. They are explicit in their understanding that economic growth requires real resources, and they have identified an important potential source of such resources. Only on the basis of such growth can the present debt be serviced. Paying less now is also a way of paying later, and increasingly, perhaps the only way.

The Latin American political economy of austerity and adjustment seems more advanced than the international one. For too long there has been rote insistence upon a division of costs of the debt bubble of the 1970s that has left the developing countries with the lion's share. Further pressure may backfire, and ill-conceived austerity programs may provoke a rejection of a sensible economic policy in favor of simplistic populism. What is at stake is the style of Latin American political and economic development and the region's relations with the rest of the world. The situation involves not only debt or democracy but also economic well-being; not only the Latin American countries are involved, but all others as well. One hopes that the lesson will be learned in time.

Notes

1. International Monetary Fund (1985):200.
2. Bela Balassa's decomposition can be found in Balassa (1981a). In contrast to Table 4.1, he uses $(P_{M1} - P_{M0}) M_1 - (P_{X1} - P_{X0}) X_1$ for his price effect.

3. For a concise and useful treatment of Mexico's response to the first oil shock, see Zedillo (1985).

4. More extensive discussion of the Brazilian experience in the 1970s can be found in Albert Fishlow (forthcoming a). Among the many Brazilian analyses is Lemgruber, Batista, and Fendt (1981).

5. On Korean policies, see Balassa (1981b) and for a different and longer-term perspective, see Haggard (1983).

6. These data on debt characteristics are taken from the World Bank (1983).

7. International Monetary Fund (1983):196ff.

8. Inter-American Development Bank (1979):3.

9. Such statistical results are elaborated upon in Fishlow (forthcoming b).

10. For estimates of capital flight based on a comparison of debt levels and balance-of-payments flows, see Dooley et al. (1983).

11. This information on the deficit comes from Inter-American Development Bank (1985):66.

12. For a collection of essays expressing both the optimism of some people about the debt problem at the beginning of 1984 and the skepticism of others, see the *Journal of Development Planning*, no. 16 (1985).

13. For a description of the adjustment efforts of the principal Latin American countries, see Inter-American Development Bank (1985):63–90.

14. International Monetary Fund (1985):261ff.

15. Reparations estimates relative to income are from Machlup (1976):381–386.

References

Balassa, Bela. 1981a. "The Newly Industrializing Developing Countries After the Oil Crisis." *Weltwirtschaftliches Archiv* 117:142–194.

———. 1981b. *The Newly Industrializing Countries in the World Economy.* New York: Pergamon Press.

Dooley, Martin, et al. 1983. "An Analysis of External Debt Positions of Eight Developing Countries Through 1990." Washington, D.C.: Federal Reserve Board, International Finance Division Working Paper 227.

Fishlow, Albert. Forthcoming a. "A Tale of Two Presidents: The Political Economy of the Brazilian Adjustment to the Oil Shocks." Berkeley: University of California.

———. Forthcoming b. "Revisiting the Great Debt Crisis of 1982." Berkeley: University of California.

Haggard, Stephen. 1983. *Pathways from the Periphery: The Newly Industrializing Countries in the International System.* Berkeley: University of California. Ph.D. dissertation.

Inter-American Development Bank. 1979. *Economic and Social Progress in Latin America, 1979.* Washington, D.C.

———. 1985. *Economic and Social Progress in Latin America.* Washington, D.C.

International Monetary Fund. 1983. *World Economic Outlook.* Washington, D.C.

———. 1985. *World Economic Outlook.* Washington, D.C.

Lemgruber, Antonio C., Paulo N. Batista, Jr., and Roberto Fendt. 1981. *Choques Externos e Respostas de Politica Economica no Brasil: O Primeiro Choque do Petroleo.* Rio de Janeiro: Fundação Getulio Vargas.

Machlup, Fritz. 1976. *International Payments, Debts, and Gold.* New York: New York University Press.

World Bank. 1983. *World Debt Tables, 1982–1983.* Washington, D.C.

Zedillo, Ernesto. 1985. "The Mexican External Debt: The Last Decade." In Miguel Wionczek, ed., *Politics and Economics of External Debt Crisis: The Latin American Experience.* Boulder, Colo.: Westview Press.

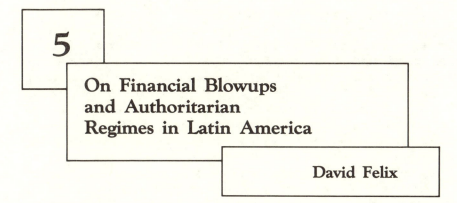

5

On Financial Blowups and Authoritarian Regimes in Latin America

David Felix

The immediate impetus for the resurgence of military regimes in Brazil in 1964 and in the Southern Cone countries in the 1970s came, it is generally agreed, from sharp upsurges of inflation and from collapsing exchange rates, accompanied by a heightening of social tensions and political radicalization that appeared to threaten basic capitalist property relations. The resulting "great fear" that permeated the propertied classes and U.S. foreign-policy makers during the precoup crises helped spawn the civilian-military plots that culminated in the military takeovers.

Once in power, the military leaders went beyond their conventional gendarme role of liquidating leftist threats. They also assumed the long-term task of overseeing a radical restructuring of economic policies designed to transform their countries' economies into more efficient engines of growth by raising the rate of capital formation and altering its composition through wage repression and strengthened trade and financial links with the advanced capitalist economies. This revolutionary development gloss has been a major focus of two prominent interpretations of the "new authoritarianism": the neoliberal (NL) one, associated with the Chicago economists and their acolytes, and the bureaucratic-au-thoritarian (B-A) one, associated with Guillermo O'Donnell and his followers.

The explosive financial crises of the early 1980s have now badly tarnished the gloss. The new authoritarian regimes have had to shift abruptly from nurturing the birth and maturation of economic miracles to depressing their countries' economies in order to squeeze out enough foreign exchange to avoid defaulting on their foreign debt. This turn of events caught the espousers of the NL and B-A interpretations unaware. Each group recognized the possibility that political failure (that is, policy conflicts between economic power groups and/or revived popular resis-

85

tance) could destroy policy coherence and cause the economic strategies of the new authoritarian regimes to falter, but neither expected economic failure to precede political failure. Moreover, financial crisis and economic depression afflict dirigiste, or interventionist, B-A regimes as well as the NL experiments of the Southern Cone. This fact suggests that the adherents of each approach misread crucial elements of the "economic reality" of Latin America and of the larger capitalist world with which the region interacts. It also suggests that one must dissect the consequences of both the dirigiste and the NL experiences to identify the elements. Since detailed dissection is much too large a task for this chapter, my shortcut is to combine a critical analysis of the economic perspectives of the NL and B-A approaches with a limited appeal to the evidence.

The chapter has five main parts. In the first, I briefly contrast the NL and B-A perspectives toward recent Latin American authoritarianism. The second part is a survey in more detail of the NL policies in the Southern Cone countries from inception to collapse, and the third part is a discussion of the shortcomings of the basic theoretical framework guiding regime policies. In the fourth part, I present a comparative analysis of the dirigiste policies of the Mexican and Brazilian B-A regimes from their initial successes to their recent financial crises. In the concluding part, I probe beyond the recent authoritarian experiences to suggest that a long-standing behavioral feature of Latin American "reality" may help account for the unusually high incidence of financial crises that have plagued the region under quite varied political regimes and economic strategies past and present.

Ideational Contrasts Between the NL and B-A Approaches

The economic perspective and the spirit of the two approaches differ profoundly. NL operates analytically within a neoclassical Walrasian theoretical framework; B-A uses a structuralist-cum-Marxist mode of analysis. NL narrowly identifies a successful economic strategy as one that produces rapid, noninflationary economic growth by shrinking the public sector and allowing free commodity, labor, and financial markets to "get prices right." The B-A criterion is lower: A successful economic strategy is any combination of economic policies, dirigiste or liberal, that sustains a high rate of capital accumulation and industrial growth. The preblowup sets of success stories of the two approaches thus intersect only partially. The NL set included the Southern Cone countries during their market liberalization years.[1] B-A analysts were doubtful about Argentina but included Brazil and Mexico in their set, the latter as a sort of honorary B-A regime because its one-party system is considered an effective surrogate for a military regime, allowing the country to pursue a consistent proaccumulation strategy behind a facade of populist rhetoric (O'Donnell 1979).

The spirit imbuing each of the two approaches differs as profoundly. The NL adherents are advocates. Some of the leading Latin American advocates were policy participants, and leading U.S. academic ones served as consultants to the NL regimes. Their analyses have concentrated on the economic rather than the political aspects of the NL strategy, with economic efficiency as the prime social-welfare criterion. Market liberalization, they contend, necessarily raises the level of social welfare, irrespective of its impact on the distribution of income and wealth, because it eliminates the price and wage "distortions" that are alleged to be responsible for resource misallocation, unemployment, and "deadweight" utility losses to consumers.[2] The truncated political analysis has been primitive: restatements of the "great fear" and an exaggerated denigration of the economic performance of preceding import-substituting industrialization (ISI) and the competence and honesty of populist regimes, which rationalize as unavoidable a prolonged intercession of authoritarianism to set things right. Such appraisals rely more on prior deduction than data.[3] Certitude about the correctness of the NL strategy necessarily rules out other explanations of resistance to its adoption than incompetence or chicanery.[4] To NL adherents, the economic collapse of the Southern Cone liberalization strategies was therefore traumatic as well as unexpected.

In contrast, analysts of the new authoritarianism in the B-A mode have been mainly sideline observers, and their economic analyses have been subordinated to their primary focus on the political dimensions of the new authoritarianism. Distaste for the economic inequities of the authoritarian development strategies and for the political repression and brutalities of their sponsoring regimes is only thinly concealed by the B-A jargon. The financial crises and collapse of the development strategies were unanticipated but not, therefore, unwelcome.

The 1970s NL Experiments in the Southern Cone from Inception to Blowup

1. Initial Stabilization

Similarity of economic objectives, policy instruments, the theoretical concepts guiding their use, and the financial crises that terminated the NL experiments of the 1970s in Argentina, Chile, and Uruguay suggest a common "stylized" pattern. Although there were differences among the countries in the intensity and the sequencing of the market liberalizing reforms, before the financial blowups NL advocates and critics alike stressed the similarities. Since the blowups, however, NL advocates have been stressing the differences among the liberalization efforts to explain what went wrong. It is useful, nevertheless, to sketch out the common pattern.

In all three countries, priority was given to stabilization as the precondition for implementing the more radical market-liberalizing reforms. The analysis guiding the initial stabilization effort was conventional monetarism. The main source of inflation was held to be the excessive growth of the money supply, caused mainly by central bank monetizing of large fiscal deficits. Adverse balance-of-payments effects were believed to be basically derivative of the monetary expansion and further worsened by the trade and exchange controls imposed to constrain an excess demand for foreign exchange. The initial stabilization policies were, therefore, also conventionally monetarist. These were, in quick detail:

a. Fiscal deficits were attacked on the expenditure side, mainly by cutbacks of public investment and social services as well as by layoffs and partial salary freezes in the public sector. On the revenue side, the initial effort consisted mainly of sharp increases in the cost of public services and improved tax collecting. The efforts produced some quick results as in all three countries, fiscal deficits fell sharply in real terms during the first two postcoup years.

b. The slowing of monetary expansion was held to a pace designed to permit financing the reduced deficits without crowding out credit to the private sector. Interest ceilings on term deposits and bank loans were, however, abolished in order to improve the "efficiency" of financial intermediation. Positive real deposit rates were expected to draw capital that had been leaving the country back into the domestic financial system, to dissuade households from purchasing real estate and consumer durables as inflationary hedges, and to raise household savings ratios. Positive lending rates were also expected to greatly improve the allocation of real resources.[5]

c. To strengthen the balance of payments, multiple exchange rates were unified and the unified rate was adjusted downward by mini-devaluations, which were tied more or less to the domestic inflation rate to avoid overvaluation. Export taxes were reduced, and quantitative restrictions and exchange controls on imports were lifted.

d. Real wages were lowered drastically during the initial stabilization effort, mainly by removing price ceilings and eliminating subsidies on wage goods and services while imposing tight limits on compensating wage adjustments. Subsequently, the limits were eased, but the weakening of protective labor legislation, unemployment, and suppression of union militancy perpetuated a shift of wage bargaining power to the employer. The real wages of skilled workers rebounded to near precoup levels during fleeting interludes near the eve of the blowups, but the wage share never did recover. What began as an anti-inflationary device persisted as a capitalization device.[6]

2. Market Reforms

Initial progress in bringing down the inflation rate encouraged the NL strategists to begin implementing more radical market-liberalizing reforms. The economic objective was to induce faster economic growth through improved static and dynamic efficiency and a higher rate of private capital accumulation. The political objective was to place the "commanding heights" of the economy more firmly in private hands as a barrier against any future retrogression toward socialism. The reforms included:

a. Sequential tariff reductions leading to a low uniform rate. After initial hesitancy, all three countries adopted preannounced schedules of reductions in order to give firmer long-term signals to private investors.

b. Lifting of controls on international capital movements. This procedure was done step by step and included removing legal restrictions on the entry of foreign-owned banks and their range of domestic operations.

c. A more generous foreign investment code to improve the climate for foreign investment, which was expected to be a major contributor to private capital formation and dynamic efficiency.

d. "Supply-side" tax reforms to promote private domestic capital accumulation, such as reduction of taxes on income and wealth, consolidation of the indirect tax system, and increased reliance on the value added tax.

e. Shrinking of the public sector by selling off public firms, cutting back public housing programs, and opening service areas that had been previously dominated by the government to private initiative. Privatization was the most conflictual aspect of the liberalization effort as the ideological predilections of the NL strategists grated against the nationalistic proclivities of the military. In Chile, the "Chicago boys" were able to set a fast pace of privatization; in Argentina and Uruguay, NL strategists had to move slowly and gingerly in the face of resistance within the military.

3. Prefixed Exchange Rates

Confidence that the stabilization policies initially put in place would progressively squeeze out inflation and level off the exchange rate soon proved unwarranted. After a decline, the inflation rate leveled off on a high plateau in all three countries, which meant that minidevaluations had to proceed at an unexpectedly rapid pace. It also became evident that, contrary to conventional monetarist theory, the inflationary stimulus from devaluation was, despite lagging money wages, quickly wiping out the hoped for balance-of-payments improvements. The policy response was to convert the liberalizing reforms into additional anti-inflationary instruments by accelerating the pace of their implementation.[7]

All three countries adopted *tablitas cambiarias* (preannounced fixed-date schedules of diminishing minidevaluations) and attempted with varying intensity to accelerate the pace of tariff reductions. These measures were expected to progressively reduce the domestic rate of inflation on internationally traded goods. On the premise that traded and nontraded goods were substitutes, lowering price increases in the first group would shift demand away from the second group and pull down its inflation rate as well. It was believed that preannouncing the diminishing devaluations and tariff cuts would also hasten disinflation by dampening the inflationary expectations of the private sector. In sum, the earlier sequencing of inflation and devaluation was reversed. Avoiding exchange rate overvaluation now meant that the inflation rate had to be adjusted to the pace of devaluation.

4. Liberalizing Financial Markets

Liberalizing financial markets from restrictions on international capital transactions was also quickened in hopes of reducing real interest rates. This procedure may have been motivated in part by a belated heterodox suspicion that the rising cost of credit was an important force behind the persistence of inflation (see Taylor [1981] for a heterodox theoretical elaboration of this relationship). Mainly it seems to have been a reaction to the failure of other erroneous anticipations of the NL strategists: that the stabilization recession would be brief because the improved financial intermediation and savings incentives would hold real interest rates to only moderately positive levels and that private investment would respond so vigorously to the liberalization program that overall investment and growth rates would soon accelerate, despite the reduced public investment.

In fact, domestic and foreign private investors responded sluggishly, and the economic boom did not materialize on schedule.

The accelerated liberalization, however, did catch the rising tide of enthusiasm of U.S. and European banks for lending to less-developed countries (LDCs) at full flood. In the three Southern Cone countries, large domestic banks and foreign-owned banking subsidiaries were able to obtain loanable funds easily and more cheaply abroad than from local depositors. Real interest rates on domestic loans and deposits dropped while central bank monetizing of the inflow of foreign funds ballooned official exchange reserves, reinforcing private sector confidence that, despite their weak dampening effect on domestic inflation, the exchange rate targets of the *tablitas cambiarias* would be met. The financial inflows fueled the belated two-to-three-year economic booms that crowned the NL experiments as well as the financial crises that terminated the booms and the experiments.

5. Industrial Stagnation During the Boom

During the boom years, it was the rapid expansion of finance, commerce, and private residential and commercial construction that accounted for the augmented GNP growth. The financial boom was induced by the high profitability of arbitraging between foreign and domestic money markets. Established banks expanded rapidly, and new financial enterprises sprang up to exploit the persistently large spreads between foreign and domestic real interest rates and between domestic lending and deposit rates. The commercial expansion was in response to the speeding up of tariff cutting and the widening gap between domestic price increases and the devaluation pace of the *tablitas.* Increased access to foreign consumer goods and increased foreign sources of inputs by local producers provided lush opportunities in wholesale and retail trade. The commercial construction boom mainly serviced current and anticipated space needs of the rapidly expanding financial and commercial sectors. With public housing programs in eclipse, the residential construction boom responded mainly to the housing demands of the middle and upper classes, the prime recipients of rising real income during the NL experiments.

The conditions nurturing the boom in finance and commerce retarded expansion in the goods producing sectors. Trade liberalization and the shift to foreign sources hurt the demand for major segments of manufacturing producing consumer durables, other middle- and upper-class consumables, and intermediate and capital goods. Demand in the industries processing basic foods and other wage goods was held down by the lagging wage share, and the augmented demand for domestic building materials for the private construction boom was largely offset by reduced public construction. The industrial share of the gross domestic product (GDP), indeed the share of the entire goods producing sector, which had already declined during the initial years of the NL experiment, fell further during the boom years. Industrial capacity utilization and employment, depressed by the initial stabilization effort, recovered marginally during the boom years, but the ratio of investment in the goods producing sectors to GDP did not.

Some squeezing of industry through the opening up of domestic markets to foreign competition and the elimination of various industrial subsidies was a planned component of the liberalization strategy. This tactic was expected to assist disinflation by reducing monopolistic pricing and forcing greater production efficiency. Over time, it was also expected to rationalize the productive structure by redirecting investment to activities that could operate profitably at international relative prices in the domestic and export markets. Other components of the strategy were expected, however, to soften the squeeze and to hasten the structural transformation: notably, reduced real wages and taxes, liberalized access to foreign sources and finance, and generous foreign investment codes. A prolonged weak industrial response was not anticipated by the strategists.

Part of the retardation of output in the goods producing sectors was caused by the sluggish response of the inflation rate to the *tablita cambiaria* tactic. An increasingly overvalued exchange rate compressed the profitability of nontraditional industrial and agricultural exporting and gave unwanted reinforcement to the planned price-cost squeeze on industry. Some industrial firms protected their profitability by deindustrializing, i.e., shutting down production lines and shifting to direct importing and marketing of their products. Others concentrated on laying off workers, speeding up work, retooling with more modern imported equipment, and altering their product mixture. The latter responses, the desired ones from the NL perspective, did have some drawbacks. Reduced cash flows forced many of the firms to increase their dependence on debt financing, mainly from banks, for their restructuring. Firms thus moved toward an increasing share of short maturity credits, which required frequent rollovers in order to acquire low turnover assets. This strategy left them vulnerable to severe cash flow problems if future interest rates rose faster than their product prices. Agricultural firms, with most of their prices tethered to the exchange rate, also became financially more fragile during the *tablita cambiaria* period.

The financing problems of the goods producing firms were further intensified by the persistence of high spreads between lending and borrowing rates. This situation mainly reflected market segmentation in the financial sector. Large banks and commercial and industrial firms could obtain direct credit lines in foreign money markets; the rest had to rely on more expensive local finance. Liberalizing international capital movements thus led to the formation of two-tiered credit markets, with privileged access to the cheaper tier giving a substantial competitive advantage in home markets to the large firms. Industrial concentration was further impelled by a burgeoning of conglomerate firms. Centered around the lead banks and with access to the cheaper credit tier, the conglomerates engaged aggressively in taking over firms that were in financial difficulty. Cheaper tier credit from the lead bank then enabled the firms that had been taken over to expand their market shares at the expense of their less financially advantaged competitors.[8] Although the aggressive conglomerate expansion also depended on extensive debt leveraging, the financial fragility was disguised during the boom years by explosive increases in share prices and real estate values.[9]

Contrary to NL expectations, foreign direct investment did little to facilitate the desired industrial transformation. The NL strategists failed to appreciate the extent to which multinational manufacturing investment in Latin America had depended on the very protectionist and subsidy system they were dismantling. New foreign equity capital was used to a limited degree in buying up distressed firms, but some established multinational corporate (MNC) subsidiaries "deindustrialized." Despite the generous foreign investment codes, labor controls, and the inviting free enterprise rhetoric of the NL strategists, foreign investors oriented toward exports preferred locations with less overvalued exchange rates than those produced by the *tablitas cambiarias*. Foreign investment flows remained disappointingly low, and most went into financial, commercial, and mineral projects.

6. Signs of Financial Fragility

Bemused by the alleged allocative efficiency of the liberalized market forces, the NL strategists largely ignored the structural fragility of their respective economic booms. They were bothered by the sluggish decline of domestic inflation and the resulting trend toward exchange rate overvaluation, but they comforted themselves by believing that these were transitional phenomena. Furthermore, the NL strategists deduced that they could shorten the transition period by stepping up the pace of liberalization even further. The Chileans did so with abandon. In 1979, that country's fiscal deficit was eliminated, the tariff rate on all items save large motor cars was reduced to 10 percent ad valorem, the final exchange rate of the Chilean *tablita cambiaria* was instituted six months ahead of schedule (and then kept frozen until the financial blowup), and the minimum maturity allowed on foreign loans was shortened further. The Argentine and Uruguayan step-ups were hindered by military and business resistance and thus were more limited. These countries had to concentrate mainly on removing remaining regulatory restrictions on international borrowing.[10]

Dazzled by the insights of global monetarism, the NL strategists paid little heed to salient indicators that their economic booms were financially fragile. These indicators included:

a. Growing balance-sheet weakness of many of the goods producing firms and the conglomerates, brought on by heavy debt leveraging and reliance on short-term credit to finance long-term positions.

b. Increasingly risky liability structures of the domestic banks, brought on by their avid dollar borrowing at the adjustable London interbank borrowing rate (Libor) or U.S. prime rate plus interest rates. These terms shifted the interest rate as well as the exchange rate risk to the borrower and rendered banks with large dollar liabilities highly vulnerable to unanticipated devaluation or interest rate increases in foreign money markets.

c. Fissures in the boom such as rising bankruptcy rates and the collapse of a few of the burgeoning conglomerates. To NL strategists, these problems were merely stochastic perturbations, manifestations of the normal corrective disciplining of the market. However, when the conglomerate collapses enveloped the lead banks, the authorities prudently deviated from global monetarist theory and brought in the central bank as lender of last resort to allay the incipient financial panic.

d. Widening trade and current account deficits, sparked by rapidly growing imports and rising debt service requirements. These deficits were rendering the economy increasingly vulnerable to adverse risk-return reassessments and lending cutbacks on the part of foreign banks.[11]

7. Financial Blowup

Events described in 6b initiated the spiraling interactions that produced the financial blowups and the deep economic depressions that terminated the NL experiments. Schematically, the financial spiral ran initially from 6b to 6a to 6c to 6b, etc., but 6d soon joined the chain. At that point, the financial spiral began interweaving with a downward spiraling of real aggregate demand, output, and employment. The rapid declines of output and employment; the waves of de facto and legal bankruptcy that enveloped the goods producing, construction, and financial sectors; and the overwhelming difficulties of servicing the foreign debt forced the NL strategists into ad hoc interventions to stem the spiraling. These actions led to a de facto abandonment of the NL strategy, which soon became de jure when the military rulers replaced the NL strategists with dirigiste-minded tacticians.

The upsurge of interest rates in international money markets toward the end of 1979 meant that the Southern Cone banks were confronted with abruptly increased servicing costs on their overall dollar liabilities. They sought to meet these costs by raising domestic lending rates and by additional dollar borrowing. Goods producers, whose price-raising power was constrained by rapid inflows of competitive imports under the *tablita cambiaria* exchange rates, debt leveraged further to meet their rising financial costs. When this tactic proved inadequate, they fell back on production cutbacks and unilateral suspension of their tax and debt payments. These actions increased the *carteras vencidas* (nonperforming loans) of the domestic banks, which pushed them into an additional defensive borrowing of dollars. Rising tax delinquency and falling output and employment augmented the fiscal deficits, which the NL strategists financed at first by more dollar borrowing and running down the official reserves to avoid crowding out of borrowing by the hard-pressed domestic enterprises. Swelling current account deficits, diminishing foreign exchange reserves, and rapidly augmenting foreign debt servicing undermined private sector confidence in the viability of the *tablita cambiaria* and set off anticipatory flights to the dollar. International money markets, nervously following these developments, became cautious. Risk premiums on new and rollover loans were raised sharply, and new loans became increasingly difficult to obtain. The domestic banks, desperate for dollar liquidity, cut back on investment financing, drew more heavily on central bank dollar reserves, and squeezed domestic borrowers harder. The cash flow problems of the latter worsened, which generated more output retrenchment, nonperforming loans and outright bankruptcies, and a more rapid decline of effective demand that further worsened the cash flow problems.

The interweaving of the upward spiraling of debt with the downward spiraling of output presented the NL strategists with a set of Catch-22 choices. Tariff liberalizing and the *tablitas* were keeping output on the skids and threatening to exhaust the foreign exchange reserves. Abandoning the *tablitas*, however, would not reduce the oppressive foreign debt service requirements and would risk pushing the more-dollar-indebted domestic banks and firms into open insolvency. Moreover, the reactive increases in the domestic financial costs were likely to wipe out most of the improvement in the price-cost margins of the exporting and import-competing firms that had resulted from faster devaluation. Injecting more central bank credit to bring a country out of its domestic debt crisis would be fruitless without a parallel restoration of import and exchange controls. Such a drastic reversal of liberalization and the rising inflation would, however, destroy any remaining confidence at home and abroad in the viability of the NL experiment, which would encourage more capital flight and a still greater reluctance on the part of the foreign banks to lend.

In the event, the NL strategists opted for more devaluation, perhaps because that procedure involved less compromising with liberalization.[12] Bankruptcies and nonperforming loans did increase in number, and major banks, both private and official, did begin toppling. The central banks were impelled to take over the nonperforming loan portfolios and dollar debts of the failing financial institutions;[13] the latter at the insistence of the ideologically fickle international banks, who made the assumption of private dollar liabilities a condition for debt rollover. These efforts to stanch the financial crisis brought the privatized commanding heights back under state control, as collateral for the official bailouts.[14] The salvage operations also required larger central bank emissions of money and fiscal deficits and a return to import and exchange controls. The inflation rate rebounded, but the financial panic was dampened, and the downward spiraling of output and employment slowed. Thus ended the NL experiments. Their main heritage in all three countries was a reacceleration of inflation, the deepest depression since the early 1930s, and the imperative of remaining depressed for a prolonged interval in order to help service the oppressive accumulations of foreign debt.[15]

Postmortem NL Diagnoses of the Southern Cone Blowups

When advocating the market liberalizing strategies, the NL adherents had contended that "economic theory"—meaning the versions of neoclassical theorizing—provides firm support for such strategies. "Theory" was alleged to show that any market economy, whatever its socioeconomic structure and other initial conditions, could put itself on a stable, long-run equilibrium growth path by liberating private initiative and allowing freely functioning markets to channel that initiative toward socially efficient actions. This global claim rested, however, on comparatively static reasoning since "theory" does not specify which transitional routes to the equilibrium growth paths are feasible under different initial conditions. The NL advocates filled this theoretical gap with faith, seemingly grounded in a mixture of ideology and historical amnesia. They believed that such paths always exist and that conditions are benign enough to allow mid-course policy corrections to keep the liberalizing economies from falling over precipices.

After the blowup, however, postmortem diagnoses by NL supporters have been discovering various fatal flaws in the transitional strategies. The gist of these diagnoses is that while free-market equilibrium growth paths existed for the Southern Cone countries, the transitional routes were more treacherous and disaster prone than had been anticipated. The blowups resulted from mistakes in the sequencing of liberalization among the different markets and from a mishandling of the interplay between domestic and balance-of-payments stabilization. However, by learning from the mistakes, the Southern Cone countries should be able to do better the next time they attempt a full market liberalization strategy.

However, should these countries decide to again attempt such a strategy, which even its proponents now tacitly admit is a high-risk one, they would get no clear guidance concerning the transitional policies from the contradictory postmortem diagnoses. For example, from Ronald McKinnon, whose writings on financial repression helped shape the unsuccessful NL strategies and who served as an economic adviser in Argentina and Chile during their NL years, they would learn that the fatal Argentine mistake was to liberalize financial markets before the fiscal deficit had been eliminated and trade liberalization completed.[16] The correct order of liberalization was that followed in Chile, which, by delaying the full lifting of controls on international capital flows until the budget had been balanced, trade liberalized, and the exchange rate stabilized, succeeded in reaching a stable, fast-track growth path (McKinnon 1982). On the other hand, from another leading NL adviser, Arnold C. Harberger, they would learn that the Chileans encountered needless problems by delaying the complete removal of controls on international capital flows. The error, however, was venial; Harberger predicted continued GDP growth for Chile of 6–8 percent per annum (Harberger 1982).

The blowup in Chile, which began less than a year and a half after Argentina's, occurred while the McKinnon and Harberger papers were being printed. From the Chilean catastrophe, yet another influential NL adviser has now concluded that delaying full liberalization of foreign capital flows was a mortal rather than a venial error (Sjaastad 1982). The postmortem NL diagnoses of how the *tablitas cambiarias* contributed to the blowups give similarly contradictory appraisals.[17] Evidently the NL advocates are no better able to chart a correct transitional route now than before the failure of their strategies.

Whether such transitional routes can be found depends also on whether the destination exists. The gist of the structuralist critiques has been that the stable free-market growth path is an ignis fatuus for the Latin American economies with their assorted structural malformations and technological dependency. The NL riposte has been that if the structuralists could only understand "theory," they would see that the malformations are mainly manifestations of misguided interventionist policies rather than market failure. "Theory's" axiomatic postulates that maximizing rationality and the desire for material betterment are universal attributes of individual economic agents mean that free competitive markets to integrate and channel the individual pursuits of economic agents to socially desirable ends should work as efficiently in Paraguay as in Texas.

The intuitive insights of the structuralists turn out, however, to be closer to the findings of actual Walrasian general equilibrium theorizing than do the claims of the NL advocates.[18] Walrasian theorizing has concentrated on the search for the minimum set of constraints on the behavior and the choice sets of individual agents that would make maximizing rationality plus competitive markets logically compatible with the general existence of Walrasian equilibriums, which are also stable and unique. The search, however, has established merely alternative sets of sufficiency conditions, each incorporating various arbitrary constraints on technology and behavior, some of which are most unlikely to have general empirical validity.

The macroeconomic propositions on which the NL strategies are based have therefore only a hand-waving relationship to, rather than a firm logical grounding in, Walrasian general equilibrium theorizing. The alleged certitudes of "theory" cannot be called upon to protect the propositions against falsifying evidence. The structuralist view that the Southern Cone NL strategies were doomed to fail because no stable, free-market growth path existed for them probably has more theoretical support than does the contrary proposition that it was merely transitional errors that did the strategies in.

The financial blowups of the Southern Cone economies are extreme manifestations of a debt leveraging–debt deflation dynamic that is inherent in all private market economies. The dynamic reflects the shifting balance between profit seeking and the protection of capital values that uncertainty about the longer-term future imposes on private investment and lending decisions.[19] At any point in time, markets bind such decisions with conventions about the appropriate limits to leveraging, which serve to guide equity and credit market assessments of the relative potential of firms to meet their profit targets and debt service commitments.

Such conventions necessarily are much more shaped by recent experience than by the timeless laws of classical probability theory. They are toughened during crises and the rush to safety. They get eased during the economic revival phase because the surviving firms, with their strengthened balance sheets, absorb random shocks with a minimal incidence of liquidity crunches and bankruptcy, an accumulating experience that then tilts borrowing and lending decisions toward more venturesome profit seeking. Innovators demonstrate the gains to be obtained from skirting the current conventions, and market competition, i.e., falling market shares and takeover threats, forces follow-the-leader responses to the more-levered strategies and a modification of the financial markets' constraining rules. Partly disguised by the higher capitalization of the assets of the aggressive firms, the leveraging can progressively create the balance sheet conditions for a new financial crisis by weakening the ability of borrowers and lenders to absorb exogenous shocks easily. The shocks may then set waves of illiquidity and insolvency reverberating through the interdependent economy, which is followed by a rush for liquidity and a retightening of the leveraging norms, whose repercussions deepen the financial crisis and the accompanying contraction of investment, output, and employment.[20]

The imperfect art of central banking consists of fending off such crises by imposing regulatory constraints on financial transactions and, should the crises hit, by dampening the repercussive waves of illiquidity through lender-of-last-resort reactions. NL monetary theorists, however, reject these central bank functions as unnecessary and even counterproductive, just as they reject the need for fiscal countermeasures to sustain aggregate demand in the goods markets during the crises. Although neither of these rejections has a firm grounding in Walrasian general equilibrium theorizing, they help explain why the NL advocates grossly underestimated the risks of financial market liberalization: in particular, why they mistook the international bank lending bubble of the 1970s for a secure long-term alleviant of domestic and external financial stringencies in the Southern Cone countries.

The competitive market symmetries of the NL theory, with its ubiquitous price-taking agents, also diverted attention from the risk for the heavily indebted LDCs that the superior economic power of the creditor countries would enable them to impose the real adjustment costs after a bubble collapse asymmetrically. This risk hit home in 1982 when bankers' doubts about Latin America's creditworthiness caused them to cut off the region from ordinary access to new bank loans. Orchestrated by the United States, the leading creditor countries have stepped in with emergency packages of official and coerced commercial bank loans to cover the unpaid current interest liabilities and thus to fend off defaults. To qualify for these loans, however, debtors have had to agree to adopt policies that are designed to squeeze out a sufficient trade surplus to service the increased debt, primarily by depressing domestic real income and employment (for a recent survey of these developments, see Bank of International Settlements 1983). The priority of debt servicing over other national economic objectives has been essentially imposed on the debtor countries by their creditors. Debtors, on the other hand, have been unable to obtain an easing of their travail by extracting a parallel commitment from the creditors to change domestic policies that impede the inflow of imports from the debtors. In dancing with elephants, mice can also push, kick, and stomp. A prudent mouse would, however, consider the asymmetries of power in deciding how to respond to an invitation to dance.

The B-A Blowups in Brazil and Mexico

Brazilian and Mexican growth rates exceeded those of the Southern Cone countries during the deteriorating world trade environment of the post-1973 decade. However, since Brazilian and Mexican growth was also higher prior to the onset of sustained authoritarianism in Brazil and the Southern Cone, a longitudinal comparison is more appropriate in assessing the relative effectiveness of NL versus dirigiste authoritarianism. This comparison shows that Brazilian and Mexican growth rates averaged as high during 1947–1964 as in 1965–1982. For Brazil, this fact suggests that the postcoup cycle of growth and crisis was a repeat of the earlier postwar cycle rather than a breakthrough to a higher path (for an elaboration of this thesis, see Serra 1979). If the 1964 military coup successfully broke a political gridlock associated with the economic crisis of 1962–1964 and imposed major revisions of Brazil's economic strategy, the net growth consequences were no better than what had been implemented previously under democratic regimes.[21] Yet this record is much better than can be claimed for the NL regimes, which produced growth rates in Chile and Argentina that were distinctly lower than those of the first two postwar decades.[22]

The relative superiority of the dirigiste strategies of Brazil and Mexico survives comparison along two other dimensions of economic performance, allocative efficiency of investment and income distribution. Pre-NL growth in the Southern Cone countries, despite distortions, added much more to the long-run productive capacity and human capital than did growth during their NL period, when there was an undue concentration on evanescent commercial and financial expansion. There has not been a comparable deterioration of efficiency during the recent Brazilian and Mexican growth cycles.[23] Distributionally, the comparison is probably a standoff. The trend toward income inequality accelerated under both the NL regimes and Brazil's B-A regime while inequality in Mexico has risen, albeit more steadily, since 1950.[24]

The superiority is, of course, qualified by the denouement. In both Brazil and Mexico, current account deficits and inflationary pressures gradually worsened during the fast-growth phases of the cycle. As in the NL cases, the two countries resorted to exchange rate overvaluation and intensified foreign borrowing to prolong growth, which increased their vulnerability to exogenous shocks. As in the earlier Brazilian and Mexican growth cycles and those of the Southern Cone countries, the terminating factor was a major balance-of-payments crisis.[25] This common denouement suggests the pervasiveness of basic destabilizing forces, which neither parliamentary nor B-A regimes, whether NL or dirigiste, have been able to overcome. The final section of this chapter speculates on these forces, but first I discuss some similarities and contrasts between the Brazilian and Mexican paths to their respective blowups.

As a basic similarity, the common ideological commitment of the dirigiste development strategy of both countries throughout the postwar era was to nurture an expanding mixed economy, with the intention that the public sector's expansion would support the growth of the private domestic sector. Major lines of support included the alleviation of supply bottlenecks by public investment in infrastructure and in parastatal firms when scale and risk barriers were judged too formidable for private investment; protection against foreign competition; and subsidization of the costs of private firms through various channels, such as credit, tax exemptions, underpricing of key inputs from public enterprises, etc. To be sure, the various lines of support also tended to pull against each other to create some of the imbalances that induced further public sector expansion. Nevertheless, the added expansion, which raised the public sector's share of the total activity and also helped create the conditions for the financial blowups, was in both countries more an ad hoc than a preplanned process.

A salient difference was the greater freedom of action of the Brazilian policymakers to pursue the regime's symbiotic government-business development strategy. Not only did the 1964 military coup effectively remove the populist demands of worker and peasant groups from the policy agenda, but under the aegis of the generals, the economic bureaucrats implemented the basic development strategy in substantial autonomy from particularistic business pressures. Mexico's Institutional Revolutionary party (PRI) regimes, however, were hindered in the implementation of a similar development strategy by conflicting political commitments. One was to the urban unions and peasant and white-collar groups, the mass pillars of the PRI's formal party structure. The other was to the private business sector, formally unrepresented in the PRI but a key partner in the symbiotic development strategy. Mexico's development strategy, therefore, had a populist tinge that was absent in the Brazilian case. Much of the tinge was in the rhetoric, but some was substantive. The shift, attempted by both Echeverría and López Portillo, from stabilizing development (*desarrollo estabilizando*) to shared development (*desarrollo compartido*) was more a response to growing political discontent with the rising distributional inequities of stabilizing development than to its declining effectiveness in producing fast growth. The attempted shift put inconsistent demands on the economy that helped bring on the break-downs of 1976 and 1982.[26]

The difference in the responsiveness to populist demands is reflected in the contrasting distributive patterns that underlay the rising Gini coefficients of Brazil and Mexico.[27] In Brazil, only the top decile increased its income share, with most of the relative gain going to the upper half of that decile, while the shares of each of the remaining nine deciles declined.[28] In Mexico, the share of the eightieth to ninety-fifth percentiles rose, that of the sixtieth to eightieth held constant, and the shares of the top 5 percent as well as the lowest 60 percent declined (the estimates cover 1950–1975; for details, see Felix 1982). Unionized labor, white-collar workers and professionals, and owners of medium-sized farms fall primarily in the sixtieth to ninety-fifth percentiles.

The difference is also reflected, paradoxically, in the more extensive encroachment of the state in Brazil than in Mexico on the commanding heights of the respective economies. The government's share of gross investment in Brazil, according to Werner Baer, reached 60 percent in the mid-1970s, compared to 40 percent in Mexico (Baer 1979:100, 107; Solis 1981:Table 1.1). Brazil's avowedly probusiness regime, encroaching in a pragmatic and nonpopulist manner, aroused weak resistance from the business sector. The Mexican regimes, compelled to screen their probusiness development strategies with radical rhetoric and intermittent populist reforms in order to preserve the PRI's political base, made the business sector very wary, and it was quick to counter state encroachments with investment strikes and capital flight. These threats helped abort intermittent attempts by Mexican governments to raise their tax share of GDP and to reduce the regressiveness of the tax structure.[29] The tax share, while rising from 7 percent in the early 1960s to 10 percent in the mid-1970s, remained well below the Latin American average, with taxes on profits and other capital income staying below 3 percent of GDP (computed from Solis 1981:Tables 1.1, 3.2, 3.5).

Brazil was less of a supply-sider paradise, i.e., having low tax rates to promote investment. Its ratio of taxes to GDP rose from 18 percent in 1959 to 25 percent in 1975, with increased direct taxes accounting for much of the rising share. The direct tax increase, however, came largely from higher payroll taxes; more revenue, not progressiveness, was the objective of the Brazilian tax reforms (Baer 1979:146 and Table 24). Their effectiveness enabled Brazil to parallel its rapidly expanding public outlays with shrinking fiscal deficits, whereas Mexico's expansion of public expenditure was associated with widening deficits.

A reverse paradox is that despite greater fiscal weakness, Mexico's fast growth was accompanied until the mid-1970s by much less inflation and more stable exchanges than was Brazil's. Differences in the system of financial intermediation explain much of the paradox. Mexico's ingenious but fragile intermediation system held the country's stable, fast growth virtually hostage to price and exchange rate stability. Brazil's intermediation system was more tolerant of both instabilities.

Mexico's Road to Crisis

Mexico's intermediation strategy sought to avoid a recurrence of the inflation and balance-of-payments crises of the first half of the 1950s by increasing private voluntary savings so as to fund the private and public sectors' credit requirements for fast economic growth without recourse to major central bank emissions. Commercial banks and *financieras* were encouraged to issue an array of securities with nominal interest rates set well above those of the United States and with the issuing institutions guaranteeing repurchase on demand at the issue price. Term deposit facilities with similarly high interest differentials relative to U.S. rates and quick withdrawal rights were also created. To further sweeten their attractiveness, the securities and deposits were virtually tax exempt.

The fundamental requisite for drawing funds into the domestic financial system was, however, preserving private sector confidence so that the dollar-peso exchange rate would not fall, that the convertibility of the peso would not be impeded, and that the difference between the Mexican and U.S. inflation rates would remain below the interest rate differentials. As the instant liquidation guarantee would accelerate the speed of capital flight by allowing holders of term claims on the financial system to liquidate them en masse without capital loss, the success of the intermediation system depended crucially on the ability of the authorities to constrain inflation and avoid devaluation. This task was made more difficult because the capital flight threat embedded in the intermediation system was also used effectively by business groups to keep the authorities from enacting progressive tax reforms. The regimes were forced, therefore, to try to reconcile price and exchange stability with fast growth and the appeasement of populist demands by other means.

Until the 1970s, such reconciliation was done fairly successfully, in part because populist demands were subordinated to the requirements of stabilizing development. Private funds flowed with increasing confidence into the banks and *financieras*, whose combined liabilities rose faster than the nominal GDP, as did private domestic savings (Solis 1981:Table 1.1). Fiscal deficits were largely financed by issuing government securities, which banks and *financieras* had to hold as part of their required reserves. Since the manipulation of reserve ratios was also the central bank's chief anti-inflationary instrument, there was a potential incompatibility between the two uses of reserves. Rising fiscal deficits could undermine the symbiosis between public and private sector output growth by crowding out credit to the latter. This reaction did not occur in this period because fiscal deficits grew moderately and a slowly rising share was financed by foreign borrowing. Destabilizing tendencies were also held down by an array of supplemental polices. Central bank regulations impeded the access of private banks and firms to foreign credit markets, and the growth of the foreign trade deficit was dampened by import controls and export subsidies. Underpricing by parastatal firms of sensitive items such as fuel, electricity, and public transport and the subsidized pricing of basic foods increased public sector deficits but helped to keep down wage-price spiraling and the Mexican-U.S. inflation ratio.

The attempted shift to "shared development" after 1972 intensified the fiscal-monetary incompatibilities to the point of open crisis. Crisis might have come, albeit at a slower pace, without the strategy shift because of the growing real imbalances that were aggravating the fiscal-monetary incompatibilities. These imbalances seem to have helped motivate the strategy shift—notably because of concern about the pronounced downward trend after the 1950s of the employment/output elasticity in both agriculture and industry, the rapidly rising rate of underemployment, and the deceleration of agricultural and export growth. The main motive, however, seems to have been to revive popular support for the PRI by restoring its populist credentials, which had been badly tarnished by the neglect and inequities of stabilizing development.[30]

Shared development called for augmenting the level of public expenditure by more spending on social infrastructure, rural public works, and land redistribution. A parallel tax reform package, revenue enhancing as well as redistributive, was to finance the augmented expenditures. However, intense negotiations with leading business groups in late 1972 failed to gain their assent to even modified versions of the tax reforms. Apparently fearful of capital flight and investor strikes, Echeverría scrapped the tax effort. The higher expenditures thus generated fiscal deficits that were well beyond the capacity of the reserves of the banking system to absorb without crowding out private sector credit. Despite recourse to monetary expansion and increased foreign borrowing, the private sector's share of total credit began falling, as did the growth rate. Other incompatibilities worsened rapidly. The rising fiscal costs of holding down price increases for fuels, public services, and basic foods added to the public sector's borrowing requirement.[31] Increased inflation and foreign borrowing undermined confidence in the stability of the exchange rate, and by 1974, a flight to the dollar was under way. The government further augmented export subsidies and foreign borrowing to defend the exchange rate, which merely facilitated the capital flight. In 1975, the current account deficit reached 5.1 percent of GDP, and the wholesale price index rose 15 percent. In the fall of 1976, the exchange rate was set free to float. It sank 50 percent while the annual inflation rate rose to over 40 percent in the ensuing twelve months (Weintraub 1981:Tables 8.4, 8.6, 8.7).

After a stabilization interlude, the succeeding president, López Portillo, oversaw a replay of the Echeverría experience on a grander scale. Forced initially by Mexico's foreign creditors to turn to the IMF, his stabilization program followed the standard IMF format. During 1977-1978, public sector investment and subsidies were reduced, limits on new foreign borrowing were imposed, import restrictions were eased, and money wage adjustments were held below the rate of inflation. The mixed accomplishments were also "IMFish." Targeted reductions of the fiscal and current account deficits were met, inflation stayed above target, real wages fell, and output and employment growth hovered around the depressed rates of the last two Echeverría years.

New oil discoveries enabled López Portillo to break loose from IMF conservatism and embark on his version of rapid shared development. During 1979–1981, the ratio of public sector expenditures to GDP was 34 percent higher than the average of the Echeverría years while the GDP growth rate matched that of the best triennium of the stabilizing development era. Inflation also rebounded, but rising oil exports eased the tight dependence of the financial system's stability on low inflation rates. That stability remained, however, closely dependent on confidence in the stability of the new exchange rate. Diminishing confidence during 1981 instigated the massive capital flight and financial crisis that terminated López Portillo's experiment with shared development.

How did the oil revenues diffuse throughout the financial system? First, rising Petróleos Mexicanos receipts (PEMEX, the parastatal oil monopoly and initial recipient of the oil export receipts) transformed the public sector's foreign current account balance from a deficit averaging 2 percent of GDP in 1976-1977 to a surplus of nearly 1 percent of GDP in 1981. Yet PEMEX's chronic overall income-expenditure deficit had also risen to an unprecedented 2.25 percent of GDP by 1981 (Gil Diaz 1983:Tables 7, 11). The chief cause was the gross domestic underpricing of PEMEX's products. The implicit subsidy to domestic buyers from petroleum underpricing had risen from an average of 2.5 percent of GDP during 1968–1977 to 5.3 percent by 1980 (Gil Diaz 1983:Table 12). Other public sector diffusion channels were increased underpricing of electricity and public transport, reduction of import and export taxes, and increased export subsidies (for statistical estimates, see Gil Diaz 1983:Tables 12, 17, 18). As there were no important offsetting tax increases, the expansion of the public sector was accompanied, despite the rising oil revenues, by a rising fiscal deficit.

Some of the deficit was financed by raising required bank reserves for the compulsory purchasing of government securities, which increased further the public sector's share of total domestic bank credit. To mitigate the crowding out of private borrowers, the government also raised its foreign borrowing, lifted restrictions on foreign borrowing by private nonbank firms, and allowed banks to set up dollar deposit accounts and to lend in dollars. During 1979–1981, the foreign debt of the public sector rose $27 billion and that of the private sector $15 billion, with two-thirds of the latter representing nonbank liabilities (Green 1983:Table 8). Encouraged by the petroleum-fueled boom, the larger Mexican private firms raised their debt-equity ratio 27 percent between 1978 and 1981 while their ratio of debt payments to sales rose 156 percent. Confident of the continued stability of the exchange rate, they leveraged mainly in dollars; the ratio of dollar to total debt rising from 30 percent in 1978 to 63 percent in 1981.[32]

Most of the public and private foreign borrowing flowed out again to finance the rising trade and current account deficit of the private sector, which rose from 2.8 percent of GDP in 1978 to 7.5 percent in 1981. Mexico's overall deficit on current account rose less, from 4.5 percent to 6.6 percent in the same interval, because of the public sector's current account surpluses (computed from Green 1983:Tables 7, 10).

Thus, the export oil revenues during the boom years supported output and the consumption expansion of the private sector through two main channels. The actual revenues were transferred to the private sector via selective tax cuts and increased pricing subsidies. Optimistic projections of oil revenue increases provided the psychological collateral for a burst of public and private foreign borrowing, largely from international banks, which financed the rapidly rising current account deficits of the private sector.

By mid-1981, however, these deficits and an unexpected sag in international petroleum prices had eroded confidence in the stability of the exchange rate. Private firms cut back on new foreign borrowing, and holders of peso assets began a run to the dollar. To defend the exchange rate, the government further accelerated its foreign borrowing. In 1981 and the first eight months of 1982, the government added $31 billion to its foreign debt, one-third of it short term. This addition was at the upper bound of the range of estimates of capital flight during the same interval. Inadvertently, the government was widening the capital account channel for transferring its oil-linked foreign receipts to the private sector.

In August 1982, the international banks blocked that channel by refusing further loans, which brought Mexico's simmering financial crisis to full boil. In a Samsonian act, López Portillo then nationalized the private banking system, which he accused of actively promoting the capital flight. The tottering financial intermediation system of the *desarrollo estabilizando* era was now in complete shambles, although López Portillo's act of frustration also brought quiet relief to the nervous international bankers since it meant that the Mexican government was now legally responsible for the dollar commitments of the nationalized banks. Under the new IMF agreement, the succeeding de la Madrid government also assumed responsibility for the dollar debts of the private nonbank firms. The strength of the symbiosis between the private and public sectors is not easily exhausted.

Brazil's Road to Crisis

Domestic financial panicking and capital flight were not important proximate causes of Brazil's blowup. Until the foreign credit crunch hit in mid-1982, the authorities in Brazil were able to wield tax powers and to control wages, foreign exchange, and credit allocation to shield the economy from a major financial breakdown despite rising inflation and balance-of-payments deficits. Credit manipulation rather than price subsidies, as in Mexico, was the main instrument for guiding the private sector along the lines of a growth strategy. The tactic was used with considerable skill to erect the productive structure that is now tripping over its own external imbalances.

The tax, wage, exchange, and financial powers formed an interlocking set, each depending on the others for some of its prolonged effectiveness toward the implementation of a growth strategy. The financial system, however, also had two key features that helped make it less sensitive to inflation and capital flight than the Mexican system. These were Brazil's policy of monetary correction, i.e., widespread indexing, of financial claims and liabilities generated within the formal financial system and the dominant role that the government assumed over that system. The two features were interconnected. Indexing promoted the dominance of government banks, which in turn kept indexing from breaking down under financial stress until the blowup in 1982.

Indexing was initially intended to advance the military regime's objective of making the private sector the country's main engine of growth. Efficiently functioning credit and capital markets were considered to be essential, and indexing in Brazil's inflationary milieu was viewed as a transitional mechanism, useful for maintaining positive real interest rates until inflation was brought down to single-digit rates. Imminent phasing out, however, was not expected, since "corrective inflation," i.e., the lifting of rent ceilings and the prices of public services to reduce fiscal deficits and "get prices right," was also a major facet of the initial strategy. A series of decree laws during 1964–1967 extended to a widening range of public and private entities the right to sell debt indexed to the wholesale price index.[33] Minimum wages, arbitrated union wage settlements, and public sector wages were also indexed but to the *anticipated* rise in consumer prices—with the economic authorities doing the anticipating. The results were falling real wages and a rising profit share during the first seven to eight years after the coup, implementing the implicit Marxian strand of the conservative strategy while also helping to pull down the inflation rate.

Prior to 1968, success was mixed. Indexed claims rose from 9 percent of the money supply in 1964 to 36 percent by 1967, but without a parallel rise of the private investment rate or a revival of the GDP growth rate. Virtually all the long-term indexed claims taken up by the public were government securities, and most indexed term deposits were held by government banks. With the growth of public sector spending also being held back in line with the pro-private-sector strategy, fiscal deficits shrank while the indexed government debt rose.[34] Indexing was not fueling the private sector's growth engine, and the government's engine was idling.

These mixed results reflect one of the dark sides of indexing. Except in the world of textbook monetarism, indexing is not an effective incarnation of that mystical monetarist concept, perfectly predictable inflation. Indexing doesn't eliminate the inflation risk but merely concentrates it asymmetrically between private and government borrowers. For private borrowers, indexing increases the variance between future debt payment commitments and cash flows, which heightens illiquidity and bankruptcy threats, whereas the government can cover unexpected net revenue shortfalls by money creation. Since private borrowers in Brazil were unwilling to assume the inflation risk, the issuing of indexed debt devolved on the government. As Werner Baer puts it, "Brazilians have been happy to have assets with index-linking, but never liabilities" (Baer 1982:268). Despite the intentions of its proponents, therefore, indexing promoted government dominance of the Brazilian financial sector. Moreover, since private banks and firms continued operating in nonindexed debt, private asset shifting to indexed deposits and securities caused crowding out problems and a high interest rate volatility in the nonindexed part of the financial sector. Thus, the restrictive aspects of the stabilization policy during 1964–1967, in conjunction with the shift of loanable funds to indexed assets, sharply raised interest rates and reduced credit availability for private firms' working capital financing, which helped perpetuate the slow output growth and high rates of industrial excess capacity of that period (cf. Morley 1971).

Antonio Delfim Netto, who took over economic policy management in mid-1967, finessed these problems for a time by policy adjustments that supplied the financial underpinnings for the "miracle years," 1968–1973. A more accommodating rate of central bank credit expansion lowered interest rates and increased credit availability in the nonindexed financial markets. These results were supplemented by a strategy of frequent, small devaluations—minidevaluations—that caused the rise of the cruzeiro-dollar rate to lag moderately behind the domestic inflation and indexing rates. This strategy cheapened the cost of foreign credit relative to domestic credit, which encouraged public entities and private banks and firms to borrow abroad. Voluntary indexed deposits in government banks were supplemented by an expanding system of forced indexed savings. The latter, compulsory pension and profit-sharing funds financed by payroll and related taxes, were placed as indexed deposits in government banks. In the course of the miracle years and beyond, these compulsory deposits came to exceed indexed voluntary deposits (Baer 1982:Tables 58, 59).

The rapid output growth and decelerating inflation of 1968–1973 were facilitated by the rising capacity utilization that Delfim's expansionist credit policies activated. From 1967 through 1972, industrial capacity utilization rose 6 percent per annum, accounting for much of the 25 percent decline of industry's capital-output ratio during that interlude. Soon after full capacity was reached in 1972, the capital-output ratio began rebounding (estimates are from Bonelli and Malan 1976:Table 5). But in more basic ways, the successes of the miracle years were front-end benefits of the "grow now, pay later" thrust of Delfim's financial and growth policies.

On the output side, the familiar story requires only a quick summary. Consumer durables (including passenger autos), repeating the pattern of the 1950s, led industrial growth in 1968–1974 by a considerable margin.[35] The growth was quite import intensive, and dollar outlays for capital goods and intermediate goods imports rose faster than the consumer durable output, as did outlays for petroleum imports even prior to the 1973 oil shock.[36] Most of the import intensity was linked to supplying equipment and current inputs for consumer durable production and for the expanding private and public sector infrastructure that serviced the rising consumption of those durables (Bonelli and Malan 1976:391–392). Industrial exporting, which was encouraged by tax and credit subsidies, offset only part of the increase of industrial imports. During 1968–1974, industrial exports in constant prices rose 17.5 percent per annum compared to 25.8 percent for industrial imports (Bonelli and Malan 1976:Table 6).

Thus, contrary to B-A theorizing, Brazil's authoritarian regime was not imposing a form of right-wing Stalinism but facilitating right-wing consumerism. Despite the increased income concentration, the private domestic savings rate hardly rose during the miracle years (Baer 1982:105–106). Neither was Brazil's authoritarian regime attempting to overcome the crisis of import substitution by deepening ISI. The overall import coefficient reached a postwar peak of 0.13 in 1974, far outstripping the 0.08 export coefficient of that year (the previous high for the import coefficient was 0.09 in 1949; see Baer 1982:121). A closer linkage with foreign capital, also emphasized by B-A theorizing, was evident. The fast-growing durables and the domestic equipment industries supplying them were dominated by foreign firms while foreign portfolio lending covered most of Brazil's rising current account deficits. The linkage served, however, to erect a productive structure whose import dependence rendered it more rather than less vulnerable to external shocks (see Weisskoff 1980 for an interesting attempt to disaggregate and measure the various linkages).

Monetary, fiscal, and foreign exchange policies dovetailed during most of the period, which allowed the boom to be financed by decelerating inflation. The lagged minidevaluations encouraged a shift to foreign sources for domestic capital and intermediate goods. Fiscal deficits declined steadily, becoming surpluses after 1972, despite a 13 percent annual growth of price-deflated government expenditures. The shrinking deficits were due to increased tax revenues and the indexing of the public sector debt, the *short-run* effect of which was to greatly lower interest costs. As a result, the price-deflated money supply grew only slightly more than the 10.1 percent growth rate of GDP during 1968–1974 whereas the price-deflated private sector credit rose at a 22 percent rate (see Bonelli and Malan 1976 for the monetary data; see Baer 1982:Table 56 for the fiscal budget data).

The credit flows were also guided by selective controls and tax and credit subsidies to the priority sectors. Consumer durable purchasing was promoted by measures that eased installment credit terms and encouraged the flow of funds to the acceptance bill (*letras de cambio*) market, the main source of funds for consumer finance companies. The forced savings of the social security funds were channeled to residential construction, mainly for middle- and upper-class housing and ancillary municipal infrastructure (Reynolds and Carpenter 1975). Agricultural credit at negative real interest rates, mainly from the Bank of Brazil, promoted the rural consumption of consumer durables as well as agribusiness expansion.[37] Nontraditional agricultural and industrial exports also received concessional credits as well as tax subsidies, and as already mentioned, the lagged minidevaluations encouraged the substitution of imported for domestic capital and intermediate goods.

The pay-later consequences began appearing with the first oil price shock. Brazil's current account deficit jumped to 113 percent of export receipts in 1974 while inflation doubled, arousing expectations of more acceleration to come. Private holders shifted dramatically from nonindexed to indexed financial assets, which caused a major loss of liquidity, a flurry of bankruptcies among private banks, and a sharp rise of interest costs to private nonagricultural firms.[38] The consumer durable and overall industrial growth rates dropped precipitously during 1974–1975, per capita GDP growth somewhat less so, thanks to an offsetting rise of agricultural output.[39]

These events forced the authorities to alter the focus of monetary policy from decelerating inflation to accommodating higher inflation. More central bank funds were pumped into commercial banks, and to allay panic, full restitution was extended to holders of large time deposits of the failed banks. The largest of the social security funds was transferred from the National Housing Bank (BNH) to the National Economic Development Bank (BNDE) and used to supply investment credit to private as well as to state enterprises. The loans, indexed at rates well below the inflation rate during 1975–1976, were basically credit subsidies. To further ease the debt problems of the private sector, the BNDE bought equity in selected private firms. Some that required frequent new injections of BNDE funds passed later to the public sector as the alternative to liquidation; i.e., "lemon socialism" became yet another impetus for expanding the public sector. Private banks were allowed to borrow abroad, which lowered their funding costs since the lagged minidevaluation policy remained in place and exchange-rate-adjusted Euromarket interest rates were lower than the unindexed Brazilian term deposit rates. In sum, the financial crisis of 1974–1975 was overcome by greater monetary expansion, increased financial intermediation and credit subsidization by the public sector, and augmented foreign borrowing. GNP and industrial output growth revived in 1976–1978, though remaining well short of the rates during the miracle years, while the annual inflation rate stabilized at more than double the rate of that boom era.

The 1974–1975 experience brought out clearly that with the financial sector divided into indexed and nonindexed markets—the first supplying longer-term credit, the second short-term commercial credit and working capital loans—financial market stability required maintaining parity between the expected purchasing power of indexed and nonindexed deposits of equivalent liquidity. A rise of inflationary expectations would shift funds to indexed deposits, causing turbulence and credit crunches in the nonindexed markets, a profit squeeze on private banks and firms, economic slowdown, and the danger of financial panic. Since these events, if allowed to unfold, would undermine the chief economic claim to legitimacy of the military regime by thwarting its trickle-down fast-growth strategy, the authorities felt impelled to react with expansionist financial measures to restore liquidity to the nonindexed market. This reaction validated the expected higher rate of inflation, which became incorporated in the value of indexed deposits and securities through monetary correction. Conversely, scrapping indexing to break the spiral would induce outflows of indexed deposits and securities, which would require either cutbacks of public sector activities or enlarged sales of nonindexed government debt, and that could set off turbulence and have crowding out consequences in the financial markets. Both alternatives would depress the real economy. The third alternative, central bank financing, might avoid depression but would leave the inflationary spiral intact. After 1974, the authorities experimented cautiously with partial de-indexing, mainly of loans, not deposits—except for some chiseling on the monetary correction of compulsory social security deposits (Baer and Beckerman 1980). The exception, a brief experiment in 1980 with across-the-board partial de-indexing, produced disastrous results that justified the earlier caution.

Indexing had become an integral part of the inflationary spiral rather than the transitional mechanism for facilitating disinflation that its promoters had intended it to be. It is not at all clear that inflation would have been lower sans indexing, but what the experience with indexing does bring out clearly is that the savings propensities of Brazil's affluent classes were too low to sustain a noninflationary fast-growth strategy. Despite indexing and increased income concentration, the private voluntary savings ratio to GNP scarcely rose during the miracle years and trended downward subsequently (see Table 3.2). One aid to slower inflation was the power of the military regime to raise the public savings ratio by higher taxes, forced savings, and the full pricing of goods and services of government firms. This capacity slowly eroded after 1973 as the public sector became increasingly enmeshed in credit and tax subsidizing, and in its place was a rising dependence on foreign borrowing to finance fast growth and to keep a lid on the inflation spiral. The substitute served well during 1974–1978, thanks to unusually favorable conditions in the Eurocurrency lending markets. Thereafter it became an additional source of financial turbulence.

The 1973 oil shock also brought home to the authorities the risks of continuing their import-intensive consumer-durable-led growth strategy. The second national development plan, initiated in 1975, attempted a mid-course adjustment to reduce import intensity and increase exports. To this end, the plan projected a major buildup of capacity in intermediate goods—such as steel, nonferrous metals, and petrochemicals—fuel and energy, capital goods, inorganic minerals, and agricultural processing. Supplementing these buildups were major transport programs: improved airports, road and public transport projects to relieve urban congestion and extend the rural road network, an expansion of the fluvial and maritime merchant fleet, and enlarged capacity in shipbuilding and the production of small commercial aircraft. Many of the programs included huge, indivisible projects suggestive of Soviet gigantism. The second development plan thus could be seen as a turn to right-wing Stalinism, and hence belated support for B-A theory, except for one crucial difference. The input underestimates and cost overruns were met not by cutting back on consumer goods production in order to stay on course, but by a combination of more foreign borrowing, construction stretch-outs, and program cutbacks.

Under the plan, the government was expected to fund the infrastructure projects while downstream projects would be funded according to the "one-third rule": one-third participation each by the government, foreign investors, and domestic investors. The added capital costs of the stretch-outs and overruns in sequential programs tended to fall, therefore, chiefly on the government, the supplier of the front-end capital. This fact plus the unwillingness of private Brazilian capitalists to take up their full one-third share, gave an unplanned boost to the already rising public sector share of gross fixed investment during the post-1974 years (state companies accounted for 65 percent of Brazilian investment in 1981; see Baer 1982:144). The added capital costs led to added foreign borrowing by the state companies in charge of the planned programs. By 1982, they had accounted for 72 percent of the public sector's foreign debt, which made up two-thirds of Brazil's overall foreign debt of $87 billion (Tofaneto 1983).

Trade deficits declined during 1975–1978, but increased import substitution and export growth resulting from the plan's projects probably accounted for less of the gain than did the recovery of Brazil's commodity terms of trade. The indivisible, long-gestation projects were not to go on stream until the end of the 1970s, and with the subsequent stretch-outs, the expected completion dates for some are now in the late 1980s or beyond. In the interim, project-linked imports and debt servicing have contributed more to the rising current account deficit since 1975 than completed projects have subtracted from it.

With the second surge of oil prices in 1979–1980 and the sharp rise in dollar interest rates, the fragile mechanisms for reconciling fast growth with stable inflation came unstuck once more. During 1979–1981, the dollar value of oil imports rose 153 percent, but interest payments rose 283 percent—by 1981 the latter was larger than Brazil's oil import bill.

This time, efforts to reglue the fast growth–stable inflation mechanism at a still higher level of inflation failed. During 1979–1980, economic growth held up, but inflation accelerated. During 1981–1983, output and employment fell while inflation kept accelerating. Another Brazilian growth cycle had encountered its crisis phase.

The crisis, moreover, is still unfolding. Through most of 1982, the authorities were able to keep financial turbulence from instigating major capital flight and waves of bankruptcy. They did so by further raising the private sector's share of government bank credits, by fiscal incentives to encourage private banks and firms to shift further to foreign borrowing, and by forcing state enterprises to slow down expenditures and seek foreign credit even more extensively. These actions were accompanied by intensified export promotion to buoy foreign confidence in Brazil's creditworthiness.

However, the Catch-22 aura of the post-1979 policies suggests that desperate ad hocism had replaced policy coherence. Thus, to dampen inflation, the lag in the minidevaluations was increased in 1980, and only partial monetary correction was applied to indexed deposits. A major deposit withdrawal ensued, and much of the money flowed into the purchase of consumer durables, which set off a brief industrial boom. This situation induced a sharp increase of imports, further facilitated by the exchange rate overvaluation, but brought no deceleration of inflation. With exports threatened, full monetary correction was restored in 1981, and the devaluations increased until they were greater than inflation. The trade balance turned positive in 1981, but inflation rose further, real GDP fell, and the liquidity of banks and firms with foreign debts was severely weakened.

The authorities responded by removing interest ceilings on nonindexed securities, which allowed real interest rates to shoot up to unprecedented levels (40 percent and upward in 1981). This change restored liquidity and profitability to private banks but seriously worsened those aspects for private domestic firms. To ease that squeeze, state firms were made to retrench and to rely still more on foreign financing in order to shift more public sector credit to the private sector. Retrenchment, however, depressed sales of the private capital goods and construction materials firms, whose main customer had come to be the state enterprises. The cash flow of these firms was further depressed by payment delays from the state enterprises, which sought thereby to bypass their budget ceilings (Baer 1982:132). In contrast, state firms with good access to foreign loans funneled some of their liquidity to hard-pressed suppliers by excess purchasing and inventorying of their goods.[40]

The narrowing of the authorities' freedom of action because of increasingly contradictory political demands did not, as in populist crises, account for much of the policy incoherence. To be sure, full indexing of lower-echelon wages was begun in 1980, apparently to facilitate the military regime's strategy of gradually restoring a limited parliamentarianism purged of radicalism. However, the negative effect of full wage indexing on the cash flows of firms seems to have been minor, the main effect being rather an intensification of wage-price spiraling. It was primarily the cumulative imbalances that the growth strategy had embedded in Brazil's productive and financial structures that forced the authorities to draw and discard cards frenetically from their policy deck to keep growth going and, when that proved no longer possible, to stave off a major financial breakdown.

The refusal of international banks in the summer of 1982 to make additional loans ended that effort. That action led quickly to a complete rundown of Brazil's central bank gold and foreign exchange reserves, a curtailment of foreign trade credit, the beginnings of a flight to the dollar, and a bankruptcy wave. In October 1982, the authorities were forced to turn to the IMF, which added a new dimension to the policy game: how to get IMF conditionality, needed for new credits and a debt rollover, without collapsing the economy.

The performance requirements incorporated in the first IMF agreement, signed in February 1983 and violated shortly thereafter, highlighted Brazil's desperate alternatives. Under the agreement, Brazil was to cut the 1983 rate of credit expansion 30 percent below that of 1982, which represented a 30 percent cut in price-deflated credit, given the inflation projection of the agreement. The public sector borrowing requirement was to be frozen at the 1982 nominal amount, and to be included in the requirement was a rise in the public sector debt due to indexing. In addition, wage indexing was to be cut to 80 percent of the inflation rate. The agreement projected a 3.5 percent fall of real GDP and a 10–15 percent drop in the inflation rate.

However, if the agreement had been carried out faithfully with debt indexing kept intact, the massive fall of real public sector expenditure would, according to Brazilian critics, have reduced real aggregate demand and GDP by 15 percent rather than 3.5 percent (Bacha 1983). It is unlikely that the highly leveraged private sector could have absorbed such a shock without major bankruptcies, given the reduced real credit target of the agreement.[41] Scrapping debt indexing would ease the government borrowing constraint but fan the financial turbulence. Cutting down wage indexing would, according to one prominent Brazilian macromodel, have a minor impact on the inflation rate, which the model projected, thus far accurately, would be 60 percent higher than the IMF's estimate.

In the event, the Brazilian authorities tried the option of accepting the IMF terms and then fudging on the performance requirements. The IMF then held back its loan installments, and protracted renegotiations ensued. In the interim, rising unemployment, bankruptcies, and food riots in Brazil have popularized a fourth alternative, a unilateral debt moratorium. Begun as a proposal from the left, this alternative is gaining strong support within the frightened business and political establishments. Whether this is a Samsonian bargaining weapon or a serious option no one knows.

Conclusion

Latin America has been an embarrassing statistical outlier for social scientists who postulate positive linear or parabolic linkages between per capita income and such nice things as political democratization, more equitable income distribution, declining malnutrition, and more stable economic growth. The experiences detailed in this chapter add to the embarrassment.

Industrializing "middle-income" LDCs worldwide have been afflicted by comparable external shocks since 1974: rising fuel costs, a slackening growth of the capitalist center, increased terms-of-trade fluctuations, etc. All faced the temptations of the international bank lending bubble. Yet the incidence to date of debt crises and financial blowups among the middle-income LDCs has fallen disproportionately on the Latin American countries, whether authoritarian, parliamentary, or quondam-parliamentary.[42] Did they succumb more than the other middle-income LDCs to the temptation to borrow beyond their means? The comparative statistical record gives contradictory answers. At the end of 1981, the ratio of net disbursed foreign debt to GNP for all of Latin America was below the average ratio for all LDCs. Of the thirteen major LDC borrowers, the 1981 ratios of Argentina, Brazil, Chile, Mexico, and Venezeula were at or below the median. On the other hand, the 1981 net debt to export ratio of Latin America was moderately above the LDC average, and of the above-mentioned five countries, three had 1981 debt to export ratios in the upper half of the thirteen-country array.[43]

The second set of statistics lends some support to a neoclassical indictment: distorted prices, inward-looking policies, etc. Yet, as I have shown in this chapter, the Southern Cone countries were engaged con brio in removing trade restrictions, liberating relative prices, eliminating negative rates of protection, holding down real wages, and other activities designed to open up the economy. In its dirigistic way, Brazil was promoting exports with lavish tax and credit subsidies, and the oil boom gave Mexico an unusually fast rate of export growth during 1976–1981. Why did import expansion overtake export growth in all these countries?

A historic perspective helps to sharpen the question. The current balance-of-payments crisis in each of the countries is only part of a series that extends far back in time. In the authoritarian countries today, the military seized power in the context of a previous crisis. Earlier, other takeovers terminated the early post–World War II import booms and the severe post-1929 crises. In 1914, a youthful John Maynard Keynes wrote, "Men are born of two kinds (except in South America, where all are of the second), mercantilists and inflationists—those who believe that a sufficiency of solid gold is a cure for all financial ills, and those who believe that a sufficiency of cheap credit and paper money will promote unlimited prosperity for us" (Keynes 1914:631). With no Latin American consumer or wholesale price indices extant in the prewar era to motivate Keynes's remark, it was undoubtedly based on the region's reputation for depreciating exchanges, a policy that was already well established during the area's nineteenth-century export-led growth era. The worsening of income inequality in the Southern Cone countries, Brazil, and Mexico during the years covered in this chapter also follows a pattern reaching back to the nineteenth century: rising inequality during most growth periods, partial reversals during contractionary periods, and, on the whole, a secular trend of rising inequality.[44]

The persistence of patterns through eras of inward- and outward-looking policies, oligarchic and populist politics, rusticity and urbanization, and primary and industry-led growth implies the workings of similar socioeconomic causal mechanisms. In some earlier writings, I have put forth as a persisting mechanism the impact on Latin American productive structures and balances of payments through the various epochs since the early colonial years of the intense addiction of the elites to European—more recently, North American—status goods (see Felix 1983 for bibliographical references). That is, in those writings, I attempted to transform the "international demonstration effect" (IDE) from a staple of Latin American pop sociology to an analytic tool by giving it more economic specificity and historic and cultural dimensions. Three inferences from this effort are especially relevant for understanding the persistence of unstable growth and weak trickling down.

The first is that trade liberalization and "getting prices right" need not, in the presence of a strong IDE, improve the market disciplining of consumer behavior since the effect of a greater availability of imported status goods may dominate the relative price and income effects. The weak household savings behavior and the orgy of consumer imports that helped topple the NL experiments in the Southern Cone countries should have been anticipated. A prerequisite for such anticipation, however, would be abandoning a basic axiomatic underpinning of neoclassical price disciplining policy prescriptions, the immaculate conception of the indifference curve, i.e., the exogeneity and fixity of consumer preferences.

A second inference is that turning an intense demand for foreign-designed status goods inward to spark an industrial boom led by consumer durables, Brazilian style, may alter but need not ease excessive pressures on the balance of payments. Such an effect depends on the interaction between the speed with which new foreign-designed status-laden goods displace older ones and the speed of development of domestic backward-linkage activities supplying the successive new products. There is no automatic market mechanism to coordinate the two speeds, other than balance-of-payment overload and foreign exchange crises. Alertness to this possibility also requires scrapping the "immaculate conception" axiom.

A third inference is that the strength of the IDE varies among LDC regions, reflecting differences in the local norms that award status to specific consumption goods. Latin America's elites, initially the products of European conquest and subordination of indigenous cultures and replenished over the centuries mainly by European recruitment, developed an intense IDE well before J. Walter Thompson and Coca-Colaization. Asians, who industrialized later, were much more addicted to indigenous status goods, an addiction embodied in an extensive craft sector to service elite demands. The shift in the twentieth century to foreign-designed goods has occurred in Asia at a more measured pace than in Latin America, allowing much larger segments of the craft sector to survive, accumulate, and modernize the technology and easing balance-of-payments pressures. Trickling down has been stronger, growth less unequalizing and less unstable.[45]

Yet deep-rooted though Latin America's IDE may be, it is still primarily the product of endogenous social processes. Perhaps the current financial blowups will finally force onto the Latin America policy agendas consideration of how to slow the IDE to a more economically digestible pace.

Notes

Reedited for publication February 1984. My thanks to Sam Morley for his many helpful criticisms and suggestions on the original draft, some of which I've used.

1. Postcoup Brazil was hailed for a time as an NL success story because of its indexing of bank deposits and loans, mini-exchange rate devaluation policy, and openness to foreign investment—e.g., Larry Sjaastad (1974). Brazil was subsequently dropped from the set for dirigiste deviationism, but when the expulsion took place is unclear. In the summer of 1974, Arnold Harberger, on one of his consulting-

lecturing visits to Chile, was still holding up Brazil to the Chileans as the exemplar of a glowing future under economic liberalism.

2. Actually, the Pareto superiority of a policy change requires an accompanying tax-subsidy mechanism to redistribute welfare gains so as to ensure there are no losers from the policy change. The Southern Cone NL strategy included no such commitment, but the writings of its advocate-interpreters show no concern at the oversight.

3. Thus, Ronald McKinnon dismissed the statistical evidence that Chile's economic growth and domestic investment rates averaged lower after the 1973 coup than during the preceding two decades by appealing to the "common classroom theory of immiserizing growth. . . . Import substitution so reduces the efficiency of foreign trade that welfare could decline in the economy as industrialization proceeds" (Cline and Weintraub 1981:144).

4. Exposés in the Southern Cone countries are revealing extensive conflicts of interest, nest feathering, and chicanery involving high military figures and NL economic policymakers; e.g., "BIR Tumbles Down—Who Comes After?" (1980); "Tinkering with the Rules of Monopoly" (1980); "Black Hole of Private Debt Threatens Chilean Model" (1983); "He That Is Without Sin Among You . . ." (1983); and Ruiz-Tagle (1983).

5. The concern to get real interest rates above zero quickly distinguishes the initial monetarist stabilization efforts of the NL experiments from earlier monetarist efforts in Latin America. The latter had taken a gradualist approach to creating a positive real interest rate structure, with interest ceilings and quantitative limits on new bank lending used as transitional instruments.

6. The industrial sectors, however, did not share in the increase. Thus, in Argentina, the wage share of industrial value added rose from 1978 to 1980. This change reflected a substantial decline of industrial relative prices and a rise of financial costs as well as a partial recovery of real wages, although in 1980, real wages measured against the consumer price index were still about 11 percent below those of 1977. The aggregate rate of surplus value had increased, but the gains flowed primarily to the burgeoning service sector, chiefly to finance and commerce. The pattern was similar in Chile and Uruguay during their brief boom years.

7. In Chile, the skill of the "Chicago boys" in exploiting policy failures to accelerate liberalization led some observers to dub them "Marxists of the right" (see O'Brien 1981).

8. The concentration of asset ownership went furthest in Chile. By 1978, the five largest conglomerates were already in control of 53 percent of the assets of the 250 largest Chilean firms, and nine conglomerates controlled 82 percent of the assets of the financial system (estimates by Dahse 1970). This concentration was considerably aided by the sale of state-owned firms to the conglomerates at subsidized prices. In a sample of forty-one such sales, the sale price averaged 30 percent below balance sheet net worth (estimate by Foxley 1980:19, Cuadro 8).

9. The *price deflated* index of the stock market prices in Chile rose sevenfold between January 1978 and December 1980 (Harberger 1982:124).

10. Uruguay was more successful than Argentina in cutting back the fiscal deficit during its boom.

11. In a May 1981 seminar in Santiago for visiting bankers, current and past Chicago-influenced presidents of the Chilean central bank reassured the visitors that the private sector's debt could never be excessive since its acquisition was always for profitable purposes. For the same reason, the large current account deficit was no danger since it was merely a reflex of private borrowing and would decline automatically if the profitability of private investment were to fall (*Ercilla* 1981).

12. Uruguay stuck the longest with its *tablita cambiaria*, abandoning it only in November 1982. Chile abandoned its *tablita* in the summer of 1982; Argentina, early in 1981.

13. By March 1983, the nonperforming loans of the Chilean private banking system totaled more than its capital and reserves (Leiva Lavalle 1983:344, Cuadro 3).

14. In Chile, virtually the entire banking system has been taken over by the government and is now operated by government-appointed managers. A wisecrack, popular in structuralist circles, is that the transition from Allende to Pinochet has been a transition from utopian to scientific socialism, since the means of production are ending up in the hands of the state.

15. Jose Dagnino Pastore, the Argentine economist and ex-finance minister, reports that the three main uses of the increment in the foreign debt during Argentina's NL experiment were, in decreasing order of importance, capital flight, foreign tourism, and the purchase of nontraditional imports. He concludes that "the asset counterpart of the increased liabilities has not added significantly to the capacity of the country to generate foreign exchange" (Dagnino Pastore 1982:14–15). On the unproductive use of Chile's capital inflows, see French-Davis (1983).

16. This modifies McKinnon's earlier view put forth in his influential *Money and Capital in Economic Development* (1973). In that work, financial liberalization is presented unqualifiedly as a policy that will bring quick and pervasive efficiency gains to all "financially repressed" LDCs.

17. McKinnon's judgment is negative; Harberger's and Sjaastad's are not. Most other NL and non-NL appraisals are negative. Dornbusch, who believes the *tablitas* were a disaster, also points out that "fixed nominal exchange rates or pre-announced target paths of the nominal rates" were considered by NL strategists to be "integral parts of the stabilization efforts." They were applications of the general Chicago belief that preannounced fixed "rules" minimize policy shock in the marketplace (Dornbusch 1982:703).

18. An economy is in Walrasian equilibrium if supply equals demand in all its markets for commodities and factors at positive prices. The equilibrium is unique if there is no more than one array of quantities associated with each array of market clearing prices. The economy is stable if it returns to equilibrium after a supply or demand shock.

19. In the Arrow-Debreu specification for competitive equilibrium, uncertainty occurs because future markets covering all future contingencies do not exist (Arrow and Debreu 1954).

20. These observations draw heavily on the seminal work of Hyman Minsky on the "financial instability hypothesis" (see Minsky 1975 and 1982).

21. Mexico's growth also slackened in the late 1950s and early 1960s, leading to an internal regime crisis and a moderate shift of economic strategy. The crisis was resolved, however, without a toppling, or even a fracturing, of the PRI-controlled political institutions.

22. Uruguay's 1973–1982 growth rate exceeded that of the preceding decade but was lower than that of the 1940–1960 decades.

23. For Brazilian sectoral growth data, see Baer (1979:Tables 22–25); for Mexico's, see Solis (1981:Table 1.3).

24. For a summary of evidence of rising inequality during the 1970s in the Southern Cone countries, see Foxley (1981:202–203). For Brazil and Mexico, see Morley (1982:Table 3.2) and Felix (1982).

25. E.g., Brazil's ratio of debt service to exports in 1962 reached 0.42, access to new foreign credits was cut off, and inflation peaked at 125 percent in early 1964 (Morley 1982:7). By 1982, the Brazilian debt service to export ratio had risen beyond 0.42, and the inflation rate approached 150 percent. The current financial plight of Brazil appears more desperate than the crisis that helped spawn the 1964 military takeover (see Bacha 1983).

26. Solis (1981) provides a critically sympathetic assessment of the Echeverría period by a participant observer. Weintraub (1981:271–296) treats the Echeverría episode as an idiosyncratic deviation and the IMF-directed stabilization program of 1977-1978 as a successful return of the Mexican economy to "stabilizing development." The subsequent tilt back to *desarrollo compartido* by López Portillo suggests, however, that the political push for that program transcended presidential idiosyncracies.

27. The Gini coefficient is a statistical measure of income inequality. An increase in the coefficient indicates a rise in inequality.

28. Based on Langoni's estimates for 1960-1970, as summarized in Morley (1982:Table 3.2). According to a 1975 estimate, the share of the top 10 percent rose further at the expense of the other deciles ("Brazil's Morning After" 1983).

29. Vernon (1963) describes the aborting of Lopez Mateos's tax reform project early in the 1960s. Solis (1981:Chapters 2–3) details the aborting of the tax reform efforts under Echeverría.

30. Cf. Solis (1981) Chapters 2 and 3 for a discussion of both motives by a high-placed participant observer in the Echeverría government.

31. The estimated cost of these price subsidies rose from 2.1 percent of GDP in 1969–1972 to 5.3 percent in 1973–1976 (Weintraub 1981:277).

32. The debt figures are from a survey of 2,200 Mexican firms conducted by the Office of Economic Advisors to the President and summarized in Gil Diaz (1983:Table 15). Direct evidence of the confidence in the continued stability of the exchange rate is the fact that very few firms made use of a central bank facility that allowed them to convert a dollar debt into a peso debt at the prevailing peso exchange rate (Gil Diaz 1983:26).

33. The formula differed for short and long maturity debts. For details on the early evolution of indexing and other features of the post-1964 financial market reforms, see Ness (1974) and Baer and Beckerman (1980).

34. The cumulated fiscal deficit during 1965-1967 totaled only 70 percent of the rise in the outstanding fiscal debt (computed from Baer 1982:Tables 38, 39).

122   David Felix

35. During 1968–1974, consumer durables expanded at an annual rate of 22.8 percent compared to 13.7 percent rate for all industry (Bonelli and Malan 1976:Table 2). For the pattern of the 1950s, see Serra (1979:Table 3).

36. Outlays on imported capital goods rose 32 percent per annum; on imported intermediate goods, 49 percent per annum. Outlays on petroleum imports in 1968–1973 rose 27 percent per annum, then shot up to 287 percent in 1974 (Bonelli and Malan 1976:Table 2).

37. Most of the credit went to the wealthiest 5 percent of the farmers who used part of it for consumption, as evidenced by the positive correlation between variations in credit flows and sales of autos in rural areas (Baer 1982:327–329).

38. The share of gross domestic savings in nonindexed financial assets dropped from 0.24 in 1973 to 0.09 in 1974 while indexed assets rose from 0.10 to 0.19 (Baer and Beckerman 1980:Table 8).

39. The annual growth rate of consumer durables declined from 21 percent in 1973 to 2.1 percent in 1975; industrial growth fell from 15.8 to 3.7 percent (Bonelli and Malan 1976:Table 3). Annual GDP per capita growth fell from 10.8 to 2.8 percent (Baer 1982:Table 22).

40. Petrobrás (Petróleo Brasileiro, S.A.), the giant state oil company, was especially active in such bailout purchases (see *Latin American Regional Reports: Brazil*, January 7, 1983).

41. Between 1971 and 1981, the debt-equity ratio of Brazil's 500 largest firms rose 125 percent while return on equity fell 21 percent (Kanitz 1983).

42. Since 1981, twelve Latin American countries have signed conditionality accords with the IMF (see *Latin American Weekly Report*, 1983).

43. Net debt is disbursed debt outstanding less foreign exchange reserves. The comparative data are in World Bank (1983).

44. The sketchy but, I believe, plausible evidence is summarized in Felix (1983).

45. Asian commentators currently refer to the Philippines as Asia's only Latin American economy, a left-handed way of making the same point.

References

Arrow, Kenneth, and Debreu, Gerard. 1954. "Existence of an Equilibrium for a Competitive Economy." *Econometrica* 22 July:265–290.
Bacha, Edmar L. 1983. "The Prospects for Adjustment in Brazil." In *Prospects for Adjustment in Argentina, Brazil, and Mexico: Responding to the Debt Crisis*, ed. John Williamson. Washington, D.C.: Institute for International Economics, May.
Baer, Werner. 1979. *The Brazilian Economy: Its Growth and Development*. Columbus, Ohio: Grid Publishing Company.
———. 1982. *The Brazilian Economy: Growth and Development*. 2d ed. New York: Praeger.
Baer, Werner, and Beckerman, Paul. 1980. "The Trouble with Indexing: Reflections on the Recent Brazilian Experience." *World Development* 8 September:677–703.
Bank of International Settlements. 1983. *Fifty-third Annual Report*. Basel: June 13:85–188.

"BIR Tumbles Down—Who Comes After?" 1980. *Latin America Regional Reports: Southern Cone* (London), April 18:5.

"Black Hole of Private Debt Threatens Chilean Model." 1983. *Latin America Regional Reports: Southern Cone* (London), February 4:1-2.

Bonelli, Regis, and Malan, Pedro S. 1976. "Os limites do possivel: notas sobre balanco de pagamentos e industria nos anos 70." *Pesquisa e Planajamento Economico* 6 August:353-406.

"Brazil's Morning After." 1983. *Economist* (Special Survey, London), March 12:17.

Cline, William, and Weintraub, Sidney, eds. 1981. *Economic Stabilization in Developing Countries.* Washington, D.C.: Brookings Institution.

Cohen, Benjamin J., and Basagni, Fabio. 1981. *Banks and the Balance of Payments.* Atlantic Institute for International Affairs Research Volume. Montclair, N.J.: Allanheld, Osman.

Dagnino Pastore, Jose M. 1982. "An Anti-Inflammatory Experiment: Argentina, 1979-1981." In "Symposium on Liberalization and Stabilization: Recent Experience in the Southern Cone." Mimeograph. Washington, D.C.: World Bank, May 20-21.

Dahse, F. 1970. *Mapa de la extrema riqueza.* Santiago: Editorial Aconcaqua.

Dornbusch, Rudiger. 1982. "Stabilization Policies in Developing Countries: What Have We Learned?" *World Development* 10, no. 9:701-708.

Ercilla. (Santiago). 1981. June 3.

Felix, David. 1982. "Income Distribution Trends in Mexico and the Kuznets Curves." In *Brazil and Mexico,* ed. Sylvia Hewlett and Richard Weinert, pp. 265-316. Philadelphia: Institute for the Study of Human Issues.

———. 1983. "Income Distribution and the Quality of Life in Latin America: Patterns, Trends, and Policy Implications." *Latin American Research* 18, no. 2:3-33.

Foxley, Alejandro. 1980. "Hacia una economia de libre mercado: Chile: 1970-1978." *Collección Estud CIEPLAN* (Santiago: Corporacion de Investigaciones Economicas para America Latina), no. 4:5-37.

———. 1981. "Stabilization Policies and Their Effects on Employment and Income Distribution." In *Economic Stabilization in Developing Countries,* ed. William Cline and Sidney Weintraub, pp. 191-225. Washington, D.C.: Brookings Institution.

French-Davis, Ricardo. 1983. "The Monetarist Experiment in Chile: A Critical Survey." *World Development* 2, no. 11:905-926.

Gil Diaz, Francisco. 1983. "Mexico's Path from Stability to Inflation." Mimeograph. Mexico City: Institute for Contemporary Studies, April.

Green, Rosario. 1983. "Mexico: Crisis financiera y dueda externa: El imperative de una solucion estructural y nacionalista." *Comercio Exterior* 33 February:99-107.

Harberger, Arnold C. 1982. "The Chilean Economy in the 1970s: Crisis, Stabilization, Liberalization, Reform." In *Economic Policy in a World of Change,* ed. Karl Brunner and Alan H. Meltzer, pp. 115-152. Carnegie-Rochester Conference Series on Public Policy vol. 17. Amsterdam: North Holland Publishing Company.

"He That Is Without Sin Among You . . ." 1983. *Latin America Regional Reports: Southern Cone* (London), March 11:7-8.

Jaffe, William. 1977. "The Normative Bias of the Walrasian Model." *Quarterly Journal of Economics* 91 August:371–389.

Kanitz, Stephen C. 1983. "Brazilian Companies Performing Well." *Wall Street Journal*, Special Advertising Section, January 31.

Keynes, John Maynard. 1914. "The Prospects for Money, November 1914." *Economic Journal* 24 December:610–632.

Latin America Weekly Report. 1983. September 16.

Leiva Lavalle, Jorge. 1983. "El Derrumbe del sistema financiero." *Mensaje*, July.

McKinnon, Ronald. 1973. *Money and Capital in Economic Development.* Washington, D.C.: Brookings Institution.

_____. 1982. "The Order of Economic Liberalization: Lessons from Chile and Argentina." In *Economic Policy in a World of Change*, ed. Karl Brunner and Alan H. Meltzer, pp. 159–186. Carnegie-Rochester Conference Series on Public Policy vol. 17. Amsterdam: North Holland Publishing Company.

Minsky, Hyman. 1975. *John Maynard Keynes.* New York: Columbia University Press.

_____. 1982. *Can It Happen Again?* New York: M. E. Sharpe.

Morley, Samuel A. 1971. "Inflation and Stagflation in Brazil." *Economic Development and Cultural Change* 19 January:184–203.

_____. 1982. *Labor Markets and Inequitable Growth: The Case of Authoritarian Capitalism in Brazil.* Cambridge: Cambridge University Press.

Ness, Walter L. 1974. "Financial Market Innovation as a Development Strategy: Initial Results from the Brazilian Experience." *Economic Development and Cultural Change* 22 April:453–472.

New York Times. 1983. July 5:30.

O'Brien, Philip. 1981. "The New Leviathan: The Chicago School and the Chilean Regime, 1973–1980." *IDS Bulletin* (Brighton, Eng.: Institute of Development Studies) 13, no. 1, December:38–50.

O'Donnell, Guillermo. 1979. "Tensions in the Bureaucratic-Authoritarian State and the Question of Democracy." In *The New Authoritarianism in Latin America*, ed. David Collier, pp. 285–318. Princeton: Princeton University Press.

Reynolds, Clark W., and Carpenter, Robert T. 1975. "Housing Finance in Brazil: Toward a New Distribution of Wealth." In *Latin America Urban Research* 5:147–174.

Ruiz-Tagle, Jaime. 1983. "Del Derrumbe financiera a la crisis externa." *Mensaje*, March-April:88–90.

Sampson, Anthony. 1981. *The Money Lenders.* New York: Penguin Books.

Serra, Jose. 1979. "Three Mistaken Themes Regarding the Connection Between Industrialization and Authoritarian Regimes." In *The New Authoritarianism in Latin America*, ed. David Collier, pp. 99–163. Princeton: Princeton University Press.

Sjaastad, Larry. 1974. "How to Contrive a Miracle: Brazil Since 1965." *Nebraska Journal of Economics and Business* 13 Autumn:43–73.

_____. 1982. "The Failure of Economic Liberalism in the Southern Cone." 1982. Bateman Memorial Lecture, University of Western Australia, September 23.

Solis, Leopoldo. 1981. *Economic Policy Reform in Mexico.* New York: Pergamon Press.

Taylor, Lance. 1981. "ISLM in the Tropics: Diagrammatics of the New Structuralist Macro Critique." In *Economic Stabilization in Developing Countries*, ed. William Cline and Sidney Weintraub, pp. 465–503. Washington, D.C.: Brookings Institution.

"Tinkering with the Rules for Monopoly." 1980. *Latin America Regional Reports: Southern Cone* (London), May 23:6–7.

Tofaneto, Antonio. 1983. "Government Seeks to Diminish State Role in Brazilian Economy." *Wall Street Journal*, Special Advertising Section, January 31.

Vernon, Raymond. 1963. *The Dilemma of Mexico's Development: The Roles of the Public and Private Sectors*. Cambridge: Harvard University Press.

Weintraub, Sidney. 1981. "Case Study of Economic Stabilization: Mexico." In *Economic Stabilization in Developing Countries*, ed. William Cline and Sidney Weintraub, pp. 271–292. Washington, D.C.: Brookings Institution.

Weisskoff, Richard. 1980. "The Growth and Decline of Import Substitution in Brazil—Revisited." *World Development* 8 September:647–675.

World Bank. 1983. *World Debt Tables: 1982–1983*. Washington, D.C.

Part 2

Military and Civilian Regimes: Spectacular Failures and Moderate Successes

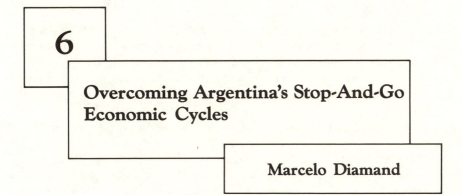

6

Overcoming Argentina's Stop-And-Go Economic Cycles

Marcelo Diamand

For decades, the performance of the Argentine economy has been poor because of economic policies that have swung like a pendulum between two opposing poles—the expansionist/populist and the orthodox, or neoclassical, approaches. The two principal objectives of the expansionist policy are to reduce inequality of income distribution and to attain full employment. The first objective is sought by granting larger social benefits and generous wage and salary increases. The second objective—full employment—is sought by assuring a high level of demand. Other principal instruments of expansionist, or populist, economic policy include manipulating foreign exchange rates and controlling the prices of goods and services rendered by both the private and the public sectors to keep the cost of living low.

Expansionist periods frequently begin with an increase in real salaries, cheap credit, increased economic activity, and optimism in the industrial and commercial sectors. This stage seldom lasts long. The budget deficit grows, the balance of trade is thrown into disequilibrium, accelerating inflation erodes real wages, and unrest develops in the labor unions. The process culminates in the exhaustion of central bank reserves and a crisis in the balance of payments. Expansion comes to a halt, and a chaotic economic situation emerges. As time passes, the opposition of influential sectors of society increases, and finally, the people in charge of the government's economic policy are ousted, which generally means the chief executive as well.

Although the populists admit to some errors and excesses, they tend to minimize their importance. They offer as the principal reasons for their failure an insufficiency of political power to control the key factors of the economy and the resistance of powerful national and international economic interests.

The failure of the populist program always provokes an abrupt turn toward economic orthodoxy. The power goes to economic policymakers who are strongly influenced by the neoclassical economic theories that prevail in the universities, governments, financial circles of the highly industrialized countries, and the international financial institutions. The orthodox ideas emphasize order, discipline, efficiency, and balancing of the budget as well as confidence of investors, the attraction of foreign capital, and the virtues of popular sacrifice.

In countries like Argentina and the rest of the Southern Cone, the new economic teams generally come to power in the midst of a balance-of-payments crisis. Their responses include large devaluations (which automatically bring about large increases in the income of the agricultural sector), a lid on increases in urban money wages, drastic monetary and credit restrictions, and an intensified effort to attract foreign capital. Invariably, the first effects are a wave of business failures, increased unemployment, and a fall in real wages—in short, a recession. The economic team regards these effects as a temporary, but unavoidable, sacrifice that must be endured in order to put the economy on a sound basis for revival and growth for the benefit of the entire population.

In Argentina and other countries with similar economies, however, this revival and recovery has not materialized. The orthodox policy does achieve certain successes in the beginning. The rate of inflation, which always increases initially after devaluation, usually diminishes later on; financial capital flows in from abroad; and real salaries recover to some extent. Nevertheless, at some point in the process, a crisis of confidence appears. The flow of foreign capital is reversed, and loans that had come in from abroad begin to slip away. This situation results in great pressure on reserves of foreign currency and a crisis in the foreign exchange market, compelling the government to effect a sudden devaluation. Real wages then fall, aggregate demand falls off, the rate of inflation accelerates rapidly, and the economy again falls into a recession, usually even deeper than the previous one.

The reaction of orthodox-school proponents to their lack of success has always been similar to that of the populists. Though the former may admit some errors in the execution of their economic policy, they attribute failure primarily to not having enough political power. The lack of this power, they always insist, made it impossible for them to bring about the improvement in public administration that was necessary to eliminate inefficient public enterprises and to keep wages depressed for a period long enough to generate a self-sustaining growth process.

The Political Standoff

The pendulum swings between populist and orthodox economic policies have led many political observers to believe that what counts is not so much the nature of policy but the fact that whatever policy is chosen, its proponents must have enough political power behind them to give the policy enough time to work.

My thesis in this chapter is that this view is erroneous. Although it is true that any economic policy needs to be accompanied by political support in order to be successful, neither the populist policy nor the orthodox policy, as carried out in the past, would have been able to achieve its stated objectives even if it had been accompanied by total political power. This is so because neither had intrinsic feasibility. Both policies were and are condemned to failure for purely economic reasons. The lack of viability of both policies is due to the inadequacy for semi-industrialized countries of the intellectual models on which the policies are based—the Keynesian in the case of the populist model and the neoclassical in that of the orthodox model.[1]

The determination of the cause of the stop-and-go cycles in Argentina has great political importance. If, on the one hand, the real cause is the more or less equal political strength of the populist and the orthodox schools, which prevents either from having adequate time to carry out its policies, an authoritarian government should be capable of overcoming this standoff. Regardless of the program chosen, an authoritarian government should be able to carry it out despite resistance, confident that in time, the correctness of the policy will be proved and the government's firmness will be justified.

On the other hand, if neither of the policies has intrinsic feasibility, then the disorder, inflation, shortages, and cessation of foreign payments that have nearly always characterized the populist program and the recession, foreign debt, and crises of confidence associated with the orthodox program are not chance phenomena. Rather, they are inherent faults of the respective policies. In this case, the resistance of the affected sectors—independent of the fact that it could constitute a defense of their interests—ought to be interpreted as a healthy defensive reaction of society. And if this is so, then government leaders who aspire to give their nation an economic solution should not only be concerned about getting the necessary amount of power but, above all, should concentrate on formulating an intrinsically viable economic policy. These statements do not refer only to Argentina. The struggle between the two opposing economic policies, both divorced from reality, has been reproduced in several similar Latin American countries, and the analysis of the Argentine situation can, to a great extent, be applied to them as well.[2]

Industrialization and Comparative Advantage

Argentina belongs today to a large group of primary exporting countries in the process of industrialization. All of them first developed their economies by specializing in the production and exportation of certain primary products, in which they were highly efficient thanks to nature's bounty: fertile soil, favorable climate, or an abundance of mineral resources. In this stage, the countries have virtually no manufacturing industry since they compete in this area on the international scene. The cause of the problem is the low initial productivity of the industrial sector.

In contrast to the productivity of the primary sector, industrial productivity does not depend on more or less favorable natural conditions but on the degree of development of the country. The first requisite of industrial productivity is a high density of capital—plant and equipment—in the industry itself and in the economy within which it operates. The second requirement is the mastery of technology obtained through "learning by doing."

Third, industry is not a simple aggregate of activities, but rather a complex interdependent system, the productivity of which depends on management's capacity to coordinate, synchronize, and control the multiple stages involved in the manufacture of an industrial product. Fourth, productivity depends upon government behavior—the efficiency of the basic services provided by the state and the coherence and stability of the rules of the game that the state creates and that determine the capacity of the public and private sectors to plan for and make long-term investments in machinery and technology.

Finally, industrial productivity depends on scale. Modern technologies of mass production are characterized by low direct costs and high fixed costs: amortization of capital plant and equipment and the employment of staffs for design, engineering, marketing, procurement, production, and quality control. To keep operating, manufacturing firms must have a certain minimum volume of production.

None of the conditions, therefore, that could create a comparative advantage in favor of industry is provided by nature. Nor is comparative advantage a genetic endowment of a few lucky countries. Success depends upon the degree of development of the industrial structure. In other words, a nation can become an efficient industrial economy only by means of the industrialization process itself.[3]

All of these factors mean that in the first decades of development, industrial productivity will necessarily be very low and at a net disadvantage when compared to the primary sector, which is favored by nature. To overcome this disadvantage, the manufacturing sector requires protection.

The Free Trade–Industrialization Controversy

Traditional neoclassical thought is opposed to such protection. According to the principle of comparative advantage, all countries ought to abide by the principles of free trade, even if for many developing countries this doctrine means renouncing industrialization. According to this theory, those countries should dedicate all of their resources to primary production and use the foreign currency earned to import the necessary industrial goods. In this way, presumably, they would assure the most efficient use of their resources and the greatest welfare for their populations.

The neoclassical argument is based on a very simplified theoretical model that does not adequately reflect the conditions of the real world. In practice, the countries that are exclusively dedicated to primary production encounter serious economic problems not recognized by neoclassical theorists.[4]

The first of them is the problem of employment. Even those primary activities that count on a sustained world demand, as was the case until recently with the production of petroleum, can never give employment to an entire population. In the second place, world demand is rarely maintained on a stable basis. The market for primary products generally expands much less than is needed to assure the economic growth to which the producing countries aspire. Moreover, the prices of primary products tend to be highly variable, which means the foreign exchange earnings of the exporting country are highly unstable. In the third place, it is risky to base all of the economic life of a country on one or two products because of the possibilities that their source of supply may dwindle or that they may become obsolete (possibilities that occurred in the cases of the Peruvian anchovy and Brazilian natural rubber).

Finally, and most important, there is the problem of the dynamic quality of industrial productivity. In order to reach a high level of industrial productivity, it is necessary to begin the industrialization of a country at low levels of productivity. The theory of the international division of labor, which underlies the principle of free trade, is totally static and would freeze the initially low industrial productivity of a developing country. Under the free trade scheme, a country that exports primary products is condemned to reject the only route that would enable it to eventually have a more efficient industry and a diversified export sector. A developing country must seek, therefore, to develop a manufacturing sector and to give it just enough protection to enable it to become an efficient exporter of manufactured products.

The infant-industry controversy is well known, going back to the debates of more than a century ago between U.S. and German protectionists and British free traders.[5] The United States and Germany are industrial powers today and not agricultural countries because of the fact that at some time in the past, the supporters of protection were able to translate their ideas into policy. In the same way, the present processes of industrialization in the primary exporting countries result from the fact that in all of them, there was at some point a political decision to industrialize and to make use of protection.

In light of the present problems of countries like Argentina, their decisions to industrialize seem to have been less successful than the similar decisions that the industrial countries of today made at the inception of their industrialization. I argue that the problem now afflicting the industrializing countries is due, not to the fact that the decision to industrialize with protection was mistaken, but to the inconsistency with which this decision was implemented in practice.

Moreover, though the manufacturing sectors of Argentina and several other Latin American countries are not internationally competitive, they have greatly raised the level of employment in their countries, developed a substantial technological base, and trained a skilled labor force. The root of their problem is that in the process of industrializing with high protection, they have also created a new economic model. This model, which is very little understood and is quite different from the traditional neoclassical model that forms the basis of prevailing economic thought, has its own set of problems.

Unbalanced Productive Structure

I call this new model an unbalanced productive structure (UPS).[6] A UPS economy is composed of two principal sectors that have very different levels of productivity: a primary sector (agriculture in the case of Argentina) that competes effectively in world markets and an industrial sector of much lower productivity that, because its costs and prices are substantially higher than world market prices, is confined to producing primarily for the domestic market.

In general, in today's world, the industrializing countries do not realize that they are working with a new and different dual sector model, and they continue to apply traditional ideas that conflict with this new model. The results are a profound disorientation in the UPS countries and a virtual incapacity to overcome the problems that arise in the development of their economies.

The first characteristic of UPS that is not well understood refers to high industrial prices, which are generally attributed to industrial inefficiency. However, the inability of the industrial sector to compete internationally has relatively little to do with the efficiency or inefficiency of the industry in absolute terms. The price of any export good in dollars depends in part, it is true, on the efficiency or productivity with which it is produced. But it also depends on the rate of exchange—that is, the price of the dollar in national money—that is used to translate domestic prices into international prices.

In traditional economies, this rate of exchange, which results from either the marketplace or government action, is established at a level that permits domestic goods and services to compete internationally, whatever their productivity. This automatic mechanism of exchange adaptation is what makes it possible for countries with very different degrees of productivity to compete with each other in the world market. As a result, Korea, Taiwan, and Hong Kong, despite the low productivity of their industries at the beginning of their development, were able to inundate the world market with their cheap exports. They were able to do so because they set a low value on their currency in terms of dollars, which enabled them to bring their prices down to internationally competitive levels at a cost of depressed real salaries and a low standard of living.

The lack of competitiveness of UPS countries like Argentina arises because the mechanism of exchange adaptation does not function properly. Since there are two sectors with entirely different degrees of productivity—the primary and the industrial—the rate of exchange can adequately represent only one of them at the international level. Given that in Argentina the exchange rate is habitually based on the costs and prices of the highly productive agricultural and cattle industries of the fertile pampas, conversion of the "pampean dollar" into pesos does not provide enough pesos to cover the costs and prices of consumer and capital goods manufactured for the home market. The pampean dollar is even too low to cover the cost of cotton from the Chaco or sugar from San Miguel de Tucumán. This is the reason why the prices of industrial products as well as those of many regional agricultural products (i.e., those not grown on the pampas) as expressed in pampean dollars are higher than international prices. The agricultural sector, accordingly, sets a standard of exceptional productivity that is impossible for the rest of the country to reach.[7]

This illusion of industrial inefficiency leads to the first problem confronting Argentina and many other UPS countries. The failure of their industries to compete in the international market generates hostility within some influential groups in the countries themselves toward the whole process of industrialization. The conviction that domestic industry is inefficient leads immediately to another adverse conclusion: Argentina's industry could be more efficient if only it wanted to be; Argentina's entrepreneurs must be incompetent or lazy because they do not compete more effectively. Protectionist measures come to be seen as instruments that create and perpetuate inefficiency; they are imposed by politicians to benefit "inept" entrepreneurs to the detriment of the rest of the population. An anti-industrial stereotype is thus sustained. Periodically, this stereotype gives rise to "efficiency" drives that not only destroy industrial productive capacity but also thwart economic policies that would lead to greater efficiency.

The stereotype is founded upon false premises. The fact that domestic industrial prices in dollar terms are higher than international prices does not support the argument that industry is less efficient than it ought to be at the present level of the country's development. The only valid conclusion that can be drawn is that the industrial sector does in fact operate at a comparative disadvantage in relation to the primary sector.

Given that this disadvantage is repeated in all of the primary exporting countries in the process of industrialization, it is unlikely that all their domestic business people can be charged with alleged deficiencies. It is more logical to conclude that these countries are all facing differences in productivity that always arise between the primary and industrial sectors during the first decades of industrialization. One may disagree with an LDC's decision to industrialize while disregarding the principle of comparative advantage. Once, however, a country embarks on this model of industrialization, it should accept the disparity of relative prices between its two sectors as a fact of life in the short run and then devise an approach that will enable the less productive sector to compete internationally.

Strangulation in the External Sector

The main problem that the UPS countries suffer from is recurrent foreign exchange crises. Industrialization entails a growing need for imported intermediate products, raw materials, and capital goods. In other words, the growth of industry demands a constantly increasing supply of foreign currency.

At the beginning of the process of industrialization, these new needs for foreign currency are counterbalanced by the foreign exchange savings that import substitution brings. But this substitution, which is rapid and easy when it involves only final goods, becomes much slower when it comes to raw materials and capital goods. Huge investments are required to develop the potential sources of raw materials and to achieve economies of scale for capital goods so the rhythm of foreign currency saving slows. Finally, the situation is reached in which substitution barely manages to offset the growth of imports necessary for technological progress. Under these circumstances, the need for foreign currency soon surpasses the foreign exchange earnings of an economy that still must rely principally on its primary sector exports.

If, as happens in the industrialized countries, the new industrial sector were to export a part of its production, these exports would generate the foreign currency necessary to pay for the new foreign exchange needs that the sector generates. But since the prices of manufactures produced in UPS economies are higher than the international prices, the industrial sector, unless it has special incentives in its favor, cannot export, and the primary sector remains by far the main generator of foreign exchange.

The primary sector, however, cannot increase its production and its exports so quickly and easily as the potential growth of industry would demand, and even if it could, the world market might not be there for the additional output. Accordingly, in periods of industrial expansion, the requirements for foreign currencies grow much more rapidly than their supply. The economic development of UPS countries is thus characterized by a chronic disparity between the demand for foreign currency and its generation. As a result, each period of expansion terminates in the exhaustion of international reserves and a crisis in the balance of payments. If such a country does not possess sufficient reserves to supply its productive system, production in one way or another must decline to the level of the foreign exchange available. A considerable part of the productive capacity remains unused, the living standard of the population declines, the employment level falls, and the process of investment stops—and all of these conditions are the result of the limitations imposed by the external sector.

In this manner, the type of limitation prevailing in the economic system changes. The production of goods and services ceases to be restricted by the productive capacity installed, as in the classical model, or by global demand, as in the Keynesian, but is limited by the "bottleneck" in the external sector.[8]

To be accurate, this description of the model is greatly simplified. Since the mid-1960s, the treatment of industrial exports in Argentina— as in many other countries—has become more flexible, incorporating some incentives to stimulate them. Nevertheless, at least in Argentina, the government has never considered that these incentives are an important instrument for the economy as a whole but believes they are simply one more concession to the inefficiency of industry. Because of this fact, these incentives have never been of sufficient magnitude or maintained long enough to stimulate the entrepreneurial sector to make the investments necessary to modify the country's external imbalance.

In short, developing an economy with two sectors of different productivity—the primary sector, which operates with international prices, and the industrial sector, which has prices that are higher than the international ones—the impossibility or difficulty on the part of the industrial sector to export, the consequent disparity between the demand for foreign currency and the capacity to provide it, and a recurring tendency to develop bottlenecks in the external sector have led to repeated Argentine crises. In addition, as we shall see, these factors have promoted many other disturbances such as great devaluations, battles over the distribution of income, hyperinflation, and cumulative foreign debt.

To successfully confront this set of problems, an appropriate theoretical model is needed. Unfortunately, neither the Keynesian nor the orthodox model is adequate for the Argentine situation. On the one hand, the Keynesian model ignores the possibility of problems in the external sector, since it was elaborated on the foundation of a simplified hypothesis of a closed economy. On the other hand, the neoclassical model postulates that external imbalances are always resolved by means of a suitable action of the market. When imbalances appear, they are interpreted as mere symptoms of internal disorder and excessive state interventionism. Accordingly, without adequate conceptual models to guide them, the governments of UPS economies will remain incapable of adopting policies that could combat these imbalances.[9]

The Populist Movement and the External Sector

Until now, the coming of a populist movement to power in Argentina has always coincided with a fortuitous accumulation of foreign exchange reserves in the central bank, owing to a favorable international economic situation or to a previous recession. The economic expansions initiated by populist administrations have always been nourished by using these reserves. But in order for the expansion to continue, the populist governments should have acted vigorously to counteract the gravitation of the economy toward external disequilibrium. Instead, the populist governments have generally ignored the problem and taken actions that frequently exacerbated it. Thus, in order to maintain low food prices, populist administrations have frequently postponed devaluation and kept agricultural prices below production costs. As a result, both agricultural production and agricultural exports have been discouraged, thus aggravating the foreign exchange problem.

Nor do industrial exports receive support since, because of a series of ideological prejudices, populist governments have a strong propensity to believe there is a contradiction between production for the internal market, which they favor, and production for the export market, which they do not. At the same time, import substitution generally lags, not only because of intrinsic difficulties, but also because of the lack of new investments in basic segments of the economy. Since such crises occur so often, business firms are reluctant to invest in an environment that is marked by labor unrest, decapitalizing price controls, and often dilatory state action vis-à-vis concrete investment projects.

When the foreign reserves are in danger of exhaustion, the populist administrations then turn to controls to economize on foreign exchange and channel it selectively. The mechanisms used are, however, seldom efficient. Instead of carefully selecting imports on the basis of their degree of necessity and the extent of value added by domestic industry, quantitative quotas are generally applied. Instead of regulating which products are to be imported, governments attempt to regulate the quantities to be imported and to choose the firms that will be allowed to import, a policy that leads to charges of arbitrariness and favoritism.

Finally, in an attempt to stem the inevitable outflow of capital, exchange controls are imposed. These controls effectively restrain the outflow of officially managed capital, but the quick appearance of a parallel market creates strong incentives to overinvoice the prices of imports and underinvoice those of exports. In this way, a part of the foreign currency earned finds its way to the parallel market. Controls on interest rates lead to negative real rates and thus offer further incentive for domestic capital to flow abroad. The gap between the official quotation of the dollar and the parallel quotation grows even larger, and therefore the incentives to overinvoice and underinvoice become greater, thus increasing the drain of foreign exchange.

Sooner or later the controls become ineffective, the country finds itself on the brink of a stoppage of foreign payments, and physical shortages follow. The utilization of productive capacity falls because of the country's incapacity to pay for the indispensable raw materials, semifinished goods, and machinery that must be imported. The contractionary process continues until production falls to the level permitted by the reduced availability of foreign exchange.[10]

Recessive Plans of Stabilization

The crisis in the balance of payments generally leads to a change to an orthodox-minded government. This kind of government makes use of two policies. The first consists of contractionary stabilization programs designed to solve the balance-of-payments problem. These programs generally follow the lines recommended by the International Monetary Fund, but they do not always involve a formal agreement with this institution. The second policy, adopted when the balance-of-payments problem is less acute, is to increase borrowing from abroad.

Stabilization programs always begin with an abrupt devaluation. In accordance with prevailing economic theory, such devaluation should stimulate exports, discourage imports, and thus reestablish the external balance. These results of devaluation may well be realized by highly industrialized countries, given the high price elasticity of both their exports and their imports. In these countries, it is the industrial sector that accounts for the bulk of exports; therefore, devaluation, by making a wide range of potentially available industrial products more competitive, automatically stimulates an increase in the exporting of those products. On the other hand, many goods that are not essential for the functioning of the economy and are imported because their price is lower than comparable domestic products are replaced by nationally produced goods when devaluation raises the price of imports.

In contrast, in Argentina and other UPS countries, imports and exports are very inelastic with regard to price, especially in the short run. As far as industrial exports are concerned, their price is too far above the international level for even a substantial devaluation to make them competitive. Thus, unless industrial exports can count on important differential incentives, no significant increase can be expected in this sector. With respect to agricultural exports, the increase in production necessary to increase their supply cannot come about quickly. Consequently, these exports respond very slowly to any depreciation of the exchange rate, at least in the short run. Finally, imports are largely either indispensable or their replacement by national products would be difficult and complex.

External equilibrium is finally restored primarily because of the income effect, which is similar to the old effect of the gold standard and different from the price effect that conventional theory presupposes. The depreciation of the exchange rate provokes an increase in the cost of all imported products. This increase is quickly transmitted to prices, first those of imported products and then to those of many basic raw materials that are produced locally and in direct competition with the imports. Finally, the increase in income that the exporters of agricultural products receive in domestic currency stimulates, also by a "pulling" effect, similar increases in the internal market, which are translated into a rise in the price of foodstuffs.

Thus, in three simultaneous ways costs and domestic prices increase sharply. Real salaries fall, and a transference of income in favor of agricultural producers and traditional exporters occurs. Owing to differences in the propensity to consume, this transference in itself brings about a significant decline in aggregate demand.[11]

In addition to this first automatic contractionary mechanism, a second deliberate mechanism appears, introduced by the monetary authorities who refuse to expand the quantity of money in circulation on a par with the increases in costs and prices. The rise of interest rates that follows reinforces the recessive effect.[12]

The resulting recession causes consumption, production, and investment to decline. Consequently, imports of finished products, capital goods, raw materials, and intermediate products also decline. A surplus is then realized in the current account, and the external sector returns to equilibrium because of the decrease in the level of economic activity.

But monetary restriction and recession, besides reducing the demand for foreign exchange, have another purpose as well—the stimulation of agricultural production. This objective, although not possible in the short run, is feasible in the longer run providing the relative advantage for agricultural prices that is gained by the devaluation can be kept intact for a reasonable length of time. This proviso can be met only if the prices of the nontraded products and wages do not move in correspondence with the exchange rate, and unfortunately, that situation is possible only if the recession continues. Finally, monetary restriction has a third simultaneous objective, which is to discourage the outflow of domestic capital and stimulate an inflow of foreign capital, a theme to which I shall return.

Thus, the equilibrating function of the traditional stabilization programs requires that monetary tightness be maintained for three reasons: to reduce production and imports, to maintain the rise of the exchange rate and of agricultural prices relative to other domestic prices and salaries, and to attract foreign capital. The resulting decline in production to the bottleneck level in the external sector, brought about by the deliberate lessening of demand, constitutes the indirect manner through which the external constraint works (an earlier description of a similar process can be seen in Eshag and Thorp 1965).

Exchange Inflation

In real life, the evolution of contractionary stabilization plans does not follow the traditional or IMF schemes. Devaluation raises costs and prices substantially and thus has a strong initial inflationary impact. The abrupt reductions in real wages and in the relative prices of products not traded internationally that result arouse great social resistance. The people affected—employers and wage earners in the industrial and service sectors—demand the recovery of their customary share of the national income. Even in the midst of a recession, they always manage to get back, albeit partially, their prices and real wages and thus prolong the initial inflationary impact. At the same time, pressures mount against the policies responsible for the recession. These pressures emanate from different sectors of the economy as well as from within the government itself, particularly the Ministries of Labor and Social Welfare and the presidency. Finally, the recession becomes difficult to enforce because of the inevitable increase in the budget deficit. In their stabilization proposals, the IMF and other proponents of the conventional wisdom insist almost obsessively that the budget deficit be eliminated. Beyond the rationalizations that are employed, the real reason for this insistence is the need to limit monetary expansion, which would reactivate the economy and cancel the contractionary process that is considered necessary to keep the external sector in balance.

However, one of the main effects of the decrease in economic activity is a decline in the tax base of the country and the consequent decline in government revenues. In addition, since tax collections are always made in the prices of the previous period and spending is done in current prices, the former lag more with respect to the latter because of the abrupt increases in costs and prices as a result of the devaluation. Because the fall of state revenues is greater than the reduction of expenditures, despite the fact that the government usually does what is possible to lower fiscal expenditures, the budget deficit always grows. Sooner or later it becomes necessary to resort to monetary expansion to finance the deficit. The feared reactivating effect follows, and wages begin to rise. The inflationary spiral, unleashed by the devaluation, tends to continue, and the agricultural sector loses the advantages it gained during the recession.

To restore the contractionary balancing mechanisms of the external sector, the government has to devalue again, which initiates a new spiral and unleashes a special type of inflation, characteristic of UPS economies, that is quite distinct from traditional demand inflations. This phenomenon, which I call *exchange inflation*, belongs to the family of structural inflations or bottleneck inflations. Its origin is the specific imbalance between the demand for scarce foreign currency and its supply, which causes a rise in the price of the foreign currency, or, stated in another way, makes a devaluation obligatory. The characteristics of this exchange inflation are a rise in domestic prices that is simultaneous with the fall in real wages, a lack of liquidity, and a decrease in the level of business activity. This type of inflation also coincides with a budget deficit, but, in contrast to what occurs in demand inflation, the deficit is not the cause of the inflation but rather a phenomenon induced or at the very least aggravated by it on account of the reduction in state revenues.

In general, inflation in Argentina has had different causes and motives at different times, but the worst outbreaks have occurred precisely because of attempts to correct the imbalances of the external sector by means of large devaluations and the consequent transfers of income from one sector to another. This procedure, when resisted by the lagging sectors, always causes long periods of a pendulumlike struggle for income, giving rise to very violent inflationary phenomena which are extremely difficult to control. The most virulent inflations in Argentina broke out in 1959, 1962, 1971-1972, 1975, and 1981—in every case after very large devaluations brought about by crises in the balance of payments.[13]

To sum up, the main difficulty that confronts contractionary stabilization programs in the long run is that they come into conflict with an income distribution acceptable to society. The pressure from the lagging sectors and the virtual impossibility of avoiding monetary expansion make it difficult to maintain the sought after configuration of relative prices. To the extent that governments try to restore such a configuration by new devaluations, the result is an ever greater acceleration of exchange inflation.

It is for these reasons that just as soon as the balance-of-payments situation brought about by the recessive process permits, governments forsake their contractionary programs and go back to the pattern of lagging devaluations with respect to domestic prices. In this way, they produce a slight redistribution of income from the agricultural sector to the urban sectors, and in particular to the wage earners, and the economy is again reactivated.

But as recovery proceeds, imports again increase. At the same time, the lag in devaluations with respect to inflation causes the agricultural sector to continue losing the price advantages it had obtained by virtue of the initial devaluation. Thus, two of the three mechanisms that helped to balance the external sector during the recessive period disappear, and the only balancing mechanism that remains is foreign borrowing. In this way, programs of contractionary stabilization enter their second phase, that of accumulating foreign debt.

The Accumulation of Foreign Debt

A common characteristic of UPS countries is the unrelenting search for investments and financial loans from abroad. Contrary to what is generally believed, the importance of these contributions lies, not in the necessity of complementing national savings with foreign capital, but in the fact that, by coming into the country in the form of foreign currency, they provide a solution to the external imbalance.[14]

Nevertheless, obtaining money from abroad is never a solution; it is at most a sedative that brings temporary monetary relief to the problem but at a price of making it fundamentally worse. The loans (or the investments) enter in foreign currency. As a consequence, amortization costs and interest (or dividends) must also be paid in foreign currency. If these foreign contributions were invested in new export capacity or channeled into the import substitution sector, they would increase the country's availability of foreign currency and thus be self-liquidating. But the most frequent destiny of foreign borrowing is to provide a temporary respite in the external sector, to delay a recession, and to make possible a continuing growth of production for the domestic market. To the degree that foreign borrowing achieves these objectives, the need for foreign currency increases still more. Furthermore, the payment of interest for the new loans is added to these expenditures, thus enlarging the initial foreign deficit.

To maintain the equilibrium in the exchange market, it is necessary for loans to be renewed each time they come due. Furthermore, to compensate for the increasing interest and amortization payments, the new credits and foreign investment in the country must expand continuously. In this way, foreign indebtedness increases until sooner or later a new crisis in the balance of payments develops, and it is more serious than the one the increased borrowing originally attempted to avoid. This process has a particularly explosive nature because of the mechanism used to stimulate inflows of foreign capital.[15]

Obtaining funds from abroad takes the form of loans to the government or loans to the private sector. In the latter case, the foreign currencies that enter the country are negotiated in the exchange market and are bought by people or groups that need to settle their external accounts. In this way, the loans are ultimately used indirectly by governments to finance imports and other foreign currency disbursements. This procedure of using private and state enterprises as "obtainers" of foreign currency is used in all orthodox stabilization programs. By restricting the quantity of money in circulation and credit, these programs raise domestic interest rates and thereby compel local firms to borrow abroad. Since the increase in real interest rates has a contractionary effect, the procedure suits perfectly the first phase of stabilization programs, in which a reduction in general economic activity is sought in order to reduce imports and to discourage wage increases.

But as orthodox administrations, ceding to political pressures or to the effect of monetary expansion that they cannot avoid, enter the second stage of their stabilization programs, the interest rates go down as a result of monetary and credit expansion. At this point, the incentives for the attraction of foreign capital disappear. Thus, nothing remains of the three balancing effects on the external sector—the fall in imports due to the recession, the increase in agricultural prices, and the attraction of capital—that are present in the first phase. However, the problem is momentarily overcome thanks to the devaluation lag.

The Devaluation Lag

To understand how the devaluation lag works, one must keep in mind that the incentives for borrowing abroad are not determined by real rates of interest as such, i.e., measured as the difference between nominal rates and inflation. What is important is the difference between domestic nominal interest rates on the one side and the sum of the international rates on the dollar market and the rate of devaluation on the other. Thus, high incentives for borrowing can be provided either by raising domestic interest rates to high levels in real terms or by decelerating the rhythm of devaluations with respect to inflation. The former procedure is characteristic of the first recessive stage of stabilization programs, but in the second stage, in which the goal of recession is being abandoned, it is no longer adequate. Delaying devaluations seems to provide a solution. As I have said before, in this second stage the devaluations begin to lag behind inflation as a result of expansionary pressures exerted by society.

Taking advantage of this lag to attract foreign capital seems to be an ideal remedy for the foreign sector disequilibrium. In offering very high yields, the lag induces a massive inflow of foreign investment into the country. The reserves in the central bank increase sharply, real wages recover, the level of business activity rises, confidence in the economy increases, and a general feeling of prosperity develops. However, in order to maintain these incentives, the devaluations have to keep lagging so the local currency becomes progressively more and more overvalued. This overvaluation has a very high economic cost since it discourages exports and encourages imports, which worsens the foreign deficit and creates a still higher need for foreign capital.

Another usual characteristic of this phase of the cycle is an emphasis on efficiency. As we have seen before, the decision to industrialize, made several decades ago in Argentina, has never been totally accepted by society as a whole and even less so by the agricultural and ranching interests and circles dependent on or influenced by them. These groups are convinced of the validity of the stereotype of industrial inefficiency and of the fact that this inefficiency can be overcome only by greater international competition. For this reason, any temporary abundance of foreign exchange always encourages attempts to reduce protection and to eliminate the government's incentives that could stimulate industrial exports. This "efficientism" stimulates an increase in imports and reduces the volume of nontraditional exports, which adds to the drain of foreign exchange that originated because of the devaluation lag. In sum, the country deliberately increases its external disequilibrium and its indebtedness for the sake of a claimed increase in industrial efficiency.[16]

Once the process of exchange rate lags is initiated, it is very difficult to halt. The longer it lasts, the greater the deficit on current account of the balance of payments becomes; the larger this deficit is, the greater the need for new foreign capital to cover it. For this reason, the need to not disturb the patterns of exchange lag that make this capital flow possible is also greater.

The process ultimately becomes very unstable. The continuity of the flow of foreign loans depends on the confidence of foreign lenders in the ability of the country to repay them. At the same time, an even greater flow of loans is necessary to maintain that ability.

In the final stages, there is a slowly growing awareness that the indebtedness is getting out of hand. For this reason, an increasing number of firms and individuals in the private sector, foreseeing an imminent maxidevaluation, begin to send funds abroad. As this capital flight also has to be covered, it is necessary to borrow even more foreign funds. Thus, the pressure increases for the "obtainers" of loans—at this stage, principally the public sector enterprises—to acquire more foreign currency. Business confidence declines. A number of short-term loans, supposedly renewable, are not renewed, and the central bank is obliged to begin selling its reserves. The lack of confidence increases, the rate of renewals decreases even more, and capital flight accelerates. Finally, the process culminates in a run on the exchange market, which can plunge an apparently prosperous country into a profound crisis within a few days. The government feels obliged to impose a new and abrupt devaluation, and its only option is to undertake a new contractionary stabilization program. The whole process is thus repeated but with a higher foreign debt level, the need for a more drastic contractionary program, and a more pronounced fall in production.

The Pendulum and Vicious Circles

There is a certain parallelism between the populist and orthodox policies. The former neglect private investment and the external sector and endure as long as the foreign exchange reserves hold out. The latter are initiated when there are few or no reserves and the country is on the brink of a cessation of payments. In the short run, the reserves are rebuilt at the price of recession and as a result of the inflow of new credits. In the longer run, however, orthodox foreign sector policy fails because its mode of stimulating the inflow of foreign exchange becomes incompatible with recovery as well as with an acceptable level of real wages. Finally, foreign loans and investments remain as the only source of external financing, and expansion and growth continue only as long as the country's capacity for foreign indebtedness can sustain them.

The prospects of success for both the populist and the orthodox approaches are not very encouraging. On the one hand, populist policies come afoul of the external sector. On the other hand, orthodox policies that aim to reform the external sector by reducing real wages and demand lead to recession and stagnation. Thus, it can be seen that the causes of the Argentine pendulum are much much deeper than the so-called political standoff. The cycles of expansion and recession are generated by the balance-of-payments problem that is inherent in both the populist and the orthodox approaches.

The worst aspect of the situation is that this pendular process is not static: It becomes increasingly unmanageable because of at least three types of vicious circles. The first of these is the growth of foreign indebtedness. Between 1959 and 1982, Argentina's external debt grew from $500 million to nearly $40 billion in nominal terms. In terms of 1975 dollars, this amount is about equivalent to a growth from $1.8 billion to $23 billion. At the same time, interest payments grew rapidly, adding to the basic external disequilibrium each successive economic team had to face, and which each tried to solve by borrowing even more.

The second vicious circle arises from the conflictive character of development. The continuous attempts to resolve the problems of the external sector through massive transfers of income provoke sectorial defense reactions that become more and more violent and lead to higher and higher rates of inflation, which themselves later become autonomous causes of economic chaos and disorder.

The third vicious circle develops in regard to industrial efficiency. Industrial productivity or efficiency depends fundamentally on the degree of development of a country. After several decades of sustained development, the initial difference in productivity between agriculture and industry should have disappeared or at least been greatly diminished. But because of erratic development caused by recessions and the destruction of industrial capacity during "efficientist" episodes, instead of sustained progress, Argentina has for every three steps forward fallen back two. After forty or fifty years, the country has advanced to a point that should have been reached within ten or fifteen years. The problems of the differences in productivity between the two main sectors and the inability of the industrial sector to compete internationally remain unsolved. The classic question of the anti-industrial sectors, How much longer are we going to support industry by maintaining it artificially? appears to be a valid one. Anti-industrial measures find greater justification and successively fall into another vicious circle, one that apparently has no solution.

The Present Situation and Prospects for the Future

The factor that contributes most to the continuation of all these vicious circles is orthodox economic policy. The last stage in the accumulation of the debt of 1978–1981, which occurred in the second phase of the contractionary stabilization program initiated in 1976–1978, is very illustrative. The model followed was conceptually the same as models followed during similar periods in the past, but during 1976–1978, it had an intensity and a destructive effect never seen previously in Argentina. On no previous occasion had there been such a wholesale dismantling of protective mechanisms and of incentives to continue nontraditional exports. Never before had Argentina experienced such a pronounced exchange lag or such a generalized destructive effect on internal productive activity. In short, orthodoxy had never before gone to such extremes (for an exhaustive investigation of the exchange lag incurred, see Llach 1982).

There were several reasons for this virulence. The first was the strong concentration of political power, which permitted the authoritarian government to impose a particularly fanatic conception of the economy on a virtually defenseless society. The second was the great abundance of easily obtainable funds in the international financial market, an abundance generated by the oil surplus that facilitated and stimulated a practically unlimited expansion of debt. The third was the international prevalence of a monetarist and free trade ideology that reinforced the local orthodoxy. This ideology coincided with the pressing need of the industrialized countries both to pass on to others their trade deficits, which had also been caused by the manifold rise in world oil prices, and to recycle the funds of the oil exporting countries that were being deposited in their financial institutions.[17]

The first outcome of this period in Argentina was the unprecedented growth of the foreign debt, which rose from some $10 billion in 1976 to nearly $40 billion in 1982, equal to about five years of exports (in terms of 1975 dollars, the debt rose from about $9 billion in 1976 to about $23 billion in 1982). It is appropriate to emphasize that the accumulation of Argentina's debt stands in sharp contrast to the way Brazil experienced a massive increase in its foreign debt. Brazil's debt grew largely because the country had to pay a sharply increased oil import bill and to pay for the increased imports of other goods needed to sustain its high rate of growth. The Argentine experience contrasts also with that of Mexico, which contracted an enormous debt to continue excessive investments. Argentina imports almost no petroleum and until the end of the period, could count on favorable terms of trade. Nor was its indebtedness increased in order to finance growth, since the country's production, particularly its industrial production, declined. Argentina got into debt above all to compensate for the growth of imports and the decrease of exports provoked by an efficientist policy.[18] One of the fundamental arguments in support of this policy during the period was that it would put an end to the chronic inflation that has plagued Argentina for decades. Instead, the inflation rate rose dramatically, from 81.9 percent to 146.3 percent annually.

Finally, with regard to increases in efficiency, which was another of the government's rationalizations for its program, the result could not have been more disastrous. The growing displacement of national goods by imports restricted the market for domestic industry, forcing sharp reductions in the scales of production and thereby increasing the burden of overhead costs. The rules of the game became chaotic, destroying the possibility of advance planning and discouraging productive investment. A large part of the country's capacity for import substitution was destroyed, and the high degree of industrial integration that had been achieved before was sharply reduced. Entire areas of domestic production were abandoned, research laboratories went out of business, and local technological innovation fell off sharply. The few exports of manufactured goods that had met with some degree of success in world markets fell off as the government incentives were eliminated. Foreign markets for nontraditional exports, so laboriously won over the years, have to a great extent been lost.

Industrial enterprises, subjected to the increasingly unbearable pressure of international competition, incurred even greater losses. To cover them, they had to go further into debt. The firms that did so in the national currency suffered the impact of variable and, in the last stages, very high positive real rates of interest that progressively decapitalized their enterprises. Those who became indebted in foreign currency suffered the decapitalizing impact of the multiple devaluations at the culmination of the cycle. The result was a tremendous deterioration of the country's industrial enterprises and the disappearance of many of them. In short, industrial efficiency—which always depends on the degree of utilization of productive capacity, the size of the market, the rhythm of technological incorporation, and investments—fell sharply, and a great part of the installed equipment was converted into scrap metal.

As to future perspectives, the experience since 1945 seems to condemn Argentina to repeat the same cycle of expansion and recession, increasingly indebting itself in the process and growing but little and only in spurts. Moreover, if Argentine society's attitude toward the country's economic problems does not change, even this bleak outlook may turn out to be overly optimistic. The severity of the problems confronting Argentina, as a result of its many failed programs and a prospect of slow growth of the world economy, may not permit even the customary Argentine economic pendulum to remain in motion.

For the first time in Argentine history, populist policymakers have taken over the reins of government without an ample reserve of foreign exchange and with half of the exports committed to the payment of interest on the debt. Also for the first time, populist policymakers lack the initial margin of maneuver their predecessors always counted on. Moreover, because the debt crisis has made international lenders very wary, it is now almost impossible for debtor countries like Argentina to obtain new credit, and even governments committed to orthodox stabilization programs no longer enjoy their usually ample foreign exchange lines of credit.

All of these factors mean that for the present, the pendulum has come to a halt. Populist expansionist policies are out of the question because of the lack of foreign exchange reserves, and economic orthodoxy is ruled out because of the inability under present circumstances of the Argentine government and the private sector to attract foreign credits or investment. If Argentina is not to remain condemned to permanent stagnation, it will have to learn how to overcome the foreign exchange bottleneck that periodically strangles the economy.

Because of the wealth of the country's natural resources and its skilled human resources, Argentina does not need miraculous cures. What it does need is to realize that virtually all the serious problems of the economy are a direct or an indirect consequence of the foreign exchange bottleneck and that this problem should finally be given the importance it deserves. Public opinion must be mobilized in support of a sound strategy for producing foreign exchange and for using it wisely (see Schydlowsky 1979b).

The task does not end there. Once the external bottleneck is overcome, it will be necessary to reactivate the economy, slow down the inflationary process by means of an incomes policy, stimulate long-run growth, reduce the budget deficit, and promote an industrial policy designed to make industry increasingly efficient.

The Bases for a New Economic Policy

Action with respect to the external sector should be based on the following strategies: (1) promotion of industrial exports, (2) stimulation of agricultural production and exports, (3) a sound, selective policy for imports and the aggressive promotion of import substitution, and (4) the rational management of external financing and the internal financial system. Argentina must abandon the ancient vice of eternally debating the alternative merits of different strategies without adopting any and adopt all of them at the same time in a very intensive manner.

Although in some cases the cost in terms of other economic variables may seem high, one must keep in mind that once unessential imports are eliminated, the marginal coefficient of imports in Argentina hardly exceeds 10 percent, which means that for every dollar earned or saved, about ten dollars worth of domestic production can be put to work. In other words, the necessary cost of obtaining each additional dollar of exports or of import substitutes should always be compared to the alternative cost that the loss of about ten dollars of domestic production would signify.

The Promotion of Industrial Exports

The high prices of Argentina's manufactured products, which impede their exportation, are the result both of the lower productivity of the industrial sector relative to the agricultural sector and of the fundamental and key factor that the exchange rate is based on agricultural parity. To protect domestic manufacturing production, taxes or import tariffs are levied that, together with the basic exchange rate, function in reality like a system of multiple exchange rates. But the serious defects of these pseudo exchange rates is that they function only for imports. For industrial exports, the nominal exchange rate based on a parity corresponding to the primary sector continues to prevail. Thus, industrial products, whose lower productivity is recognized by import exchange rates that are much higher than the nominal rate, are exported on the basis of an exchange rate that is not appropriate for them because it is set for the purpose of moving only efficiently produced primary goods. This exchange asymmetry militates against industrial exports and is responsible for the chain of events that has culminated in Argentina's economic crises and stagnation.

Choosing to determine the nominal rate of exchange on the basis of the more productive sector, which seems obvious and natural, in reality constitutes the traditional tool for preserving the equilibrium of the productive structure. When this criterion is adopted, all activities that have a relatively lower productivity than that of the sector chosen as the basis of the exchange system will have prices higher than those on the international market and—except when deliberate protection is provided—will be unable to survive because of world competition. In other words, making the exchange rate coincide with the most productive sector is the conscious or unconscious expression of an intention to assure fulfillment of the principle of comparative advantage.

The industrial development of countries like Argentina requires, at least initially, the deliberate abandonment of the principle of comparative advantage and the promotion of the relatively less efficient manufacturing sector. To continue to hold to an exchange rate system that has the implicit goal of preventing industrialization is a monumental contradiction into which most of the primary exporting countries fall during the process of industrialization. It is this contradiction, not industrialization per se, that leads to the so-called dead end of an import substitution policy—scarcity of foreign exchange and recurrent balance-of-payments crises (for an analysis of the exchange system, see Diamand 1972 and 1973).

Thus, even though the political will favors industrial development, the policies adopted because of the experience of developed countries militate against industrialization. To make this industrialization possible, industrial exports, services, and nonpampean agricultural products must have rates of exchange that bear a reasonable relationship to the effective exchange rates governing imports.

The most direct way to achieve such a situation is to maintain the nominal exchange rate at a higher level than that which agricultural production requires, to concurrently reduce import duties, and to return to the pampean exchange rate by means of appropriate taxes on traditional exports. Another possibility is to reconstruct a system of multiple export exchange rates by means of appropriate fiscal reimbursements. Still a third choice is to utilize a system of generalized drawback, which compensates for the internal high level of prices of raw materials and intermediate goods—including those of local origin.

Each one of these procedures has certain advantages and disadvantages from the point of view of internal political considerations and external relations, the latter particularly related to the country's vulnerability to charges of dumping. The important thing, however, is to understand the necessity of differential exchange rates, whatever the exact details of their structuring may be.

The difference between this procedure and the systems that have previously been tried in Argentina is that the other systems were only reluctantly and fitfully applied since they lacked a sound, conceptual basis. The incentives should not be offered in an ad hoc way, as they have been offered in the past, but rather as an integral part of a deliberate promotional program that takes into full account the difference in productivity between the agricultural and manufacturing sectors, the need to compensate for this difference, and the overriding importance of overcoming the foreign exchange problem. The export incentives should not be short-lived but assured for at least the medium term.

One objection to governmental export promotion is that the government's fiscal resources are too limited to finance an ambitious incentive program. The fiscal expenditure necessary to obtain an additional dollar of exports is, however, much less than the decline of the government's revenues caused by the recession that inevitably develops when this marginal dollar of foreign exchange is lacking. In other words, the state's financing of an export incentive system is not an ordinary budget expenditure but an investment that makes possible the expansion of the economy and produces additional revenues for the government (for the fiscal effect, see Schydlowsky 1967 and 1971).

An efficient export promotion scheme must meet two requirements. First, every peso invested in the scheme must generate a reasonable net profit in terms of foreign exchange. Second, overgenerous incentives should be avoided. The producer or exporter must not receive on a net basis a higher return on exports in the national currency than would be obtained by selling in the home market. If the goods exported sell at higher prices abroad than they sell at home, the prices of these goods in the home market will rise as a result of the competition between the two markets.

Stimulation of Agricultural Production and Exports

The second course of action should be the expansion of traditional agricultural output. In Argentina, agricultural production operates on the basis of increasing costs. The cost of growing the first ton of wheat per hectare is low because the producer utilizes the natural advantages of the very fertile central plains (pampas) and good climate. However, to produce two tons per hectare requires special care, fertilizer, and more intensive management, all of which mean higher costs. The same increased costs occur when wheat and other grains are produced on marginal lands. To increase production, the price must rise enough to cover the additional costs entailed in producing the second ton. When the price does rise, however, the intramarginal producer who did not expand output obtains a windfall because his costs have not risen. The global increase of agricultural prices thus has two effects. On the one hand, it gives farmers a greater and economically useful incentive to produce more. But on the other, it leads also to a free transfer of income to the nonmarginal producers at the expense of real salaries and other urban incomes, which fall as a consequence of this rise in prices. The challenge to Argentina's policymakers is to design a system that would separate the two effects, rewarding marginal or additional agricultural production without gratuitously rewarding production that would have taken place anyway.

This separation can be achieved by combining a substantial increase in prices with a land productivity tax that would replace all other agricultural taxes, including taxes on profits. Let us suppose that the normal output of a pampean hectare is a ton of wheat priced at 100 pesos. By devaluing the pampean dollar (or by lowering export tariffs, if they exist), this price would rise, say, to 150 pesos, but a tax on pampas land of 50 pesos per hectare would be imposed simultaneously. The first ton of wheat would then yield a net profit of 150 pesos minus 50, or, in other words, the same 100 pesos as before. In contrast, however, the second ton would yield 150 pesos net, since the land tax would already have been paid for the first ton. One might also vary the land tax in accordance with the productivity of the land, thus giving a greater incentive for nonpampean production.

Thus, the first part of the plan would aim at ensuring that the increases in agricultural prices would not transfer windfall gains to the agricultural sector. The second part of the program would consist of ensuring that agricultural prices did not cause a fall in the real income of the urban population. That is, the revenue from the land productivity tax would be transferred back to the urban consumers. One way of accomplishing the transfer would be to reduce the retail tax on sales, turnover taxes, and other taxes imposed on manufactured products and services consumed widely, thus lowering their prices. Another way of keeping urban real income from falling would be to lower social security contributions. In practice, it would probably be suitable to use a mixture of the foregoing strategies. In this way, despite the increase in food prices, a fall in the buying power of wages would be avoided.

To sum up, effective incentives to increase production can be devised without precipitating a massive transfer of income away from the urban population, which is socially unsettling and economically destructive. The tax reform would also discourage the idling and underexploitation of good land, and the entire plan would have the important additional effect of modifying relative prices. Agricultural prices would go up in relation to the prices of industrial goods, and the dollar would be set closer to the parity of the industrial sector. The imbalance between the two sectors would be reduced, and with it the exchange rate differentials for both imports and exports.[19]

Selectivity of Imports and Import Substitution

An increase in the supply of foreign exchange must be accompanied by better criteria for its allocation among competing uses. Some imports are more essential to the functioning of the economy and the welfare of the public than others. At the level of industrial inputs and capital goods, the selection process is complex, and business firms should have a large role in determining import priorities.

The instruments of a rational import policy should be import duties and the prohibition of some imports. Rationing by means of quantity quotas should be avoided at all costs as the power to determine which firms should have import rights leads to charges of favoritism, arbitrariness, and a rise in the domestic prices of rationed products. In other words, the system of selection should be limited to determining what should be imported, not what firms can import a product or how much each can import.

Similarly, import substitution should be encouraged so as to achieve a sharp reduction in the ratio of imported inputs to total inputs (the import coefficient). Although substitution opportunities are supposed to have diminished greatly, there are still many goods that Argentina does not produce which it could manufacture if potential producers were given adequate encouragement. Although import substitution efforts in Argentina have been quite intense over the years in some sectors, in general they have been rather haphazardly and sometime perversely applied. Argentine governments have wavered in their policies, sometimes helping enterprises whose costs of production are very far above world prices and neglecting those that with a little help, could quickly compete internationally. Also, periods of extreme restrictions, which sometimes prohibit even the importing of indispensable raw materials, have alternated with efficientism periods in which imports are totally liberalized and "desubstitution" is brought about in sectors where considerable success in substitution had been achieved.

The most recent period of efficientism was the most extreme in Argentine history, and it left a very low general level of protection and little differentiation in the level of that protection among the different stages of production. In addition, the experience shook the self-confidence of the business community and left it with little confidence in the ability of governments, present and future, to abide by a rational substitution policy.

There is a productive capacity, but appropriate protection is lacking or exemptions and exceptions now in force make it inoperable. In revitalizing the substitution strategy, the first step is to structure a coherent system of protection. Realistic limits should be set to the costs of substitution, limits that are compatible with the current average level of industrial costs and prices, and the substitution of all imports possible within those limits should be energetically promoted (for a more precise definition of the admissible cost of substitution, see Diamand 1973).

The foregoing implies basing import duties on rational criteria. For example, a coherent tariff system would differentiate duties according to the stages of production. Accordingly, lower tariffs would be set on raw materials, and higher tariffs would apply to technically complex finished products. Moreover, clear rules of the game should be established for granting protection to new import substitution activities.

A change of policy is urgent with respect to imports by the public sector, which are mostly capital goods. Generally, the practice in Argentina has been for the government to buy equipment domestically only if the supplying firm has already compiled a satisfactory record of performance in producing the required item. Many national firms, however, have never had the chance to become eligible for consideration because the state enterprise may be the only market for a product. To break this Catch-22 situation, the government must encourage its procurement officials to make a deliberate effort to develop national sources of supply.

Such an effort means assuring foreseeable and sustained demand by deliberate planning, establishing cooperation between the provider and the state buyer, selecting technologies in terms of their availability in the country, and creating a favorable predisposition on the part of the state buyer to parcel out large turnkey projects to domestic firms. Indeed, one of the most important goals of the policy of import substitution is to bring about such a change in attitude on the part of government agencies and state corporations.

Rational Management of External Financing and the Internal Financial System

With respect to foreign capital, a distinction should be made between risk capital and financial capital. Risk capital plays a double role. On the one hand, it fulfills the role of investment capital; on the other, it brings in foreign currency. In the long run, however, risk capital always creates greater foreign currency obligations arising from the importing of raw materials and other inputs for manufacturing, payments for technology, technical assistance, patents and trademarks, amortization, interest, and profits. As far as the balance of payments is concerned, foreign investment is a transitory palliative that in the long run, can magnify the original problem of scarcity of foreign exchange. To prevent this magnification, foreign capital should be channeled toward the expansion of activities that directly or indirectly generate foreign exchange.

With respect to financial capital, Argentine history shows that when foreign loans are contracted and basic measures to increase exports and substitute imports are not adopted simultaneously, the palliative is confused with a cure, and the country embarks upon a course of accumulating debt that within a short time, explodes in the form of a new foreign exchange crisis. For this reason, the use of external financial capital ought to be reserved either for emergencies in the external sector or to anticipate the inflow of foreign currency until simultaneous measures of export promotion bear fruit.

During such emergencies, internal financial management that encourages the inflow and retention of foreign capital is necessary, but this imperative is not limited to emergencies. It is vital, although in a less intense form, even when the country can do without foreign capital in order to deter the flight of domestic capital. Assuming a system of free exchange, there are only two ways to prevent capital flight. The first is to maintain the real domestic rates of interest at levels that are at least equal to the real international rates plus the country risk premium as the saver perceives it. The second is to adopt lower real rates of interest together with a lag in devaluation to make foreign asset holding less attractive.

Nevertheless, for the measures of import substitution and export promotion to be effective, the basic rate of exchange, once established at the appropriate level, ought to vary at the same rate as domestic inflation minus the international inflation rate. Thus, to avoid the cumulative growth of external debt, the systematic use of the exchange lag to attract or retain foreign capital should be rejected.

In this way, the objective in a system of free exchange of preventing the outflow of capital imposes a strong connection between domestic and international rates of interest. Given the wide spread between borrowing and lending rates in Argentina and the wide margin of risk perceived by investors, the equation mentioned previously leads to strongly positive real rates of interest, which are incompatible with efforts to expand demand and reactivate the economy.

For this reason, populist governments always resort to exchange controls as a method of isolating domestic interest rates from international rates. Such controls generally permit domestic rates to decline to some extent, but the domestic financial circuit continues to be associated with the foreign circuit through the parallel foreign currency market. This market, at the same time, is connected to the official one by means of manifold over- and underinvoicing. Through these practices, the market influences the volume of foreign currency that flows into the central bank, the parallel price of the dollar, and indirectly, the domestic prices of exportable products.

The foregoing indicates that even with the existence of exchange controls, it is impossible to peg the domestic interest rate in total disregard of external rates. When the domestic nominal rate is much less than the international rate, the outflow of capital through the parallel market and the consequent rise in the exchange rate of the parallel dollar become uncontrollable. Expectations of further depreciation of the peso increase the outflow of capital until it eventually pulls the official dollar along with it.

This margin can be widened. One factor restricting the margin is the risk perceived by investors. If they are persuaded of the stability and coherence of the policy, then their level of confidence will be higher, and the risk will seem to be lower. In the second place, the separation of domestic from international rates can be much greater when there is opportunity for profitable domestic investment. This opportunity implies economic expansion, favorable expectations for the future, and finally, a tax structure that favors investment and profitable reinvestment.

With the same goal of providing incentives to keep capital in the country, it is necessary to pursue strategies to increase the domestic savings rate. This goal can be partially reached by indexation so that savings and their yields will not be less than the prevailing foreign yield. It is also necessary to avoid arbitrary taxes on financial capital or taking measures that can create uncertainty in the financial markets.

The Foreign Debt

Even supposing total success in the implementation of a policy to create and save foreign currency, the seriousness of the foreign debt and of the limitations that payment of the interest on that debt would exercise on the level of domestic activity make necessary an urgent renegotiation of foreign loans. Such renegotiation refers not only to the debt per se, which is more or less automatic, but also to a large part of the interest. Here another difficulty presents itself, not because the renegotiation is particularly difficult as such, but because it is accompanied by conditions on the part of the creditors that affect the future economic policies of the country. The institution charged with formulating these conditions and verifying compliance with them is the International Monetary Fund (IMF).

The conditions can be subdivided into two large categories. First, there are the contractionary measures, which have already been analyzed. Second, there is the efficientist ingredient, which consists of reducing protection, decreasing differential incentives for industrial exports, eliminating exchange restrictions, and so on. Speaking in terms of multiple exchange rates, the general IMF requirement is that a country reduce the dispersion of these rates as much as possible and preferably to a single rate. This requirement is exactly the opposite of the policy for the external sector that I have proposed, which is based on the explicit recognition of differential productivities in the UPS countries and, therefore, calls for multiple exchange rates. Is it possible to make this policy compatible with the demands of the IMF?

I am convinced that it is perfectly possible to do so. What is needed is a thorough understanding of both kinds of needs. The first objective of the IMF, as the representative of the international commercial lending institutions, is to assure the capacity of debtor countries to pay the interest on the outstanding debt. But, since the IMF has always had a strong ideological commitment to the freedom of international trade and to the principle of comparative advantage, it cannot propose programs based on multiple exchange rate systems, which leaves contractionary stabilization plans and increasing foreign indebtedness as the only alternative. The IMF's commitment to international free trade also compels it to push for additional efficientist requirements, which always entail a pressure for unified, effective exchange rates.

But these demands work in such a way for many countries like Argentina that they defeat the basic aim of the IMF, which is to ensure the ability of debtor countries to repay their loans. The more the mechanisms for the protection and encouragement of nontraditional exports are abandoned, the greater will be the increase in imports and decrease in exports of these products and the deeper the recession necessary to obtain the sought-after surplus of foreign currency. That is, the greater the degree of efficientism, the more difficult it is to maintain in practice the contractionary mechanisms necessary to compensate for the loss of foreign currency.

In its official doctrine, the IMF totally denies that there is a contradiction, and it uses neoclassical theory to demonstrate that its measures for liberalizing foreign trade, by reestablishing the functioning of the market system, help balance rather than unbalance the foreign accounts of UPS countries. Underlying this rationale is a failure to appreciate that UPS economies are different in important respects from those of industrialized countries.

Nevertheless, at the working level of governments, the officials of the international lending agencies are conscious of the difference in structure between industrializing and already industrialized countries. In practice, they often abandon their efficientist ideological principles and do not insist on contractionary policies if they are convinced that their priority objective, which is to assure a country's ability to pay, will be fulfilled.

Given the official weight of dogma, however, unorthodox initiative can never originate with the IMF but must begin with the negotiating officials of the borrowing country. Of course, to have any chance of approval, the borrowing countries must present coherent and technically sound proposals. Experience shows that when such proposals are made, the borrowing countries are actually given great latitude in managing their economic policies.

Unfortunately, experience also shows that innovative stabilization policies are rarely presented to the international agencies by countries with UPS economies. Argentina is a clear example of a country in which there is a total confusion of ideas with respect to the foreign debt and the way to deal with it, a confusion that stems from the false dilemma of orthodox versus populist ideology.

The officials who make up Argentina's orthodox economic cabinets not only fully support the efficientist requirements of the IMF but often carry the requirements further than even the fund's officials may want. At the other extreme, the exponents of populist ideology usually reject the contractionary policies demanded by the IMF. They do so, however, within a frame of reference that tends to ignore the external sector and disregards the need for achieving equilibrium in a country's balance of payments. That is, the populists reject recession as a way of correcting external disequilibrium but do not propose a coherent alternative policy.

If Argentina's democratic government breaks with these precedents of the past and formulates a coherent program for expansion together with an array of measures in the foreign sector to support it, the government will not only have a guide for its own action but will also demonstrate its creditworthiness to the IMF and to foreign creditors. The crux of the economic problem for UPS countries, especially Argentina, is to be found in the country itself. The solution of the problem depends in the last analysis on the ability of the governing circles to correctly grasp the nature of the problems and to carry out economic policies appropriate to the structure of an economy that is, in fundamental aspects, distinct from the economies of industrialized countries and operates in a world economy that is vastly different from the one that existed when the industrialized countries embarked on their own development.

Notes

1. The theme of the struggle between economic ideologies in Argentina is described in detail in Diamand (1971b and 1973).

2. It is obvious that the struggle between the two opposing economic programs is not purely academic but constitutes an intellectual reflection of an interclass

dispute concerning the distribution of income and economic power. Another aspect is that the instability of constitutional government in Argentina, the propensity of the country to move toward military coups, and the pendular political movement between democracy and de facto regimes are also closely related to these unresolved economic conflicts (see O'Donnell 1973).

3. An interesting illustration of the theme of dynamic comparative advantages of industry is given in Katz (1983).

4. The different reasons for industrialization are given in Prebisch (1963), with emphasis put on problems on demand, and in Kaldor (1964), with emphasis on problems of employment and the dynamic nature of industrial productivity.

5. These debates can be followed in the book *The National System of Political Economy*, written more than a century ago by Friedrich List, a famous theoretician of the industrialization of the United States and Germany (see List 1922).

6. An analysis of the UPS economic model is presented in Diamand (1969, 1971b, 1973).

7. Experience shows that although this reasoning coincides totally with the prevailing economic theory, as it is taught in the universities, the conclusions to which the reasoning leads are not understood either by the general public or by the majority of economists.

8. As we shall see, this discrepancy between imports and exports is not inevitable and can be overcome with appropriate policies. To this basic cause of external imbalances are added many errors of economic policy that the two disparate ideologies habitually commit, each in its own way. Thus, the phenomenon of external disequilibrium, although largely of structural origin, can be overcome by appropriate policies. However, to elaborate these policies, previous recognition of the problem is necessary, which is precisely what is lacking.

9. The prevailing economic paradigm recognizes two alternative types of limitation: the limitation of productive capacity in the classic model, in effect when resources are fully used, and the limitation of insufficient demand in the Keynesian model, in effect when there is unemployment of resources. The possibility of a limitation caused by the external sector is generally ignored. If and when such a limitation is given a hearing, its operation is usually analyzed in terms of the two theoretical models mentioned, which in this case have little to do with reality. The resulting disorientation resembles the situation that existed before the Keynesian revolution in the face of the great crises in the industrial countries. The consequences of this disorientation in UPS economies are analyzed in Diamand (1973). The description of a similar confusion that is being repeated now at the international level because of the petroleum crisis can be found in Diamand (1978). There are exceptions to this tendency to ignore the external limitation on the part of the school of "dual economies," many Latin American structuralists, and some individual economists. See for example, Chenery and Strout (1966), Taylor (1979), Prebisch (1963), Seers (1962), Bacha and Malan (1983), and Furtado (1958). See also Hicks (1974). The antecedents can be seen in Kalecki (1970).

10. A more detailed analysis of these policies is provided in Canitrot (1975).

11. The analysis of this effect in Argentina can be seen in Diaz-Alejandro (1965). For a general model, mathematically formalized, see Taylor (1979).

12. For an analysis of this second contractionary effect, see Sidrausky (1968). For a model that contains both contractionary effects—the redistributive and the monetary—see Porto (1975).

13. The ideas that are profoundly rooted in the traditional economic model with respect to the capacity of the market to eliminate blockages of supply by means of relative price changes impede the acceptance of the existence of such blockages. These ideas interfere with understanding structural inflations that originate in such a way. But the difficulty becomes even greater when dealing with the specific case of exchange inflation originating from the disequilibrium between aggregate demand and the blocked supply of foreign currency. When this imbalance occurs, a level of demand that is perfectly suited to the installed productive capacity becomes excessive with respect to the limited supply of foreign currency, which results in an increase in the price of the latter that spreads to other prices. Despite the fact that the above situation has constituted a repetitive phenomenon in the UPS economies and also in industrial countries for the last several years, these inflations are seldom recognized as such. More or less elaborate references to the phenomenon can be found in Prebisch (1963), Diaz-Alejandro (1965), Seers (1962), and more recently and explicitly in Hicks (1974). For a detailed analysis, see Diamand (1971a, 1973, 1978).

14. Here again, the postulate of automatic external equilibrium of the prevailing paradigm erases the essential difference between foreign capital in the role of currency and foreign capital in the role of provider of savings. Thus, there is great difficulty in visualizing the inconvertibility of national savings into foreign currencies that occurs in countries with problems of balance of payments. Consequently, the impossibility of repayment of the debt and its services because of this inconvertibility cannot be visualized either. The result is a highly imprudent and irresponsible management of foreign debt. The antecedents of the confusion can be seen in Keynes's famous article about the German transfers (see Keynes 1953). For an analysis of the problem in the UPS countries, see Diamand (1970 or 1973).

15. For a mathematical analysis of the capital market under such conditions, see Frenkel (1958).

16. In the cycles of cumulative foreign debt occurring in the Southern Cone in recent years, which have been supported at the theoretical level by the monetary view of the balance of payments, this dismantling of protection for the sake of greater efficiency acquires a second significance since it is converted into a presumed mechanism of price stabilization. The stated mechanism becomes necessary for the scheme to be complete at a theoretical level—although again without any relationship to what happens in reality (see Diamand 1980 and Foxley 1982).

17. The apparently new monetary emphasis on the balance of payments is nothing more than an elegant rationalization of phase two of the stabilization programs, which in practice have been applied for decades (thus, the period 1978–1981 in Argentina has great conceptual similarity to the period 1960–1962). For the reasons why the monetary focus failed, see Foxley (1982), Schydlowsky (1979a), and Diamand (1980).

18. The 1982 GNP fell almost to the level of 1973, and the per capita GNP went down about 12 percent with respect to the same year.

19. Thus, an exchange scheme based on land tax can complement a scheme with export duties, allowing the latter to be smaller, or replace it entirely.

References

Bacha, Edmar L., and Malan, Pedro S. 1983. "Brazil's Debt: From the Miracle to the Fund." Department of Economics, Catholic University. Rio de Janeiro.

Cámara Argentina de Industrias Electrónicas (CARTA). 1966. "Proyecto de modificación de la estructura arancelario-cambiaria." Buenos Aires.

Canitrot, Adolfo. 1975. "La Experiencia populista de redistribución de ingresos." *Desarrollo Económico* 15, no. 59 (Oct-Dec):331–351.

Chenery, Hollis B., and Strout, Alan M. 1966. "Foreign Assistance and Economic Development." *American Economic Review* 56 (September):679–733.

Diamand, Marcelo. 1963. "El F.M.I. y los países en Desarrollo." *Movimiento soluciones Económicas.* Buenos Aires.

———. 1968. "El Régimen de Drawback generalizado y las exportaciones industriales." *El Cronista comercial*, September 9–10.

———. 1969. "Bases para una política industrial Argentina." *El Cronista comercial* (April-May).

———. 1970. "Desarrollo industrial, política autárquica, y capital extranjero." *Centro de estudios de coyuntura.* I.D.E.S., no. 16. Buenos Aires.

———. 1971a. "Los Cuatros tipos de inflación Argentina." *Competencia* (April).

———. 1971b. "Seis falsos dilemas en el debate económico nacional." *El Cronista comercial*, January 4–20.

———. 1972. "La Estructura productiva desequilibrada y el tipo de cambio." *Desarrollo económico* (April-June):25–47.

———. 1973. *Doctrinas económicas, Desarrollo e independencia.* Buenos Aires: Paidos.

———. 1978. "Towards a Change in the Economic Paradigm Through the Experience of Developing Countries." *Journal of Development Economics* 5, no. 1 (March):19–53.

———. 1980. "La Marcha de la economía." *Revista idea,* no. 36 (July-September). Buenos Aires.

Diaz-Alejandro, Carlos. 1965. *Exchange Rate Devaluation in a Semi-Industrialized Country: The Experience of Argentina.* Cambridge, Mass.: MIT Press.

Eshag, Eprime, and Thorp, Rosemary. 1965. "Las Consecuencias económicas y sociales de las políticas ortodoxas aplicadas en la República Argentina durante los Años de postguerra." *Desarrollo económico* 27 (April-June).

Foxley, Alejandro. 1982. "Enfoques ortodoxos para el ajuste económico de corto plazo: Lecciones de la experiencia y temas de Investigación." Mimeograph. Santiago, Chile: CIEPLAN.

Frenkel, Roberto. 1958. "El Desarrollo reciente del mercado de capitales en la Argentina." *Desarrollo económico* 20, no. 78 (July-September).

Furtado, Celso. 1958. "El Desequilibrio externo en las economías subdesarrolladas." *Trimestre económico,* no. 2.

Hicks, Sir John Richard. 1974. *The Crisis in Keynesian Economics*. Oxford: Basil Blackwell.

Hirschman, Albert. 1961. *La Estrategia del desarrollo económico*. Mexico City: Fonde de Cultura Económica.

Kaldor, Nicholas. 1964. *Exchange Rates and Economic Development. Essays on Economic Policy*, Vol. 2. New York: Norton.

Kalecki, Michal. 1970. *Estudio sobre la teoría de los ciclos económicos*. Barcelona: Ariel.

Katz, Jorge. 1983. "Estrategia industrial y ventajas comparativas dinámicas." *Cuadernos*. Eugenio Blanco Foundation. Vol. 1 (August). Buenos Aires.

Keynes, John M. 1953. *Ensayos sobre teoría del comercio internacional: El Problema de transferencias alemanas*. Mexico City: Fondo de Cultura Económica.

List, Friedrich. 1922. *The National System of Political Economy*. London: Longmans Green and Company.

Llach, Juan. 1982. "Los Precios de una década: El Tipo de cambio real y los precios relativos en la economía Argentina: 1970–1982." *Estudios* 5, no. 24 (October-December). Córdoba, Argentina: Instituto de Estudios Económicas sobre la Realidad Argentina y Latinoamericana.

O'Donnell, Guillermo. 1973. *Modernización y autoritarismo*. Buenos Aires: Paidos.

Porto, Alberto. 1975. "Un modelo simple sobre el comportamiento macroeconómico argentino a corto plazo." *Desarrollo económico* 15, no. 59 (October-December):353–371.

Prebisch, Raúl. 1963. *Hacia una dinámica del desarrollo Latinoamericano*. Mexico City: Fondo de Cultura Económica.

Schydlowsky, Daniel. 1966. "From Import Substitution to Export Promotion for Semi-Grown Up Industries." Cambridge: Development Advisory Service, Harvard University.

———. 1967. "Short Run Employment Policy in Semi-Industrialized Economies." Cambridge: Development Advisory Service, Harvard University.

———. 1971. "Fiscal Policy for Full Capacity Industrial Growth in Latin America." Cambridge: Center for International Affairs, Harvard University.

———. 1979a. "Argentina's Macroeconomic Prospects as of Early October." Mimeograph. Boston.

———. 1979b. "Containing the Costs of Stabilization in Semi-Industrialized LDC's." Center for Latin American Studies, Discussion Paper Series no. 36. Boston: Boston University.

Seers, Dudley. 1962. "A Theory of Inflation and Growth in Underdeveloped Economies Based on the Experience of Latin America." *Oxford Economic Papers* n.s. 14 (June):173–195.

Sidrausky, Miguel. 1968. "Devaluación, inflación, y desempleo." *Económica* 14, no. 1-2 (January-August).

Taylor, Lance. 1979. *Macro Models for Developing Countries*. New York: McGraw-Hill.

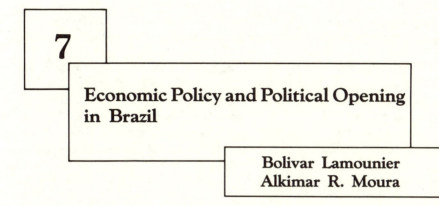

7

Economic Policy and Political Opening in Brazil

Bolivar Lamounier
Alkimar R. Moura

The performance of the Brazilian economy from 1973 to 1984 presents three important issues. The first concerns the Brazilian policy response, primarily under the Geisel government, to the impending world petroleum crisis when the choice was made to sustain the rhythm of growth, with emphasis on import substitution of capital goods and basic inputs. The second relates to the specifically political conditions at the beginning of the 1970s, which were characterized by an apparently unprecedented degree of repression. The policy response to that situation took the form of a gradualist liberalization strategy. The third concerns the inability of the first nonmilitary government in twenty years to find a politically acceptable way to cut the government deficit and slow the acceleration of inflation.

From the perspective of this chapter, the decisive question is whether the two concomitant reactions were independent of one another, or whether, on the contrary, there were significant connections between them. In effect, what were the most important features of these reactions to the economic crisis and the dilemmas of eventual democratization? What perceptions on the part of the governing group and the most influential participants constituted the foundations of their respective strategies?

Our objective, obviously, is not a theoretical discussion about the interaction of economic and political factors nor a systematic investigation of adjustment strategies or the impact of political liberalization processes in different countries. Our purpose is more modest. Beginning with a general analysis of the economic strategies of the governments of Ernesto Geisel (1974–1979) and João Baptista Figueiredo (1979–1985), we propose to identify the factors that may have been obstacles to the adoption of more rapid and consistent measures of adjustment. We accept as a valid premise that an orderly slowdown of economic growth midway through the decade of the 1970s would have assured Brazil of better choices in the management of external constraints, making the present problems less crucial.

A brief overview of the contents of our discussion is appropriate. In the first section, we present some basic data concerning the strategy adopted by the Geisel government. In the second, we discuss the economic data of the period 1979–1983, in other words, from the second petroleum and rate of interest shocks to the recession that began in 1981 to the virtual foreign strangulation of the economy in the second half of 1983. In the third section, we cover the same ground but from the political side, taking as points of reference the presidential succession (from Emilio Garrastazu Medici to Geisel) and the rigidity of the initial picture at the very beginning of the *abertura* ("opening of political system"). Reviewing the period 1973–1978, we try to point out how excessive gradualism made it difficult to create alternative bases of support that could have forced the economic policymakers to undertake a process of constructive criticism and, eventually, encourage a more orderly slowing of growth.

In the fourth section, which concentrates on the Figueiredo government, we emphasize the loss of the best opportunities to resolve the political problems inherited from the Geisel government—in particular, the new government's slowness in making viable or recognizing a political force of the center that would implement austerity measures compatible with political stability and with the continuation of the liberalization process. In this discussion, we utilize the word "austerity" in a manner that is not always very precise. Its traditional connotation may be that of orthodox contractionist measures, but we believe that the political difficulties referred to could have occurred, and perhaps to a greater degree, if the government had adopted the alternative of an incomes policy based on the European social-democratic model. The basic ideal of an austerity program is that of an orderly slowing of growth, which also implies greater selectivity of large projects, a revision of expansion plans of the major state enterprises, and so on. Finally, we describe events during the first year of the presidency of José Sarney (1985) and offer some general conclusions.

The Brazilian Answer to the First Petroleum Shock

Today, it is widely recognized that Brazil reacted with enormous delay and inconsistency to the first petroleum shock and its consequences: recession in the industrialized countries and strong price fluctuations in international commodity markets and raw materials. It can be argued that the policy implemented by the Geisel government, in addition to being slow and late, increased the disequilibrium of the economy to a great extent and thus accentuated its notorious external vulnerability.

The World Bank has made an estimate of the effects of the petroleum shock (and the responses to it) on the balance of payments, using for this purpose an analytic model proposed by Bela Balassa. This model postulates that the effect of the petroleum shock can be measured by two factors: the terms-of-trade effect and the export-volume effect. The first estimates to what extent changes in prices of imports and exports affected expenditures for imports and receipts from exports. The second captures the impact of the recession in the industrialized countries on the demand for imports from the less developed of the nonindustrialized countries. With the purpose of analyzing the response of specific countries to these two factors, Balassa's methodology takes into account four different "modes of adjustment": (1) import substitution efforts; (2) attempts to increase penetration of foreign markets; (3) external financing (i.e., the extent to which these countries turned to foreign debt to finance their growing commercial deficits); and (4) reduction of growth rates (an attempt to measure the adjustment brought about by deliberate policies to retard growth in the petroleum importing countries).

The World Bank study includes forty-seven oil-importing developing countries, divided into four subgroups according to their principal economic characteristics and the actions they undertook in terms of economic policy. Brazil is placed in a group of thirteen semi-industrialized, medium-income countries.[1] Despite the deficiencies and rather mechanical simplicity of the Balassa model, the results indicate how different groups of developing countries attempted to react to an external shock that caused dislocations of income and wealth on a world scale. Table 7.1 compares the effects of the shock on Brazil and that country's adjustment with those of its subgroup, and at least three general conclusions can be derived from the table:

1. The effect of the first petroleum shock on Brazilian GNP was 50 percent greater than that for the whole subgroup.
2. The Brazilian mode of adjustment was clearly different in regard to the relative weight of the diverse components, being strongly based on import substitution (66.8 percent), external financing (26.2 percent), increased exports by means of penetrating new markets (15.1 percent), and a reduction of growth (−8.1 percent).
3. The negative sign of reduced growth becomes particularly significant if we consider that that component was responsible for 32 percent of total adjustment in the other semi-industrialized oil importing countries.

Table 7.1

EFFECTS ON THE BALANCE OF PAYMENTS OF THE EXTERNAL SHOCK
PRODUCED BY THE WORLD OIL CRISIS AND THE ADJUSTMENTS
ADOPTED BY THE SELECTED SEMI-INDUSTRIALIZED
COUNTRIES OF MEDIUM INCOME AND BY BRAZIL
(1974-1978 Yearly Average as Percentage of GNP)

	Semi-Industrialized Countries		Brazil	
A. External Shocks	% of GNP	%	% of GNP	%
Terms of Trade Effect	.90	49.8	2.22	82.0
Volume of Exports Effect	.91	50.2	.49	18.0
Total Shock	1.81	100.0	2.71	100.0
B. Means of adjustment				
Import Substitution	.09	5.0	1.81	66.8
Export Increase	.69	38.1	.41	15.1
Economic Growth Reduction	.58	32.0	-.26	-8.1
External Financing	.45	24.8	.74	26.2
Total Adjustment	1.81	100.0	2.71	100.0

Note: Not all percentage totals sum to 100 because of rounding.

Sources: World Bank, World Development Report (New York: Oxford University Press, 1981), p. 66, and Choques (Rio de Janeiro: Fundação Getúlio Vargas, 1981), p. 17.

It is thus evident that the policies implemented by the Geisel government to confront the first petroleum shock manifested a strong preference for import substitution and a strong resistance to the option of reducing growth. This conclusion is still more evident if we consider that the Brazilian performance is being compared with the combined performance of other developing countries that were also struggling with a heavy burden of adjustment. It is clear that the Brazilian policymakers did not wish to or could not adopt policies that would have resulted in a more substantial slowing down of growth.[2]

Concerning domestic macroeconomic imbalances during the period 1974-1978, the government's economic policy, far from showing a more or less coherent pattern of evolution, appeared to alternate between expansion and retraction of economic activity. This incoherence, together with the shocks of foreign origin, produced an accentuated degree of instability in the Brazilian economy. Table 7.2 presents the annual rates of change in real terms of three important macroeconomic variables— the money supply, the estimated expenditures of the federal government,

Table 7.2

REAL RATE OF CHANGE OF SELECTED MACROECONOMIC
INDICATORS AND RATE OF INFLATION, 1974-1978

(in percentage)

	Money Supply	Government Expenditure	Rate of Exchange (US $)	Growth in GDP	Growth in Industrial GDP	Rate of Inflation
1974	.8	3.0	4.3	9.5	9.1	34.6
1975	10.3	1.0	.7	5.6	5.6	29.4
1976	-6.1	18.8	-2.7	9.7	12.5	46.2
1977	-.9	5.0	2.6	5.4	3.9	38.8
1978	1.0	1.0	-.5	4.8	7.4	40.8
Mean	.7	5.7	.8	7.0	7.7	37.9
Standard Deviation	6.0	7.4	2.7	2.4	3.3	6.3
Coefficient of Variation	872.4	129.7	307.9	34.1	42.9	16.7

Sources: Conjuntura Econômica (various issues) and Central Bank of Brazil, Boletím (various issues).

and the rate of exchange (cruzeiros/U.S. dollars)—and the last three columns show the results of the government's economic policy measured by the annual rates of growth of the real GDP and the GDP of the industrial sector as well as the rate of inflation. The coefficients of variation presented in the last line attempt to indicate the magnitude of the fluctuations observed in those macroeconomic variables in the period 1974–1978.

The data in Table 7.2 show a high level of instability in some of these indicators of economic policy, which is reflected in fluctuations in the growth of real output and rate of inflation. The government's behavior during this period could be described as an attempt to accommodate conflicting short-run economic objectives: namely, to reduce the rate of inflation while maintaining a relatively rapid rate of growth in the presence of an increasingly restrictive external environment.

We are thus supposing that the crucial question that should have been confronted by the government has to do with the speed and composition of the adjustment process that an economy should undergo in response to foreign shocks. By choosing a rhythm and pattern of adjustment that maintained economic growth at the expense of greater internal and external imbalances, the economic policymakers simply postponed the moment when the growing burden of international obligations would have to be confronted. It can be assumed that as it was able to circumvent the difficult choices of the foreign sector, the government could also avoid domestic restrictions, which would require more austere policies. In other words, once the problem of economic adjustment in the foreign sector was postponed, it was not to be expected that the administration would implement policies to restrict demand in order to achieve a percentage reduction in the rate of price increases in an economy that had already developed mechanisms of living with inflation.

In reality, as various authors have pointed out, economic policy in the five-year period 1974-1978 was clearly expansionist, despite the deterioration of the country's foreign accounts. It should not be forgotten, however, that solid economic reasons can be invoked to support the expansionist decisions of the Geisel administration. In the first place, since 1968 Brazil had chosen to implement a strategy of growth based on foreign indebtedness contracted with the private international financial system. Considering the vigorous growth of the economy in the period 1968-1974, this strategy appeared to have been successful. In that period, there was an influx of foreign loans, and among all the developing countries, Brazil was the largest individual recipient of the resources of the Western industrialized countries.

After the first petroleum shock, the connections between the Brazilian economy and the Eurodollar market became stronger, taking into account the mode of adjustment mentioned previously. Nevertheless, the fact that the country's access to international bank credit was maintained is surprising, even after the market stopped absorbing the credit demands of some low-risk industrialized countries that were also troubled with problems of financing imbalances in their foreign accounts. In truth, Brazil's share of the total of Eurobank loans to developing countries (excepting credits to developing petroleum producing countries), which had reached 20.5 percent in 1972, grew to 23 percent in 1975 and remained at about 20 percent in 1977 and 1978. The interest differentials above the Libor rate collected from Brazilian debtors were maintained at levels close to the average spread paid by debtors from developing countries except in the years 1977 and 1978 (for statistical data, see Nogueira Baptista, Jr., 1983, World Bank 1981, Moura 1981, and Bacha and Diaz-Alejandro 1981).

Thus, the availability of foreign financial capital at real negative interest rates (in the ex post sense) constituted, without doubt, a powerful stimulus to indebtedness in hard currency, which in turn favored a somewhat myopic approach to Brazil's external economic adjustment problem. Moreover, the fact that private international banks came to constitute the principal source of loans for Brazil can also explain, at least in part, Brazil's excessive foreign debt in the period 1968–1978.

In the second place, the mode of adjustment chosen by Brazil depended above all on import substitution (see Table 7.1). The second national development plan, formulated by the Geisel government, was based fundamentally on an ambitious program of substitution of imported products in the basic raw materials sectors and of capital goods. Substantial investments were made in the domestic production of nonferrous metals, iron and steel, paper and cellulose, petrochemical products, and fuel alcohol. The federal government itself invested heavily in the production of electricity and the development of transport and communications systems, in addition to granting fiscal, credit, tariff, and other incentives to import substitution projects in the private sector and government enterprises.[3] Many of these investments were projects characterized by a long maturation period and a low rate of return. Moreover, they were characterized by a high degree of indivisibility and of complementarity with other private investments and by the fact that they could display economies of scale beyond a minimum level of production. In this way, the special technical and economic characteristics of the import substitution projects led to large-scale undertakings that had a considerable impact on domestic resources, but in the initial stage, they also put pressure on the foreign exchange accounts because of the necessity of importing goods and services, and thus they led to an increase in the foreign debt.

The Strategy of the Figueiredo Government

At the beginning, in March 1979, the government of General Figueiredo seemed disposed to confront the crucial questions inherited from previous governments (external adjustment and internal macroeconomic imbalances) with greater determination and consistency than the Geisel administration had shown. Actually, from March to August 1979, some measures that seemed to presage an austerity period were tried out in the conduct of economic policy. Among them it is worth mentioning a "mini-exchange reform" that established a program of gradual reduction of fiscal incentives for the export of manufactured products, offering as a counterpart to exporters the promise of a slight acceleration of the minidevaluations of the cruzeiro. Also, the government published guidelines to oversee institutional changes that were intended to assure greater control of public sector expenditures and announced measures that were calculated to strengthen the central bank's ability to exercise effective control of monetary policy and, at the same time, promote a gradual separation of functions among the official institutions regulating the money supply. In the area of substitution of imported energy, attempts were made to accelerate the alcohol program and to increase investments in petroleum prospecting. It is symptomatic that for the first time, the term "war economy" was utilized in the official rhetoric, to denote the critical-limits situation of the economy and the sacrifices that would be required from the people to overcome it.

This period of premature adjustment lasted exactly six months, ending in August 1979 when the "recessionist" Mario Enrique Simonsén was replaced by the "developmentalist" Antonio Delfim Netto as head of the Secretariat of Planning. A new phase of economic policy was initiated that could be called "anti-adjustment" since the errors of the Geisel administration were repeated on a large scale. Short-run economic policies changed direction; public expenditure was accelerated (in the broad sense, involving indirect administrative expenses and those of state enterprises); the money supply and credit were increased; the nominal interest rate was controlled; the mini-exchange reform was abandoned; the policy of price controls on industrial goods was reinstated; tariffs on products and services were regulated; attempts to make organizational changes in the mechanism of monetary control were suppressed; and the wage-indexing policy was modified, making semiannual rather than annual adjustments and permitting a larger correction for inflation.

The only decision consistent with the necessity for external adjustment—the maxidevaluation of 30 percent of the cruzeiro relative to the dollar in December 1979—turned out to be completely neutralized by the decision to prefix the rate of exchange devaluation during 1980. In effect, the advantages of competitiveness in the foreign sector for manufactured exports were eliminated in little more than nine months by prefixing changes in the rate of exchange. Moreover, the effort to reduce the imbalance in international trade became more difficult, since imports were encouraged by the high level of domestic economic activity.

The results of the anti-adjustment policy were foreseeable and are already strongly documented by economic analysts. The economy underwent vigorous growth in 1980, sustained by the activities of the industrial, trade, transport, and communications sectors. On the other hand, a marked deterioration in foreign accounts was observed: There was a record current account deficit of $11.7 million (representing 5.2 percent of the GDP) and a loss of $2.3 million in international liquid reserves; the ratio of the foreign debt to exports grew from 2.2 (average of the period 1974–1978) to 2.8 in the two-year period 1979–1980; the gross foreign debt, including the short-term debt, reached $64.4 billion in December 1980; and the real rate of exchange increased in value, both in relation to the U.S. dollar and to the moneys of the principal Brazilian

Table 7.3

ECONOMIC INDICATORS OF THE DETERIORATION
OF BRAZIL'S EXTERNAL SECTOR

Year	Terms of Trade Index (1977=100)	Petroleum Import Index (1977=100)	International Rate of Interest (December)[1]	Real Rate of Exchange (US$) (March 1973 = 100)[2]	Real Rate of Economic Growth[3]
1978	86	101	12.31	96.3	4.1
1979	79	135	14.44	96.3	3.5
1980	65	226	16.47	98.0	1.2
1981	55	270	14.81	108.7	1.4
1982	54	259	9.50	117.3	-0.5

[1]International rate of interest rate on six-month deposits in the Eurodollar market

[2]Index of the effective real rate of exchange of the U.S. dollar; weighted by the volume of trade with the United States

[3]Real rate of growth of the GNP for OECD countries, non-OECD European countries, and South Africa

Sources: Terms of Trade and Petroleum Import indices: Conjuntura Econômica (various issues); International Rate of Interest and Real Rate of Exchange: International Monetary Fund, International Financial Statistics (Washington, D.C., various years); Real Rate of Economic Growth: Economic Report of the President (Washington, D.C.: Government Printing Office, 1983).

trade associates. On the domestic front, the macroeconomic imbalances were enlarged by the expansionist economic policy, which resulted in an increase in inflation from 77.2 percent in 1979 to 110.3 percent in 1980.

The monumental failure of this heterodox experiment in economic policy can in part be explained by the attempt to implement a strategy of economic growth, disregarding the marked deterioration of international economic conditions that occurred in 1979 and 1980 (see Table 7.3). The change in U.S. monetary policy in October 1979 and the second petroleum shock, events that in themselves would be sufficiently disastrous to affect domestic economic activity under normal conditions, had devastating effects on the Brazilian economy since the anti-adjustment policy combined with them to amplify rather than weaken their effect.

It cannot be said, however, that there was a generalized inability on the part of the government technocrats to interpret the unequivocal signs of economic difficulties resulting from changes in the international economy. Rather, their predominant attitude was to try to exorcise such demons with the optimistic rhetoric inherited from the years of the Brazilian "miracle." The resignation of Finance Minister Rischiebieter might be interpreted as one confirmation of the official position on the crisis and its effects on the Brazilian economy.

The pressure of foreign economic restrictions finally prevailed, and at the end of 1980, a radical change in macroeconomic policy became necessary because of growing difficulties in obtaining new loans from international banks. The first indicators of this change could be observed even at the beginning of the second half of 1980, when monetary policy gradually became restrictive. Nevertheless, it was only at the end of that year, when the National Monetary Council approved a series of clearly restrictive decisions, that the anti-adjustment policy was abandoned entirely. It is worth emphasizing a point that will be reconsidered later in this chapter: This change in economic strategy was not produced by the competitive power of organized political groups and supported by conventional mechanisms of representation. Rather, it came about from pressures emanating from the private international financial system, which feared an increase of "exposure" in a country that might become a high risk.

Policy Reversal

Beginning in 1981, the economic strategy of the Figueiredo government was exactly the opposite of its policy in 1980. The ostensible objective of government policy was now centered on trying to reestablish the flow of loans in Euromoney to demonstrate to bankers, who are traditionally averse to risk, that Brazil had again become a trustworthy debtor. The array of economic policy measures put into effect contained various components of orthodox stabilization programs. Among these, the following can be cited: the abandonment of attempts to prefix monetary and exchange corrections; the establishment of strict limits for the expansion of loans from financial intermediaries; the setting of realistic rates for public services; the freeing of prices in industrial sectors previously subject to official control; and the establishment of stricter limits for the government on current capital and import expenses and on domestic foreign loans by state enterprises as a whole. (From that time on, state enterprises were subject to the control of the recently created Secretariat of Control of State Enterprises [SEST], which was directly associated with the Secretariat of Planning.)[4] Other measures included a cut in real terms in direct government imports and a more intense utilization of government bonds as an instrument to secure resources for the financing of the public debt and also as a mechanism of monetary policy.

Through conventional measures, an attempt was made to raise the nominal interest rate in order to stimulate "voluntary" indebtedness in foreign currency and to promote a real devaluation of the cruzeiro. Instead of a more drastic adjustment in the rate of exchange, an unavoidable measure in any orthodox stabilization plan, the preferred alternative was to accelerate the minidevaluations of the cruzeiro (with changes in the rules of devaluation) and to turn to fiscal incentives for the export of manufactured products. With regard to measures of credit and spending containment, various highly subsidized agricultural credit programs were maintained as well as programs for export promotion and the domestic substitution of imported energy. Wage policy also remained unchanged.

Thus, the Figueiredo administration's second attempt to carry out an austerity program contained measures to reduce the aggregate level of expenditures in the economy as well as administrative measures to reallocate expenditures to benefit some sectors that were considered to be of high priority. These two objectives, the containment of the aggregate level of expenditures and considerable economic incentives for some protected sectors, led to various conflicts later on. In the case of monetary policy, for example, the need for stricter control over the factors responsible for credit expansion clashed with sectorial demands for loans at highly subsidized interest rates.

Nevertheless, the economic policy had a strong net contractionary effect, finally achieving a marked slowdown in economic activity and the level of employment during 1981. The recession principally affected the durable consumer goods and the capital goods sectors and thus centered on the most urbanized areas of the country. The level of investments in real terms decreased 10.8 percent between 1980 and 1981 and, as a percentage of total output, went from 23 percent to 19.5 percent within two years. Recent estimates show that the output gap increased fivefold, rising from 2.3 percent in 1980 to 11.5 percent in 1981 (data taken from Malan and Bonelli 1983).

From that point on, an unprecedented economic scenario took shape, one that could be described as a "negative-sum game," and it extended throughout 1982 and 1983. During these three years, the country experienced the deepest, most prolonged, and most comprehensive drop in economic activity in sixty years. In terms of per capita output, Rudiger Dornbusch has shown that the recession exceeded that of the period 1960–1967; in its observed ill-effects, it exceeded the worst years of the depression of the thirties (Dornbusch 1983).

This worsening of economic conditions occurred again due to an external shock, that of the turbulent condition of the international financial market that culminated in August 1982 with the Mexican debt moratorium. Truly a mortal blow for an economy that was extremely vulnerable to modifications in the external environment, Mexico's moratorium had an immediate contagious effect on the influx of foreign bank loans into Brazil. From that point on, the country was confronted by a totally inelastic supply curve of loans originating from private international banks, above all U.S. regional banks. Although Brazilian debtors were prepared to pay higher spreads, they were excluded from the bank loan market.[5]

It is worth pointing out that the Mexican moratorium was only the most obvious sign of a latent exchange crisis, the clearest manifestation of which was provided by the disorderly growth of short-term indebtedness on the part of the monetary authorities beginning with the first quarter of 1982. At the end of March of that year, six months before "black September," the net reserves of Brazil's central bank were already negative, indicating, therefore, the country's total inability to deal with the liquidity crisis that would emerge in the second half of 1982.

The reaction of Brazilian policymakers to this new external shock was again ambiguous. On one side, they tried to transmit to the international financial community unequivocal signs that the country would reinforce its policy of "voluntary" adjustment. In line with this effort, the monetary policy was modified, in the sense that it was made more restrictive, and an ambitious program of reduction of external disequilibrium and cutting of public sector investments was approved. Trying to show that it was a *reliable* debtor, the country aimed to maintain its share of the international bank loan market.[6] On the other hand, owing to the approaching general elections of November 1982, there was an attempt to minimize the impact of the international financial situation on the Brazilian economy. The policy of containment of public federal and state expenditures was selectively eased in some regions of the country, with the specific goal of assuring a favorable electoral return to the government.

Possibly because the severity of the international financial crisis was greater than it was thought to be, or perhaps because of the low credibility of the Brazilian economic authorities, the strategy carried out did not succeed in convincing the majority of the private creditors. An interruption of payment was avoided at the end of December 1982 only by the assemblage of an emergency financial assistance package for the country, which involved bridge loans and other kinds of operations originating with the International Monetary Fund (IMF), Bank of International Settlements, the U.S. Federal Reserve System, U.S. Treasury, and major private U.S. banks.[7]

After this dramatic situation of illiquidity, economic policy came to be dictated by the IMF, and a first stabilization program was presented to that organization in February 1983. It is important to note that the program of the IMF meant little in terms of loans, but it offered to the international financial community a certain guarantee against "moral hazard" and other risks typical of debtors in difficulty. The IMF's guarantee of the Brazilian adjustment program meant that private banks would also support the program financially.

Brazil did not succeed in fulfilling the first economic performance goals required by the IMF, which resulted in the country's inability to obtain additional loans from the fund. Consequently, the foreign banks also interrupted the flow of credit allocated to the four financing projects established in December 1982. At this point, a period of wearisome negotiations among Brazilian economic authorities, international bankers, representatives of multilateral financial agencies, supervisory bodies of national banking systems, and governments of industrialized countries began. With this internationalization of the country's illiquidity crisis, Brazil's economic policy was restricted throughout all of 1983 to a mere administrative exercise in cash management, with all preoccupations concentrated on the cash inflow of foreign money. The deterioration of this flow led to delays in commercial and financial payments and at the same time obliged the central bank to centralize exchange operations in August 1983.

At the end of 1983, Brazil submitted to the IMF yet another letter of intention, establishing quarterly goals for the principal indicators of macroeconomic performance utilized in the stabilization program sponsored by that institution. At the same time, the country attempted to obtain a new "jumbo" loan from the creditor banks of $6.5 billion in new credits to be used during 1984.

In the final year of the Figueiredo administration, some positive results of the sharp contraction of 1983 could be seen. Output began to grow again, and there was a sharp improvement in the balance of payments. The current account, which had been $14 billion in deficit in 1982, was in balance by 1984 thanks to a 30 percent rise in exports and an equivalent decline in imports, both resulting from a maxidevaluation in 1983 and the continuation of recession. Not surprisingly, this adjustment to the foreign exchange shortage exacerbated inflationary pressures. Inflation, which had hovered around 100 percent for 1980–1982, jumped to over 200 percent in 1984 and was expected to be even higher in 1985.

Political Aspects

At first glance, the poor economic performance of the Brazilian economy since the second oil shock seems irreconcilable with the image of Brazilian economic policymakers, who until recently have been praised for their technical competence and their supposed wisdom in the management of foreign debt. Given the inadequacy of Brazil's policy, above all in view of the excessive duration of the crisis and the timidity and inconsistency of the corrective efforts, even under the Geisel government, an investigation of the political substratum becomes critical. What perceptions on the part of the ruling groups and what interests and pressures on the part of other participants had advised the continuation of a policy that was so markedly developmentalist in the face of an international environment that was increasingly hostile to that orientation?

Among the possible replies to this question, one should be discarded without further ado: The choice of maintenance of growth at any price in the Geisel period did not result from populist inclinations and even less from pressures exercised through competitive channels that were eventually created or reinforced by the process of liberalization. Only in the second half of 1983 (the tenth anniversary of the first petroleum shock), did the loss by the government of its majority in the federal Congress, which was allied to dissidents within the government party itself, begin to present itself as a serious complicating element with a defined institutional base in the formulation of economic policy. The opening of Brazilian politics, recognized as incomplete by the government itself, had not produced any reduction in the monopoly of economic decisions by the federal bureaucracy. Dissent and pressure were felt, without doubt, but it was not possible to talk about negotiated change, much less of blocking those decisions that had resulted from pressures produced by the operation of conventional mechanisms of representation.

Let us reconsider, however, the question of the *diagnosis* that guided the action of the ruling groups. To what extent had they taken into account the seriousness of the crisis, that is to say, its probable long duration and the violence of its impact on the Brazilian economy? Here also, the reply is unequivocal: Consistent underestimation went on for ten years. It would not be difficult to compile evidence of this situation, beginning with the slogan "isle of prosperity" that was informally adopted by the Geisel government. More eloquent, however, are some later testimonies that insist that the root of the difficulties lies in the years 1978–1980 and not before.[8]

We do not refer, however, to purely subjective manifestations, much less to distortions that could be attributed to a lack of individual competence, but rather, to a widely held position—possibly even shared by some opposition sectors—concerning the maintenance of high rates of growth. If we discard the hypothesis that populist and/or opposition groups blocked the eventual restrictive measures and agree that the maintenance of growth remained the basic orientation of economic policy until the beginning of the 1980s, what is the analytical model that is best suited to the period as a whole? A possible reply is that we are facing an authentic "prisoner's dilemma" situation, that is to say, one in which different participants choose to maximize their profits and thus make impossible the joint adoption of a strategy of moderate profits, which leads to serious losses for everyone. It is easy to see that a cooling-off policy would not have had the support of the capital goods industries or the great construction firms, which were contemplating substantial orders in accordance with the economic strategy of the Geisel government. Nor would such a policy have had the sympathy of the durable consumer goods industry, beginning with the automobile industry, as that sector was dependent on the middle-class market, which was already quite restricted.

What can be said of the political forces themselves, for example, the opposition parties and the labor unions? We have already said that the political liberalization did not at first include even the remote possibility of their influencing economic policy. The point to be raised, therefore, is that the opposition's influence, if it had existed, would hardly have operated in the way indicated. The opposition's challenging of the "economic model," and especially the spiral of foreign indebtedness, became a clear fact from the beginning of the 1970s, but nothing compels us to conclude that in that period, and under those conditions, the opposition viewpoint could have been immediately translated into a proposal for a slowdown. Beyond its greater sensitivity to popular claims, the opposition would clearly encounter difficulties in carrying out a more selective investment policy and in allocating resources in a much more specific manner, with a view to favoring projects characterized by a lower coefficient of imports.

If these assumptions are correct, it seems clear that only the government could have modified its excessively optimistic initial diagnosis, that only the government could have gone beyond the level of sectorial preferences and proposed a more cautious strategy, and that, in short, only the government could have stimulated the emergence of a political force capable of supporting a revision of its own strategy. Those possibilities are exactly what did *not* happen under the Geisel government or during the first three years of the Figueiredo government, and thus, an unprecedented worsening of the external imbalance occurred. We now face the following options: on the one hand, to consider that what did *not* happen is not explicable, that is to say, it was the natural result of continuity or of inertia in the system of power then prevailing, and on the other hand, to seek less evident or immediate connections between the facts noted and the political process of liberalization. We will choose the second option, aware that we are merely mapping out signs and conjectures, not presenting a fully demonstrable hypothesis.

The Beginnings of Political Liberalization

In Brazil, the principal characteristics of the liberalization process have been its extreme gradualism and its rather experimental character. The process has been based on an extremely diffuse agenda, and consequently, there has been constant uncertainty as to its direction and even as to its continuation. Officially named as the candidate of the National Renewal Alliance (ARENA) for the presidency in June 1973 (which at the time was virtually equivalent to an appointment), General Ernesto Geisel let it be known in the months that followed that he would introduce modifications in the political system, possibly including some steps toward liberalization but not necessarily a process of redemocratization. There was never any specification whatever of what these steps would be, but the general sense was that they would be *sensors* capable of identifying points of tension or weakness in the system and that they would therefore help bring about a better institutionalization of the regime. The regime was searching for a political model that would be "appropriate" to the country's new situation. It was implied that this state of better equilibrium would be something different than the almost completely throttled political system of the Medici period, but there is really no adequate phrase to describe the system the regime had in mind. Rather than referring to a final objective or to a sequence of traditional stages, the language of the regime alluded simply to a *process*, somewhat undefined, of *distensão* ("relaxation of repression"), which would be both gradual and safe.

The evocation of these beginnings is indispensable here, since our objective is precisely to limit ourselves to the plausible questions about the connection between this process of political opening, as it was conceived and implemented, and the options of economic policy—in other words, the connection between the political and economic strategies.[9] As we have already said, the political liberalization did not signify any possibility of changing the economic directives by means of pluralistic competition of organized political groups.[10] We must, however, ask whether excessive gradualism and the maintenance of growth at any price were not at least in part distortions produced by the same factor, that is, the excessive rigidity of the political, institutional, and military panorama of the Medici period and the economic "miracle."

According to our hypothesis, the situation had two decisive consequences. One was the absolute necessity of sustaining optimism. The euphoria concerning the rates of expansion of the GNP, practically deified during the Medici period, and the rhetoric that Brazil would in a short time be a great power took, without doubt, a more moderate form when elaborated by the new government, but the change in emphasis never went to the point of undermining the people's confidence in growth and the success of the industrialization program. The other consequence was the extreme difficulty of calculating the support that the government could actually count on in this new phase, not to mention the difficulty of neutralizing the existing opposition because of the need to obtain new sources of support. We do not refer here to the immediate support derived from satisfaction with the economic results, since excessive dependence on these was exactly the problem inherited from the Medici government, which had combined extreme repression with the euphoria of the miracle. Rather, we are referring to support based on the legitimacy of the regime and the government. The regime's political problem had to do, also, with the vacuum that the extreme centralization of power had created and covered over with a "revolutionary" mystique, transforming into institutional fact the suspicion that people on the outside are always adversaries and that adversaries are always enemies. With Congress weakened and the press censored, the diffusion of these ideas in the previous period had led to growing government isolation, an almost insuperable rigidity in dealing with civilian elites, and an almost automatic disregard of outside spokesmen who tried to preserve their autonomy.

And thus, with some exceptions, we can accept the affirmation of Cruz and Martins, according to which the context in which the decision to liberalize was taken "could not have been more favorable." The affirmation is correct in the sense that the succession from Medici to Geisel, in the middle of 1973, was probably the least traumatic since 1964 and also in that "the polarizing divisions within the armed forces had apparently been resolved, overcome as it were by the institutional principles of hierarchy and authority."[11] Let us keep in mind, however, that four years before, in 1969, such polarization had emerged with unusual clarity in the series of events that led to the election of Medici and to the objection of the nationalist wing headed by Albuquerque Lima. It would emerge again, four years later, in 1977, with the dismissal of the minister of the army, General Sylvio Frota, which opened the way for the nomination of Figueiredo for the presidency. Between these two dates, in January 1976, General Eduardo D'Avila was dismissed from the command of the Second Army in São Paulo because of the deaths, supposedly by suicide, of a journalist and a worker who had been imprisoned and subjected to torture. These facts prove nothing in themselves, but they allow us to suspect that divisions within the military would have been considerable if liberalization had been speeded up or if there had been a sharper slowdown of the economy by the government.

We suggest, therefore, that authoritarian rigidity could not be successfully reversed in a climate of negative economic prospects. Neither can we underestimate, in this context, the personality and world outlook of President Geisel.[12] Archetype of the military technocrat and familiar with the operation of large public sector industrial enterprises, Geisel evidently would not let his presidency, described frequently as "imperial," be tainted by the accusation that it had produced a stagnant economy. His view of the Brazilian political problem was undoubtedly authoritarian, but not static and rigid like that of the right-wing military.[13] His political will was therefore clearly developmentalist, a developmentalism characterized by a certain neo-Bismarckian sense of historical urgency and by the desire to transform Brazil into a respectable world power within the shortest time possible. His sense of reality, however, certainly made him conscious that that goal could almost immediately become infeasible and that a policy of extreme austerity could become necessary. These hints allow us to understand, at least impressionistically, the composition of his ministry, which included figures as contradictory as João dos Reis Velloso, who was totally identified with the thesis of maintenance at any price of high growth rates, and Mario Enrique Simonsén, a key figure in the panoply of orthodoxy and austerity.

Considering the totality of the power system, the point of departure doubtless has to be the difficulty encountered by the government, in those first days of liberalization, in avoiding flight into the "black hole," which is to say, into superisolation and immobility.[14] De Souza and Lamounier present the same general interpretation of the liberalization. They emphasize how government isolation occurred even as a consequence of the excessive "success" of measures initially supported by the people, notably repressive actions against the guerrillas, which ended with the creation of self-sufficient security agencies within the state apparatus. The same can be said of accelerated economic growth, which created unsatisfied expectations of an equally rapid redistribution of its fruits (Lamounier 1981).

De Souza and Lamounier argue that the initial aim of the political liberalization was precisely to avoid the risk of excessive isolation by means of three measures:

1. Revitalization of the electoral process and of the party system as mechanisms suitable for distributing support and as the principal basis of legitimacy
2. Gradual liberalization of the press and of public debate on political affairs in general
3. Control of the autonomous agencies of security and repression

The above discussion helps us understand the experimental and gradualist concept that was to guide the process of distension. What can be said, however, about the impact of this concept, once effectively begun, on the economic perceptions of the Geisel government? The elements at our disposal to respond to this question are purely speculative, but they acquire some consistency when considered in the light of the first two measures cited above, the revitalization of the electoral process and the liberalization of the press.

The impact of the 1974 elections cannot be adequately understood if we do not take into account the perceptions and diagnoses that oriented the process of liberalization at its outset. The general elections of 1970 and the municipal elections of 1972 had not only overwhelmed the fragile opposition but also revealed abundant signs of distrust in representative institutions. Whether on the basis of merely "institutionalizing the authoritarian regime" or something a little more liberalizing than that, the Geisel government was convinced right from the beginning of the necessity of revitalizing those institutions. Revitalize, yes, but in a context in which absolutely no one doubted that anything could occur but a tranquil victory for ARENA (the government party). The opposite, a resounding defeat for the government party, occurred in 1974. The Brazilian Democratic movement (MDB) increased its representation in the Senate from 12 percent to 30 percent, taking sixteen of the twenty-two contested seats. In the Chamber of Deputies, the MDB increased its share from 28 percent to 44 percent.[15]

The magnitude of the opposition's gains made clear two facts that the initial planners of liberalization had not contemplated. First, there was the possibility of a new institutional impasse, given the bipartisan nature of the system and the rigidity of the initial ideological definitions. The discrepancy in the "revolutionary" rhetoric, which established only a tenuous distinction between parliamentary opposition and rejection of the military regime, assumed sharper political contours in the face of the MDB's electoral growth, which made it necessary for the governing group to preserve a minimum of cohesion.

A second finding seems incontrovertible: The opposition votes were strongly concentrated in the richest states, beginning with São Paulo, and in the large urban centers, which is to say, in the areas that had benefited most from the economic miracle and in which the possibility of regaining any degree of popular support for the government appeared to be most difficult. To this fact we can add that the opposition's gains were largely credited to the emphasis it had put on economic questions during the campaign, notably the inequalities in the distribution of income. The growing identification of the MDB as the party of the poor, or of the people, and ARENA as the party of the rich and the government was an unequivocal factor in the 1974 campaign.

These brief comments about the revitalization of the electoral process seem to lend credibility to two of our conjectures: the wisdom of maintaining a high rate of economic growth and the difficulty of promoting a realignment of political forces when the growth strategy was being revised. Warnings against a change in the growth strategy emerged from the other institution revived by the liberalization—namely, the free press.[16] Such warnings, as we shall see shortly, made possible a more visible participation of entrepreneurs in public discussion, which rapidly took the form of a campaign for a reduction in the role of the state in the economy and, indirectly, against the exaggerated growth targets of the Geisel government.

The meaning of the so-called campaign against state intervention, especially its connections with the process of political opening per se, continues to be controversial. Some people see in that clamor against state intervention—which began with the 1974 choice of Eugenio Gudin as *homen do ano* ("man of the year") by the magazine *Visão*—one of the fundamental levers of the liberalization process. This interpretation has been suggested by Bresser Pereira, who believes the campaign was an indication of the collapse of the alliance formed by state enterprises and private national and multinational firms, a collapse that began when the inevitable slowing of the rate of growth began to occur (Bresser Pereira 1978). Another position emphasizes that the political activities of the entrepreneurs, up to the end of the Geisel administration, were

notably cautious and limited, suggesting not so much an immediate impossibility of accommodating the interests of their various sectors, but rather (a) the use of an opening process already under way to try to redress a prior loss of access to decision-making centers, and (b) some sort of preventive, anticipatory repositioning, in order not to be later branded as "enemies of" the process—an outcome which could be at least as damaging to them as their limited challenges to the present order of things.[17]

If the campaign against state intervention was not part of the origins of the political liberalization and if, in fact, the economic strategy of the Geisel government consisted of sustaining, despite all external difficulties, the rhythm of growth of the economy, what then would be the significance of those first demands of the industrial entrepreneurs? To call them a "false conscience" is not an explanation, and the hypothesis suggested by Bresser Pereira, with the modifications we will propose later, seems more concrete. The accelerated industrialization that began in 1967 effectively conferred a dominant role in the Brazilian economic structure upon state and multinational enterprises. The petroleum shock, representing the end of a period of cheap and abundant energy, made it clear to the national private sector that important changes were on the way. The scarcity of petroleum and other imported elements would necessarily mean a competition between the public and private sectors, without the latter's being given the appropriate means to influence the decision-making process.[18] It is sufficient to recall that the National Monetary Council, the agency most sensitive to the pressure of the private sector, lost influence during the Geisel administration in favor of the Councils of Economic Development and Social Development, which were directly linked to the presidency.

It seems to us, then, that the dilemma of sustaining or stopping growth appeared to the industrial entrepreneurs at the beginning of the Geisel administration to be of the "damned if you do, damned if you don't" type. A policy of "cooling off" and austerity was thus easily interpreted as an incitement to compete for scarce resources under circumstances that were probably disadvantageous to the private sector. To maintain growth under such adverse conditions, above all under the hyperoptimistic second national development plan proposed by the government, would probably mean assigning an even more decisive role in the economy to state enterprises. Between these two alternatives there was space only for the government's promise that it did not intend to take over anything and the fears of the entrepreneurs, who were noisy but not always very practical.[19]

The Figueiredo Government: The Party Reform of 1979 and the Elections of 1982[20]

The main weakness of the Brazilian political system has been characterized in the preceding sections as the nonexistence of a political force capable of backing an orderly slowdown of economic growth in order to look forward to an increase in the amount of freedom in dealing with foreign constraints. The parliamentary and electoral institutions, despite the upsets and pressures to which they were subjected, retained the potential of serving as a vehicle for the constitution of such a political force, but the excessive gradualism and, as we will see immediately, the solution adopted in the face of certain specific crises prevented them from taking shape at the proper time.

The transition from the Geisel to the Figueiredo government, at the beginning of 1979, concluded one stage in the process of liberalization. Important concessions were made to the opposition (for example, the amnesty and the almost complete reestablishment of freedom of press), but, at the same time, the electoral impasse that had trapped the government was diminished when the bipartisan structure and the opposition front in the MDB came apart. Having reached this stage, we are necessarily confronted with three questions. One concerns the very nature and extent of the democratic institutionalization that was to be gradually implanted. Another has to do with the degree to which the government would have been disposed to curb the potential excesses and arbitrary actions of the repressive police and military apparatus. A third concerns the effects the new economic situation (the rate of growth of the GNP was appreciably lower in 1977-1978) had on the political situation as a whole. These three issues lead us to three pronounced developments of the Figueiredo administration in the period 1979–1982, which were interconnected in some of their ramifications:

1. The lack of viability of the Popular party, which had aspired to be a party of the center, perhaps with the characteristics of party orientation to which we have referred
2. The appearance of terrorism of the right, especially the bomb episode in Rio on May 1, 1981, which made it clear that the armed forces were not disposed to permit independent and rigorous investigations of the possible participation of military personnel in such acts
3. The virtual foreign strangulation of the economy in the second half of 1982, especially after the Mexican moratorium, and the consequent deepening of the recession

Amnesty was declared in August 1979, and the euphoria about the return of the exiles and the relaxation of constraints in the cultural sphere created the impression that the country would now put into effect a clear *democratic* transition. But the latent ambiguity of the situation soon manifested itself through a series of maneuvers that were intended to postpone the municipal elections planned for November 1980. The worsening of the economic perspectives furnished the background, and the debate at the center of the stage focused on the difficulties that the new parties would encounter in organizing municipal bases according to legal requirements in time to participate in the elections.[21]

At best, only the Democratic Social party (PDS), the party of the Brazilian Democratic movement (PMDB), and the Popular party (PP) would be able to form local directories, according to the requirements of electoral legislation and of new legislation regarding parties, in order to participate in the elections in a majority of the 4,000 Brazilian municipalities. We can therefore speculate that the postponement of the election of 1980 was in reality *contemplated* by the party reform of 1978-1979. In effect, the postponement and the consequent extension for two years of the municipal officeholders (mayors and councilmen) were actually imposed by the government by means of its parliamentary majority against little more than rhetoric on the part of the opposition parties.

Today, we can attribute at least three very serious developments to that measure. First, the more than three years without electoral contests created a political vacuum of considerable proportions. This vacuum created conditions favorable to the advancement of right-wing terrorism, which began with bomb and fire attacks on newsstands in order to keep them from selling leftist publications. Second, the postponement of municipal elections for two years (not for one, as was suggested by many of the opposition leaders) meant that all the elections (except the presidential, which continues to be indirect and took place in 1985) coincided in 1982. That overlap evidently made the elections almost infeasible, leaving the door open to speculation that they might be canceled or that new changes in the rules of the game would be imposed inexorably. Finally, the postponement caused an enormous wearing down of the parties, which for two years had to struggle to organize and adapt to legal parameters that were either too demanding or even indefinite.

It can then be said that the period 1979–1981 was very different from the period 1974–1978 in respect to the dynamics of the political liberalization. The fundamental characteristic of the latter period was that the electoral process lost importance as a focus that could bring together the elements of opposition to the regime. In part, this loss of focus is considered here as a result of the postponement of the elections of 1980 and of the fragmentation of parties. But it also had to do with a reemergence of the difficulties normally encountered by civil and professional groups when they try to unite in a so-called opposition front. Thus, especially during 1981, a division of political activity occurred among the opposition groups, which in their own self-interest turned frequently to the specific problems of each sector.

It was in this context of hesitation and exhaustion that various crises occurred during 1981, and these crises forced the government to extend even further its already over-extended gradualist strategy. The first and most serious began with the failed terrorist attempt that occurred in Rio-Centro, a popular site where an artistic show celebrating May 1 was being held. There were clear indications of the involvement of army officers in that episode, and the official explanation satisfied neither the press nor public opinion. This outcome, it has been affirmed, was one of the principal reasons for the resignation of General Golbery do Couto e Silva (the all-powerful head of the president's civil cabinet). The formalization of the general's resignation in the month of August and his replacement by the jurist João Leitao de Abreu had serious effects on political coordination in the period immediately following. In September, the president of the Republic had to take a temporary leave because of cardiac complications, and during his absence, the parliamentary opposition (with the support of dissidents from the Democratic Social party itself) succeeded in defeating the majority on two projects of vital importance to the government. One of them was a proposal to increase the contribution of wage earners to finance the enormous social security deficit. The other had to do with the so-called *sublegenda* ("sub-heading"), that is, the possibility of each party's endorsing up to three candidates for governor in each state, a tactic by which the government was hoping to accommodate the competing factions within the PDS. With the defeat of this latter proposal, the electoral perspectives of the government for 1982 became even less encouraging.

When General Figueiredo was once again able to assume the duties of the presidency, the reply was not long in coming. On November 25, in a menacing tone, the administration forced its parliamentary majority to begin deliberating the so-called November package, an electoral reform project that would drastically alter the situation, with the intention of "reestablishing equilibrium" between the government and the opposition.

The consequences of the November package should be analyzed on two different levels, the extrinsic and the intrinsic. From the first point of view, it was a discouraging interruption of the optimistic atmosphere that had formed as a result of the presence of a civilian (Vice-President Antonio Aureliano Chaves) in the presidency for the first time since 1964—he had substituted for General Figueiredo during the latter's illness. Intrinsically it was also a *recrudescimento* ("rehardening"), a reaffirmation of the rhetoric of the "revolution of 1964" that indicated once more the unwillingness or incapacity of the government to close the gap that separated it from even the moderate opposition.

With respect to the November proposal itself, its main objective was to impose a total binding of votes at all levels, or in other words, to nullify the votes given to candidates from different parties. With that measure, *all* the parties, including the small ones, were required to present candidates for all offices, including that of governor, in the states in which they aspired to present any candidates. A fragmentation of the opposition front was thus carried to the last consequences. Any and all alliances, even tacit ones, became impossible among the opposition parties, since such alliances would have had as a touchstone the support of the minor parties for candidates of the PMDB or the PP for a candidate on the state level in exchange for their support of candidates from those parties for other offices. The November package thus reinforced the position of the PDS in several states, increasing the effective power of the use of state political machines (through public works and employment concessions) and enhancing the importance of party bases in small municipalities.

The November package destroyed the PP, which, under the leadership of then-Senator Tancredo Neves, tried to reunite itself with the PMDB.

Without doubt, that attempt reduced the excessive advantage that the package had initially conferred on the administration, and it was not by chance that the reunification effort was described by government spokesmen as an attempt at confrontation and radicalization. But it is also certain that that gain, or reduction of disadvantage on the part of the opposition, was equivalent, on a more general level, to another lost opportunity with respect to the more fundamental impasses of the political system. It was as if excessive gradualism had fallen into its own trap. Brazil was once more moving toward an election that was little more than bipartisan, as in fact was verified in 1982. The plebiscitary ghost that the party reform of 1978 had tried to exorcise was back again, but now in a context of sharp recession, growing unemployment, and obvious exhaustion of leadership, which theoretically could have reinstated conditions of effective governability in the country. From this point of view, the optimism generated by the election process of 1982 was hardly more than a brief interlude and rapidly dissipated in the first half of 1983. After the votes were counted and opposition governors were inaugurated in ten states (including São Paulo, Minas Gerais, and Rio de Janeiro), it was clear that the breach remained, and the agreement with the IMF and the negotiation of foreign loans made the government even less willing than before to share control over economic policy with the opposition.

Having conserved its majority in the electoral college, the PDS, although subject to irreversible fragmentation, held to the theory of "acquired right" in choosing the successor to President Figueiredo, despite the clear illegitimacy of the procedures in force. To the institutional crisis that had been latent during the 1970s there was therefore added a crisis of succession; the whole situation drastically increased the risks of a collapse in the conditions necessary to govern the country.

Events in 1985

In the indirect elections of January 1985, thanks to a three-way split in the government party, Tancredo Neves, the candidate of the opposition PMDB, won an absolute majority in the electoral college and assumed the presidency two months later. Unfortunately, he became severely ill after intestinal surgery soon after the election and died on April 21, leaving the presidency to his vice-president, José Sarney. Sarney was in a far weaker position than Neves to carry out a strong economic program, both because of the circumstances of his assumption of power and the fact that he had only recently crossed over from the PDS to the PMDB.

For the first five months of his presidency, economic policy was paralyzed by a fight between ministers inherited from the Neves regime, some of whom believed in a continuation of the orthodox stabilization strategy that had caused a recession in 1983–1984 and others backed a more expansionary policy. Finally, in August 1985, resignations at the Treasury and central bank made it clear that the expansionist group had won out. Efforts to reduce the spiraling budget deficit were relaxed, monetary expansion was increased, real wages were raised, and the fight against inflation was shifted from contraction and recession to a wider use of price controls and lower rates of interest. These policies led to a sharp increase in output, but unfortunately, inflation rates also began to spiral upward. As had happened earlier under Figueiredo, the government did not have a sufficiently strong mandate to impose contractionary spending cuts on the public sector. At the end of 1985, rising inflation, budget deficits, and interest costs suggested that more draconian measures might be necessary in 1986.

Conclusion

The major premise of this chapter is that an orderly slowing of economic growth in the middle of the decade of the 1970s would probably have increased the amount of freedom the Brazilian leaders had to manage the country's external economic adjustment, and thereby reduce the severity of the present recession and its consequences. We then attempted to chart the course actually taken by the Brazilian policymakers, which consisted of following a dangerous program of import substitution and maintaining a high rate of growth. Among the factors that explained that course of action, we initially identified economic reasons in a strict sense, such as high international liquidity during the 1970s and the indivisibility and long terms of maturation of investments made by the Brazilian government. We immediately pointed out the political importance of developmentalism in a country that had been maintaining high growth rates for several decades, frequently transforming them into the backbone of the legitimation process.

In the transition from the Medici to the Geisel period, which corresponds to the initial stages of the political opening, the necessity of sustaining optimism again became imperative. We finally argued that the excessively gradualistic conception of the political liberalization made difficult the formation of alternative bases of support capable of backing a more austere direction for economic policy. Under the Figueiredo administration, those disadvantages of gradualism seemed to have entered a vicious circle of self-sustainment, leading to political decisions that tended to reproduce and amplify the elements of rigidity and hesitation already present in the initial picture.

It is evident that our analysis barely constitutes a first charting of ideas, highly conjectural and no doubt limited. But the result is sufficient to indicate some similarities and differences between our present analysis and previous ones on the subject of the Brazilian experience since 1973. For several years, analysis was a matter, above all, of characterizing the Brazilian regime within the frame of the new authoritarian experiments and of showing that even in the most successful cases (and here the so-called Brazilian miracle is an obligatory memory), the model of economic growth seemed not to have a solution for the persistent inequalities in the distribution of income or for the very large part of the population that still lived at the level of absolute poverty.

This chapter moves toward a conclusion that is at the same time both *more* and *less* pessimistic. It is more so to the extent that the international crisis and the exhaustion of the growth-with-debt strategy led Brazil to its present recession and the certainty that it will take many years to again reach the employment level reached in 1980. The picture is less pessimistic, however, if we take into account the facts that the liberalization process has shown itself capable of survival under extremely adverse economic conditions and that its continuity, despite its ambiguity and excessive gradualism, is gradually revitalizing the political aspects of society.

The unprecedented volume of foreign debt should not cause us to overlook the fact that the domestic problems, namely, the eradication of absolute poverty and the reduction of social and interregional inequalities, are not less gigantic. To confront them without falling back into conditions of political tyranny, it is evidently indispensable that Brazil have a plurality of institutional arrangements capable of continuously sustaining the pressures and claims of society. On this point, at least, there is hope that the country can prevail over the many failures since 1964.

Notes

This paper was translated by Doris C. Da Rosa and edited by Samuel A. Morley.

1. The thirteen semi-industrialized countries whose data are included in Table 7.1 are Argentina, Brazil, Colombia, Egypt, Israel, Mexico, the Philippines, Portugal, Singapore, South Korea, Turkey, Uruguay, and Yugoslavia. Note that all of these, including Mexico, were petroleum importers in the period under discussion. For facts about the import structure of these countries, see World Bank (1981:146–153).

2. Recourse to foreign debt as one of the responses to the first petroleum shock was not, evidently, an exclusive characteristic of Brazil. The semi-industrialized

countries, in a general way, made use of bank loans at the beginning of the period 1974–1978. According to the data of the World Bank, the percentage of private creditors in the composition of the foreign debt (public and guaranteed by the government) increased 27 percent between 1972 and 1978 in those nations. During the same period, interest and amortization on the debt as a percentage of exports of goods and services rose from 9 percent to 15 percent in that group of countries. Nevertheless, for the majority of the semi-industrialized petroleum importing countries, the utilization of the international financial market was seen as a temporary way to accommodate to exchange difficulties until structural adjustments in the economy could be promoted to confront the external shocks. It is relevant also to point out that in 1973–1974, Brazil already held first place in the absolute volume of its foreign debt compared to all the other petroleum importing countries because of the *growth with debt* strategy that had been implemented since 1968.

3. For example, the share of value of investments approved by the Council of Industrial Development (CDI) in gross fixed capital formation in the economy increased appreciably during this period. This share rose from 7.4 percent in the early 1970s to 11.8 percent in the period 1976–1978 according to statistics presented in Malan and Bonelli (1983). Note that the majority of the applications approved by the CDI were destined for projects in the capital goods and basic input sectors.

4. Although created on October 29, 1979, through decree No. 84,128, the SEST initiated its activities of elaboration and supervision of state enterprise budgets in 1980. Therefore, it was only after 1981 that it could present a more comprehensive budget for state enterprises, federal as well as state run (the public electric utilities, for example).

5. As a dramatic example of how the credit markets functioned under conditions of incomplete information, debtors who were disposed to pay higher rates of interest were considered very poor risks and were then excluded entirely from the loan market.

6. Very illustrative of this attitude are the words of the then-president of the central bank, Carlos G. Langoni, in a speech to New York bankers on December 20, 1982, at the signing of the bank loan program for Brazil: "The basic idea was that a voluntary adjustment put into practice as soon as possible would be more effective from the economic point of view and less burdensome from the social standpoint than a compulsory adjustment made at a later time, which had unfortunately been the procedure of many countries" (see Langoni 1982).

7. In June 1982, the Brazilian bank debt was approaching $55.3 billion, of which 37 percent, or $20.5 billion, was owed to U.S. banks. Of this last figure, 60 percent, or $12.3 billion, consisted of obligations with the nine major U.S. banks (*World Financial Markets*).

8. "The fundamental problem was the superimposition, beginning in 1978, of the new petroleum shock on the financial shock represented by the foreign interest rates in real terms. The immediate consequence was the impossibility of continuing with the strategy of growth with debt at growing rates, making necessary the transmission of those fiscal and financial limitations to the domestic economy with greater intensity. In this context, the slowing down of the rate of growth, especially in the industrial sector, became inevitable, and its intensity and duration will be conditioned by the ability to overcome the external imbalances" (Langoni 1981:4).

9. The principal source for the analysis of the beginnings of the process of *distensão* are dos Santos (1978), Figueiredo and Cheibub (1982), and Cruz and Martins (1983).

10. We are not referring here to the proverbial characterization of the Brazilian state according to models of "corporative" or "patrimonial" bureaucratic domination, but rather to the more tangible fact that until 1983, no political figure succeeded in exerting pressure against any aspect of economic policy through the conventional means of representation, notably Congress and the political parties.

11. Cruz and Martins (1983).

12. We thank Roberto Macedo for suggesting the "neo-Bismarckian" analysis or profile of General Ernesto Geisel. For a substantial journalistic treatment of Geisel's presidency, see do Góes (1978).

13. In this also Geisel made a point of appearing superior and pedantic: He gave to the elitism of the past a more elaborate intellectual formulation, postulating that policy should first begin with economic growth, with social welfare to follow afterward, the latter being the precondition of a healthy democratic regime. Rather than purely and simply vilifying partisan politics, he looked upon them as desirable and even praised them, but with the condition that they could only be authentic when the country had reached a high level of development and had an electorate made up of aware, rational, and socially oriented citizens (Lamounier 1981:230).

14. The term "black hole" was used on more than one occasion by the architect of the distension, General Golbery do Couta e Silva, himself. In his inauguration speech, General Geisel also affirmed that the perfecting of the regime not only depended on the will of the chief executive but required more sincere and effective collaboration from other national groups (Cruz and Martins 1983:46). Following the same line of reasoning, Celso Lafer referred to the new importance of *voice* (in Albert Hirschman's sense), which increased the rulers' ability to learn, making them aware that a reduction of autocracy was a condition for their continuing as viable political figures (IDESP 1983).

15. For the elections of 1974, see Lamounier and Cardoso (1975). Referring to the same event, Cruz and Martins (1983) say the following: "Sure of victory, Geisel invested heavily in those elections, which should have played a crucial role in the accomplishment of his program: With popular support for the 'work of the Revolution' confirmed in the ballot boxes, the following year would be dedicated to the task of institutionalizing the regime with the expected reforms. But for that to occur, these could not be elections like the others (1970 and 1972), undermined in their legitimacy by the omnipresence of censorship and by violent measures of intimidation. . . . It was necessary for the opposition to become fully involved in the contest and, given the guaranties offered, to voluntarily accept its future defeat" (Cruz and Martins 1983:49).

16. On the role of the press during that period, see Duarte (1983). Along the same lines, F. H. Cardoso alludes to the reinvention of civil society as a political force by the communications media, citing as an example the choice of the most representative entrepreneurs by the journal *Gazeta mercantil*, starting in 1977 (Cardoso 1983).

17. See Lamounier (1979:9); emphasis in original. In a similar vein, see the analysis of F. H. Cardoso (1983). The meaning of the entrepreneurial pressures

cannot be grasped without explicit reference to the fact that the Geisel government itself (since 1974, although not continuously) had thrown out the subject of "distension" for debate. When, starting in 1976–1977, the entrepreneurial sector came forward to join the debate on liberalization, these discussions already constituted the background of Brazilian policy. The voice of the industrial entrepreneurs was added to this chorus. If this group did not take the initiative, it managed to have an effect on the civil society movement. The press itself, to strengthen the clamor for liberalization, "used" the entrepreneurial leadership (Cardoso 1983:21).

18. Along these lines, see the comments of Celso Martone: "This large scale anti-cyclical policy (in reaction to the first petroleum shock) developed industries characterized by long maturation periods, high capital intensity, and high import coefficients, at least in the initial phase, and directly competed, or provoked competition, for precisely those resources that were scarcest in that period— foreign currency, fiscal capital, qualified labor, etc." (Montone 1981:20–21).

19. See, on these points, the interesting analysis of dos Santos: "Apparently the first actions of the Geisel administration hid the intention to make serious changes in the model. . . . A clarification from the government on this crucial point was becoming necessary, and continued lack of clarification of what it really intended to do finally caused a growing lack of confidence in one of the partners of the civil coalition—the private interests, national and international—meanwhile the uncertainty and the consequent progressive paralysis of the various cliques that together made up the other partner—i.e., the balkanized state bureaucracy— was growing" (dos Santos 1978:125–126).

20. In this section, we reproduce some portions of Lamounier (1982).

21. With the party reform approved at the end of 1979 by the government majority, there were now six new parties: (1) the Partido Democrático Social (PDS, Democratic Social party), the one in power and successor to the extinct ARENA; (2) the Partido do Movimento Democrático Brasileiro (PMDB, party of the Brazilian Democratic movement), successor to the former MDB, whose initials it retained through the clever strategy of adding the "P" to them since the new legislation required that all parties have the word "party" in their names; (3) the Partido Popular (PP, Popular party), which is said to have been created by Minister Petronio Portella, strategist (together with General Golbery do Couto e Silva) of the distension. It is said that Portella even gave the party the two Ps of his name. This creation represented an attempt to hold the liberal center together, with significant participation on the part of the entrepreneurial sector, in a party that also defined itself as the opposition to the regime in power but obviously was preparing for the role of a dependable partner in a future coalition government. (4) The Partido dos Trabalhadores (PT, Workers' party) was strongly concentrated in the person of Lula (José Ignacio da Silva) and in the so-called *novo sindicalismo* ("new syndicalism") of the São Paulo metropolitan area. It was formed with a show of extreme lack of confidence in all other parties. Finally, (5) and (6), two other parties were formed that contested the use of the old initials PTB (Partido Trabalhista Brasileiro), actually or supposedly the depository of the laborite symbolism of Getulio Vargas. The use of the initials finally rested in the hands of

Ivete Vargas, using the influence and inspiration of the ruling group, as all indications suggest. This supposition was confirmed by the negotiations of this party with the government after the 1982 elections. The Partido Democrático Trabalista (PDT, Democratic Workers party) originated with Leonel Brizola's refusal to share his political plan, which was oriented toward European-style democratic socialism, or the initials PTB with Ivete Vargas's groups.

References

Bacha, Edmar L., and Diaz-Alejandro, Carlos F. 1981. "Mercados financeiros internacionais: Uma Perspectiva Latino-Americano." *Estudos econômicos* 2, no. 3.

Bresser Pereira, Luis Carlos. 1978. *O Colapso de uma aliança de classes.* São Paulo: Editora Brasiliense.

Cardoso, Fernando Henrique. 1983. "O Papel dos empresarios no processo de transição." *Revista dados* 26, no. 1.

Central Bank of Brazil. n.d. *Boletím.*

Choques Externos e Respostas de Política Econômica no Brasil—Primeiro Choque do Petróleo. 1981. Estudos Especiais IBRE no. 3. Rio de Janeiro: Fundacão Getúlio Vargas.

Conjuntura Econômica. n.d. Rio de Janeiro: Fundacão Getúlio Vargas.

Cruz, Sebastião C. Velasco e, and Martins, Carlos Estevam. 1983. "De Castello a Figueiredo: Uma Incursão no pré-história da Abertura." In *Sociedade e política no Brasil pos-64,* ed. Bernardo Sorj and Maria Herminia Tavares de Almeida. São Paulo: Editora Brasiliense.

de Souza, Amaury, and Lamounier, Bolivar. 1981. "Governo e sindicatos no Brasil: A Perspectiva dos anos 80." *Revista dados* 24, no. 2.

do Góes, Wálder. 1978. *O Brasil do General Geisel.* Rio de Janeiro: Nova Fronteira.

Dornbusch, Rudiger. 1983. "A Stabilization Program in Brazil." Mimeograph.

dos Santos, Wanderley Guilherme. 1978. *Poder e política: Cronica do autoritarismo brasileiro.* Rio de Janeiro: Editora Forense Universitaria.

Duarte, Celina R. 1983. "Imprensa e redemocratização no Brasil." *Revista dados* 26, no. 2.

Economic Report of the President. 1983. Washington, D.C.: Government Printing office.

Figueiredo, Marcus Faria, and Cheibub, José Antonio Borges. 1982. "A Abertura política de 1973 a 1981: Inventario de um debate." *BIB Boletim informativo e bibliográfico de ciencias sociais* (Rio de Janeiro), no. 14.

IDESP. 1983. "O Sistema político brasileiro hoje: Tendências e perspectivas." *Textos,* no. 1.

Lamounier, Bolivar. 1979. "Notes on the Study of Redemocratization." Working Paper no. 58. Washington, D.C.: Wilson Center.

———. 1981. "Representação politica: A Importancia de certos formalismos." In *Direito, Cidadania, e Participação,* ed. Bolivar Lamounier, Francisco Weffort, and Maria Vitória Benevides. São Paulo: T. A. Queiroz Editora.

———. 1982. "As Eleições de 1982 e a abertura política em perspectiva." In *Brazil em perspectiva: Dilemas da abertura política*, ed. Hélgio Trindade. Porto Alegre, Brazil: Editora Sulina.

Lamounier, Bolivar, and Cardoso, Fernando Henrique, eds. 1975. *Os Partidos e as eleições no Brasil*. Rio de Janeiro: Paz e Terra.

Lamounier, Bolivar, and Faria, José Eduardo, eds. 1981. *O Futuro da aberturas: Um Debate*. São Paulo: Cortez Editora.

Langoni, Carlos G. 1981. "A Estrategia de ajustamento de setor externo." Lecture presented at the seminar Perspectivas de Economia Mundial in the headquarters of the Central Bank of Brazil in Brasília. *Jornal do Brasil*. September 27: 4 (Caderno Especial).

———. 1982. Speech to New York bankers. *Jornal da tarde*, December 24.

Malan, Pedro S., and Bonelli, Regis. 1983. *Crescimento econômico, industrialização e balanco de pagamentos: O Brasil dos anos 70 aos anos 80*. Rio de Janeiro: IPEA, IPES.

Martone, Celso. 1981. "Comments." In *O Futuro da abertura: Um Debate*, ed. Bolivar Lamounier and José Eduardo Faria. São Paulo: Cortex Editora.

Moura, Alkimar R. 1981. *A Politica cambial e comercial no periodo 1974–1980*. Núcleo de Pesquisas e Publicações, Relatorio de Pesquisa no. 16. São Paulo: Fundacão Getúlio Vargas.

Nogueira Baptista, Paulo, Jr. 1983. *Mito e realidade da divida externa brasileira*. Rio de Janeiro: Paz e Terra.

World Bank. 1981. *World Development Report*. New York: Oxford University Press.

World Financial Markets. n.d. Morgan Guaranty Trust Company.

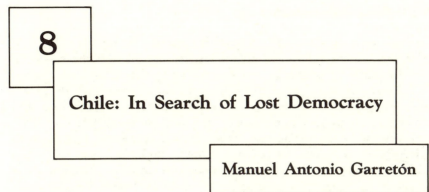

8

Chile: In Search of Lost Democracy

Manuel Antonio Garretón

In recent years, there has been a decline of authoritarian or military regimes in the Southern Cone, a phenomenon accompanied by a total failure of these regimes to solve the fundamental problems of their societies as well as to resolve the prolonged crisis of hegemony that has characterized the Southern Cone nations since the collapse of the oligarchic state.[1] In this context of democratic renewal, the Chilean case stands out: Historically one of the more stable democracies on the continent, it is now experiencing a relatively significant delay in terms of ending its military dictatorship and reestablishing democracy. A cruel paradox appears to be operating in which conditions that helped make democracy possible in Chile are now factors that make an exit from dictatorship more problematic.

To avoid the temptations of the "crystal ball" or of wishful thinking, an analysis of the recovery or rebuilding of democracy in Chile should be undertaken from three perspectives. First, what conditions or features were characteristic of Chilean democracy in this century? Second, what caused the collapse of that democracy? Third, what sociopolitical transformations have occurred under the military regime, and what would be the possible scenario of a transition? I shall try to answer these three questions in broad and schematic terms.

The Chilean Political System

In broad strokes, the political system in effect until 1973 possessed the following general characteristics:

1. Each democratic regime was accompanied by a process of capitalist modernization and industrialization known as the development model of growth via the internal market, in which the state played a central role.

To the memory of René Zavaleta.

There was also a process of "substantive democratization," which led to a continuous incorporation of different social groups into the economic life of the country, political participation, and sociocultural advantages. Political democracy and substantive democratization were both restricted. Peasant and marginal urban sectors were excluded until the 1960s, and the Communist party was politically excluded between 1947 and 1958. Also, until the 1960s only a third of the population effectively participated in the political-electoral life of the country, and the organized urban popular sectors were in a clearly subordinate position. Despite these limitations, the political system offered "visibility" for the expectations of the different social groups, thereby reducing antisystem tendencies.[2]

2. The presence of the state as the principal focus of social demands and claims and as a vehicle to satisfy popular expectations favored a particular type of relationship between the state and society that was characterized by the relevance of the party system. The party system served as the main arena for the integration of social groups and for the mediation of the demands of organized social groups. On the one hand, the political parties were essentially structured on the national level (right, center, and left) before the masses were incorporated into the political and social arena. As a result, the newly incorporated groups found clearly established channels for participation. New participants could thus be brought in without causing serious institutional disruptions, which provided further stability to the party system.

On the other hand, to the extent that opportunities to influence the state depended on the degree of organization and social weight of each sector, the type of organization most likely to succeed was one that linked partisan political leadership to the representation of a social base. The student movement, the labor movement, and the peasant and mass organizations of the 1960s are all examples of this particular overlapping of party and social bases. Thus, for a party to effectively articulate, channel, mediate, and represent the demands of a social group, there had to be a highly politicized, party-linked citizenry. The counterpart to this requirement was a weak and dependent role for the other organizations of civil society. This kind of articulation between social bases and a party system, which favors a particular kind of social integration, constituted the essence of the Chilean political system, the backbone of Chilean society.

3. In a society that is characterized by a dependent capitalist industrialization, compatible up to a point with an unequal and conflictive process of democratization, and in which the state plays a central role in the development process, the political system becomes the arena or principal battlefield of the class struggle. The social classes are thus principally political forces and have only a weak structure at the level

of civil society. This "state of compromise" was characterized in Chile by the fact that, in spite of the country's predominantly capitalist character, no particular social class was capable of imposing its hegemony over the others; the system succeeded, although in an asymmetrical fashion, in integrating the interests of the dominant classes, the middle classes, and, in a subordinate role, the organized working class. The exclusion of other sectors such as the peasantry until the 1960s can be explained by the fact that the compromise rested on the intangibility of the agrarian system and the immutability of the social structure of the hacienda or latifundio—in other words, on the absence of agrarian reform. This fact, combined with the foreign ownership of the country's basic resource, copper, characterized what has been called the "incomplete reformism" that prevailed until the 1960s (see Moulián 1982).

The dominant classes were a fusion of industrial, financial, commercial, and agrarian interests, and there were no sharp distinctions between the modern and traditional sectors on political or ideological issues. Given the unchanged system of land ownership, the dominant classes never generated an effective program of modernization. Instead, they devoted their energies to defending their privileges and to obtaining benefits from the state. All projects for modernization within the capitalist framework came from groups that represented the middle classes, never from the dominant capitalist sectors. One weakness of the latter sectors is reflected by the fact that their political representation came from the right, the historic Liberal and Conservative parties. The right governed the country only from 1958 to 1964; most of the time it resigned itself to promoting defensive policies in Congress and to wielding its influence on the political center, the Radical party.

The so-called middle classes were composed of heterogeneous groups united by a common link to the state and to the educational system. During the long period from the 1930s to the 1960s, they were identified with the process of state expansion and the democratization of the system, viewing these changes as the guarantor of their continued growth and mobility. They played a progressive role in the 1930s, but the fact that they became the major beneficiaries of the system made them increasingly more conservative and inclined to defend a social order that appeared threatened by the emergence of the popular sectors. Representation of the middle classes was undertaken by the political center, principally the Radical party. Playing a crucial role until the 1960s, this organization was a pragmatic and somewhat pendular political force, which led to great flexibility in dealing with crises.

The urban popular classes—industrial and mining—were included ambiguously in the political system. Their participation was of a fragmented and subordinated character, and they were able to gain only minimal conditions of subsistence. They achieved political expression mainly through two parties. One was the Socialist party, more a popular than a working-class party and not very homogeneous. Although hampered by a lack of organizational unity, it was characterized by a rich and diversified ideological base. The other was the Communist party, fundamentally a workers' party. Socially and ideologically homogeneous, this party was affiliated with the international communist movement and Marxist orthodoxy. These two parties had an ambivalent relationship to the political system: They were participants in it, not antisystem forces, but at the same time, they supported and developed projects for a radical change of the social system.

4. The interaction between the state and society and especially the prominent role of the political parties favored the strengthening of a relatively large and ideologically diverse political class that guaranteed the normal operation of political and social institutions on the national level. Furthermore, the evolving institutional system resulted in a continuous process of negotiation and the adoption of strategies for gradual change in order to avoid threatening the prevailing balance of interests. All of these characteristics permitted the utilization of agreed-upon formulas to resolve conflicts on the institutional level, avoiding any appeals for the intervention of external elements such as the armed forces.

With respect to the armed forces, the politicians maintained an attitude of distance and distrust in the absence of a clear policy. This situation led to a "cloistering" of the armed forces, which had little interaction with the civil sector, and to the development of a military ideology that rested on professionalism and constitutionalism. This ideology, in turn, generated within the armed forces a high level of internal cohesion and hierarchical legitimacy. Finally, these developments led to a process of military modernization and ideological socialization that was dependent on U.S. hegemony in Latin America after World War II (on the armed forces, see Varas 1980).

The Crisis of the Political System

The political system in Chile underwent a series of changes in the 1960s. In certain respects, these transformations would become more pronounced in the period 1970–1973.

Phase One: 1960s

According to the perception of the principal political participants, the compatibility between the capitalist system of development and the process of substantive democratization appeared to be coming to an end. The massive incorporation of new sectors into the political arena between 1958 and 1964 suggested the transition to a more inclusive democracy and an increasing legitimization of views calling for social change. The political right seemed to have lost legitimacy following its first direct government after several decades (the presidential term of Jorge Alessandri Rodriguez [1958-1964]), and in the political center a new political force replaced the Radical party. This was the Christian Democratic party, which defined itself in highly ideological terms by a program that sought profound changes in the capitalist system. This new force distanced itself as much from the political right, which it characterized as reactionary, as from the left, which it accused of being classist and supportive of a socialist program that was lacking in originality as an alternative to the Soviet model. The inability of the political right to offer its own alternative to meet the threat of a leftist victory in the presidential elections of 1964 led it to support the successful Christian Democratic candidate, Eduardo Frei Montalva (1964-1970).[3]

The Christian Democrats' plan was to complete modernization in two critical areas: transform agrarian relationships by destroying the latifundio system (agrarian reform) and recover the country's basic wealth by "Chileanizing" the copper industry (as the process of seminationalization was called). This two-pronged modernization project also portended a forward leap in industrialization through an important flow of foreign capital, with which a "modern bourgeoisie" was supposed to be associated, and through expansion of internal and external markets. But this program wasn't simply a modernization project, for its advocates also wanted it to be consistent with a broadening and a deepening of the process of substantive democratization, especially with reference to the peasant and marginal urban groups. In other words, it was an attempt to end the exclusions that had characterized the state of compromise until that time and to complete the process of modernization the state had not yet accomplished. These goals required changing the key participants of the compromise, sacrificing the interests of the landowning classes, and developing as a counterbalance the interests of a modern national bour-geoisie associated with the state and the interests of the middle sectors. They also meant incorporating the interests of the peasants and the marginal urban groups and neutralizing the sectors of the organized working class that expressed themselves via the left.[4]

It is now clear that the Christian Democrats introduced a relative rigidification into the political party spectrum and contributed to its polarization. On the one hand, their organizational style and political discourse, with its messianic content and inflexible tone, would prevent their playing the classical pendular role of a political center, which establishes alliances with either side of the political spectrum to obtain the majority necessary to prevent accelerating crises. In this sense, the Christian Democratic party would be a "center" that acted very differently from the Radical party, and the government during the Frei period was an illustration of this tendency toward inflexibility. On the other hand, the fact that one of the basic pillars of the party's political plan was agrarian reform meant that for the first time, the intricate web that had maintained the state of compromise was being threatened. This reform could not be carried out without alienating the entire capitalist class, which saw in such action the destruction of the principle of private property in the hands of an all-powerful and arbitrary state. The fluid bonds joining different sectors of the capitalist class coalesced into a unified reaction against the government.

With agrarian reform and peasant unionization, an entire economic, social, cultural, and political world was perceived as collapsing. This belief stimulated the reorganization of the right, which came together in the National party to develop a rhetoric and a program that were now more nationalistic, more authoritarian, and less democratic. This party incorporated into its ruling elite elements that came from nationalistic groups, to the detriment of the liberal-conservative leadership.

The Christian Democrats also became isolated from the left, with which they were unable to make the agreements necessary to bring about great changes. Furthermore, the Christian Democrats did not succeed in "stealing the left's show," as they had originally aspired, for the left radicalized its positions, denounced the capitalist and limited character of what it called "Christian Democratic reformism," and maintained its influence on that part of the urban industrial proletariat that had not been co-opted by the Christian Democrats' project. This radicalization of the left occurred in an ideological climate that was very conducive to such developments. The climate included the impact of the Cuban Revolution and the wave of reformism unleashed by the U.S. government (Alliance for Progress) to neutralize that impact, as well as the Christian Democrats' rhetoric of transformation and the bogging down of their program halfway through the presidential term.

There were two principal changes on the left in the decade of the 1960s: the introduction into its traditional components, the Socialist and Communist parties, of radicalized groups that originated from the center, the Radical party, the Movement for Unitary Popular Action (comprising dissident Christian Democrats), and later the Christian left and the unification of all these components behind a classic Marxist-Leninist vision. Although accepting the idea of a "peaceful road" for Chile, that vision included a plan for the transition to socialism as the only way to overcome capitalist underdevelopment in the framework of bourgeois democracy.

Thus, the backbone of Chilean society—i.e., the articulation of relationships between the state and civil society provided by the overlapping of the party system and social organizations—underwent significant changes in the 1960s. On the one hand, the country's "social base" was modified and extended by the inclusion of the peasantry and marginal urban sectors and with the attainment of a mass democracy. On the other hand, the state significantly enlarged its role as an agent of development and change and of social redistribution of resources. Finally, between the social base and the state, the party system underwent a process of "tripolarization," with a reunified right swinging toward undemocratic, more-authoritarian positions to preserve capitalism in crisis; a rigid political center, which was unable to form alliances and was as isolated from the right as from the left; and a left that, while maintaining its participation in the democratic process, politically and ideologically radicalized its project to replace capitalism.

Two fundamental elements that had maintained the political system for decades were altered during this period. First, the change in the agrarian social structure radicalized authoritarian positions on the right, pushing the latter toward encouraging the breakdown of the democratic system. Second, there was a growing tendency toward the separation of the middle and popular classes, the two sectors that together, had made politically feasible the compatibility between political democracy and a process of more general democratization. This separation was expressed at the party level in exclusive platforms for change from the center and the left and in the loss of flexibility in the system to handle crises as the tripolarization developed.

Phase Two: 1970–1973

In some ways, the period 1970–1973 saw an intensification of certain features of the political system that had appeared in the 1960s. At the beginning of the 1970s, Chilean society seemed to be facing a historical choice between a deepening of capitalism, which would require paralyzing or reversing democratic tendencies that created demands on the state and on capital accumulation, and an intensification of democratization, which would require altering the existing pattern of capitalist development. This choice appeared in the context of a crisis of legitimacy of the capitalist model and of a relative disintegration of the state of compromise—however, the legitimacy of the democratic regime as a place for the resolution of conflicts remained unchallenged. In this framework, the triumph of the leftist coalition, the Popular Unity, and of Salvador Allende Gossens in the presidential election of 1970 signified the beginning of a process that reflected the second choice.[5]

The core of the Popular Unity's program was the expropriation of the monopolistic sector of the economy by the state in order to redirect any surplus toward another model of development, the completion of agrarian reform and the nationalization of resources accompanied by a vast program of redistribution. The project could be defined as one of "noncapitalist democratization," inasmuch as the theoretical and ideological tradition of the left designated it as a "transition to socialism." From its inception, elements of the private sector in Chile, the public sector in the United States, and groups on the Chilean political right, considering their interests affected, attempted the overthrow of Allende by both legal means and insurrectional tactics. Initially, these attempts did not find support in Chile on the part of the middle class, the political center, or the armed forces. The legitimacy of the democratic regime led the first two groups to seek to neutralize the Allende government's program, forcing it to moderate the pace and content of the intended transformations in order to capitalize on its weakening in the middle term. With respect to the armed forces, regime legitimacy led them to accept their role as "guarantors" of the constitution. Thus, the delegitimization of the political regime was critical if the strategy of overthrow was to take precedence over that of neutralization. To that end, it was necessary to generate in the middle class a perception of catastrophic crisis that seemed to pose a threat to their existence. The right devoted all of its efforts toward achieving this end, using a variety of tactics.

As far as the Popular Unity coalition was concerned, its revolutionary rhetoric, which was directed almost exclusively to the working class, and its strategy of expropriations, which was perfectly legal although threatening to the traditional principles of negotiation and gradualism in that it was not conducted through Congress, had the effect of alienating the middle classes. These sectors, along with the political center, were drawn into a strategy of regime overthrow. Ideological radicalization, polarization in all aspects of political and social life, the use of boycott and terrorism by the right, and the Popular Unity government's intransigent pursuit of its program of change were eroding the legitimacy of the consensual mechanisms of conflict resolution. The armed forces, which in October 1972 had taken the political position of supporting the constitutional government, increasingly found conditions favorable for their autonomous intervention, which implied not only the overthrow of Allende but also the destruction of the entire political system that had developed during several decades. Having no clear political goal beyond a consensus that the existing situation had to end and a self-defined role as "saviors of the nation in crisis," the military regime that followed the overthrow of democracy in September 1973 came to be defined primarily by the brutality of its intervention, its hierarchical cohesion, and its activation of a latent ideology of national security.

In terms of the principal features of the political system that was described at the beginning of this chapter, the period between 1970 and 1973 witnessed, on the one hand, an overflowing of traditional party channels by the social base (producer associations with respect to the right, middle-sector associations and organizations with respect to the Christian Democrats, and new popular associations with respect to the left). On the other hand, a clear break emerged between the middle and lower sectors, a division expressed by the alignment of the political center with the strategy of overthrowing the regime and of a right that had abandoned all democratic pretense and was relying on the breakdown of the system to rescue its dominant class position. Finally, there was a considerable extension of state activity, but simultaneously, there was also a growing fragmentation and autonomy of its components, especially the armed forces.

In summary, the following factors provided a framework for the tasks the military regime would assume: a process of disintegration of the capitalist system; state fragmentation; a loss of legitimacy of the political mechanism of conflict resolution; and an extreme polarization of society characterized by the active organization and mobilization of the masses as well as of the middle and ruling classes. The tasks of the new regime would be, therefore, nothing less than the restructuring and reorientation of the capitalist system and the disarticulation of the existing mechanisms of social and political organization—which were to be replaced by a national military-state system of control and repression.

The Military Political System and the Problems of Transition to Democracy

The Military Political System

The military regime that came to power after Allende's overthrow in 1973 and resolved the political crisis in favor of the capitalist bloc did more than put an end to the democratic system and to processes of substantive democratization; that is to say, the new regime not only reacted against the preceding order but also tried to reconstruct a new social and political order based on a development scheme that was profoundly contradictory to that which had characterized the country until 1973. From the beginning, the military government was marked by a growing personalization that unified the political leadership with the head of the institutional hierarchy of the armed forces (General Augusto

Pinochet Ugarte). It was also characterized by the elimination of all forms of mediation and representation that had been instituted during the democratic period. This elimination was accomplished by means of numerous forms of repression that have been continuously in effect during the regime's rule.

The first phase of the military regime (until 1976 or 1977) was characterized by unrestricted repression, the consolidation of personal power by General Pinochet, and the formation of a ruling government nucleus that comprised the personalized military leadership and a team of technocrats (the "Chicago boys"). Along with some intellectual groups, these technocrats had the responsibility of providing the regime with an ideological and a programmatic content, which the armed forces were unable to do since they had no political goal other than to put an end to the preceding political developments.

During the second phase (1976/1977–1981/1982), the military regime was to lay out its plan of social transformation without abandoning the repressive dimension. The plan consisted of an attempt to restructure capitalism, although the leadership was not to be provided by the capitalist class as such, owing to its traditional hegemonic weakness. This time, the project of capitalist transformation came from the technocratic sector, which relied upon all the coercive resources of the state. It was a model of outward development characterized by an unrestricted opening of the economy, a reduction in the role of the state, a replacement of the latter by the private sector of the economy, and the expansion of market mechanisms (see Moulián and Vergara 1980). The apparent initial success of this economic model, measured by its own parameters, was due to the flow of foreign capital, which was devoted to speculation and luxury consumption, not productive investment. At the level of societal organization, the leaders sought to end the redistributive role of the state, to extend the logic of the market to all spheres of civil society, and to break up and weaken social demands. This was the "modernizations phase," according to official terminology, and it was expressed in reforms of territorial organization, health and public welfare, education, and professional and interest associations.

The culmination of this phase was the political institutionalization expressed in the new constitution approved by the plebiscite in 1980. In that constitution, two political "models" are consecrated. The first involves the extension of the military regime for nine years and the possibility of prolonging it for another eight years. The military regime, having established the position of authority defined for it after the coup of 1973, would then ensure that a second political model came into play. This second "model," as established by the constitution of 1980, would conform to the special characteristics of an authoritarian but not necessarily a military regime: a political arena with restricted representation, exclusion of certain social and political groups, and an armed forces' power of guardianship or veto, among others.

Beginning in 1981 or 1982, the military regime entered a third phase, which can be described as one of recurrent crises initiated by a total failure of the economic model (see Vega 1984). As a result, the sociopolitical plan and the effort to create a new social order to replace the previous societal backbone were left without an economic base. The prominent features of this period have been the disintegration of the ruling group in the government, the isolation of Pinochet, the splintering of support from civilian society, the adoption of erratic and contradictory emergency policies under the prevailing model, a renewed wave of repression, and a reactivation of the opposition. Having failed in its attempt to restructure capitalism and create a new articulation between the state and civil society, the rationale of the regime has become one of mere survival in terms of the time periods and mechanisms imposed by the constitution. In this effort, the regime can rely upon the institutional cohesion of the armed forces, the internal legitimacy provided by the constitutional framework, the ambiguity of a political right that is still reorganizing itself with regard to its loyalty to democracy, and Pinochet's stubborn will to remain in power regardless of the means.

The economic crisis affected the middle sectors to such an extent that they distanced themselves from the regime. This segregation provided an opportunity for the popular sectors and their political associations to express their discontent with the regime during the national protests that erupted in the middle of 1983. For the first time in many years, the middle and popular groups joined forces under the same political banner. This situation forced Pinochet to try to rebuild his fragmented support bloc and to encapsulate or channel the opposition, efforts that gave rise to the so-called political opening. By the end of 1984, however, neither objective had been met, and the government declared a state of siege and canceled the "opening." From the point of view of the military regime, a combination of such "openings" and "closings" is probable in the future, depending on the regime's assessment of its survival needs in the context of the 1980 constitution.

Opposition to the Regime

In the first phase (1973 to 1976 or 1977), opposition to the military regime consisted almost solely of the sector overthrown in the coup, the left. Most of the repression was directed against this sector, whose principal oppositional goal was to protect the lives of its members and to maintain its organizational apparatus.[6] During this phase, the Catholic church filled the existing political vacuum. It was within the church that the defense of the persecuted was organized and sociopolitical organization was rebuilt. At the same time, the church was the principal actor opposing the power of the military state until 1983.[7]

By the time the second phase began, the Christian Democrats had already aligned themselves with the opposition. The predominant themes were unity of opposition and social opposition to the sectorial changes of the regime, especially in the labor and union areas. In the plebiscite of 1980, an opposition bloc was active although there were disagreements regarding which tactics should be employed. From 1980 until mid-1983, a process of an organic reconstitution of the political parties and of a precarious rearticulation between them and social and professional organizations developed. In this period, also, there began to be talk of the end of the military regime, or more specifically of its overthrow, with the Communist party leaning toward a more insurrectional (violent) line.

The national protests, which were initially headed by the labor organizations (although with some participation on the part of political leaders), forced the government into an erratic and a reversible "opening." This action led to the eruption of political opposition and the formation of large political blocs. This organic and partisan activity produced the first widening of the "social world" of the protests, which had previously been concentrated among the youth in the marginal urban classes.

On the other hand, the perception of an imminent fall of the regime relieved the opposition of the task of formulating a precise consensual formula for a transition to democracy. This task was replaced by implicit schemes for a social mobilization that would impel the armed forces to depose Pinochet and to negotiate with the civilians or a social mobilization that would provoke a collapse of the military regime and replace it with a provisional opposition government. There were also formulas that took for granted the departure of Pinochet, and a kind of mythologizing of "social mobilization," which attributed to such a movement the role of a panacea for all problems and assigning to it the power to overthrow the regime, which it could not possibly have done. Instead, what occurred was that as the mobilization called for a maximalist goal (the end of the dictatorship) it did not have the capabilities to reach and because any intermediate political objectives related to that goal were lacking, the movement weakened and was reduced to its militant base. The broad social spectrum of the opposition did not succeed in becoming an effective political force.

Structural Transformations

From the perspective of an articulation between the state and civil society, the regime's effort to create a new "backbone" failed. However, this fact does not mean that important transformations did not occur. The first of these was the disappearance of channels for processing societal demands as the relationship between the political party structure and the state was broken. A second was the partial disruption and precarious reconstruction of the relationship between the party-based political structure and the social base. As for the state, its role as an agent for development and redistribution was significantly reduced, and its power to coerce and repress was greatly increased (see Vergara 1980).

Regarding the social base, two significant changes took place. First, there was a reduction and an atomization of the structural bases of many social actors (industry, state apparatus, agrarian structure, educational system, etc.). The significant increase in the number of "independent" workers (see Martinez and Tironi 1983) reinforced the atomized quality of society. The result was a weakening of the role of previous social actors with no new ones to take their place. Second, this organic weakening of the social structure was reinforced by the military's repression of political parties, organizations, and their leaders, which created tremendous problems in the relationship between the political party structure and the social base, all of which aggravated the crisis of representation.

With respect to the party system, it was neither eliminated nor replaced by a new one, as was intended. The old system continued with a few changes in composition. The political right, which had dissolved itself in 1973 to identify with the military regime, remained greatly fragmented until 1983. In that year, two groups appeared on the right. One was closely identified with the program of the new regime and considered itself the natural heir to that regime. The other, although somewhat ambiguously, avoided identification with the regime and leaned toward a democratic orientation. Thus, the organizational future of the political right remains an open question. The Christian Democratic party remains in the political center, but it is now more amenable to forming alliances with the left, although not with the Communist party. There is also in the political center a group with social democratic leanings that has yet to crystallize organizationally. On the left, two major tendencies are in a process of consolidation. One is socialist, renewed but still fragmented; the other is classically orthodox, represented principally by the Communist party. The consolidation of a party spectrum with four points (the democratic right, the Christian Democrat center and social democrats with leftist inclinations, the unified socialist left, and the Communist party) might be a fundamental element in the establishment of a future democracy.

Although it is not possible to draw definite conclusions, the structural transformations that have taken place as well as the adjustments the political leaders have made to the new realities of social organization suggest that a new model of interaction between political and social entities may be emerging. These relationships do not merely replace those of 1973; rather, they reveal a tendency toward greater mutual autonomy. The evidence, however, is insufficient and different for each social sector.

Transition to Democracy?

The crisis of the military regime and its failures in all areas reopens the question of an alternative to it and the means by which this alternative can be reached. It seems obvious that such a change cannot come about only with regard to the nature of the political regime, since the crisis brought about by the dictatorship affects all the spheres of society and society as a whole. Thus, the establishment of political democracy by itself would be insufficient as a means to reconstruct the nation. The existing disruptions and inequalities demand structural transformations and global democratization, processes that have been interrupted and set back by the dictatorship. Despite these conditions, there are others that make a military overthrow or breakdown or military fragmentation highly improbable. These include the hierarchical structure and the cohesion of the armed forces, their intense solidarity due to a shared responsibility for the repression, in which they have invested enormously to transform it into a modern instrument, and the existence of a large and diversified middle class. Thus, it is not possible to associate the end of the dictatorship with the triumph of a revolution capable of producing a "great social change." That change will have to be the task of majorities that emerge within the context of a future democratic system.

Democratic restoration appears to be the goal that attracts the greatest support and urgency. On the other hand, unless the dictatorship is defeated or collapses, it will end only if the armed forces deliberately decide to abandon the government. The general problem for the opposition is how to provoke the armed forces into making such a decision. To accomplish this aim, the opposition must transform its capacity to mobilize the citizenry into a solid political force. From this perspective, the conditions and problems of a period of transition, as well as of the social actors, are different from those of a process of democratic consolidation.

In Chile, the problem of transition is even more complex because the armed forces have already decided upon the deadlines and mechanisms to be employed (for more details, see Garretón 1985). The armed forces are the only unifying element of the bloc in power, and there is no internal alternative program to that of the constitution that was approved in 1980. Moreover, the "transition" prescribed by the constitution, to which the military dictatorship refers, is a transition, not to a democratic regime, but to an authoritarian regime. Therefore, in Chile, the problem of a transition to democracy is not only one of forcing the armed forces to withdraw from power but the more difficult one of forcing them to change a decision they have already made.

In this profound crisis of legitimacy, there are no mediating institutions or arenas for conflict resolution. Thus, in the confrontation between the dictatorship and the opposition, the former is favored because of the power resources it controls. The principal aim of the opposition currently is to create an arena or space in which the conflict of legitimacy can be resolved in its favor. In other words, the transition to democracy in Chile implies a change in the institutional framework imposed by a constitution that was dictated by the military regime and submitted to a vote that deceptively claimed to recognize the principle of popular sovereignty. To progress toward a transition, the opposition must put its mobilizational capacity behind an agreed-upon transitional formula that is capable of avoiding an institutional vacuum and that can obtain support from the broadest social and political spectrum possible. The fact that such progress has not yet occurred is partially a result of the diversity of concepts about the transition process that the various opposition forces hold.

Summary and Conclusion: Prospects for Democracy

I believe that the prospects for democracy in Chile should be analyzed in connection with the conditions and circumstances that made democracy historically possible, the causes of its collapse, the transformations that have taken place under the military regime, and the scenario of its transition. My arguments can be summarized and extended as follows:

1. With respect to the conditions and traits of Chilean democracy until 1973, one could say that it was based on the compatibility between capitalist industrialization, with strong participation of the state, and the incomplete process of substantive democratization and on the creation of a backbone or a particular mode of constituting social forces, which was characterized by the articulation between the political party system and social organizations. This situation led to the establishment of a large political class that was capable of representing, coordinating, and reflecting the hegemony of the middle sectors of society, as well as the subordinated but autonomous presence of the popular sectors, and the defensive actions of the capitalist bloc. This political class was also able to keep the military under control by "cloistering" it.

2. With respect to the crisis of Chilean democracy, key components were the increasing incapacity of the socioeconomic system to sustain a

process of substantive democratization and the inability of the political class to reach an agreement that would provide a political basis for the transformations necessary for such democratization.[8] This inability was manifested in the fragmentation and hostility of the sectors that had combined to build democracy since the 1930s and had brought about progressive social changes: the middle sectors and the popular classes; on the political level, the center and the left. This antagonistic situation permitted the emergence of the armed forces as an autonomous force and the creation of the conditions that allowed them, with the support of the capitalist bloc—which feared a terminal crisis—to end political democracy and reverse the process of democratization.

3. The military regime attempted to undo the preceding political order in order to construct an authoritarian social and political organization by means of a long period of military rule and economic transformation. The facts that elements of the preceding political system remained— particularly the political parties—and the Catholic church emerged as a substitute for the former political actors made it difficult for the regime to realize its utopian designs. These goals then completely disintegrated with the collapse of the economy model in 1981–1982. This failure left the personalized military regime with no program other than to fight for its own survival within the framework imposed by the constitution of 1980, to which all its short-term actions are linked. These factors notwithstanding, there has been a certain disarticulation in the relations between the state and civil society and a weakening of the historic social actors. The crucial problem is the relationship between the political world of representation and coordination and the social world of protest and mobilization.

4. The problems associated with the transition to political democracy in Chile do not conform to the classical model (defeat of the military, provisional government, and new sociopolitical order)—that is, in a revolutionary model in which the end of a military regime and the creation of a new society coincide. A military collapse seems unlikely. Thus, the problem is how to provoke a military decision that would alter the regime's previous decisions. These decisions consist of the deadlines and procedures incorporated into the constitution of 1980, which guarantees the continuation of the military regime until 1989 and an authoritarian conservative regime after that date. The tasks of the opposition are to struggle for an arena or political space that will permit a resolution of the conflict of legitimacy that afflicts the country and to extend the crisis into the institution of the armed forces. From an operational viewpoint, such a need will require linking a consensual formula for transition with social mobilization, elements that until now

have not been combined and, thus, the opposition has not been able to develop a strategy.

5. Whichever scenario for the transition to political democracy is eventually enacted—in all probability, it will not differ from other such contemporary processes, especially those in the Southern Cone—the prospect for attaining democratic stability will depend on the country's ability to overcome some extremely difficult initial conditions. On the one hand, a new regime would inherit a deep economic crisis, which would mean that democratic consolidation would have to coincide with economic reconstruction—a problem that allows little room for maneuver in a context in which all conventional models for development seem to be unsuitable. On the other hand, a generalized support for democracy could be precarious inasmuch as such support from the middle-sector groups is primarily the result of the failure of the earlier regime's economic policy; from the urban masses, it stems from cautious acceptance, for they remain suspicious of institutional procedures for negotiating and reaching consent. In the third place, the armed forces—undefeated, uncommitted to democratic values, and isolated from the rest of civil society—have enormous power to pressure the state. Finally, unlike the decade of the 1930s, numerous challenges must be confronted with the masses already having won their right of incorporation into the country's political life and with the simultaneous presence of old, unresolved problems and of new ones generated by the effects of modernization and social differentiation.

6. Beyond the initial conditions needed for a future political democracy, the prospects for a democratic consolidation in Chile depend on the resolution of four basic problems. First, a developmental model must be formulated that could play a role similar to the one played by the process of industrialization and state participation that served as a basis for the constitution of social actors, thus facilitating a global democratization. Second, a new backbone must be developed that will permit a redefinition of the relationship between political parties and social movements. The fundamental principles should be autonomy and mutual tension on the one hand and democratic control on the other, which will require a renovation of the political system to replace the prior model of sub-ordination of the social movements to the parties. Third, the power of the armed forces must be subordinated to political power, which pre-supposes a greater penetration of the military by society and thus a different model than the cloistered one followed until 1973.

Fourth, once a transition that involves other types of political agreements or pacts is completed, the outcome should be the creation of a political framework with a democratic right; a center favorable to social change, and therefore progressive; and two political lefts—a renovated socialism and a classical communist branch. Within this arrangement, the stability of democracy will rest on the creation of a sociopolitical majority similar to that of the popular fronts of the 1930s but with a composition and a content compatible with the new historical conditions. This sociopolitical majority can only be obtained on the basis of a new relationship among the sectors that historically made possible the survival of political democracy and, to a lesser extent, a democratization of society—and whose earlier break initiated the collapse of the democratic regime—the popular classes and the middle sectors.

On the political level, I am referring to the center and the left, with various possible coalitions. The reluctance of the Christian Democrats to understand the necessary presence of the Communist party as a member of this bloc, the fragmentation of the socialist left, and the ambiguity of the Communist party regarding the revolutionary or reformist character of the transition are factors that currently conspire against the creation of that sociopolitical majority. But it seems clear that without such a majority, which would link political democracy and social change, any future democracy will be defeated by conservative forces, as occurred in 1973.

Notes

The author thanks the collaboration of Paulo Hidalgo, research assistant at the Facultad Latino-Americana de Ciencias Sociales (FLACSO). The Spanish version circulated as a working paper of the Centro Estudios del Desarrollo (CED). This paper has been translated by Doris da Rosa and edited by Jonathan Hartlyn. For the U.S. reader, the editor has added a few suggested references in English—these are appropriately identified below.

1. An analysis of these authoritarian regimes and of their relationship to the problem of hegemony appears in the second part of Garretón (1983) and in Chapter 1 of Garretón (1984). A relatively complete discussion can be found in Collier (1979). A more extended analysis of some of the topics discussed in this chapter can be found in my two books listed above.

2. On political developments of this period, see, among others, Pinto (1971) and Moulián (1982). For a complementary bibliography on particular issues discussed here see Garretón (1983:37, 38).

3. On the period 1964-1970, in addition to sources already mentioned, see Molina (1972) and de Riz (1979).

4. Ed. note: For some additional sources in English on the Christian Democratic party, see Fleet (1985); on economic policy, see Stallings (1978); on the agrarian structure and land reform, see Kaufman (1973) and Loveman (1976); and on the copper industry, see Moran (1974).

5. For the period of the Popular Unity, see Garretón and Moulián (1983), Bitar (1979), and Valenzuela (1978). Ed. note: Additional sources in English from varying

perspectives include Gil, Lagos, and Lansberger (1979), Roxborough, O'Brien, and Roddick (1977), and Sigmund (1977).

6. On the evolution of repression and the defense against it, see Fruhling (1981).

7. Ed. note: For a general view of the Catholic church in Chile, see Smith (1982).

8. A synthesis of the current controversy over the causes of the crisis of the democratic system can be found in Tironi (1984).

References

Bitar, Sergio. 1979. *Transición socialismo y democracia: La experiencia chilena.* Mexico City: Siglo XXI.

Collier, David, ed. 1979. *The New Authoritarianism in Latin America.* Princeton: Princeton University Press.

de Riz, Liliana. 1979. *Sociedad y política en Chile: De Portales a Pinochet.* Mexico City: Universidad Nacional Autónoma de México.

Fleet, Michael. 1985. *The Rise and Fall of Chilean Christian Democracy.* Princeton: Princeton University Press.

Fruhling, Hugo. 1981. "Disciplinando la sociedad." Mimeograph. Santiago.

Garretón, Manuel Antonio. 1983. *El proceso político chileon.* Santiago: FLACSO.

———. 1984. *Dictadura y democratización.* Santiago: FLACSO.

———. 1985. *Chile: La Transicion bloqueada.* Santiago: Mensaje (January-February).

Garretón, Manuel Antonio, and Moulián, T. 1983. *La Unidad Popular y el conflicto politico en Chile.* Santiago: Editora Minga.

Gil, Federico C.; Lagos E., Ricardo; and Lansberger, Henry A., eds. 1979. *Chile at the Turning Point: Lesson of the Socialist Years, 1970–1973.* Philadelphia: Institute for the Study of Human Issues.

Kaufman, Robert R. 1973. *The Politics of Chilean Land Reform, 1950–1970.* Cambridge: Harvard University Press.

Loveman, Brian. 1976. *Struggle in the Countryside: Politics and Rural Labor in Chile, 1919–1973.* Bloomington: Indiana University Press.

Martinez, J., and Tironi, Ernesto. 1983. *Estratificación y cambio social en Chile en la década de los sesenta.* Santiago: CEPAL.

Molina, Sergio. 1972. *El Proceso de cambio en Chile: La Experiencia 1965–1970.* Santiago: Editorial Universitaria.

Moran, Theodore H. 1974. *Multinational Corporations and the Politics of Dependence: Copper in Chile.* Princeton: Princeton University Press.

Moulián, Tomás. 1982. *Desarrollo político y estado de compromiso: Desajustes y crisis estatal en Chile.* Colección Estudios CIEPLAN no. 8. Santiago.

Moulián, Tomás, and Vergara, P. 1980. *Estado, ideologia, y políticas económicas en Chile.* Estudio CIEPLAN no. 3. Santiago.

Pinto, Aníbal. 1971. "Desarrollo económico y relaciones sociales en Chile." In *Tres ensayos sobre Chile y América Latina,* ed. Aníbal Pinto. Buenos Aires: Ediciones Solar.

Roxborough, Ian; O'Brien, Phil; and Roddick, Jackie. 1977. *Chile: The State and Revolution.* London: Macmillan.

Sigmund, Paul. 1977. *The Overthrow of Allende and the Politics of Chile, 1964–1976.* Pittsburgh: University of Pittsburgh Press.

Smith, Brian H. 1982. *The Church and Politics in Chile: Challenges to Catholicism.* Princeton: Princeton University Press.

Stallings, Barbara. 1978. *Class Conflict and Economic Development in Chile, 1958–1973.* Stanford: Stanford University Press.

Tironi, Eugenio. 1984. "Clases sociales y acuerdo democrático." Documento de Trabajo no. 14. Santiago: CED.

Valenzuela, Arturo. 1978. *The Breakdown of Democratic Regimes: Chile.* Baltimore: Johns Hopkins Press.

Varas, Augusto. 1980. *Chile, democracia, fuerzas armadas.* Santiago: FLACSO.

Vega, Humberto. 1984. "Crisis económica, estabilidad y du eda externa." Programa Economica de Trabajo no. 33. Santiago. (August).

Vergara, Pilar. 1980. "Las transformaciones del estado Chileno bajo el régimen militar." Mimeograph. Washington, D.C.: Wilson Center, Latin American Program.

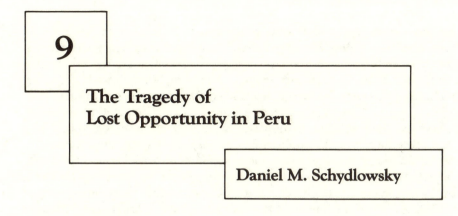

9

The Tragedy of Lost Opportunity in Peru

Daniel M. Schydlowsky

The Present Disaster

For the Peruvian economy, 1983 was the worst year of the century. The GNP fell 12 percent in real terms, and inflation rose to 125 percent, the highest rate ever observed in the country. There was a slight recovery in 1984 and the first half of 1985, with a real growth of 3–4 percent, but then inflation accelerated, and the balance-of-payments situation and government finances became precarious. Despite strenuous efforts to cut government expenditures, the deficit averaged 6.5 percent of GNP during 1983–1984. Meanwhile, Peru's public foreign debt of over $13 billion cannot be serviced, and the new government of Alan García has unilaterally announced that it will pay no more than 10 percent of the country's export earnings as interest.

The most immediate cause of the current situation is the severe balance-of-payments problem. The lack of foreign exchange forced the Belaúnde government to follow a very tough deflationary policy designed to reduce domestic aggregate demand and thereby to depress the country's import level. The result was a recession accompanied by a sharp increase in inflation. Neither the balance-of-payments situation nor the inflation rate came out of nowhere. It is true that in 1983, Peru was hit by several natural disasters: terrible rains in the north and a severe drought in the south. However, these disasters at most accounted for a drop of 4 percent in the GNP. The remaining 8 percent drop, as well as the slow growth in previous years, cannot be assigned to an "act of God." Rather, Peru's current economic situation is the result of a cumulative process that began many years ago and has been steered at various times by different economic teams.

The following sections of this chapter review the various policy decisions that were taken at different strategic moments, explore their rationale and consequences, and question why alternatives that were available at the time were not adopted. As an introduction, the nature and dynamics of the import-substituting industrialization (ISI) strategy will be laid out as they provide

217

the necessary key to understanding a major part of Peru's economic tribula-
tions. The later sections focus on the successive periods of Peruvian economic
history when policymakers had the option of breaking out of the ISI pattern
but did not do so. In each case, an attempt is made not only to describe the
policy followed but to analyze its rationale, its shortcomings, and the apparent
reasons why policymakers rejected the alternatives. This review covers the
policy flexibility available in the devaluation year of 1967; the new policy
departures chosen by the autonomous military government during Phase 1,
1969-1975; the reversal of policy under pressure during Phase 2, 1976-1978;
the use of balance-of-payments and fiscal latitude during Phase 3, 1979-1980;
and the fresh start made by the civilian constitutional government during
1980-1983. Given the nature of the task as well as the limitations of space,
the analysis covers the high points and the broad sweep of policy rather than
going into minute detail.

The Latin American Prescription for Economic Disaster

The popular economic strategy of Latin America has been that of import-
substituting industrialization. The rationale is simple: Latin America has
plenty of labor, and it can mobilize savings, but it does not have enough land
to occupy all its workers; therefore it must industrialize. National savings
should be invested in industry, and the most obvious things to produce are
those consumed by Latin Americans themselves. Import substitution means
making use of a ready market, and also one that is safe. Moreover, by protecting
against import competition, infant domestic industrialists can be given a
chance to learn their trade and to solidly establish themselves. Since import
substitution will save foreign exchange, this strategy will also contribute to
improving the balance of payments.

Implementation of the strategy is also quite straightforward. In the initial
stage, tariffs or quantitative restrictions are imposed on the import of finished
goods, thus raising the profitability of their domestic production. After a
range of imported products has been domesticated, the production process
is integrated backward to intermediate goods. At this point, it is the turn of
the intermediate goods producer to receive protection. However, this protection raises the cost of domestic finished goods, and their producers request
and receive additional protection in turn. The process of successive backward
integration generates an escalator in the protection system, with every
successive stage of backward integration of a domestic industrial process
requiring higher levels of protection for the later stages of transformation.
As the process continues, the domestic cost structure becomes more and
more different from that obtaining in the developed world.

The development of the protection system has no negative impact on domestic profitability, since domestic prices move along with the additional protection. The only difficulty experienced in the domestic market is that this market is relatively small, and therefore the economies of scale in industrial production cannot be realized. Instead, firms diversify their product mixture and thus become less specialized, and markets become increasingly monopolistically competitive.

On the export side the situation is quite different. Industrial producers who make quite reasonable (or sometimes quite high) profits on sales in the domestic market are completely unable to compete in the export market. The reason is that high input prices raise the costs of the products well above those of the world market. Lack of competitiveness in the export market, however, is taken as an indication of inefficiency. Combined with the generalized view that high protection in the domestic market also indicates a lack of competitiveness and therefore inefficiency, the conviction gradually grows among industrialists, government officials, and the public alike that Latin American industry is inefficient.

Much of the conviction that industry is inefficient is based on a mistaken calculation. Efficiency is measured in a simpleminded way by looking at the costs of production in local currency, dividing by the exchange rate, and then comparing the resulting cost figure to the import price (excluding tariff) of comparable goods. On this basis, indeed, domestic industry in Latin America has typically been high cost and "inefficient." However, there is something fundamentally wrong with this calculation. When a country levies a tariff, it is essentially devaluing for the particular good on which the tariff is levied, because what matters for trade and for domestic production is the total cost of an import after all payments of taxes have been taken into account.

Thus, if a Latin American country's exchange rate is ten soles to the dollar and the import of widgets is taxed with a 50 percent import duty, it is as though the exchange rate for widgets were fifteen, with no duty levied. Likewise, if the tariff for broomsticks is 80 percent, it is as though broomsticks had their own exchange rate of eighteen soles to the dollar. It follows that the system of differentiated tariffs in fact produces the equivalent of a multiple exchange rate system. Therefore, in order to properly compare domestic costs with international prices, it is necessary to convert cost figures in local currency to dollars at the exchange rate that actually affects those costs. Now, since in the process of industrialization many imports have tariffs on them and are therefore produced domestically at prices that reflect exchange rates higher than the "financial" rate, it also turns out that the "cost" rates are all higher than the financial rate. Of course, when costs are converted to dollars at the financial rate, which is lower than the cost rates, the costs in dollars are going to be overstated and look high. Much of the conviction of industrial inefficiency therefore is an illusion, properly called the "industrial inefficiency illusion" (for early statements, see Diamand 1973 and Schydlowsky 1972).

What is not an illusion, however, is the lack of export competitiveness of domestic producers. This lack is policy induced too, however, as it results from the fact that there are no offset sales to the high cost exchange rates for export sales. Thus, although tariffs on outputs are typically higher in the domestic market than the tariffs on inputs, such is not the case for export sales. Traditionally, these sales are based on the same exchange rate as all financial transactions, and therefore they are effectively subject to an exchange rate that is lower than the one that affects their costs. The lack of export competitiveness naturally locks domestic industrial producers into the domestic market.

Now consider what happens as an economy is made to grow. The strategy is to have industry lead the growth process, which means that industry must grow faster than the rest of the economy. However, industry needs imported raw materials to produce, and therefore the demand for imports will have to grow rapidly. But the supply of foreign exchange is provided by the primary sectors, which are growing more slowly—as they are intended to do. At some point, the growth in demand for imports is going to exceed the growth in the supply of exports, and a foreign exchange crisis will result. The fundamental cause of this crisis is the divergence in growth paths between the foreign exchange–using sectors (industry and services) and the foreign exchange–producing sectors (agriculture and mining).

Unless and until the foreign exchange–using sectors can be made to earn their own foreign exchange, this sectorial imbalance will strangle growth. If this structural problem is misdiagnosed as a cyclical one, and the economy is deflated to repress the balance-of-payments problem, nothing is solved. The only benefit that does occur is that for a time, foreign exchange reserves are built up again, but as soon as the economy begins to grow the problem reappears—to the increasing frustration of the policymakers who have treated the fever but not the disease.

Setting the Peruvian Stage: The Missed Opportunity of 1967

Peru embarked upon its explicit phase of import-substituting industrialization with the Industrial Development Law of 1958. Before that date, Peru had begun to industrialize, but this law provided systematic tariff incentives and a liberalization of material inputs designed to raise the profitability of industrial investment and to boost the domestic supply of industrial goods.

The military government of 1962, and then the regime of Fernando Belaúnde Terry that followed it a year later, adopted as their planning criteria the fundamental tenets of the Economic Commission for Latin America (ECLA): expansion for the domestic market, modification of price signals through deliberate government policy, and the expansion of domestic demand through government investment. However, there was no recognition of the inherent but self-limiting nature of the strategy.

Quite independent of this ISI strategy, the deliberate and explicit adoption of a planning approach made external assistance available to Peru under the Alliance for Progress. Also, and coincidentally, growing export revenues from earlier investments in copper (*toquepala*) and from newly "discovered" fish meal were available.[1] Thus, the foreign exchange requirements of the inward-looking industrialization policy became available.

The Belaúnde regime followed a generally expansionary policy during its first two years and began to fuel a demand-driven inflation. By 1965, a number of signs indicated that the exchange rate was becoming overvalued, and the required planning for an orderly devaluation began in the central bank, the responsible government organ. Nonetheless, through 1967, every attempt was made to hold the exchange rate at the existing level, including adopting substantial increases in import duties, which reinforced the import-substituting nature of the country's policy.

By 1967, it was quite clear that the exchange rate could not be maintained for very long. In August of 1967, the central bank's international reserves ran out, and it withdrew from the foreign exchange market, thereby allowing the sol to depreciate against the dollar.[2]

One member of the small group at the central bank that conducted the technical studies leading to the devaluation had had experience in Argentina, and he persuaded his colleagues that the exchange rate system had acquired an anti-export bias because of the gradual increase of import duties with no symmetric analogue on the export side. The dangers of locking the industrial producer into the domestic market were thus perceived, and the leaders resolved to try to use the devaluation as an occasion to modify the situation.

The exchange rate at the time was 26.80 soles to the dollar, and it had been at that level since the beginning of the decade. The internal projections of the central bank indicated that an exchange rate of approximately 33.50 soles would be appropriate for traditional export production. However, it was also believed that a somewhat higher rate would be needed if capital flight were to be reversed. Moreover, the conviction existed that a devaluation to 33.50 would cause some degree of domestic price increase and that it was therefore desirable to devalue somewhat more in order to offset in advance some of the domestic price increases that the devaluation itself would bring about. It was thus felt that a rate in the neighborhood of 38.00 would be appropriate. However, adopting such a rate would give a substantial windfall to export producers, who only needed an exchange rate of 33.50 to be competitive. It was therefore decided to levy an export tax of one-third of the exchange rate difference in order to pick up most of the exporters' windfall. Since this export tax would only affect traditional exports, the full rate of 38.00 or so would be available to industrial and other nontraditional exporters. This provision would make it more possible for them to overcome their cost disadvantage, particularly since the most recent tariff increase would be rescinded with the devaluation.

The policy proposed, therefore, was a partially compensated devaluation, i.e., one that partially compensated for the inflationary effects of the devaluation by lowering tariffs and retaining some of the windfall given to traditional exporters. A substantial cost push still remained in the policy, however, since neither food nor industrial inputs were affected by the compensation measures. The only direct domestic consumption item that would be subject to price restraint as a part of the policy was sugar, which at the time was an important export product for Peru. Its limitations notwithstanding, the policy would have gone a long way toward correcting the existing anti-export bias in the country's industrial policy and toward beginning the process of making Peruvian manufacturing export oriented.

The proposal wound its way through the bureaucracy, where it was largely perceived as an ingenious way to cover the yawning budget deficits. It thus gained acceptance throughout the executive branch as a revenue-raising measure. However, the administration had no legal power to impose an export tax, and since congressional approval was unobtainable, particularly in advance, the solution found was to create an "export retention" to be paid into an economic stabilization fund.[3]

As can be imagined, Congress and the exporters rose in anger at the proposed export tax. Congress formally declared it illegal, and the executive rescinded the tax two weeks after it had been imposed. However, the export tax was not completely dead: The fiscal crisis made one imperative. Accordingly, two months later, the tax reemerged, this time as a 10 percent forced loan from exporters, repayable over a period of eight years and deductible as a current cost. In effect, then, it became a tax of some 6 percent. It lasted on the books for about eight months when it was again abolished.

A measure that had the potential of changing the trend of Peru's industrial growth thus became entangled in a major political struggle on how to finance the government deficit (see Kuczynski 1977, Chapter 8, for a vivid account of these battles). In the process, it completely lost its long-term policy character and became transformed into a mere revenue-raising tax. As such, it had only the appeal of easy collectibility. Moreover, instead of being part of a compensated devaluation involving an offsetting reduction in import duties, it coexisted for the short duration of its life with an import surcharge! Thus, even if it had survived, its long-term effect would have been quite different from the one intended.

The question now is, Why did this first attempt to balance Peru's trade policy end so badly? It would appear that the reason was the far-too-narrow base of understanding on which the policy initiative was based. At best, half a dozen people really understood what long-term objective was being pursued by the export retention. A far wider group of people thought of it as merely a tax-gathering device. But the handful of people who understood the purpose were concerned simultaneously with monitoring a wide number of issues surrounding the implementation of the devaluation, which was being resisted, among others, by the president of the Republic. In such a context, "implementation overload" occurred, and a number of things had to be sacrificed. Unfortunately, one of those things was righting the trade policy for long-term gain. It might therefore be concluded that along with the fact that many Peruvians were unaccustomed to complex economic analysis, the root cause for this missed opportunity was Peru's far-too-narrow technocratic base. Fortunately, the very small group of technocrats that did exist had recognized that problem and had set in motion mechanisms that over the long term, would very substantially multiply the base of technicians on which any future Peruvian government team could draw. Of course, nobody could guarantee that these technocrats would do better when their turn came! But that is getting somewhat ahead of the story.

Strategic Mistakes of the Peruvian Revolution, Phase 1: 1968–1975

The Peruvian Revolution, phase one, set out to create a new Peruvian reality. The country was to have an economy able to grow autonomously and in a sustained fashion. It was to be an economy more modern than in the past, and much more independent of the rest of the world. Industrialization was an obvious choice of strategy, but it was balanced with very large investments in mining projects with long gestation periods. Thus, import substitution on the one hand and mineral exports (including petroleum) on the other were intended to produce a very strong balance of payments. Equity would be improved through changes in the control of enterprises: agrarian reform, industrial legislation, etc. Moreover, all would be held together by strong government control of the commanding heights of the economy. Direct ownership, import licensing, and exchange control were the tools of implementation.

The identification of the objectives to be achieved and the strategy of a frontal attack to break through to these objectives were consistent with the military mind. However, little thought was given to protecting the flanks; there was a total disregard for secondary consequences. Yet, quite soon, the Peruvian economy produced pernicious and cumulative by-products, which ultimately engulfed the whole operation and exploded in an unmanageable balance-of-payments problem.

The military leaders picked up in 1968 pretty much where they had left off in 1963, even allowing for Belaúnde's continuation of the industrialization policy. They viewed the world in terms of ECLA's import substitution doctrine. However, they also knew that Peru had enormous riches beneath its soil, and thus they regarded the development of mining as absolutely essential. Since they believed (not altogether incorrectly) that constraints are removable by human effort, they pursued industrial development and mining expansion at the same time. Their promotion of industry was by far the most vigorous ever known in Peru, and it was perhaps more vigorous than that undertaken in any comparable period in Latin America.

The procedure was simple enough. The import of anything that could be produced in Peru was prohibited; all that was required to trigger a prohibition was for a domestic producer to appear on the scene. The result was that the foreign exchange–saving period of import substitution, i.e., that period when the existing imports are reduced as domestic output expands, was compressed to a year and a half or two because all it took was the announcement of domestic production for import reduction to occur. From then on, any domestic production was, in fact, foreign exchange using, for it would require imported inputs. Thus, the military regime concentrated all its foreign exchange savings in the first two years and left for later the foreign exchange–using parts of its industrial development effort.

The mining development program for all practical purposes had a similar time profile. All foreign exchange saving occurred at the beginning when the existing foreign enterprises were nationalized and the previously existing profit repatriations were retained in the country. Thereafter, all new mining activity involved heavy expenses for exploration and expansion. These were in very large measure foreign exchange expenses. Thus, increasingly, the mining sector was absorbing the foreign exchange it was earning through its own expansion program. Evidently, the new investment would pay off in foreign exchange earnings, but only after a long gestation period and well into the future. Moreover, the foreign exchange intensity of the mining efforts was increased further by virtue of the lack of experience on the part of the government enterprises involved. Finally, it is also likely that the foreign exchange revenue realized from current exports of minerals was lower than it would otherwise have been as a result of the ineptitude of the government marketing corporations, which needed to learn their trade in the school of hard knocks. Oil from the jungle was the principal source of new foreign exchange; however, the quantities involved turned out to be well below expectation.

As far as the productive sectors are concerned, the development strategy was clearly headed for the classical type of trouble that Latin America's import substitution pattern generates, as discussed earlier. However, other policies of the Peruvian Revolution aggravated the situation substantially.

Pursuing fairness in agriculture led to an agrarian reform in 1969 that broke up the large sugar and cotton estates and reduced the output of this major foreign exchange producing sector, thus aggravating the imbalance between foreign exchange production and foreign exchange usage. The "industrial community" legislation of 1970 had the same effect. It provided very strong incentives for the substitution of labor by capital, but the capital goods were largely imported so the import intensity of new industrial investment rose substantially. Moreover, the exchange controls of 1970, which accompanied the trade policy, made it very attractive to overinvoice machinery and to operate with imported inputs, also preferably overinvoiced, in order to expatriate assets the private sector feared would ultimately be confiscated in any case. Thus, the foreign exchange intensity of current industrial production went up, once more aggravating the trend toward a structural balance-of-payments explosion.

The income redistribution policy added the final touch. Income was distributed from the top 5 percent to the following 15 percent of the population. This policy gave the middle class a substantial increase, which resulted in a substantial change in the composition of final demand in the country as the demand for the more modern industrial goods increased significantly. These, however, are precisely the goods that have a high import component. Thus, the income distribution further reinforced an already unsustainable trend.

Once Peru's development policies were set, the countdown to a collision between the demand for foreign exchange and the availability of such foreign exchange was under way. The terms of trade and foreign bankers came providentially to the rescue, or so it seemed initially. Impressed by the superficial order and purpose of Peru's government policy, and later awash with Eurodollars from the first oil shock, international bankers lent Peru large amounts of foreign exchange, at least in comparison to the amounts that had previously been customary. From 1970 to 1974, export prices rose, and Peru's foreign debt doubled. The combined effect of the price rise and the capital inflow was to postpone the moment of explosion concerning the balance of payments, but by the same token, when that explosion did come, it was much larger than it would have been earlier. Export prices fell, and the balance-of-payments problem exploded in 1975.

While all the foregoing events were occurring on the main stage of the Peruvian economy, a very minor sideshow was going on as well. This story began in 1969, at the beginning of the military government, when General Angel Valdivia, a man with strong roots in the 1962–1963 military government, was minister of finance—but before the central bank had been purged of its leading technocrats of the Belaúnde administration. In January 1969, a team from the central bank approached General Valdivia with the notion that the new Peru might benefit substantially if it balanced its industrial development strategy. To that effect, it would be necessary to create an export promotion instrument, akin to the tariff, that would raise the number of soles obtained by an industrial exporter on sales abroad to something approximating the number that could be obtained on the local market. The argument was buttressed by calculations to show how, given Peru's depressed economy of that time, fiscal support of exports would be largely a self-financing venture, thanks to the fiscal consequences of a high foreign trade multiplier. The minister was not completely convinced of the multiplier analysis, or its conclusion that promoting exports with tax refunds was a more profitable venture when the economy was depressed than when it was booming, but he nonetheless accepted the general notion. Thus, the Certex (Certificado de reintegro tributario a las exportaciones) was created. However, before the implementation regulations could be drawn up, the minister and the civilian technocrats of the central bank were fired, and the Certex passed temporarily into oblivion.

A set of regulations for the Certex did appear eventually, and the Certex began to be used cautiously, but persistently, by the bureaucrats charged with directing Peruvian trade whenever they thought that export sales could be increased with some additional support. And thus, under the protection of a very cautiously administered Certex, Peru's nontraditional exports grew from $34 million in 1970 to $108 million by the time the balance of payments exploded in 1975.

There is little question that, the Certex sideshow notwithstanding, the Peruvian economic strategy of phase one was one of import substitution to the hilt. What is perplexing is why this strategy should have been the one followed. The self-limiting nature of import substitution had by then been recognized by a number of writers (ECLA 1964; Diamand 1971; Diaz-Alejandro 1965; Felix 1968, to name just a few) and had even been documented thoroughly in a study by the Organization for Economic Cooperation and Development (Little, Scitovsky, and Scott 1970). A part, albeit a minor one, of the government was timidly supporting a strategy of export promotion instead, and a number of highly placed civilians in the economic team were certainly acquainted with the notions of comparative advantage and the limitations arising from systematic violations of comparative costs. Still, the strategy of import substitution was adopted.

One major element was certainly ideology. The military leaders who were running the show had been trained in the early and middle sixties at the Center for High Military Studies (Centro de Altos Estudios Militares, CAEM), and lecturers there were almost invariably of a left-wing persuasion since right-thinking civilians at that time did not bother to lecture at the military institute. Moreover, the students at the CAEM carefully analyzed ECLA's doctrines, and ECLA at that time had not yet swung from import substitution to export promotion.

The second element was the conviction of the military leaders that Peru was not an industrial country. They were willing to take risks in the area of mining, even to the extent of expropriating the property of foreigners, people more timid minds would have thought indispensable to run the operations. The military leaders were willing to take enormous risks in agriculture, believing that farm cooperatives could run the complex enterprises as well as their capitalist owners had done. But they were profoundly convinced that Peru was not able to produce industrial outputs that would be competitive in the world markets in price and quality.[4] They also feared that Peruvian industry would fall prey to the marketing capabilities of multinational enterprises. Of course, the illusion of industrial inefficiency generated by the existing trade policy structure reinforced their belief, thus providing apparent empirical justification for their conviction.

The Certex program in that context was truly a sideshow as it took place quite outside the main attention span of the economic team. No members of that team would in their wildest dreams have thought that Peru's industrial growth could be outward looking. The timidity of those wildest dreams brought about the nightmare of the crisis of 1975–1978.

Orthodox Stabilization: 1976–1978

The balance-of-payments explosion of 1975 made it impossible to continue with the same economic strategy. Indeed, it made it impossible to continue with the same people at the head of the Peruvian government. Thus, by the beginning of 1976, most of the key players had changed. With the new players, and under considerable pressure from the international financial community, a new set of ideas began to take hold. These ideas were not easily accepted by the successive Peruvian government teams of 1975 to 1978, but they ultimately became the basis of government policy.

The basic scheme was the standard one of the IMF: Peru was diagnosed as having an overheated economy that needed to be cooled off, which involved a reduction of government expenditure and a reduction of credit expansion. The situation also required that the shackled Peruvian markets be freed, starting with the exchange rate, which was thereupon devalued by 350 percent over thirty months. However, price controls of various sorts, subsidies on food and other goods, etc., all had to go.

Thus, a diagnosis derived from the workings of a well-balanced economic structure was applied to an economy with severe structural distortions fostered by an unusually vigorous import substitution program.[5] The plan confused scarcity of foreign exchange with scarcity of overall productive capacity. It presumed high elasticities of substitution of domestic goods for imports when the reality was that this substitution had been removed by legislation.[6] It presumed the capacity of the economy to adjust flexibly to major price changes when rigidities had been built into the system with extraordinary vigor.

The only way to bring the balance of payments into equilibrium under such conditions was to induce a substantial deflation. The only way to do that was to substantially reduce real income. That reduction, in turn, required a substantial inflation and a lag in the adjustment of nominal wages. In other words, stagflation was needed, and it was indeed achieved with the massive devaluations of those years. GNP fell in per capita terms from 1976 through 1978, and inflation increased year after year to reach 80 percent.

An alternative approach was certainly possible. Rather than cutting back the demand for foreign exchange, its supply could have been increased. Given Peru's very large unutilized industrial capacity at that time (see Abusada-Salah 1975 and Smitmans 1975 on this point), vigorous export promotion could have contributed to a very quick increase in foreign exchange earnings (for estimates, see Schydlowsky and Wicht 1979:97ff. or 1983:132ff.). But once again, efforts to increase foreign exchange earnings were a sideshow and by no means integrated into the mainstream of economic policy.

The sideshow was run properly enough by the Ministry of Trade, which instituted a reform of the Certex in 1976 that generally substantially raised the export subsidy rates and made the whole administrative system much more flexible. The deputy minister of trade, the man largely responsible for this sideshow, was a man of unusual pragmatism, who correctly saw that a dollar earned with industrial products was as good as a dollar earned with mining exports. However, raising the Certex subsidy was not enough. The economy at that time was strangled by an import licensing system as well as by credit restriction. It happened quite frequently that an industrial producer had an export market but not the import license to procure the necessary material inputs, or a producer might have the import license but not the credit required for working capital. At the same time, others who did not have a market would have the import licenses or the credit. Despite this confused situation, the sideshow became gradually more important. Nontraditional exports grew from $137 million in 1976 to $344 million in 1978.

It is now necessary to ask why the policy shift was so pendular between the two phases of the military government. The answer lies in good part in the dichotomous nature of the economic explanations of the country's situation. The ECLA-type view had had its day and failed; therefore, the orthodox IMF-type view had to be correct. Another, and reinforcing, part of the answer lies with the nature of the new team of technocrats. Again the ECLA-trained, interventionist-oriented team had had its chance; it was now the turn of the U.S.-trained, market-oriented economists. Furthermore, international pressure also played a major role, and the views of the funding agencies (particularly the IMF and the World Bank) and the banks were quite orthodox. And Peru had to listen if it wanted to be financed!

These factors all produced a policy climate in which restricting demand was favored while expanding supply was neglected and sectorial selectivity was deliberately avoided in the conviction that a broad macro policy was what the country needed.[7] Leaning against such a massive swing of opinion, phase one bureaucrats were able to drag their feet but not do more.

The False Respite of Phase 3: 1979–1980

The crunch of 1975–1978, the massive devaluations of those years, the fall in real wages, and the 1976 increase in the Certex subsidy all combined put the sideshow of nontraditional exports on the main stage by 1979. Between 1976 and 1979, nontraditional exports grew by a stunning 453 percent from $137 million to $756 million. Industrialists who had never thought they could penetrate foreign markets suddenly found themselves exporting substantial amounts not only to neighboring countries but also to the United States and Europe. Government officials, who had been convinced that Peruvian industry was hopelessly inefficient, began to think otherwise. Long-held convictions about Peru's limitations as a potential industrial producer were suddenly abandoned and reversed. Peru seemed to be on the verge of breaking out of its structural balance-of-payments problem. The exporters association even lobbied effectively for the passage of a new export law, which contained numerous improvements related to incentives and guaranteed the stability of the export incentive system for a decade.

Then destiny intervened. The prices of Peru's minerals doubled, and with this increase, traditional exports soared from $1.6 billion in 1978 to $3.1 billion in 1980. Suddenly, the country was overrun with foreign exchange. In 1978, Peru's problem had been a shortage of foreign exchange;

by the end of 1979, the problem was widely diagnosed as having too much foreign exchange.

The economic team members, principally the minister of economics and the president of the central bank, were in the forefront of those people who worried that the balance-of-payments surplus resulting from the commodity boom was going to fuel an unmanageable internal inflation. Indeed, the money supply rose by 70 percent in 1979, the 1979 price increase on a December-to-December basis was 68 percent, and it appeared that that increase would continue at the same or a higher rate in 1980.

Unfortunately, the economic team looked only at the country's massive increase in foreign exchange income. It did not look at who received this income, nor did it look at what kind of supply capacity was available in the country to respond to an increase in demand. Had the team done so, it would have found that the overwhelming part of the increase in foreign exchange income wound up in the government's coffers and was effectively sterilized. To begin with, an export tax of 17.5 percent accrued directly to the Treasury. Thereafter, about half of the mining revenue accrued to the government enterprises, which were instructed to prudently squirrel away this windfall until appropriate investment projects could be found. Another quarter or so of the revenue accrued to the Southern Peru Copper Corporation, which used the funds to repay its debt, to pay additional taxes to the Peruvian government, and to repatriate the balance. Only 20 percent or so accrued to small and medium miners who in turn spent a part of their additional income within the country (and some on imports of new equipment).

Thus, directly and indirectly, some 60–70 percent of the additional foreign exchange revenue accrued to the Treasury and was sterilized while another 10–15 percent left the country in the form of dividend remittances or payments for other imports. The remaining 15–30 percent was expansionary, but the economy was depressed, and there was a very substantial underutilization of existing capacity, even in comparison to past normal levels. Under such circumstances, the accumulation of monetary balances was a counterpart to the accumulation of surpluses by the public enterprises, not a sign of expansionary pressure. In turn, inflation was driven largely from the cost side as a result of successive devaluations and the resulting attempt by wage earners to catch up combined with a world increase in food prices. Moreover, as the recession deepened and unsold inventories increased, producers widened their markups in order to be able to pay for current financial costs on the basis of smaller volumes of sales.

All these circumstances notwithstanding, the government was convinced that it was facing a demand-pull inflation that originated in an excessive accumulation of foreign exchange reserves. Therefore, it set about to try to reduce those reserves. The tools were quite simple: Imports had to be raised, and the growth of exports had to be slowed down. The former involved dismantling import controls that had been inherited from the previous phases of the military government. This dismantling involved two steps: first, a consolidation of import duties by removing a wide variety of ad hoc exemptions and second, removing quantitative restrictions and relying exclusively on tariffs. Both of these measures were slowly but surely implemented; however, the barriers against imports were still quite high, and imports grew quite slowly. On the export side, the main policy tool used was to limit the amount of export credit available, thus slowing down the rate of growth of nontraditional exports. The net effect of all of these measures did not reach the desired goal. When the outgoing military government handed over power to its elected successor, Peru still was running a surplus and had a substantial accumulation of foreign exchange reserves.

The mineral price boom and ensuing bonanza of foreign exchange once again pushed nontraditional exports to the side and made inflation the primary concern. Nontraditional exports did not become the sideshow again, however, because in volume they were now about 20 percent of exports and also because the exporters association had become an effective and articulate pressure group. Nonetheless, it is interesting to reflect on why the boom of 1979–1980 should have been considered so inflationary and why such efforts should have been made to squander the foreign exchange reserves that might have served well on a later and rainier day.

One element in the puzzle seems to have been the wrong conviction that the world prices of minerals would not soon fall, thus guaranteeing very high foreign exchange revenues to Peru for a fairly long period of time. Had a cyclical downturn in commodity prices been foreseen, one might have expected less of an attempt to spend current foreign exchange revenues and more of an attempt to maintain alternative sources of foreign exchange earnings through nontraditional exports. As it was, the government saw a need to sterilize a significant part of the foreign exchange revenue in order to prevent a massive inflation from taking place. However, once having undertaken sterilization measures on the fiscal side, the consequences of these measures for the interpretation of the monetary balance sheet seem not to have been comprehended. Having underestimated the amount of sterilization accomplished, and also feeling that more could not be done in this direction, the government's only remaining policy option was to "burn up the reserves."

Another possible element in this context might have been the aggregate monetarist framework of analysis that had been gradually adopted by the economic teams during phase two and believed in firmly by the economic team of phase three. An aggregate view by explicit intent, this model is, by construction, incapable of accommodating different behavior for different subgroups within an economy. It therefore does not prompt its users to inquire as to the actual behavior of distinct groups of economic agents.

In the middle of 1980, when the military's economic team handed over the reins of the economy to the economic team representing Belaúnde's second administration and headed by Manuel Ulloa, the conviction that it was essential to "burn up" the dollars in order to stop inflation was very well established.

Getting the Prices Wrong:
The Technocratic Disaster of 1980–1984

The credentials of the economic team taking over in mid-1980 were outstanding. A Harvard Ph.D. in economics became president of the central bank and a Cornell Ph.D. in economics became deputy minister of trade while experienced international bankers staffed various executive positions. Moreover, economic decision making was concentrated in the hands of the Ministry of Economics and Finance, which became the Ministry of Economics, Finance, and Trade. The addition of the Secretariat of Trade to the Ministry of Economics was of particular significance since the power to set tariffs and export promotion levels was one of the crucial levers of economic power in the country.

The new economic team applied a very clear and coherent policy consisting of two essential elements: getting the prices "right" and keeping President Belaúnde's spending urges under control. Getting the prices right had as its objective the unraveling of the substantial distortions of the Peruvian economy. The team felt that Peru had overprotected its infant industry, it had encouraged excessively capital-intensive activities, it had discriminated against the countryside in favor of the city, it had discriminated against savers in favor of borrowers, and all these factors had caused a very substantial distortion in the economy. To straighten the situation out, subsidies on food and gas prices needed to be removed, and those prices needed to reach their appropriate (and higher) levels; real wages, which were too high to generate full employment, should ideally come down, but since that would cause serious social unrest, the best that could be done was to prevent them from rising. The real interest rate needed to rise to make sure that scarce capital was properly applied; moreover, higher real interest rates would at least get the relative price of labor and capital more into line, particularly since wages could not be depressed. Tariffs needed to be lowered, and the structure of tariffs made as uniform as possible; the Certex needed to be reduced to prevent excess export profits. The exchange rate needed to be devalued more quickly, to at least to keep it in line with domestic inflation but if possible to effectuate a real devaluation.

Each one of these policy elements had individual merit and could be justified in terms of the market toward which it was oriented. Taken as an interactive package, however, these policies added up to a whole that had quite different effects. The first of these was the creation of an inflationary spiral. The circle started with the removal of subsidies on food and gasoline. As the prices of these rose, the cost of living increased, which required a rise in the nominal wage in line with the policy objective of keeping real wages constant. At the same time, however, a higher domestic price level required a devaluation in order to prevent the occurrence of overvaluation. The devaluation, in turn, caused an increase in the price of imported food and in the base price of gasoline, which required a further increase in the domestic prices of these goods, which in turn required further wage increases and devaluation. The economic team called the initial steps of this process a "corrective inflation." Unfortunately, however, after a while only the inflation part of the label remained.

The second consequence of the package was a substantial movement toward the deindustrialization of the country. The reduction of tariffs brought in a wave of imports as the consuming public satisfied an accumulated hunger for foreign goods. Correspondingly, the market for domestic producers shrunk abruptly, with a consequent impact on their profit-and-loss statements and balance sheets. This loss of cash flow caused a substantial increase in the demand for loans on the part of local businesses. Faced with a higher real interest, the result was a decapitalizing sequence, which has still not been arrested. On the export side, the reduction in the Certex caused a substantial fall in nontraditional exports, the overall effect of this reduction in foreign sales amounting to some 1 percent of GNP. Moreover, the major argument buttressing the reduction in export supports was the need to reduce government expenditures. However, the fall in the tax base was such that any reduction in government expenditure was nullified by the fall in government revenue. Thus, the 1 percent fall in GNP was not even compensated for by any improvement in government finance (see Schydlowsky, Hunt, and Mezzera 1983, Chapter 5, for a detailed discussion).

The second major element of economic policy—keeping Belaúnde's spending under control—was rooted in the conviction that Peru's inflation was demand driven. Under such circumstances, if Belaúnde were allowed to pursue his public works ambitions unchecked, it was believed that inflation would reach three digits. Consequently, every effort was made to keep expenditure in check during 1980. As might be expected, however, political forces eventually overcame the economic team's resistance, and by the end of 1981, the dam had broken, and public investment was shooting up. However, the higher public investment was financed by foreign borrowing rather than by the country's own foreign exchange. This method of financing was necessary because the trade policy (tariff and Certex reductions) meant Peru was earning less foreign exchange from nontraditional exports and spending more of the foreign exchange it had on newly available imports. Moreover, the export prices of traditional exports fell in 1981, thus further reducing the availability of foreign exchange.

The phasing of government expenditures therefore was the worst possible. Had Belaúnde been allowed to spend during the first year of his term and phased down thereafter, particularly in conjunction with a more conservative trade policy, the country might well have been able to finance the public works program with its own foreign exchange and not have needed to go further into debt. Moreover, the diagnosis of demand-pull inflation could not hold up in view of the substantial excess capacity that existed in broad sectors of the economy and that was reinforced by the apertura policies being pursued by the government.

The logical culmination of the policies adopted since mid-1980 occurred in 1983. Government finances collapsed toward the end of 1982, the possibility of further foreign borrowing evaporated, and the foreign lenders insisted on very tough cuts in government expenditure. With a change in the minister of economics, a competent manager arrived on the scene who was able to actually implement the cuts. The ensuing fall in government expenditure converted an existing recession into a substantial depression, knocking some 12 percent off the country's GNP. However, the cut in government expenditure did not do much to cure the government's deficit. The depression caused a reduction in the tax base; as the level of activity in the "modern" sector of the economy fell, a substantial fraction of business became "informalized" and thereby evaded taxes; and another fraction of business took to financing itself by not paying the taxes that it owed, thus compensating for the lack of availability of credit. The sum total of these three factors signified a substantial fall in government revenue, leaving the deficit virtually unchanged at some 8 percent of GNP. The depression took its toll in other ways as well, as the financial solvency of enterprises continuously deteriorated.

The economic team did not have a lack of alternatives facing it in 1980. It had the Southern Cone experience available to it, particularly the unraveling that was already taking place in Argentina. Moreover, it received upon assumption of power a set of memoranda rising out of a conference held in April 1980 that had reviewed policy options for the new government (Schydlowsky, Abusada-Salah, and González 1980), and it received extensive private and public input on the probable consequences of its policies within the first six months of having implemented them (see, for instance, Pennano 1981 and Schydlowsky 1982). Unfortunately, many of those predictions turned out to be only too accurate. The question, therefore, is why the policies that were adopted were chosen and why they were adhered to so persistently.

A combination of factors suggests itself. One of them is the ambition to straighten out Peru's economic problems once and for all. In this sense, the Peruvian economic team apparently shared the evangelical mystique of their counterparts in the Southern Cone. The second is the recognition that straightening things out once and for all requires toughness, patience, and staying power. These two elements together account for the team's willingness to be drastic in policy measures and to be persistent in the face of short-run results that do not agree with the long-term objective.

However, even with this mind set, the substance of the policy could have been different. The problem seems to have lain on the one hand with a faulty diagnosis of the underlying conditions of the economy and on the other with an inappropriate policy design, which was based on a partial rather than a general equilibrium analysis. The faulty diagnosis was inherited to a substantial extent from the preceding economic team: the view that Peru's inflation was of the demand-pull variety and that the accumulation of international reserves was the cause of the trouble. If that view were correct, it would seem plausible that one should try to increase imports and decrease exports while cutting back government expenditure. If the accumulation of international reserves results from a bottling up of the income generated by export and if demand is low compared to full capacity production, rather than high, then of course quite the opposite policies are required.

What is so wondrous is how a new and competent economic team could so misdiagnose the situation. The only partial answer available is that the diagnosis chosen was the one closest to economic orthodoxy in the international agencies and in the textbooks. Yet this explanation is only very partial for one would hope that any practicing economist and responsible government official would go beyond simple tradition in making a diagnosis. In addition, a key member of the economic team, the deputy minister of trade, had previously done extensive research to document the extent of underutilization of installed capacity in Peru's industry, a finding quite at variance with the demand-driven explanation for inflation (Abusada-Salah 1975, 1976).

The lack of any coherent instrumentation of the policy and the lack of perception of the explosive nature of the interactions among different policy elements should perhaps be set down to inexperience. The members of the economic team who had previous experience with major executive responsibility in a policymaking capacity had been away from macroeconomic analysis or the design of packages of economic policy for about a dozen years. In the interim, Peru's economic problems had become very much more complex: The "simple truths" of the 1960s were not applicable to the complicated 1980s. Thus, some members of the economic team wound up updating their skills and others wound up learning their skills by operating on the live body of the patient. Unfortunately, the patient got worse rather than better.

In solving the underlying structural problem of Peru, i.e., in allowing the country to industrialize in a self-sustaining manner, the technocratic experience between 1980 and 1982 was a failure. Rather than getting the prices right and eliminating the distortions in the economy, the economic team got the prices wrong and created the worst depression in Peru's economic history—bringing a major portion of the economic agents to the brink of bankruptcy to boot.

Is the Lesson Finally Being Learned?

October 1983 witnessed an unusual spectacle in Peruvian economic history. The exporters association held its sixth convention of exporters and invited all the major figures of the economic team to speak, including the president of the central bank and the minister of economics, finance, and trade. The presentations of these economic officials were remarkable. The president of the central bank, who had participated actively over the previous three years in the deindustrialization and anti-export policy, declared that nontraditional exports were the economic salvation of the country. He asserted that little could be expected from foreign borrowing. Nor was he optimistic about the prospects for Peru's traditional exports. He concluded that Peru had to do everything it could to promote nontraditional exports. The minister of economics reiterated the theme and declared that his portfolio would be most receptive to suggestions that the business community might have to solve the country's crisis situation.

Action followed upon words, and the Certex for agroindustrial products was reestablished forthwith to the levels that had existed before the reductions of 1981. Promises for additional export credit were made, and additional export promotion incentives were studied.

Pressed by the immediacy of the foreign exchange crisis, nontraditional, particularly industrial, exports finally came into their own. But was the policy change the desperate grab for a life preserver on the part of a drowning man or the true conviction that the country's long-term growth required balanced industrialization? Only an upturn in the prices of raw materials will give the answer to this question.

In April 1985, the Belaúnde government and its party, Acción Popular, was repudiated in the presidential election won by Alan García, the thirty-six-year-old candidate of the APRA party, a nationalist and populist party that has always been an anathema to the conservatives and the military. After assuming the presidency in July, García, copying Argentina, announced a new economic program to deal with the deteriorating economic situation. Rejecting the neoliberal and orthodox stabilization policies of his predecessor, García imposed import and foreign exchange controls to reduce the current account deficit and vowed that Peru would allocate no more than 10 percent of its export earnings to interest payments on its foreign debt. Domestically, he laid out a development strategy that represented a sharp change from that of the previous government. He raised real wages, set up an ambitious program of employment creation, and argued that Peru should direct its development to the satisfaction of national needs—of which the most pressing was self-sufficiency in food production. To that end, he prohibited the import of many food products while granting more generous subsidies for domestic agricultural production. To reduce the government deficit, he cut back on military spending, promised to sell off some government enterprises, and raised taxes from 15 percent to 20 percent of GDP. He also abolished payroll taxes, which allowed real wages to rise by 4 percent with no inflationary impact, and he forced big firms to buy government bonds with low real interest rates to help finance the government deficit.

García's foreign policy was nationalistic. He threatened to pull out of the IMF, announced strong support for Nicaragua, and imposed strict limits on profit remittances by foreign firms. By the end of the year, García's program appeared to be both popular and effective. He was supported by the vast majority of the public, inflation had dropped from a 50 percent to a 20 percent annual rate, interest rates had declined, and both industrial production and foreign reserves had begun to recover from their steep declines during the previous two years. It is too early to tell whether García's more populist and interventionist strategy is viable in the long run, but the short-run indicators are encouraging.

In conclusion, Peru appears by no means to be out of the economic woods into which it wandered in the late fifties and early sixties. It may yet provide another instance of the sad Southern Cone phenomenon of a country plunging from one extreme economic policy to another without ever finding its way onto a balanced and sustainable growth path. If such a sad outcome occurs, it will not be because Peru is short of technicians, as in 1967; or because the limits of planning are not known, as in 1968–1975; or because the free market and orthodoxy have not been tried and found wanting, as occurred in 1976–1978, 1979–1980, and 1980–1984. It will be because the various competing economic groups that make up the Peruvian economy cannot coalesce sufficiently around a coherent consensual policy that will promote everyone's interest to some extent and no one's interest to another's detriment.

Notes

1. *Toquepala* generated substantial export revenues beginning in 1960, and the volume of fish meal exports almost quadrupled between 1959 and 1962.

2. A very interesting, almost blow-by-blow account of this period can be found in Kuczynski (1977).

3. In the event, 40 percent of the export windfall was to be paid into the fund.

4. Their industrial programming approach to the Andean Group illustrates this point well.

5. This view is also taken in Schydlowsky and Wicht (1979, 1983). However, Cline (1981) argues that a standard IMF-style stabilization program was suitable; indeed, it should have been applied earlier.

6. Cline (1981:313–315) adduces econometric evidence to the contrary, estimating the exchange rate elasticities at 0.5 for exports and -1.05 for imports. Running the export regression in percentage changes instead of shares makes the elasticity come out insignificant and with the wrong sign. A more complete econometric analysis of imports, which segments the data fully by period, also makes this elasticity statistically indistinguishable from zero (see Schydlowsky 1981:329–330).

7. Although export promotion may seem a "broad macro policy," it is conventionally viewed as a policy that narrowly discriminates in favor of selected inefficient producers who need subsidies to compete in world markets.

References

Abusada-Salah, Roberto. 1975. "Utilización de capital instalado en el sector industrial peruano." Mimeograph. Boston.

———. 1976. "Capital Utilization: A Study of Peruvian Manufacturing." Ph.D. dissertation, Cornell University.

Central Reserve Bank of Peru. "Cuentas nacionales del Peru." For 1950–1967 and 1960–1974, see *Memoria* (various issues) and *Boletín* (various issues).

Cline, William R. 1981. "Economic Stabilization in Peru, 1975–1978." In *Economic Stabilization and Developing Countries*, ed. William Cline and Sidney Weintraub, pp. 297–326. Washington, D.C.: Brookings Institution.

Diamand, Marcelo. 1971. *Seis falsos dilemas del debate económico nacional.* Cuadernos del Centro de Estudios Industriales no. 5. Buenos Aires.

————. 1973. *Doctrinas económicas, desarrollo, e independencia.* Buenos Aires: Paidos.

Diaz-Alejandro, Carlos F. 1965. "On the Import Intensity of Import Substitution." *Kyklos* 18:495-509.

Economic Commission for Latin America (ECLA). 1964. "The Growth and Decline of Import Substitution in Brazil." *Economic Bulletin for Latin America* 9, no. 1:1-59.

Felix, David. 1968. "The Dilemma of Import Substitution—Argentina." In *Development Policy—Theory and Practice,* ed. Gustav F. Papanek. Cambridge: Harvard University Press.

International Monetary Fund (IMF). *International Financial Statistics.* Various issues.

Kuczynski, Pedro-Pablo. 1977. *Peruvian Democracy Under Economic Stress: An Account of the Belaúnde Administration, 1963-1968.* Princeton: Princeton University Press.

Little, Ian; Scitovsky, Tibor; and Scott, Maurice. 1970. *Industry and Trade in Some Developing Countries: A Comparative Study.* London: Oxford University Press.

Macario, Santiago. 1964. "Protectionism and Industrialization in Latin America." In *Economic Bulletin for Latin America* (Economic Commission for Latin America) 9, no. 1:61-101.

Pennano, Guido, ed. 1981. *Economía peruana: Hacia donde?* Lima: Universidad del Pacífico.

Schydlowsky, Daniel M. 1972. "Latin America Trade Policies in the 1970's: A Prospective Analysis." *Quarterly Journal of Economics* 86, no. 2 (May):263-289.

————. 1981. "Comment on Cline." In *Economic Stabilization and Developing Countries,* ed. William Cline and Sidney Weintraub. Washington, D.C.: Brookings Institution.

————. 1982. "Comentarios sobre la política económica." In *Conferencia de Marzo 1981.* Lima: Universidad del Pacífico.

Schydlowsky, Daniel M.; Abusada-Salah, R.; and González Izquierdo, J. 1980. *Propuestas para el desarrollo peruano (1980-1985).* Lima: ADEX.

Schydlowsky, Daniel M.; Hunt, S.; and Mezzera, J. 1983. *La Promoción de exportaciones no tradicionales en el Peru.* Lima: ADEX.

Schydlowsky, Daniel M., and Wicht, Juan J. 1979. *Anatomia de un fracaso económico Peru: 1968-1978.* Lima: Universidad del Pacífico.

————. 1983. "Anatomy of an Economic Failure: Peru 1968-1978." In *The Peruvian Experiment Revisited,* ed. C. McClintock and A. Lowenthal. Princeton: Princeton University Press.

Smitmans, Patricio M. 1975. "The Intensive Use of Capital in Industrial Plants: Multiple Shifts as an Economic Option." Ph.D. dissertation, Harvard University.

Toledo, Alejandro. 1983. "Empleo e ingresos en el contexto de la crisis: Peru 1983." Mimeograph. Lima: Ministerio de Trabajo y Promoción Social, Banco Central de Reserva, PREALC-OIT (October).

Table 9.1
STATISTICAL APPENDIX

	1960	1961	1962	1963	1964	1965	1966	1967
1) Real GDP 1970 prices in millions of US$	3634	3940	4296	4470	4790	5023	5373	5566
2) Real GDP 1970 prices annual growth rate (%)	--	8.42	9.03	4.07	7.14	4.88	7.05	3.51
3) GDP per capital 1970 prices in US$	377	398	421	426	444	453	471	474
4) Exports FOB in millions of US$	433	496	540	541	667	667	764	757
5) Imports CIF in millions of US$	379	469	537	556	580	729	817	811
6) Current Account Balance in millions of US$	8	-8	-36	-81	16	-138	-234	-282
7) Total Foreign Debt in millions of US$								
8) Public Foreign Debt Service in millions of US$								
9) Terms of Trade Index (1981=100)	61	60	63	67	76	74	84	85
10) Taxes/GDP (%)	13.7	14.6	14.2	15.0	15.0	15.4	15.3	15.4
11) Government Expenditure/GDP (%)	13.0	14.9	15.3	16.8	18.6	20.3	20.6	20.7
12) Central Government Deficits/GDP (%)	0.7	-0.3	-1.1	-1.8	-3.6	-4.9	-5.3	-5.3
13) Inflation (CPI) (%)	2.4	8.8	4.8	8.8	11.2	14.9	7.7	19.1
14) Devaluation (%)	-1.2	-1.8	0.0	0.0	0.0	0.0	0.0	48.0

(Table continues)

241

STATISTICAL APPENDIX

	1968	1969	1970	1971	1972	1973	1974	1975
1) Real GDP 1970 prices in millions of US$	5565	5795	6219	6538	6919	7348	7852	8040
2) Real GDP 1970 prices annual growth rate (%)	-0.03	4.14	7.31	5.13	5.84	6.20	6.86	2.39
3) GDP per capital 1970 prices in US$	460	466	486	497	511	529	551	550
4) Exports FOB in millions of US$	866	866	1065	893	944	1049	1503	1330
5) Imports CIF in millions of US$	630	601	622	753	797	1019	1531	2551
6) Current Account Balance in millions of US$	-23	2	202	-34	-32	-192	-807	-1535
7) Total Foreign Debt in millions of US$			3681	3692	3832	4132	5237	6257
8) Public Foreign Debt Service in millions of US$			173	223	219	433	456	474
9) Terms of Trade Index (1981=100)	87	95	106	96	88	133	128	88
10) Taxes/GDP (%)	15.6	16.5	16.4	15.9	15.9	14.8	15.2	16.0
11) Government Expenditure/GDP (%)	19.7	18.2	19.0	20.1	20.5	18.7	18.4	21.6
12) Central Government Deficits/GDP (%)	-4.1	-1.7	-2.6	-4.2	-4.6	-3.9	-3.2	-5.6
13) Inflation (CPI) (%)	9.5	5.6	5.6	7.4	4.3	13.8	19.1	24.0
14) Devaluation (%)	9.2	0.5	-0.4	-0.1	0.0	0.0	0.0	3.7

(Table continues)

STATISTICAL APPENDIX

	1976	1977	1978	1979	1980	1981	1982	1983
1) Real GDP 1970 prices in millions of US$	8307	8285	8139	8489	8727	8989	9071	8002
2) Real GDP 1970 prices annual growth rate (%)	3.33	-0.26	-1.77	4.30	2.81	3.00	0.91	-11.79
3) GDP per capital 1970 prices in US$	554	539	516	525	526	529	520	447
4) Exports FOB in millions of US$	1341	1726	1972	3676	3916	3249	3293	3015
5) Imports CIF in millions of US$	2037	1911	1959	1820	2499	3447	3601	2548
6) Current Account Balance in millions of US$	-1072	-783	-164	953	-101	-1728	-1609	-850
7) Total Foreign Debt in millions of US$	7384	8567	9324	9334	9594	9638	11340	12443
8) Public Foreign Debt Service in millions of US$	485	622	702	825	1323	1756	1600	1769
9) Terms of Trade Index (1981=100)	100	105	84	110	120	100	86	90
10) Taxes/GDP (%)	14.5	14.6	15.7	17.7	20.5	17.9	17.6	14.1
11) Government Expenditure/GDP (%)	20.8	22.1	20.8	18.3	23.3	22.8	21.6	22.8
12) Central Government Deficits/GDP (%)	-6.3	-7.5	-5.1	-0.6	-2.8	-4.9	-3.9	-8.7
13) Inflation (CPI) (%)	44.7	32.4	73.7	66.7	60.8	72.7	72.9	125.1
14) Devaluation (%)	54.2	89.6	49.5	27.5	36.6	45.4	90.7	135.5

(i)   Row (2) calculated from row (1)
(ii) For rows (7) and (8) consistent data begin in 1970
(iii) Row 9 is calculated as Price Index Traditional Exports/External Price Index of Imports
      The series for 1960-73 is constructed applying the percentage variation of the terms of trade series from Instituto
      Nacional de Planificacion to 1974 figures from Banco Central de Reserva del Peru
(iv) Row (10) excludes revenue from social security taxes

Sources: Instituto Nacional de Estadistica, 1950-80; Banco Central de Reserva del Peru, 1950-67 and 1960-74; International
         Monetary Fund, International Financial Statistics (Washington, D.C., various years)

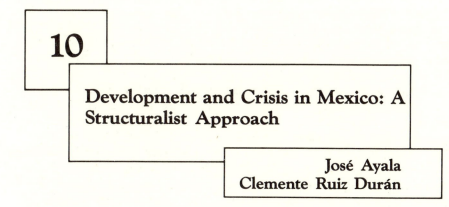

10

Development and Crisis in Mexico: A Structuralist Approach

José Ayala
Clemente Ruiz Durán

By the end of the 1960s, Mexico had enjoyed two decades of rapid growth, GNP per capita had almost doubled, inflation had been controlled, and the exchange rate had been constant for sixteen years. Unlike the other countries of Latin America, Mexico appeared to have solved the difficult problem of producing rapid noninflationary growth despite one of the area's highest population growth rates.

Beneath this promising facade of growing prosperity, however, the structural problems inherent in the import substitution growth strategy followed by Mexico could already be dimly seen. The most obvious symptom was the growing imbalance in the nation's external accounts. Despite rapid import substitution and export growth that was large by Latin American standards, the growth of imports outstripped that of exports. The current account deficit grew from $324 million in 1960 to over $1 billion ten years later and from 2 percent to 3 percent of GNP. That deficit was financed by foreign borrowing and direct foreign investment, but its size suggested that Mexico was having increasing difficulty generating the internal savings necessary to match the rising level of investment expenditures necessitated by capital-intensive import substitution activities.

A second symptom was the increasing inability of the agricultural sector to provide the food needed by a rapidly growing population. Whereas agricultural production had averaged over 5.5 percent growth during the period 1950–1965, it fell to 2.1 percent in the period 1965–1970. According to the World Bank, per capita food consumption in Mexico declined by 5.5 percent in the 1960s. This decline implied, among other things, rising food prices, underemployment in the agricultural sector, rising nutritional inadequacy, and a lack of internal demand from this key sector for the products of national industry.

Third, Mexico did not develop a national capital goods industry. Like other Latin American countries, Mexico had followed an industrial import substitution strategy that proceeded backward by stages from light consumer goods to intermediate goods and finally to capital goods. Because the capital goods sector was still in its infancy in 1970, most capital goods had to be imported, which had several unfortunate implications. For one thing, it meant that growth would require plentiful foreign exchange for the importation of capital goods and that import substitution had not really reduced Mexico's dependence on the international economy. This dependence in turn weighed heavily upon the economic sequence of investment, domestic demand, profits, and new investment and limited to a substantial degree the possibilities of long-run sustained accumulation. Another implication was that without a national industry capable of generating manufacturing technologies more appropriate to national conditions, Mexico suffered from severe technological dependency. Indiscriminate adoption of foreign technologies limited the development of labor-intensive production techniques and the absorption of the unemployed.

Fourth, there was a growing concentration of income and wealth in Mexico. In 1965, 40 percent of the labor force worked in agriculture at less than the minimum wage. Also in 1965, the bottom 20 percent of the labor force earned 3.4 percent of the total income, a percentage that was to fall further in subsequent years. The distribution of land was equally skewed. In 1982, 38 percent of the farms controlled 87 percent of the total farmland and 52 percent of the cropland while the smallest two-thirds of the farms controlled only 1.1 percent of the total farm area and 3.6 percent of Mexico's cropland (Furtado 1976:262). This concentration of wealth and power could be seen in all areas and was a source of deterioration of a model that had combined growth with political stability. The student movement of 1968 spearheaded a challenge to the existing type of development and demanded that the government implement reform.

One might summarize by saying that Mexico had not developed an internal, self-generating growth process. Growth was unbalanced with the dynamic sectors being consumer durables and other import substitutes. But both agriculture and capital goods production lagged. Thus, rather than providing a mutually reinforcing expansion of demand and supply, Mexico's unbalanced growth led to rising food prices and balance-of-payments deficits. Demand was sustained by rising government deficits, part of which financed capital formation. But this process was not sustainable in the long run, since it had led directly to growth in the current account deficit and to a rising foreign debt. When the government deficit and foreign debt became unacceptably large, the government was forced to induce recessions by cutting back on its expenditures. The recent stabilization in Mexico is only the latest of these occurrences: Previous ones were in 1954, 1970, and 1976. In each case, the stabilization effort has caused a sharp slowdown in the growth of the economy until equilibrium was reestablished in the balance of payments.

Toward a Change in the Model of Development, 1970–1976

The change of administration in 1970 presented the possibility of an economic and political reorientation of the model of development. The government of Luis Echeverría Alvarez (1970–1976) sought to confront the deteriorating economic and political situation with a new approach, which it presented to the public as "shared development." The fundamental thesis of the new growth strategy was that of incorporating marginal groups into the process of development, in contrast to the idea of the previous decade which was growth first and distribution later. This change signified a profound reaccommodation of power, since it presupposed broadening the material bases of production in the system to the greatest extent possible and achieving a kind of "democratic opening." However, that political program had its own limits and contradictions since the traditional political forces had accumulated privileges (which they were not inclined to give up) and had consolidated a style of political domination. These limitations were important in spite of the fact that modernization would benefit the very institutions that had allowed the political system to maintain sociopolitical cohesion.

The economic program of the new government gave priority to energy, agriculture, and public welfare and relied to a large extent on public expenditures to achieve its goals. There were massive increases in government spending, which rose from 21 percent to almost 34 percent of GDP between 1970 and 1976 (see Table 10.1). A substantial part of this additional spending was directed toward social welfare programs. Unfortunately, the government never had time or support enough to bring about the reforms in the tax system that were necessary to finance such a large increase in spending. As a result, there was an explosion in the government deficit, which grew from 2.5 percent of GDP in 1970 to 9.9 percent in 1976.

On the distribution front, Echeverría moved to raise the minimum wage and to raise labor income. Over the years of his administration, it is estimated that labor's share of the national income rose from 35.5 percent to 40 percent. The share of profits fell by an equivalent amount.

The net result of the massive government demand stimulus, egalitarian wage policies, and excessive monetary expansion was a short period of

Table 10.1

EVOLUTION OF THE MEXICAN ECONOMY, 1971-1976

	1971	1972	1973	1974	1975	1976
I. ECONOMIC GROWTH (%)						
Gross Domestic Product	4.2	8.5	8.4	6.1	5.6	4.2
GDP per capita	0.8	5.0	4.9	2.8	2.4	1.2
II. SECTORAL DISTRIBUTION OF GDP (%)						
Primary Sector	12.1	11.1	11.6	11.6	11.2	10.7
Secondary Sector	32.1	32.2	31.9	33.4	33.1	32.8
Tertiary Sector	55.8	56.7	56.5	55.0	55.7	56.5
III. INCOME DISTRIBUTION (%)						
Salaries	35.5	36.9	35.9	36.8	38.1	40.3
Profits	59.7	58.2	59.1	58.6	56.2	54.4
Indirect Taxes Minus Subsidies	4.8	4.9	5.0	4.6	5.7	5.3
IV. INCREASE IN PRICES (%)						
Gross Domestic Product Deflator	5.9	6.2	12.8	22.8	15.7	19.6
V. FOREIGN SECTOR (Millions of dollars)						
Current Account Deficit	928.9	1,005.7	1,528.8	3,226.0	4,442.6	3,683.3
Capital Movement	234.9	475.5	-879.4	-1,082.3	-1,061.6	-3,197.7
VI. PUBLIC SECTOR (percent of GDP)						
Revenue	18.4	18.7	20.2	21.1	23.1	23.8
Expenditures	20.9	23.6	27.0	28.3	33.2	33.6
Deficit	2.5	4.9	6.8	7.2	10.1	9.8

Sources: Mexico, Secretaria de Patrimonio y Fomento Industrial, *Principales variables macroeconomicas periodo 1970-1982* (Mexico City, 1983); International Monetary Fund, *International Financial Statistics* (Washington, D.C., various years).

rapid economic growth followed by a steady increase in the inflation rate and a severe balance-of-payments crisis. The current account deficit quadrupled, and there was massive capital flight. Private sector entrepreneurs were not in sympathy with the Echeverría program because of the redistribution of income away from profits, and they showed their opposition by increasing their capital transfers out of the country and reducing their rate of investment in the Mexican economy. As a result, the growth rate of installed capacity slowed, which contributed to a growing rigidity of supply and rising inflationary pressures. By the end of his administration, Echeverría was faced with an unprecedented fiscal deficit, rising inflation, and a severe balance-of-payments disequilibrium. All of these factors combined to trigger a financial crisis in 1976, which culminated in the signing of a stabilization agreement with the IMF and a 60 percent devaluation of the peso.

Options for Development: 1977–1982

The José López Portillo government (1976–1982) was ideologically in agreement with the orthodox stabilization program supported by the IMF. The central thesis of this orthodox approach was to conceive of the government's fiscal deficit as the cause of the crisis that the entire economy was experiencing. This thesis sidestepped the real causes and absolved speculation as the triggering mechanism of the country's financial deterioration. From the orthodox perspective, the solution consisted of reducing government intervention in the economy and eliminating the government deficit. The ultimate goal was to reactivate the power of the market as a mechanism of economic recovery. The reasoning that lay behind this thesis was in itself exceedingly simplistic, since it presumed that government interference was the fundamental cause of the decrease in private investment. It argued that overextension of the government had crowded out private investment and that the solution was to seek a permanent reduction in the government's share of the economy. This policy coincided with the proposals of the IMF and reinforced the arguments in favor of a stabilization policy.

In contrast to the IMF position, which was supported by the most conservative elements in the country, other groups in the Mexican government and society proposed an alternative strategy. They asserted that the crisis had a structural origin and that its solution required profound changes to avoid falling again into an expansion-contraction cycle. Their alternative policy postulated the following as its objectives:

1. To increase domestic production at a rate sufficient to absorb the growth in the labor force and to reduce existing unemployment and, at the same time, to gradually modify the productive structure to orient it toward the production of socially and nationally necessary goods and services
2. To center the strategy of national development on the satisfaction of basic necessities for the majority of the population
3. To make a greater commitment to the redistribution of income

4. To consolidate economic independence
5. To strengthen the mixed nature of the economy by means of dialogue and the closest possible cooperation among all the productive sectors of the nation

Both economic policy options were based on the possibilities of development derived from the new petroleum wealth that was opening up a real opportunity for short-run recovery, since international conditions were exceptionally favorable to the consolidation of a buyers' market and a rise in international petroleum prices and the exploration effort of the previous government had put the country on the road toward formulating a program to increase petroleum exports. Obviously, however, the path of recovery was different for each option. According to the orthodox plan, the strengthening of public finances was to be accomplished by means of an accelerated growth of the petroleum export industry combined with an increasingly open economy, on the assumption that national industry would become more competitive and thus less costly for the national consumer. This position was based on a conservative view of petroleum development that would maintain the fundamental relationships of the economy and the power structure rather than planning for structural change. In other words, the orthodox strategy attempted to maintain the status quo by an intensive exploitation of the petroleum resources.

The proponents of the other option proposed to develop the petroleum industry according to a plan that would connect the growth of the industry to economic recovery. This strategy supported a gradually accelerating growth that would permit a rational utilization of the financial resources derived from petroleum exports. It proposed structural change in the productive sector as well as in the financial sectors in order to lay the groundwork for more balanced growth without cyclical fluctuations.

The Implementation of the Development Option

The process of confrontation and definition between the alternative models of development did not take on an immediate and precise form, but it gradually became clear in the daily activities of the López Portillo government and in the organization of society. The conservative approach slowly and tenaciously gained ground in the main centers of power, and the financial sector gradually succeeded in imposing its criteria, not only on specific quantitative objectives but also on the long-run perspectives of the economy. In the process, the federal budget moved away from being an instrument of planning and took on the traditional role of guaranteeing sound financial management.

Thus, a kind of "debt purification cycle" was generated, consisting at the outset of reducing public expenditure, not to consolidate the government's position, but to reestablish a more balanced relationship between the servicing of the public debt and the totality of public expenditures. This policy led to a reduction of expenditures in the first year of the government while adjustments were made in the revenue base to increase the volume of collections without effecting substantial changes in the fiscal structure. With these measures, the deficit as a percentage of GDP and government intervention in the economy were both reduced. The policy favored the financial world and produced domestic and foreign financial equilibrium, but at the cost of a decline in the rate of economic growth and an increase in income inequality.

The government's program consisted of a proposal for an "alliance for production" that called for a truce among the principal social groups to stimulate production and encourage economic recovery, with an explicit sacrifice of workers' incomes. The official workers' organizations declared they were solidly behind the government in the effort to combat the crisis—their agreement was made easier by the wage gains made during the Echeverría administration. The Confederation of Mexican Workers (CIM) and the great national unions associated with government enterprises were the groups that played the most important part in the alliance with the government. On the other hand, other organizations, like the Confederación Obrera Revolucionaria (Union of Revolutionary Workers, COR) and the Confederación Revolucionaria de Obreros y Campesinos (Revolutionary Union of Workers and Peasants, CROC) maintained a less active position in the alliance. Thus, popular support for the program was based on working-class people organized at important levels of national and foreign enterprises and in the financial circles of the government. The guiding principle of the new program was the rehabilitation of the economy through reductions in public expenditures and in the average real wage, which in the inflationary context induced a redistribution of income toward the management sector and raised profits in real terms. In this way, 1977 was characterized as a year of low growth and a reconcentration of income in order to return "confidence" to the management sector (see Table 10.2).

The relative stagnation of the economy and its most immediate consequences underlined the necessity of promoting growth through government action. The government became the principal agent in the process because there was no possibility of a meaningful reaction from the private sector, which had shown in the past that it was incapable of becoming the driving force for growth. The government relied on petroleum and a potential expansion of the foreign resource base for recovery.

Table 10.2

INDICATORS OF THE NEW POLICY TAKE-OFF
(Annual Rate of Growth)

	1976	1977
Gross Domestic Product	4.2	3.4
Government Expenditure	-0.6	-3.7
Real Wages	9.9	-3.2
Private Profits	2.5	6.3

Sources: Mexico, Secretaria de Patrimonio y Fomento
Industrial, Principales variables macroeconomicas
periodo 1970-1982 (Mexico City, 1983); International
Monetary Fund, International Financial Statistics
(Washington, D.C., various years).

During 1977 and 1978, when the true size of the oil bonanza became apparent, a debate began both inside and outside the government about the proper amount of petroleum to export and how to use the financial resources coming from the oil industry. The contrasting views elicited by this debate were socially and politically opposed with respect to the social model conceived and particularly to the use of petroleum resources.

Within the framework of the policy plan derived from the agreement signed with the IMF in September 1976, one side viewed petroleum as the most useful and efficient instrument for combating the recession and external imbalances. At the same time, the other side had a nationalist-reformist orientation, because its supporters believed domestic autonomy in decisions concerning economic policy had been surrendered and economic and social inequality would be aggravated by the passive stabilization policy. Members of this group considered the exploitation of hydrocarbons to be an important element in the achievement of a more integrated and socially less-regressive economic development. However, they did not accept the notion that massive exports of petroleum resources could constitute an automatic and sufficient solution for the crisis pervading Mexican society. Rather, they argued that petroleum should be used to promote a more integrated industrial development program within the framework of a newly oriented, comprehensive economic policy.

With many shadings and variations, this latter alternative was supported by a broad spectrum of opinion, including that of a large part of the Mexican academic community, the liberal sectors, the leftist political parties, and even the official unions, which were becoming increasingly involved in the comprehensive political-economic debate. In 1977 and 1978, this coalition of forces became the most conspicuous standard-bearer in the search for a new model of development and economic reform that would be adequate to cope with the socioeconomic conditions prevailing in the country.

The Debate on the Petroleum Program

The production-exportation platform had the effect of synthesizing the discussion about petroleum, because it involved defining the government's role in placing Mexico's petroleum resources in an international context in order to promote the reorganization of the country's industrial base. This debate was initiated within the government and afterward filtered down to other groups until it became a national discussion.

The labor movement and the leftist opposition played central roles in the discussion. In 1978, at a national meeting of the Congress of Labor (Congreso del Trabajo, the most prestigious labor organization) the following proposals for the utilization of hydrocarbons were made:

> Exports should consist only of surpluses depending on the relationship between domestic needs and reserves . . . the income derived from hydrocarbon exports should be devoted directly to promoting development without becoming part of the regular fiscal reserves or being applied to the payment of foreign debt.
>
> The financial surpluses generated by the exportation of hydrocarbons should be channeled into a national employment fund, as an autonomous unit of public administration, with equal participation of workers and the government in its administration and operation. Ways must be found to assure that the income from hydrocarbon exports is earmarked for this fund, whose fundamental purpose will be to invest in programs and projects included in the National Development Plan according to the priorities established by it, especially the following: the occupation of workers, the establishment of capital goods industries, agricultural enterprises and industry based on agriculture and forestry, the production of socially necessary consumer goods, and support for strategic sectors in national economic development, such as the petrochemical, the metallurgical, equipment for mass transport of goods and persons, fertilizers, agricultural machinery, and the food industry. [Congreso del Trabajo 1978]

Labor's stance significantly influenced the direction of the discussion in that it emphasized development for domestic needs rather than for the requirements of the international economy, especially those of the

United States. This line of reasoning met with opposition, especially from managerial groups, who argued that huge increases in foreign sales of hydrocarbons constituted the economic solution to the crisis to the extent that they would bring about a rapid increase in the supply of foreign currency and thus eliminate the deficit in the current account of the balance of payments (*El Dia*, February 12, 1977:7). Although the managerial groups added that an excessive use of petroleum exports to balance foreign trade would be irresponsible, they insisted that it would also be irresponsible to leave the petroleum in the subsoil (*El Sol de Mexico*, March 2, 1978). The abundance of petroleum as well as the closeness of the U.S. market as an outlet for it should be exploited to overcome the economic crisis (*Excelsior*, March 2, 1978). However, PEMEX (Petróleos Mexicanos, the parastatal oil monopoly), which finally stated the government's position, declared, "Either we produce petroleum now, without delay and without infantile fears . . . or very soon we will regret not having been in step with the historic moment that we are living" (*El Dia*, March 19, 1978:1).

The political parties of the Mexican left, especially the Mexican Worker's party, called attention to overdependence on oil, pointing out that "the massive exportation of petroleum would bring about the premature exhaustion of reserves of a nonrenewable resource, which compromises the economic and political independence of our country, thus challenging the nationalistic nature of our former petroleum policy" (*Uno más uno*, June 1, 1977). They added, "The expansion of the petroleum industry and the accelerated growth of hydrocarbon exports would result in the worsening of domestic imbalances among various branches of production and may be used as a substitute for the essential structural reform that the entire economy demands" (*Uno más uno*, June 1, 1977, and *Excelsior*, November 18, 1978).

This very complex debate appeared to be resolved in favor of the nationalist position, which was restated in the National Plan of Industrial Development that appeared at the beginning of 1979. This plan contained the "assumption that at the end of 1980 the capacity for extraction of crude oil and hydrocarbon resources would reach a level of 2,250 million barrels a day. Beyond that level, production would increase only to satisfy the growth of domestic demand, with the volume of exports remaining constant" (Mexico, SEPAFIN 1979:3).

The National Plan of Industrial Development contained a policy definition that proposed using petroleum according to the economy's capacity for absorption in terms of national use, not according to the interests of the oil-consuming countries. However, the plan also said: "Recent events in the hydrocarbon field permit us to set more ambitious goals for the country. Today it is possible to think of reaching growing and sustained rates of economic development of 8–10 percent in order to combat poverty, to create an economic and social infrastructure, and to invest in selected areas of activity" (Mexico, SEPAFIN 1979:9). However, the plan explicitly pointed out that "the economic expansion it foresees will take place only if, from this point on, investment in the economic infrastructure is accelerated . . . and that this generally has a long gestation period" (Mexico, SEPAFIN 1979:35). The "internationalizing" position was not, however, completely rejected in the policy compromise of the National Plan of Industrial Development, because other pressure groups in the government insisted on the need to free trade through Mexico's participation in the General Agreement on Trade and Tariffs (GATT) and on redefining the place of the national economy in the world economy.

In reality, this free trade proposal again put in doubt the possibility and viability of utilizing petroleum to undertake an autonomous national road to development. Under these new circumstances, a renewed debate began, with the use of petroleum resources as the center of discussion. The workers' movement pointed out in a "manifesto to the nation," which appeared in October 1979, that it was necessary "to struggle for energy resources to become an instrument in bringing about change in economic structures and for them to be channeled toward the realization of that objective" (*Excelsior*, October 30, 1979:14). The Congress of Labor indicated that "the generalized elimination of barriers and the reduction of tariffs would lead to massive imports of all kinds of products." It added that

> the fact that income derived from petroleum exports will in the next few years allow us to overcome, to a great degree, the distortion of the Mexican balance of trade, does not mean that the economy has been freed from structural problems that limit its development, and that it is in condition to compete satisfactorily with industrialized countries. On the contrary, the foreign currency that petroleum will attract holds forth the possibility of implementing a National Plan of Development which, above all, assures permanent improvement of the people's living standard and sustained economic growth in the long run. [Congreso del Trabajo 1978]

This new discussion concluded in terms that were favorable to the national development program. On March 18, 1980, the president announced that

> after receiving varied and contradictory opinions, we have decided that this is not the appropriate moment for Mexico to enter a free system of trade. GATT does not provide the essential elements of protection and the stimulus that our

flexible economic system requires, in conformity with our global plan and sectoral plans. Its advantages are more apparent than real, even though it purports to solve the fundamental problems of liberalization of international trade. [López Portillo 1980:15–16]

On that occasion, the level of the petroleum program was also ratified, with the indication that a margin of flexibility of "about 10 percent more was granted to guarantee supplies and exports and to give our country the capacity to respond to and resolve any contingency or additional risk" (López Portillo 1980:8). Concurrently, the initiation of the Sistema Alimentario Mexicano (Mexican Nutrition System, SAM) was announced, as well as a forthcoming global development plan that would encompass all sectorial plans. The policy definition of the president of the Republic in a government characterized by a strong president indicated support, at least in principle, for the use of petroleum surpluses in a development plan that aspired to be national. However, profound contradictions would develop in the real use of petroleum as a fortifying element in national development.

Developments in the Mexican Economy, 1978–1982

The macroeconomic orientation of the National Plan of Industrial Development assumed a growing and sustained effort to expand the economy as a whole during the period 1978–1982 combined with growth in all productive sectors, especially the petroleum industry and manufacturing, and a decrease in the current accounts deficit (see Table 10.3). But that is not the way things turned out. The oil bonanza unleashed a deluge of spending by both the government and the private sector, much of it financed by foreign borrowing. Rising demand sparked a recovery in the economy, and up to 1980, the actual growth rates exceeded those forecast in the plan.

The petroleum industry came close to matching the ambitious goals laid out in the plan as production rose from 900,000 barrels per day in 1977 to 2.3 million barrels in 1981. But the rate and composition of growth in the manufacturing sector was disappointing (see Table 10.4). Up to 1979, that sector's growth rate exceeded the plan, but then it began to fall well below the planned rates. Considering that the pillar of restructuring the economy was supposed to be manufacturing, this decline was unfortunate. Expansion was limited to the traditionally vigorous areas (see Table 10.5), and there was no restructuring of supply. Instead, the old model of development and accumulation was reaffirmed. Dependency on external stimuli was maintained, or even increased, and there was little progress toward a better national integration of the productive apparatus.

Table 10.3

NATIONAL PLAN FOR INDUSTRIAL DEVELOPMENT

Projected Rates of Growth

(in percent)

	1978	1979	1980	1981	1982
GROSS DOMESTIC PRODUCT	6.5	7.1	8.2	9.5	10.6
Primary Sector	0.8	2.5	2.7	2.9	3.5
Petroleum Industry	36.5	38.3	24.6	22.0	8.9
Manufacturing	6.4	6.6	8.2	9.7	12.4
Construction	14.4	6.6	10.4	11.4	13.4
Electric Power	9.0	9.9	11.1	12.5	14.7
Balance in Current Account-millions of dollars	-2,544	-1,653	-802	-477	+26

Source: Mexico, Secretaria de Patrimonio y Fomento Industrial, Plan nacional de desarrollo industrial (Mexico City, 1979), p. 820.

When compared with the goals of the industrial plan, the behavior of the manufacturing sector shows that, with the exception of the automotive, electrical, electronic, and chemical areas, expansion was below projected growth. How can this slow growth be explained? We will argue that it was essentially caused by problems of supply and that when such problems were encountered, they were due to lack of investment. The result was bottlenecks and rising imports.

The uneven flow of investments put pressure on the productive limits of installed capacity, reducing the possibilities for increased production in the short run and causing an increase in the general level of prices. The elements that, in our judgment, explain this process of uneven flow of investment are essentially commercial liberalization, overvaluation of the peso, and the failure of the government to marshal its financial and planning resources to help big industries.

Trade liberalization occurred despite Mexico's refusal to join GATT. The impact of the liberalization was made more significant for the domestic

Table 10.4

EVOLUTION OF THE MEXICAN ECONOMY, 1977-1983

	1977	1978	1979	1980	1981	1982	1983
I. ECONOMIC GROWTH (%)							
Gross Domestic Product	3.4	8.2	9.2	8.3	7.9	-0.5	-4.5
GDP per capita	0.5	5.2	6.1	5.4	5.1	-3.1	-7.3
II. SECTORIAL DISTRIBUTION OF GDP (%)							
Primary Sector	10.5	10.2	9.2	8.4	8.1	7.3	
Secondary Sector	34.0	34.0	34.9	37.2	36.5	36.3	
Tertiary Sector	55.5	55.8	44.1	54.4	55.4	56.4	
III. INCOME DISTRIBUTION (%)							
Salaries	38.9	37.9	37.7	36.1	37.4	35.8	
Profits	55.3	56.2	55.6	55.6	54.5	54.3	
Indirect Taxes Minus Subsidies	5.8	5.9	6.7	8.3	8.1	9.9	
IV. INCREASE IN PRICES							
Gross Domestic Price Deflator	30.4	16.7	20.3	28.7	27.2	61.2	94.2
V. PUBLIC SECTOR (percent of GNP)							
Revenue	24.2	25.3	26.2	27.8	27.7	30.4	
Expenditures	30.9	32.2	33.6	35.6	42.4	48.8	
Deficit	6.7	6.9	7.4	7.8	14.7	18.4	
VI. GROWTH RATES							
Manufacturing	3.5	9.8	10.5	7.0	6.7	2.9	-8.3
Petroleum Industry	10.1	17.6	18.4	24.0	16.7		

Sources: Mexico, Secretaria de Patrimonia y Fomento Industrial, Principales variables macroeconomicas periodo 1970-1982 (Mexico City, 1983); International Monetary Fund, International Financial Statistics (Washington, D.C., various years).

economy by the rising level of oil exports and the inflows of foreign capital. Both of these factors kept the exchange rate from rising to fully reflect rising inflation. The resulting overvaluation of the peso made imports increasingly cheap and reduced the profitability of domestic production. Domestic industry was no match for imports at an exchange rate determined by oil exports and capital inflows. In the absence of government intervention, it is therefore not surprising that private investment failed to fulfill the sectorial plans. Thus, the lack of a well-

Table 10.5

GROWTH OF THE MANUFACTURING INDUSTRY

(1977-1981)

	Average Annual Growth (%)	Standard Deviation
Low Rates of Growth Industries		
Food, Beverages and Tobacco	5.7	1.5
Other Industries	5.7	5.0
Textiles, Garment and Leather	6.3	3.1
Non-metallic Mineral Products	6.3	5.4
Average Growth Industries		
Paper and Sub-products	7.1	3.5
Lumber Industry	7.7	3.2
High Growth Industries		
Basic Metal	8.0	6.8
Metallurgic Products, Machinery and Equipment	10.3	6.8
Chemical Products excluding Petrochemical	11.0	5.5
Total	7.5	2.8

Sources: Mexico, Secretaria de Patrimonio y Fomento Industrial, _Principales variables macroeconomicas periodo 1970-1982_ (Mexico City, 1983).

designed system of protection worked against the goals of modernization, diversification, and industrial integration. The nationalist development program was increasingly being replaced by a situation characterized by disorder and a lack of focus.

With the advantage of hindsight, it is clear that the main macroeconomic problem of the López Portillo government was excessive demand stimulus. The large investment demands of the petroleum program and other projects, plus continued subsidies, boosted government spending as a

Table 10.6

SOURCES OF INSTABILITY IN THE FOREIGN SECTOR
(millions of dollars)

	1977	1978	1979	1980	1981
Deficit in Current Account	1,596	2,693	4,871	7,223	12,544
Capital Outflow	981	600	2,506	4,645	10,975
Sources of Financing:					
Foreign Debt	2,907	3,342	7,014	11,765	23,342
Foreign Investment	327	385	782	1,254	1,189

Source: Bank of Mexico.

share of GNP by five percentage points between 1977 and 1981. Over the same period, the investment ratio rose from 25 percent to 31 percent. This increase caused a tremendous surge in aggregate demand, which had two results—both unfortunate. First, it increased inflationary pressure. Second, it led to a big jump in import demand, which was not surprising, given the import liberalization that had taken place and the overvaluation of the peso caused by rising inflation rates.

The industrial plan assumed that by 1982 the balance-of-payments deficit would be eliminated. But in reality, the opposite happened as the current account deficit ballooned from $1.6 billion in 1977 to $12.5 billion in 1981. There was an increase in the trade deficit to $4.5 billion in spite of the fact that oil exports rose from $1 billion in 1977 to $14.6 billion four years later. But that was not the only problem. There was also a growing deficit in financial services due to the rising nominal interest rate being charged on Mexico's growing foreign debt. By 1981, financial services alone cost the country $7.5 billion. Perhaps more serious, there were very large capital outflows, particularly in 1981 and 1982 (see Table 10.6). In those two years, the outflows were so large they practically offset foreign capital inflows, which implied that the increase in foreign debt, rather than financing development, was being used by the private sector to finance the transfer of resources abroad.

These factors, consequences of the freedom granted in the use of foreign currency, prevented the country from advancing toward financial self-determination, produced effects contrary to the national development program, and caused a waste of resources that should have been used for productive purposes. Thus, the country did not succeed in creating an infrastructure in the export area to operate independently of petroleum. As a result, the Mexican economy today, instead of progressing toward financial self-determination, has arrived at a monoproduct dependency on petroleum as an export while accumulating one of the largest foreign debts in all the Third World.

Toward the end of 1981, the situation worsened considerably when the petroleum market went through an acute contraction of demand, which reduced Mexico's export earnings and caused the current account deficit to rise to 5.4 percent of GNP. Even more serious, the fall of oil earnings abruptly curtailed Mexico's ability to obtain foreign credit. Unfortunately, the government's economic policy did not adapt with flexibility and speed to the serious and complex conditions of the new economic situation; even more, there was a true "crisis of management of the crisis."

The situation required that the government resolutely apply a policy package that would control foreign and domestic financial imbalances. However, the financial authorities decided to retreat and then return to orthodox policy by relying primarily on market signals.

In February 1982, the government devalued by 67 percent and implemented a package of measures aimed at limiting the government deficit, reducing aggregate demand, and controlling inflation. These measures were

1. A budget reduction of 3 percent
2. Import liberalization
3. A large wage adjustment (in March)
4. Price controls
5. Increases in the interest rate to maintain equivalence with rates in other countries
6. A system of minidevaluations

Unfortunately, the plan did not work, and conditions continued to deteriorate. The freeing of market forces led to banking speculation and converted the capital outflow into an explosive process. Meanwhile, inflation accelerated while both investment and production declined. As speculation against the peso mounted, the country's international reserves dwindled rapidly, and a foreign exchange crisis ensued. Finally, the process became highly politicized, and speculation threatened the very existence of the state.

In September 1982, in response to the rapidly worsening foreign reserve position, the government made two momentous policy decisions.

It nationalized the banks, and it established exchange controls for the first time in Mexico's history. The nationalization that was applied as a remedy against the forces of reaction soon became an important element in the realignment of political groups since, for decades, financial capital had formed the basis for economic control. The process of nationalization thus led in a new direction since it was replacing traditional capital, which until then had organized both the accumulation and the production processes. In this way, a political crisis over the realignment of power contributed to the crises of disintegration, of dependence on an inefficient trade and financial structure, and of inequality. It was not simply a matter of recovering the foundations of sustained growth that had permitted continuous expansion since 1932. Rather, the entire strategy of development was under scrutiny.

The Program of the New Government

It was in this context of crisis that the administration of Miguel de la Madrid Hurtado came into power in December 1982 and proposed a program with two characteristics: first, an immediate reordering of the economy and second, the long-run reorganization described in the National Development Plan (PND). The program for immediate reorganization of the economy consisted of a package of short-run economic policies. These were founded on financial orthodoxy, which assumes that the control of demand is the basis for emergence from economic crisis. With the goal of reducing aggregate demand, a package of restrictive monetary and fiscal policies was proposed whose four main measures were to

1. Decrease public expenditure
2. Increase public revenues to halt the extraordinary growth of the deficit
3. Raise the interest rates
4. Reduce the liquidity of the financial system

Implicit in this plan was a departure from the idea that government intervention in the economy was the basic cause of financial disequilibrium and that reduction of government participation would reduce such imbalances, as had been stated in 1977. Rather, the government deficit was seen as the problem. The new administration proposed a reduction of the public deficit/GDP ratio by 17 percent in 1982, 8.5 percent in 1983, 5.5 percent in 1984, and 3.5 percent in 1985.

In the area of monetary and credit policy, the basic idea behind the reorganization package was that an excess of liquidity was stimulating consumption and leading to new inflationary pressures. Thus, to restrict the growth of consumption, it proposed to reduce the financing of the nonbanking sectors, which would make resources scarcer for individuals as well as for firms. This reduction undoubtedly discouraged consumption, but it also became an obstacle to production since many firms were unable to generate sufficient resources with their cash flows and, faced with restrictions on bank credits, chose to reduce their lines of production. In addition to the measures to control demand, another fundamental element of the program was the proposal to restructure the foreign exchange market through direct monetary control. In practice, this proposal meant, on the one hand, a liberalization of the exchange market and, on the other, a monetarist management of the exchange rate, making it flexible and devaluing it and thus imposing a high cost on production.

When former administrations faced problems in applying contractionary measures, goals were often relaxed to soften the impact of the measures. The present administration, although it has been more persistent with respect to the assumed success of its economic reorganization program, also foresaw the possibility of adjusting its budgetary goals for 1984, explicitly stating its intention to increase expenditures in case the economy did not recover within the first six months. In this case, the goal of achieving a public deficit/GDP ratio of 5.5 percent by 1984 was to be adjusted to avoid greater social tension. This flexibility would appear to indicate that the Mexican government manages its relationship with the citizenry more in terms of maintaining social balance than of adhering to traditional economic doctrines.

We turn now to the longer-run plan (PND) of the de la Madrid government. This National Development Plan seeks to unite economic reorganization and structural change, or, in other words, to establish compatibility between economic stability and productive expansion. Structural change is expressly defined as the strategy that seeks to destroy the roots of structural imbalances in order to construct the foundations of sustained economic development. Stabilization and structural change should be simultaneous and mutually supportive. It is assumed as a fundamental principle that the economy cannot recover without stability, but without structural change, the conditions that led to the crisis will remain, and crises will recur. The aim of the PND is to establish the structural conditions for a new macroeconomic stability.

The strategy of the PND recognizes the uncertainty of the present but expects a gradual recovery of the economy without presenting an outline of its general characteristics. An official responsible for economic policy gave a preview of some of these (Córdoba 1983:819). In the first place, he said the recovery will be endogenously stimulated by the private sector rather than exogenously by public expenditure. The latter will support recovery but will not be its moving force. The expected recovery will be slow, but balanced. There will be an extensive replacement of inventories, a recovery of private consumption when real wages are stabilized, a strengthening of private investment with improvement in expectations, and a moderate growth of public expenditure after a decrease in the relative burden of domestic debt. With respect to private investment, greater uncertainty exists regarding its future form because of the high prevailing rates of interest, the low level of utilization of installed capacity, and lack of confidence. These factors are in contrast to the accommodations derived from substantive modifications in relative prices (rate of exchange, energy, and capital/labor).

The above-mentioned official has proposed a possible framework for structural change. He maintains that a strategy based on the expansion of aggregate demand, which seeks to achieve full employment, will destabilize the markets of foreign currency and domestic finance. The result will be recurrent crisis, devaluation of the currency, acceleration of inflation, and contraction of economic activity—in short, acute stop-and-go cycles. Movement to a new level of macroeconomic equilibrium requires a sectorial and regional orientation of the productive and distributive systems that will allow a permanent equilibrium of the finance and exchange markets at the high levels demanded by the full employment goal. This orientation should be accompanied by a redirection of investment in a way that generates more employment and consumes less foreign currency per peso invested and by a restructuring of final demand in those areas of greater mass consumption. A sustainable recovery also requires an agricultural sector that is able to supply the nutritional needs of the masses. It will undoubtedly take many years of effort to achieve a complete remodeling of the economy that includes the creation of a nationally integrated, competitive industrial sector.

The economic logic of the program rests on an assumption of "strategic optimism," in which a return to stable growth was expected in 1985 and then an "equilibrium" rate of growth is to be achieved; that is, a new floor to growth will be established so that no market unbalances the others. The strategy to achieve this equilibrium rate consists essentially of a radical modification of relative prices to promote nonpetroleum exports and an efficient substitution of imports. What is questionable about this program is, not its goals, but the mechanism that will make it work. We can see two problems—demand and employment. We know from the plan that public investment and government expenditure are discounted as the moving forces of demand stimulus. But Mexico is not likely to get much of a boost from exports either. Given the stagnant oil market, the international situation, and protectionist pressures in the developed countries, a significant expansion of trade is highly unlikely.

That essentially leaves private investment as the main exogenous source of demand stimulus. But investment is unlikely to play that role in a stagnant economy in which neither government spending nor exports are growing rapidly.

Employment creation is another problem. The PND foresaw a GDP growth rate of 5-6 percent in 1985. But that rate, even if it had been achieved, would have been insufficient to absorb the growth of the labor force, which was estimated at 3.8 percent. The employment strategy of the plan consists of import substitution and a drastic change in relative factor prices, meaning an increase in the interest rate, a decrease in real wages, and a devaluation. There are several reasons to doubt the efficacy of that strategy. In the first place, there is little empirical evidence that factor demand is very sensitive to the modification of relative factor prices. In the second, import substitution in the past, especially as practiced by the multinationals, has led to a rise in capital intensity instead of the reverse. Thus, the future of slow and uncertain growth leaves Mexico with the prospect of high and rising levels of disguised and open unemployment.

It should be the goal of Mexican policymakers to seek a growth strategy that offers a more optimistic future. Although we cannot spell out here what the characteristics of such a growth strategy might be, we feel sure they will involve a far more central role for "economic leadership" in strategic sectors and activities by the state.

As the "developer of last resort," the state should intervene selectively to bring about a restructuring of the economy so that it is capable of more rapid, self-sustaining growth. The principal mechanisms at the state's command are the budget, sectorial plans, the nationalized banking system, and its control over the exchange rate. The joint mobilization of all these policy instruments should allow a recovery from the current crisis with fewer social costs than a program that relies essentially on the private market.

Notes

Translated by Doris C. Da Rosa and edited by Samuel A. Morley.

References

Bank of Mexico. *Indicadores económicos.*
Congreso del Trabajo. 1978. "Reunión nacional ordinaria: Tomo III, Plan económico nacional y comercialización social." Mimeograph. Mexico City.

Córdoba, José. 1983. "Desafíos e incógnitas del desarrollo sostenido." *Comercio Exterior* 9 (September):811–817.

Furtado, Celso. 1976. *Economic Development of Latin America*. Cambridge: Cambridge University Press.

International Monetary Fund. *International Financial Statistics*.

López Portillo, José. 1980. "Petroleo, GATT, y alimentos." Speech given by the president of Mexico on the forty-second anniversary of the expropriation of petroleum. *Cuadernos de filosofia politica* 30 (March). Government of Mexico, Secretaria de Programacion y Presupuesto.

Mexico, Secretaria de Patrimonio y Fomento Industrial (SEPAFIN). 1979. *Plan nacional de desarrollo industrial*. Mexico City.

_____. 1983a. *Estadísticas hacendarias del sector público, cifras anuales, 1965–1982*. Mexico City.

_____. 1983b. *Sistema de cuentas nacionales de Mexico: Principales variables macroeconómicas periodo 1970–1982*. Mexico City.

11

Colombia: Moderate Economic Growth, Political Stability, and Social Welfare

Edgar Revéiz
María José Pérez

Colombia is currently undergoing a serious economic and political crisis, and economically, this is one of the most critical periods for the country since the depression of the 1930s. The Colombian state appears to be losing control over some of the most dynamic sectors of the economy, a change that is particularly significant since it is occurring in a country that has been a symbol of political stability since the late 1950s. However, the system of political co-optation established by the National Front in 1958, which has largely ensured this stability, may now be in serious crisis.[1] Thus, the fundamental challenge the political regime faces today is to seek to strengthen and to democratize the Colombian economy while continuing to guarantee the country's democratic politics.

Notwithstanding the country's current problems, the central element of Colombian development in the past several decades has been one of continuity and moderation. Indeed, Colombia is an atypical case in the Latin American context as it has had greater possibilities of combining alternative means of development than many other countries. Thus, it differs not only from countries that have only certain agricultural, mining, or energy-related resources, and in which state economic policies are largely determined by these resources, but also from countries that are poor in natural resources but have abundant labor, and in which state policies often play a more significant role in determining the country's development pattern.

Colombia has maintained a centrist model of a mixed economy without pursuing radical extremes of either neoliberalism or socialism. It has obtained better results than most Latin American countries since 1960 with regard to economic, social, and political goals, without sacrificing economic growth. Its average annual growth rate of per capita income was 3.2 percent between 1960 and 1981, and the country's current population growth rate is 2.1 percent, indicating that it has gone through the difficult demographic transition. Although on the basis of its current per capita income ($1,400) Colombia is classified by the World Bank as a country with medium-low income, many of its social indicators correspond to countries with medium-high income.[2]

There is increasing agreement among economists, both orthodox and less orthodox, of the need to include political factors in their analyses. This inclusion is necessary as more than simply a reflection of economic factors, as was traditionally the case in the neoclassical and classical Marxist schools. There is no necessary "rule of correspondence" between political crisis and economic crisis; they often are not simultaneous because of the relative separation of the state and the economy. It is useful to analytically delink the economic and political present, viewing the two processes as separate in order to understand the role of cultural, historical, and ideological factors in the contemporary crises. However, an analysis of the relationship between economics and politics is essential to an understanding of the specific forms of regulation that are established in different periods in response to the struggle for redistribution among different economic and social groups. Studying the state—how it operates and how decisions are made within it—the complex system of coalitions within the state, and the manner in which the economic system functions and reproduces itself is more important than building models to show how the economy should function.

For some analysts, the nation—the internal market and political structure—was viewed as the primary obstacle to effective capitalist development in the 1960s when the world economy was booming. In the 1970s, when the economy was more open, the state was viewed as the principal obstacle largely because of the fiscal deficit. In this chapter, because of the level of economic and political development in Colombia, we view the state itself as the principal site of conflict for the major economic and social forces in the country. Because of economic, historical, and political factors, explored in the next section, we argue that no social group has been able to attain a hegemonic role within the state.

In Colombia, even when people who believe in neoliberal economic models have been in control of economic policy, the state apparatus has never been dismantled. Economic debates have focused more on the efficiency of state administration and on the means of transferring power and resources from the center to the departments and municipalities. State policy has been the result of a delicate process of transactions and equilibrium among different economic sectors and regions of the country. Historically, the state has found itself limited in its ability to rationalize its operation and to formulate and execute distinct economic projects because it has been unable to bring together the country's principal social and economic forces. In recent times, such a task has become even more difficult as these forces have become increasingly more diversified. However, certain interests have had primacy over the national interest, and some of them have been able to "socialize" their losses and "privatize" their gains at the expense of state efforts to regulate the economic, social, and political processes in the country.

As we discuss in greater detail below, two major groups can be identified in the redistributive struggle among the different capital sectors. There are those sectors that, because of their political and economic power, have been capable of pressuring the state to ensure their major risks. The most important of these are the coffee sector and the savings banks linked to housing construction (*corporaciones de ahorro y vivienda*). For a second, more vulnerable set of economic sectors, there are no clear institutional safeguards that allow them to eliminate their risks. The economic sectors in this group strive by a wide variety of means to influence different state mechanisms of economic and social policy to ensure their continuing profits and process of accumulation.

Economic Regulation and Political Stability

The two central historical features of Colombia's economic and political development are coffee and the two-party system. Both of these factors have helped lead to a certain "ambiguity of the state," that is to say, a difficulty in distinguishing the public interest from the private interest both in the practical exercise of power and in the mental framework of Colombians. At the same time, state officials have had considerable discretion in adopting macrodecisions and in giving concessions to certain private-sector interests within the context of a system of highly politicized and institutionalized control, which leads to modifications as governments change.

The leading sector of national development, the coffee sector, was begun with national capital. Its creation, which began around 1870, established a middle class whose new purchasing power provided the basis for the country's industrialization. Unlike other Latin American countries, industrialization did not proceed from an "enclave" created and controlled by foreign capital, and as this difference extended itself to other regions of the country, it played an important role in providing economic and political stability. For a long period of the country's history, coffee policy was the country's macroeconomic policy, rather than just a sectorial policy, as coffee dominated the economy. This group had a profound impact on the structure of the state, and even today, the coffee sector is involved in general macroeconomic decisions that affect other sectors of the economy.

A complex set of institutions was created to manage the country's coffee policy. A number are dispersed throughout the state apparatus, but the minister of finance participates in all of them. However, some key aspects of policy, such as international negotiations, have essentially been turned over to the legally private representative of the coffee sector, the Coffee Federation (Federación Nacional de Cafeteros de Colombia, FEDERACAFE). This federation's board of directors has six private members and five government directors. It is the country's only producer association that is a part of the cabinet-level National Council of Economic and Social Policy (Consejo Nacional de Políticas Económicas y Sociales, CONPES), which is headed by the president.[3] Because of its unparalleled access to the state, the federation historically has been able to ensure that profits are retained by the coffee sector while losses are borne by the state. It has done so by manipulating the various instruments of coffee policy: the National Coffee Fund, the coffee retention tax, the ad valorem tax, internal price supports, and other mechanisms.

Although coffee has played a crucial role in the country's economic development, the political evolution has been dominated by two parties formed in the mid-nineteenth century, the Conservative and Liberal parties. Particularly since the 1950s, these parties have demonstrated little ideological diversity. With the establishment of the National Front in 1958, initially in response to the danger of continued interparty violence, they have established themselves as barriers to the entry of other groups to political power. The "golden rule" of the coalition governments established by the National Front has been "everyone in government." The trade in coffee was supplemented by the politics of the National Front, which cooled the political passions and the violence that had been devouring the country. Although this process of political co-optation has been an important factor of stability, it has also prevented access to the decision-making processes of the state by a large portion of the population, including new economic and social forces.

The National Front system created an adequate political framework for economic and social development by eliminating party conflict over control of the state apparatus. It was preceded by the civilian dictatorship of Conservative Laureano Gómez (1950–1953) and the military one of General Gustavo Rojas Pinilla (1953–1957). These governments coincided with a period of world economic boom and with a coffee bonanza that lasted from 1950 to 1954. Political factors, especially those related to *la violencia*, caused the fall of the first; economic and political factors led to the fall of the second, which coincided with a decline in coffee prices between 1957 and 1958. The National Front arrangement kept all people who were not members of the traditional parties out of government posts, and it fostered clientele-type structures that, given a state incapable of reaching all marginalized sectors of the population, served as an imperfect substitute for social security. At the same time, the National Front depoliticized the country to a certain extent, establishing an "implicit consensus" that eliminated any sense of opposition, or even of pluralism.

Economic and Political Factors of Stability

The first years of the National Front, from 1958 to 1965, coincided with an increase in import-substituting industrialization in the country, and the creation of the front also anticipated by a few years the creation of the Alliance for Progress. However, the state created by the National Front was not a strong state with a bureaucratic apparatus independent of society. Rather, it set up a *weak* state with important links to the country's economically powerful groups. Only during the presidency of Carlos Lleras Restrepo (1966–1970) were the bases for a stronger state established.

Another critical step taken during the administration of President Carlos Lleras was the creation of a framework facilitating a partial shift to a model of export promotion by decreeing a new trade and exchange law (Decree Law 444 of 1967). This law established a crawling peg devaluation and a series of incentives for exports of noncoffee products. Under the previous system of fixed exchange rates from 1948 to 1967, the country had experienced numerous devaluations that were politically tumultuous. The establishment of a crawling peg devaluation and the turn toward export promotion played an important role in promoting the country's continued political stability. Diversification of the country's economy and of its export sector in the 1970s decreased the vulnerability of its external sector and strengthened the political system, for diversification made it more difficult for any group to play a hegemonic role. Manufacturing exports grew at an annual rate of 20.1 percent between 1967 and 1974.

A greater number of centers of economic power began to appear in the 1950s and 1960s as industrialization advanced due to both market forces and state support (credit, tariff, and exchange measures as well as little oversight of the financial sector). Beginning in the 1950s, there was a veritable explosion in the number of specialized producer associations. These associations and the country's different regions have been particularly sensitive to any government policy that appears to discriminate against them, thus preventing policy extremes and generating a greater degree of stability in the country. Economic diversification and the more complex ties between the state and the private sectors have been factors of relative political stability and have promoted gradual change. Important decisions involving high transaction costs have taken place over a long period of time, in contrast to what normally occurs in more specialized economies. At the same time, Colombia's different governments have implemented a wide variety of alternative development policies, as shall be seen in the more detailed discussion of different presidential periods.

One of the single most important factors of political stability in Colombia has been regional development. In contrast to other Latin American countries, Colombia's urban population is dispersed in a number of different cities, though urban concentration is increasing. The country is approximately two-thirds urban and has four cities with over 1 million inhabitants. There is considerable diversity in the structures of land tenure, types of urbanization, and degree of social development. Competition among regions and between these and the country's center have led to an emphasis on regional conflicts over class conflicts. Even when class conflicts have existed, they have often appeared to be regional ones. The dialectic begun in the nineteenth century between centralism and federalism has been a means of decentralizing conflicts. The growing process of centralization in the country has been fostered by the development model based upon international financing channeled through the public sector as international agencies prefer to negotiate with one minister than with twenty-three departmental governors.

At the same time, there has been a strengthening of the process of co-optation—of the complex rules, traditions, and procedures that determine membership in different groups. A particularly important form of co-optation has been political clientelism, which has served as an imperfect substitute for social security and the provision of public goods to population groups that are otherwise not reached by the state. Another factor promoting political stability has been the near-total monopoly over the means of communication by private interests with strong links to the political parties. Even on the state-controlled television, different news programs have been parceled out to major factions of the two major parties.

One of the causes of the country's economic and political stability has been that, on the basis of trial and error, the country has established its own set of economic orientations and those orientations are substantially less ideological than in many other countries, those of the Southern Cone, for example. In fact, a theory and an economic policy particular to Colombia was created, both based on "leading sectors." These leading sectors—coffee and then construction—are the ones that have found themselves institutionally represented within the state and protected by it while other economic sectors have had to seek a variety of means to influence state policy.

A surprising diversity of development strategies and anticyclical economic policies have been tried in the country since the 1940s, a little-studied phenomenon that appears to be due to a number of factors. Most important, the country's rich resource base has permitted a variety of development options, and increasingly, this variety has provided economic policymakers with greater latitude in their decisions. In addition, the legacy of the anticyclical policies, which have consisted of employing fiscal deficits as a counterweight to recessionary economic forces, has been important. Another important factor has been the increase in state intervention, which in the long term has complemented the economy's regulation based upon the coffee sector. Other important factors have included an appropriate management of external debt and "learning" about exchange policy from the country's several coffee bonanzas.

Economic Diversification and Modernization of the State: 1950–1970

From the 1950s to the 1970s, general objectives of the country's economic management were to focus more on controlling inflation than unemployment; to manage the exchange rate in prudent fashion; to balance the influence of producer groups and of political and regional interests in monetary, fiscal, and budgetary policy; to rely on external debt, particularly from international agencies; and to abstain from manipulation of the economy in the short term for electoral gain. The period since the early 1970s has been characterized by a greater struggle for redistribution and weaker political stability.

Since the 1950s, the country's monetary policy has been relatively less autonomous in contrast to its fiscal policy, in part because a substantial share of public investment traditionally has consisted of external credits. Especially since 1967, the dual processes of strengthening state institutions and increasing centralization have been a response to the belief that the country needed to administer in a more efficient fashion the large quantities of foreign loans the public sector was receiving. The management of short-term fiscal policy in Colombia usually has been accomplished by means of controlling public expenditures and not public revenues, which tends to increase the public deficit. The country's development plans usually have consisted of government plans for public investment prepared by the National Planning Department and approved by Congress. Yet, there has often been a separation between these plans and the government's economic policy, in which the minister of finance and producer associations have greater influence. The complex interactions between economic regulation and political stability from 1950 to the present can be divided into four stages: 1955–1966, 1966–1970, 1970–1982, and 1982 to the present.

The two principal power structures that have had the most influence on the country's economic policies and planning have been the coffee sector and international financial agencies. Their influence was particularly being felt by the late 1940s. By that time, the country had also gained valuable experience in exchange and monetary policy and in state interventionism by means of industrial promotion and housing and construction agencies.[4] In this fashion, the institutional bases for the country's economic regulation began to be established. During these years (1948–1967), the country experienced high rates of population growth (an annual rate of 3.1 percent) and slow growth of GDP per capita (1.6 percent). There was slow but steady improvement in the minimum wage, and import-substituting industrialization advanced. In the second half of this period, from 1958 to 1967, the industrial sector grew at an annual rate of 7.5 percent while exports grew 18 percent and imports 11.8 percent.

These years were characterized by considerable exchange instability. Six devaluations by means of adjustments to fixed exchange rates were carried out between 1948 and 1967. Probably the most important institutional advance was the creation of the Junta Monetaria in 1963, which improved the government's control of monetary policy. Under the influence of the United Nations Economic Commission for Latin America (UN/ECLA), government planning began to be stressed. However, the first major development plan of the National Front, the Plan Decenal, was never implemented, and planning was overshadowed by short-term management of economic policy. Not only were the 1950s a period of considerable political instability, but the National Front had to face a major challenge during the presidency of Guillermo León Valencia (1962–1966) in the form of a threatened labor strike and military coup in 1965, reflecting in part the country's balance-of-payments problems. However, the first two administrations of the National Front—those of Alberto Lleras Camargo (1958–1962) and Valencia—eliminated party struggles for control of the state and ended much of the remaining violence in the countryside, thus laying a foundation for stable economic policy. This foundation was built upon in significant ways by the subsequent administration of Carlos Lleras Restrepo.

During the Lleras presidency, numerous new state institutions and agencies for economic regulation and intervention were established. With the 1968 constitutional reform, the planning capabilities of the state were strengthened, as well as its administrative capabilities. This was a period of "state capitalism," though obviously "in transition to capitalism" in the sense of the state intervening not only by supplying credit but also by direct capital investments. The state supported efforts to build a more efficient capitalist structure in the country, one that was capable of competing in world markets, without changing the social structures of production. The state Institute for Industrial Promotion (Instituto de Fomento Industrial, IFI) acted as a source of government financing and as a government oversight agency. Planning was restructured, and the president took personal charge of economic policy, including active direction of the National Council of Economic and Social Policy. The National Planning Department assumed responsibility for evaluating and controlling all direct foreign investment. The public sector, in terms of structure and size, expanded to a position similar to that in equivalent economies. There was vigorous expansion of foreign trade, and the country's balance-of-payments problems were effectively addressed by means of the crawling peg exchange rate (for balance-of-payments data from 1967 to 1981 see appendix Table 11.A1).

The originality of the modernization of the state that occurred during these years rested on the adequate reconciliation of the traditional forms of economic regulation (by means of monetary, exchange, and financial policies) and increased planning (principally by means of fiscal policy). This combination strengthened the country's mixed economy and prevented any single group from becoming hegemonic.

During these years, there was significant growth in school enrollments and vigorous housing construction for middle- and lower-middle-class groups. The minimum wage was institutionalized and steadily improved in real terms, and the urban middle class was strengthened. Industrial growth continued at a healthy average rate of 9.2 percent between 1967 and 1974, the result of both continued import substitution and export promotion. The annual rate of growth of industrial exports during the period was 20 percent while imports grew at 4.9 percent.

However, there were also problems during this period, symbolized by the difficult elections of 1970, which Rojas and his National Popular Alliance (ANAPO) party lost by a narrow margin. Fear of agrarian reform had prevented more significant improvement in the agricultural sector, even while there was considerable expansion in credit to commercial growers. With the 1968 constitutional reform, much of Congress's power to determine public spending passed to the executive branch, which upset many politicians. In addition, departmental and municipal governments and agencies lost considerable power and autonomous spending capacity to executive branch agencies. These changes threatened the power base of many regional politicians and caused a significant polemic between technocrats and politicians.

The National Front as a political entity established important bases for economic stability, principally in exchange and fiscal policy. However, the loss of power by the Congress, the failure of agrarian reform, the weak or nonexistent redistribution of income toward the poorest groups in society, and the emergence of new political groups all led to new forms of economic and political regulation in the 1970s.

The Struggle for Redistribution and Weak Political Stability: 1970–1982

From a strictly economic point of view, the period 1970–1982 encompasses the second half of the expansionary cycle, from 1967 to 1974, and then, as a result of the oil shocks and world inflation and recession, a contractionary cycle from 1974 to 1980. The previous diversification of Colombia's economy contributed to an intensified struggle for shares of the country's income as the country's economic and social structures overran its institutional structure. Nevertheless, no social group was able to achieve a hegemonic role, for no group can have a privileged relationship with the state in a mixed economy.

The struggle for income redistribution was inevitable because of the economic shocks of the 1970s. The struggle was related not only to the inflationary process but also to the economic cycle, as economic and social forces sought to take advantage of the accumulation process during the expansive phase of the economic cycle and to protect themselves as the value of capital and labor declined during the depressive phase. These forces also attempted legitimately, but with unequal power, to influence the state. They sought to influence various instruments of state intervention such as those related to state planning and public investment as well as those regulating or controlling private sector activities, such as exchange, monetary, fiscal, trade, wage, price, and government purchase policies.

A series of gaps in the decision-making process within the Colombian state developed along three different dimensions. One dimension was the unequal degree of influence over economic policy between those sectors with institutional representation within the state (especially coffee and construction) and those without such direct influence. The second was the greater influence of the private sector in state institutions that determined short- and medium-term economic policy—including monetary, exchange, financial, and price-control policies—and, as a counterweight, the greater influence of politicians and regional interests in the establishing of fiscal policy and the channeling of state expenditures. These expenditures, increasingly more redistributive in their impact,

Table 11.1

COMPOSITION OF THE PRINCIPAL BOARDS OF DIRECTORS OF INSTITUTES,
AGENCIES, AND COMMITTEES RESPONSIBLE FOR SHORT-TERM
REDISTRIBUTIVE MACROECONOMIC POLICY AND
SECTORAL POLICY, 1978
(Percent Distribution)

	State Represen- tation	Private Sector Represen- tation	Labor and Consumer Represen- tation	Congres- sional and Other	Total	N
Short-term redistributive policies	63	30	4	3	100	152
Sectoral policies (excluding Committees)	72	20	3	5	100	421
Industrial Committees	62	34	1	3	100	162
Sectoral policy (including Committees)	69	24	3	4	100	583

Source: Prepared by María José Pérez on the basis of information on boards of directors. For a listing of the institutes, agencies, and committees, see Edgar Revéiz, "La Concertacíon: experiencias y posibilidades in Colombia," in Controversia sobre el Plan de Integracion Nacional, PIN (Bogota: Facultad de Economía - CEDE, 1981), pp. 56-60.

were supported by the National Planning Department and international multilateral lending agencies. Thus, efforts to force reductions in state expenditures were perceived as directly affecting lower-income groups and, to a lesser extent, politicians and regional interests.

Finally, there was a growing dispersion in the forums in which bilateral domestic agreements were reached without any effective national coordination. As indicated by Table 11.1, these forums have tended to be dominated by the state and to a lesser extent by producer associations, depending upon the sectors and the topics under discussion. There has been considerably less representation by the labor unions. In some cases, leaders of producer associations or other business people have been appointed as state representatives. The increasing importance of these forums in policy- and decision-making suggests that the country may be moving, without the enunciation of an explicit policy, toward a more corporatist state that will coexist with the electoral democratic processes. The forums also have represented an effort by private-sector groups to control and channel state expenditures, thus reducing politicization. The growth in the number and importance of the forums suggests that the power of many different economic groups has increased, preventing any one of them from acquiring hegemonic power over the state. The state does not appear, as it does in Brazil or Chile, as a bureaucratic apparatus independent of economic and social groups; instead, in Colombia it has been integrated into them.

This system has created a certain vacuum regarding state legitimacy in its decision making. Producer associations have played key roles in decisions from which they will directly benefit. The state has not been able to autonomously implement decisions to increase its revenues or even increase tariffs on public railways. The flexibility of particular governments to change the direction of state expenditures has also been sharply limited because over half of all public expenditures have been predetermined. These expenditures have been provided for by earmarked taxes, which can be modified only by new legislation. This policy has had clear costs in terms of efficiency, but efforts to change the system by implementing more formal methods of economic coordination have so far met with little success.

Probably the most important factor of economic and political instability during the decade of the 1970s was the financial crisis that resulted from the takeover of the industrial sector by the financial sector. In a process that began in the 1950s and accelerated in the 1970s, industrial firms and other stock companies preferred to raise capital, not by the emission of stock, but by direct borrowing. This policy allowed the original owners to maintain tighter control of their firms. Furthermore, not only was credit often subsidized by the state but special tax benefits often made this option preferable.

In the 1970s, two processes interacted to strengthen the position of the financial sector over industry. One was a state policy that essentially consisted of handing over management of savings as a concession to the private sector, with fewer and fewer state controls, combined with the state's continuing to assume part of the risk for financial failures. The other process revolved around the continuing need of the industrial sector for guaranteed financing; it was stimulated by the oligopolistic structure of the market for goods in the country and helped lead to the formation of financial conglomerates, which consisted of financial institutions, insurance firms, and industrial companies.

During this period, as well, there were significant changes in the way local conflicts and social issues were regulated. Politicians, especially in small- and medium-sized cities, began losing the capacity to channel popular demand. Increasingly, demands were articulated by more permanent labor and communal organizations. Three different periods, representing the presidential terms of Micael Pastrana (1970–1974), Alfonso López Michelsen (1974–1978), and Julio César Turbay Ayala (1978–1982), can be identified. Each of these periods was characterized by a different approach to development and economic policy.

The Four Strategies: 1970–1974

Under President Pastrana, the focus on coffee was to a certain extent superseded as housing construction was emphasized as the "leading sector" in the government's new development plan, entitled "the Four Strategies." The plan was developed by Lauchlin Currie, a U.S. economist, and implemented in spite of congressional opposition by presidential fiat, Pastrana thus employing unintended constitutional powers resulting from the 1968 reform. For the first time in the country's history, there was considerable coordination between a development plan and an administration's economic policy. In sharp contrast to the Lleras administration, the private sector played an active role in the implementation of the plan.

To carry out the new development plan, a special financing mechanism was created that would encourage savings to be channeled into construction. The state essentially laid the legal foundation for the formation of new kinds of savings institutions whose deposits would earn interest at a rate indexed to the inflation rate. This action established institutional protection for another economic sector in addition to coffee. The creation of this new system can be understood in part as the reaction of two important groups that had felt excluded by Lleras's statist reforms: regional politicians and many elements of the private sector that feared growth of state interventionism. However, the new influence on government of part of the private sector was a prelude to the struggle for improved state access and hegemonic control on the part of other economic groups, which, so far, have had no success. This period was also the beginning of a process of increased interaction and consultation between producer associations and the state. One indication of this process was the growth in the number of heads of producer associations who occupied high positions in the executive branch and vice versa.

The economic results of the period were mixed. The country's economic growth rates were relatively high—6.7 percent in 1970, 5.5 percent in 1971, 7 percent in 1972, and 7.1 percent in 1973—but the minimum salary in real terms declined between 1970 and 1976. In spite of the emphasis on construction in the development plan, unemployment in the large cities increased even as salaries declined. Furthermore, export diversification faltered, in part due to the 1973 oil shock. The possibility of agrarian reform that included a significant redistribution of land came to an end as commercial agriculture producing for export increased in importance.

Coffee Bonanza and the López Years: 1974–1978

Throughout most of its postwar history, Colombia has confronted problems of exchange scarcity. Beginning in 1975, because of a dramatic escalation in the price of coffee combined with a boom in drug trafficking, the country's international reserves expanded to unprecedented levels in spite of a growth in imports. The price of coffee jumped from $0.65 a pound in 1975 to $2.00 a pound in 1977 because of significant frosts in Brazil. In spite of government attempts to control the money supply, it expanded between 20 percent and 30 percent each year. Although the debate as to whether this sustained previous inflationary pressures or initiated a new cycle of inflation has not been settled, it is clear that during this period, inflation became a chronic problem.

Although the coffee and drug bonanzas benefited the country's balance of payments, other negative economic consequences in addition to inflation were brought about. The peso became overvalued for noncoffee exports and all imports. In contrast to the previous period's expansion in manufacturing exports of over 20 percent, the volume of these exports grew at an annual rate of only 8.2 percent from 1973 to 1980. The government delayed investments related to its development plan, entitled "To Close the Gap," which would have favored lower-income groups (particularly in the rural sector) through a national nutrition and food plan. The conflict, seen in previous administrations, between continuing with public investment plans or preserving the real income of coffee exporters emerged again. In addition, the industrial sector suffered during this period due in part to the sector's technological backwardness and the relative import liberalization that occurred in conjunction with the world recession. There were, however, some positive elements. Agricultural production, especially that of commercial agriculture, grew. A coherent policy for energy exploration was established, and it had the promise of benefiting several backward regions of the country.

The López government substantially reduced state interventionism in the country's financial markets. Distortions in interest rates and in savings rates were eliminated, the development funds linked to the central bank were also brought under closer control, and the money supply was the principal instrument for stabilization. Some state subsidies, particularly one on gasoline, were eliminated or substantially reduced. Such measures have led some people to argue that a neoliberal model was being implanted in the country. In our view, this is an exaggeration. The López government was forced to adopt a series of short-term monetary and fiscal measures in order to adjust an economy that suddenly confronted a balance-of-payments surplus. For example, the government enacted a wide-ranging tax reform with redistributionist intentions that was clearly interventionist.

In spite of the coffee bonanza and the fact that real wages began to improve slightly in 1975, the government confronted its most serious crisis in 1977: a national strike that brought together for the first time all the major labor confederations. Following the strike, the government had serious problems with public sector unions, particularly the teachers' union. With growing unity within the labor movement, symbolized by the strengthening of the National Labor Council (Consejo Nacional Sindical), an implicit system of indexation of salaries and prices was established.

Although government policy did not comprise a neoliberal model, it was apparent that the state showed a certain weakness in negotiating with the coffee sector. This weakness led the other producer associations, along with the labor unions, to join together in protest against the government's policy of the "coffee bonanza for the coffee growers." Nevertheless, from today's vantage point, the prudent management of the country's international reserves during this period appears to have been a key factor in explaining the country's current relative exchange stability, in spite of its numerous pressing problems.

The Plan of National Integration: 1978–1982

When Turbay became president in 1978, the public sector itself became the "leading sector" as the private sector had not responded to the country's sudden abundance in foreign exchange resulting from the coffee bonanza. The state and the private sector now shared the financing of the new development plan, which was an excellent anticyclical tool. In contrast to earlier plans, this one focused on transportation, communications, mining, energy, and regional development. A crisis of accumulation emerged in the industrial sector, and one of confidence in the agricultural and financial sectors. During this period, there was a process of corporate concentration.

The country's economic indicators began to decline, slowly in 1979 and more precipitously by 1981, although the government's development plan was largely executed. Public construction increased 5.4 percent in 1979, 14.9 percent in 1980, 12.3 percent in 1981, and 5.8 percent in 1982. Both the mining and communications sectors grew substantially. Nevertheless, the economy grew only 4.2 percent in 1980, 2.5 percent in 1981, and 1.4 percent in 1982, the last being the lowest figure since World War II. International reserves also began to fall. The industrial and financial sectors entered into serious crisis because of the high levels of debt within the industrial sector and the speculative activities of various financial groups or conglomerates. The crisis was exacerbated by certain "financial innovations" introduced by some of these groups. These innovations represented an attempt to evade restrictive state monetary policies, which had been imposed as part of the government's stabilization package to countervail the inflationary effects of the country's foreign exchange bonanza. Manufacturing grew only 1 percent between 1978 and 1982, and agricultural growth reached only 2–2.5 percent, which was just over half the rate of previous decades.

One effect of the coffee and drug bonanzas was an increase in the influence of financial groups in the country's economy. The bonanzas increased the money resources of the economy, leading these groups to seek to capture more and more resources for their own expansion. This attempt was facilitated by measures enacted previously by the López government, which had removed state controls and other obstacles to the continued growth of the financial groups. However, some of the consequences of this process certainly were unintended. The financial sector became less competitive, higher inflation created incentives for a variety of financial innovations, and the new high interest rates led to changes in the relative profitability of different portfolios. Financial intermediaries tried to reduce the opportunity cost of their reserves, forcibly placed in low-interest-earning deposits in the central bank or in forced investments. They sought various means to evade the government's efforts to regulate the sector in the context of the state's overall macroeconomic policy. As a result of their largely successful efforts, combined with strict government efforts to control the expanding money supply, a large proportion of the stabilization costs resulting from the coffee bonanza was shifted to the industrial sector. This shift also accelerated the direct control of the financial sector over the industrial sector, a process that had begun earlier. By the last year of Turbay's government, a financial crisis appeared inevitable.

In the period from 1975 to 1979, industrialists tried to maintain their firms' growth rates in a period of declining profits. The government's need to finance its development plan had forced it to seek additional domestic borrowing. Competition for credit among enterprises and between the state and the private sector in the context of a restrictive monetary policy led to an increase in interest rates. Most firms acquired higher levels of debt rather than issuing new stock in order to not lose control over their companies; however, as the indebtedness of these firms grew, financial groups began taking them over. It became increasingly more difficult to maintain profit rates and continue to service debts in a context of domestic and international recession. In effect, industries relied upon inflation to lower wages and to reduce the true cost of money because interest rates on deposits were fixed at relatively low levels. The people who were hurt the most were households and small savers. By 1981, the industrial recession had worsened, and the financial crisis broke into the open. In this context, financial groups that had acquired industrial interests could not comply with withdrawal requests from their depositors.

By the end of the Turbay government in 1982, several crises that had been accumulating over the years had been aggravated: The two-party system of political co-optation appeared to be exhausted; the financial sector's domination of the industrial sector, which had begun in 1950, was peaking; frustrations accumulated as a result of the lack of agrarian reform led to renewed violence, specifically guerrilla violence in certain areas of the country; the struggles to control inflation and to increase decentralization became more bitter; and the state had serious budget deficits (around 3–3.5 percent of GDP) as well as an undesirable inter-relationship among monetary, exchange, and fiscal policies. One result was that the seriously divided Liberal party lost the presidency in the 1982 elections.

The Current Economic Crisis and the Betancur Government: 1982–1986

Economic and political crises do not necessarily coincide. This fact is especially evident in Colombia today. The country confronts its most serious economic problems since World War II, but because of dramatic presidential leadership, it finds itself in one of its best political-ethical moments. Because of Belisario Betancur's leadership, both structural and short-term problems that could have created serious political crises for other governments have been avoided.

Among the most critical initial efforts of the Betancur government have been the control and regulation of the financial sector. The state has managed the crisis in two different ways. The financial institutions of the "bad bankers"—who it was felt were involved in illegal or questionable practices, including the extension of unsupported loans to subsidiary companies and, in some cases, the legalization of funds of undeclared and questionable origin—were nationalized or their admin-istration was forcibly changed by the state. The Banco del Estado (a private bank), for example, was nationalized in an innovative fashion to ensure that the people who were responsible for illegal practices would not benefit from state support: The state assumed the administrative responsibilities of the bank but determined that it would purchase bank equity only under special circumstances. The losses of the "good" or "traditional" bankers were absorbed by the state, and these banks were strengthened and then left in the hands of their original owners. A special "democratization fund" was created to facilitate the placing of bank stock with the general public in order to disperse ownership more widely.

The government's development plan, "Change with Equity," is a compilation of old initiatives and new ideas: import controls, public housing, university education by correspondence, and strict control on housing rental costs to control inflation. Thus, as a decade earlier, the strategy of making housing construction a leading sector again plays a role in the government's effort to stimulate the economy. The demand for housing between 1982 and 1983 responded dramatically as loan approvals for July–August 1983 were 350 percent higher than for the same period in the previous year. One effect was a drop in the rate of unemployment from June to September 1983, although the rate in September was still higher than it had been in September 1982.

The government also restructured the country's special exchange account in order to clarify the nation's current income and avoid further increases in the fiscal deficit. Municipal and departmental treasuries were strengthened, and taxes on the middle and upper classes increased and those on the lower class lowered. For housing that was not financed under the new savings system, rents were to be determined by the property tax assessment. The purpose was to establish a basis for increased fiscal revenues as these assessments increased. The result, however, has been paralysis and crisis in the rental market and serious harm to urban lower- and middle-class landlords.

The country's most significant current problem revolves around foreign exchange. Colombia's challenge is how, after a long period with no external constraints, to manage the next several years of severe problems in the external sector. It is difficult to have a durable internal economic expansion without adequate adjustment in the country's balance of payments. Management of the crawling peg exchange rate, essential to the country's economic and political stability since 1967, has once again become the key tool of economic policy. Economic policymakers must attend to continued internal struggles over the shrinking economic pie and deal with high interest rates in the United States, which affect the continued recession in Latin American countries.

The temptation for the Colombian government to employ economic policy for electoral purposes will almost certainly increase. Until 1974, the National Front arrangement made such tactics unnecessary. After 1974, in part because of the stabilization policy placed in effect to manage the coffee bonanza and in part because the Liberals were certain they would retain power in the period from 1974 to 1978, it does not appear economic policy was so utilized. Since 1978, as suggested by the discussions about the political origins of the fiscal deficit and then the inauguration of a Conservative government, it seems more likely that the country has entered into such a period.

Concluding Reflections

The country currently confronts a difficult period. Betancur has had to manage a large number of accumulated and short-term crises, among which are the collapse of a number of financial conglomerates, the extreme concentration of stock ownership, a resurgence of the crisis in agriculture, an international recession, foreign exchange problems, and a drop in revenue from drug trafficking. The country's loss of international reserves has been further aggravated by the decision to transfer large quantities of dollars into European currencies under the erroneous assumption that the dollar would weaken. In addition, industry is in the midst of a restructuring process due to a reversal in import substitution and a crisis in the accumulation process. In 1984, the public sector's fiscal deficit was expected to reach 6 percent of GDP, an extremely high figure by national standards.

The Colombian state is partially at a disadvantage because it lacks adequate information. Because of power fragmentation and tacit alliances between state sectors and their respective private economic sectors, information is often disarticulated. In addition, the means of communication have fallen under the control of a small number of financial conglomerates because the reduction of state control to some extent left a vacuum that has been filled by private interests.

An effort to duplicate previous efforts to achieve economic regulation by means of bilateral agreements between the state and the most important economic sectors cannot be efficient under the current circumstances because the economic sectors have unequal access to the decision-making centers of the state and recessionary conditions make it impossible for the state to provide the macroeconomic conditions that would enable all of them to flourish. In addition, the three major forms of social mobility by means of property ownership appear at risk. Stock ownership remains highly concentrated in spite of recent government measures directed at the financial sector. The distribution of agricultural land is once again a problem as the resurgence of guerrilla activity suggests, even as government efforts to seek an amnesty continue. And, the market for urban real estate is currently in critical condition. Social pressures are building as the standard of living in both urban and rural areas declines.

Government efforts to seek a "democratic opening" by establishing a legal framework that would end the pattern of coalition governments and provide greater assurances for opposition movements outside of the two major political parties have not progressed, nor have related efforts to diversify the means of communication and information. The country confronts its most serious economic situation in decades. The president appears to base his strength on an "ethical-political" position of negotiation with the armed guerrillas. This situation is somewhat analogous to the years of serious economic difficulty under Rojas Pinilla, which immediately preceded the creation of the National Front. In that period, it was necessary to create a new political consensus to obtain the conditions for economic and social development in the country. The country's current challenge is to create a new scheme similar to the 1950s political compromise of the National Front in order to fortify the country's political democracy and improve its economic prospects.

Notes

The authors thank Bernardo Guerrero and Juan Gonzalo Zapata for their research assistance. This chapter is a synthesis of a book in press by the same title and was translated and edited by Jonathan Hartlyn with the collaboration of Satya Pattnayak.

1. Ed. note: In order to remove the military from the government and to ensure against continued partisan conflict (la violencia), the country's two major political parties, the Conservative and Liberal, agreed through a series of party pacts (eventually approved by a national plebiscite in 1957) to form a series of coalition governments—the National Front. The agreement called for alternation in the presidency and parity in the executive, legislative, and judicial branches of the government through 1974. A constitutional reform in 1968 established competitive elections for Congress and the presidency in 1974 and reinstituted them for local elections in 1970. It also extended parity in the executive branch until 1978 and stated that subsequently, the party receiving the second highest number of votes had to be offered "adequate and equitable" participation in government. Thus, since 1958, all governments have comprised elements of both parties.

2. Ed. note: Such indicators include life expectancy at birth, infant mortality rates, and adult literacy rates. Income distribution data presented in Table 11A.1 suggest that in the period from 1960 to 1975, the proportion of income corresponding both to the top 20 percent and to the bottom 40 percent of the population declined to the benefit of the middle-income group. In 1975, the top income group still had a proportion of income five times greater than that of the bottom income group.

3. Ed. note: This council, created in 1968, is the central coordinating body for the state's development efforts and economic policies. Chaired by the president, its members include, in addition to the manager of the Coffee Federation, the

ministers of finance, development, agriculture, foreign relations, labor, and public works; the directors of the National Planning Department and of the Foreign Trade Institute; and the manager of the Banco de la República (the country's central bank).

4. Specifically, the Institute of Industrial Development, Central Mortgage Bank, and Institute of Land Credit.

References

Ayala, Ulpiano. 1981. "El empleo en las grandes cuidades." CEDE Document no. 065. Bogotá.

Ayala, Ulpiano, and Rey de Marulanda, Nohra. 1978. *Empleo y pobreza*. Informe presentado al Departamento Nacional de Planeación. Bogotá.

Baer, Werner. 1979. *The Brazilian Economy: Its Growth and Development*. Columbus, Ohio: Grid Publishing.

Chenery, Hollis B., and Syrquin, Moisés. 1978. *La Estructura del crecimiento económico. Un Análisis para el periodo 1950–1970*. Madrid: Editorial Tecnos, Banco Mundial.

Chica, Ricardo. 1982. *Una descripcion de la evolución de la estructura industrial colombiana 1958–1980*. CEDE Document no. 0170. Bogotá.

Colombia, Department of National Planning. 1979. *Plan de integración nacional 1979–1982: Tomo 1*. Bogotá.

Currie, Lauchlin. 1983. *La Situacion macroecónomica de Colombia*. Bogotá: Seminario Internacional, Universidad de los Andes, Facultad de Economía.

Drake, Paul. n.d. "Primera misión Kemmerer a Colombia: Prosperidad al debe 1923–1928 y segunda misión Kemmerer a Colombia: Postración al Debe 1929–1933." Manuscript.

Feige, Edgar L. 1980. "Nueva perspectiva sobre teoría macroeconómica: Causas e ingerencias de la economía no registrada." Paper presented at the conference of the American Economic Association and the International Taxation conference, Fraser Institute, Vancouver, Canada.

Fonseca, Luz Amparo. 1982. "Los Paros cívicos en Colombia." *Estudios laborales, desarrollo, y sociedad*, Cuaderno no. 3 (May).

Friedman, Milton. 1976. *Capitalisme et liberté*. French translation. Paris: Robert Laffont.

Hayek, Friedrich A. 1948. "Economics and Knowledge." In Friedrich A. Hayek, *Individualism and Economic Order*. Chicago: University of Chicago Press.

Hirschman, Albert O. 1982. "Rival Interpretations of Market Society: Civilizing, Destructive, or Feeble?" *Journal of Economic Literature* 20 (December):1463–1484.

Junguito, Roberto. 1979. "Financiamiento de la industria manufacturera en los años 80: Aspectos crediticios y tributarios." In Carlos Caballero, ed., *El Sector financiero en los años 80*. Bogotá: Asociación Bancaria.

Keynes, J. M. 1974. *Teoría general de la ocupacion, el interes y el dinero*. Tr. Eduardo de Hornedo. Mexico City: Fondo de Cultura Económica.

Kravis, Irving B. 1975. *System of International Comparisons of Gross Product and Purchasing Power*. Baltimore: Johns Hopkins University Press.

Leijonhufvud, A. 1973. *On Keynesian Economics and the Economics of Keynes: A Study in Monetary Theory*. Oxford: Oxford University Press.

Londoño, Juan Luis, and Uribe, José Dario. 1981. *Ensayos críticos al Informe Weisner—BIRD*. Bogotá: Universidad de los Andes, Facultad de Economía.

Melo, Héctor. 1983. "Las Cien Empresas más grandes de Colombia." *El Espectador* (August 31).

Montenegro, Armando. 1983. "Inovaciones financieras y política monetaria." In *El Sector financiero: Estructura, desarrollo, y perspectivas*. Bogotá: Asociación Bancaria de Colombia.

Nordhaus, William D. 1972. *The Political Business Cycle*. New Haven: Cowles Foundation, Yale University.

Ocampo, José Antonio. 1982a. *Evolución general del sector y lineamientos de política económica*. Bogotá.

———. 1982b. "Política cambiaria y de comercio exterior." Manuscript.

Poulantzas, Nicos. 1977. "L'etat, les mouvements sociaux, le parti." *Revue dialectiques*, no. 28.

Ranis, Gustav. 1980. "Distribución del ingreso y crecimiento en Colombia." *Desarrollo y sociedad*, no. 3 (November):67–96.

Revéiz, Edgar. 1974. *Ensayo sobre la planeación concertada en Colombia*. CEDE Document no. 21. Bogotá.

———. 1980. "Evolución de las formas de intervención del estado en la economia en America Latina: El Caso colombiano." In *El Estado y el desarrollo (Colombia-Alemania-Chile)*. Colección Debates-CEDE no. 3. Bogotá.

———. 1981. "La Concertación: Experiencias y posibilidades en Colombia." In *Controversia sobre el Plan de Integración Nacional, PIN*. Bogotá: Facultad de Economía-CEDE, CIDER-Uniandes and Fenalco.

———. 1982. *Función de la informacion científica y tecnológica en la planificación del desarrollo económico y social en colombia*.

Revéiz, Edgar, and Montenegro, Santiago. 1983. "Modelos de desarrollo, recomposición industrial y evolución de la concentración industrial de las ciudades colombianas, 1965-1980." *Desarrollo y sociedad*, no. 11 (May):93–153.

Revéiz, Edgar, and Ocampo, José Antonio. 1980. "Bonanza cafetera y economía concertada (1975-1977)." In Edgar Revéiz, ed., *La Cuestión cafetera: Su impacto económico, social, y político-Colombia, Costa Rica, Costa de Marfil*. Colección Debates-CEDE no. 1. Bogotá.

Revéiz, Edgar, et al. 1977. *Poder e información: El Proceso decisorio en tres casos de política regional y urbana en Colombia*. Bogotá: Editorial Antares.

Sandoval Peralta, Diego. 1975. *El Manejo electoral de la política económica durante el Frente Nacional*. CEDE Document no. 19. Bogotá.

Selowsky, Marcelo. 1981. *Who Benefits from Government Expenditures? A Case Study of Colombia*. Oxford: Oxford University Press.

Stigler, G. J. 1977. "La economía de la información." In D. M. Lamberton, ed., *Economía de la información y el conocimiento*. Mexico City: Fondo de Cultura Económica.

Urrutia, Miguel. 1980. "La Creación de las condiciones iniciales para el desarrollo: el café." In Edgar Revéiz, ed., *La Cuestión cafetera: Su impacto económico, social, y político—Colombia, Costa Rica, Costa de Marfil.* Colección Debates-CEDE no. 1. Bogotá.

———. 1983. *Gremios, política económica, y democracia.* Bogotá: Fondo Cultural Cafetero.

Villegas, Jorge, and Yunis, José, eds. 1979. *La Guerra de los mil dias.* Bogotá: Carlos Valencia.

Wiesner Durán, Eduardo. 1980. *Devaluación y mecanismos de ajuste en Colombia.* Centros de Estudios Monetarios Latinoamericanos (CEMLA) no. 43. Mexico City.

World Bank. 1983. *Informe sobre el desarrollo mundial 1983.* Washington, D.C.

Table 11.A1

COLOMBIAN BALANCE OF PAYMENTS, 1967-1981
(Millions of U.S. Dollars)

	1967	1968	1969	1970	1971	1972	1973	1974
Exports (f.o.b.)	558	609	672	788	752	979	1,262	1,494
Imports (f.o.b.)	-464	-615	-648	-802	-900	-849	-982	-1,510
Trade Balance	94	-6	24	-14	-148	130	280	-16
Profits, Interest	-105	-113	-144	-180	-176	-196	-215	-192
Services	-78	-72	-93	-135	-163	-159	-156	-198
Balance	-183	-185	-237	-315	-339	-355	-371	-390
Net Transfers	22	31	38	36	34	35	35	55
Balance on Current Account	-67	-160	-175	-293	-453	-190	-56	-351
Private Capital								
Direct Investment	40	48	50	39	40	17	23	36
Loans	24	26	39	63	19	7	-15	-9
Short-term Capital[2]	-41	29	34	115	161	-48	-108	28
Total	-23	103	123	217	220	-24	-100	55
Public Capital	44	90	143	124	120	215	277	191
Balance on Capital Account	67	193	266	341	340	191	177	246
Errors and Omissions	51	12	-45	-18	90	113	26	-15
Banco de la República: Financing of Deficit (+) or Absorption of Surplus (-)	-51	-45	-46	-30	23	-114	-147	120

(Table continues)

Table 11.A1 (continued)

	1975	1976	1977	1978	1979	1980	1981[1]
Exports (f.o.b.)	1,747	2,255	2,727	3,270	3,581	4,401	3,366
Imports (f.o.b.)	-1,425	-1,665	-1,979	-2,564	-2,996	-4,332	-4,788
Trade Balance	322	590	748	706	585	69	-1,422
Profits, Interest	-263	-313	-272	-301	-255	-269	-334
Services	-187	-106	-67	-92	134	-154	-63
Balance	-450	-419	-339	-393	-121	-423	-397
Net Transfers	48	51	46	73	101	123	115
Balance on Current Account	-80	222	455	386	565	-222	-1,704
Private Capital							
Direct Investment	32	14	43	67	104	234	209
Loans	-8	-39	-6	-32	104	57	403
Short-term Capital[2]	-133	64	-252	21	209	365	441
Total	-109	39	-215	56	417	656	1,053
Public Capital	249	118	172	25	465	736	611
Balance on Capital Account	140	157	-43	81	882	1,392	1,664
Errors and Omissions	37	217	225	131	113	71	197
Banco de la República: Financing of Deficit (+) or Absorption of Surplus (-)	-97	-596	-637	-598	-1,560	-1,241	-157

[1]Preliminary

[2]Includes commercial bank operations

Source: José Antonio Ocampo, Evolucion general del sector y lineamentos de política económica (Bogota: n.p., 1982).

Table 11.A2

COLOMBIA: ECONOMIC AND SOCIAL INDICATORS

	Gómez (1950-1952) 1950	Rojas & J. Militar (1953-1958) 1955	Lleras C. (1958-1962) 1960	Valencia (1962-1966) 1965
Population (millions)	11.6	13.5	15.9	18.5
GDP per capita (1964 US$)	188	216	222	239
Gross internal fixed capital (% GDP)	14.9	16.1	18.1	18.7
Government income (% GDP)	9.6	12.9	11.9	11.2
Tax receipts (% GDP)	9.2	10.4	11.1	12.1
Expenditures on education (% GDP)	6.0	8.0	11.5	12.1
School enrollment (% 5-19 year population)	20.9	29.2	31.9	35.0
Private consumption (% GDP)	76.9	76.81	73.24	74.81
Public consumption (% GDP)	5.51	7.1	6.2	6.5
Urbanization (% total population)	38.89	41.1	49.06	52.79
Birthrate (live births per 1,000)	43.15	45.0	45.12	41.19
Income distribution: Top 20% (% income) Bottom 40% (% income)	---	---	64.66 12.22	57.70 14.97

(Table continues)

Table 11.A2 (continued)

	Lleras R. (1966-1970) 1970	Pastrana (1970-1974) 1975	López M. (1974-1978) 1978	Turbay A. (1978-1982) 1980
Population (millions)	21.1	23.8	25.5	---
GDP per capita (1964 US$)	270	310	358	370
Gross internal fixed capital (% GDP)	18.7	19.3	21.0	22.9
Government income (% GDP)	16.2	14.6	16.1	---
Tax receipts (& GDP)	15.1	14.6	162	---
Expenditures on education (% GDP)	14.0	11.3	10.6	---
School enrollment (% 5-19 year population)	50.3	56.5	58.0	---
Private consumption (% GDP)	72.0	74.27	68.42	70.2
Public consumption (% GDP)	7.64	7.37	7.03	10.1
Urbanization (% total population)	58.85	65.77	70.25	---
Birthrate (live births per 1000)	36.39	31.01	27.40	---
Income distribution: Top 20% (% income) Bottom 40% (% income)	55.00 11.20	58.20 11.50	--- ---	--- ---

Sources: National accounts from Banco de la República; other data from Colombia, Contraloría General de la República (various years); for income distribution, Gustav Ranis, "Distributión del ingreso y crecimiento en Colombia," Desarrollo y sociedad, no. 3 (November 1980).

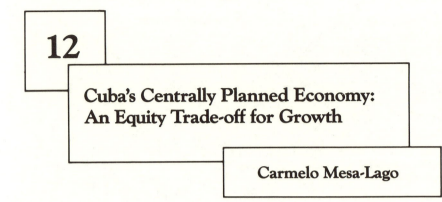

12

Cuba's Centrally Planned Economy: An Equity Trade-off for Growth

Carmelo Mesa-Lago

Cuba's Centrally Planned Economy

Since the early 1960s, Cuba has had a command economy although central planning was not thoroughly and steadily applied until the mid-1970s. After a brief and unsuccessful attempt with the Soviet model of economic organization from 1962 to 1965, Cuba experimented with an unconventional, highly idealistic model that was influenced by Mao's Great Leap Forward and Ché Guevara's ideas and freely adapted by Fidel Castro. The experiment ended in failure, and in the 1970s, Cuba returned to the more pragmatic Soviet orthodox model.[1]

According to Marx's terminology, the Cuban economy should be in the transitional stage between capitalism and communism. Soviet ideologists have divided the transitional stage into three steps (building the foundations of socialism, full socialism, and communism) and have placed the USSR in the highest echelon. In the 1966–1970 period, the Cuban leaders claimed that they were simultaneously building socialism and communism and that their country's transition was at a higher step than that of the USSR. The failure of Mao-Guevarism forced both a recantation of the Cuban boast as an idealistic error and a grumbling acceptance that the island economy was really on the first step of the socialist ladder, two below the USSR. In theory, since Cuba is closer to the capitalist stage than the Soviet Union, the former's economy should utilize more market mechanisms than the latter's. In practice, this theory is not true, although since 1968 Cuban leaders have reintroduced some market tools and launched a new system of economic administration and planning (SDPE) that closely resembles that of the USSR. In any case, the Cuban economy is more collectivized and centralized than the economies of Hungary and Poland and considerably more than Yugoslavia's. Within the Latin American context, Cuba is the only fully socialized economy, far more collectivized than that of Nicaragua.

All economic activity in Cuba is directed by the state, which owns and runs all enterprises and farms except for less than 20 percent of the agricultural land. During the Mao-Guevarist period, family plots on state farms were abolished, private farms had to sell practically all their crops to the state *acopio* (marketing board) at low government-fixed prices, and there were no free markets where peasants could sell their products directly to consumers. The remainder of all private enterprises (including small artisan and repair shops and street vendors) were nationalized, and material incentives (e.g., wage differentials, production bonuses, overtime pay, author's royalties) were gradually replaced by moral (nonmaterial) incentives. The trend toward collectivization has been somewhat reversed since the 1970s: Free peasant markets have been allowed, new incentives to private farmers include higher prices for the *acopio* and better credit facilities, self-employment in services— including the operation of small shops—is permitted, state managers can hire and fire workers more freely, the SDPE emphasizes profitability of enterprises, and material incentives have returned and replaced moral stimuli.

Still, Cuba's economy remains basically collectivized, and the small private agricultural sector is gradually being eliminated by natural attrition and state pressure to integrate the small farms into cooperatives. In 1967 there were 233,679 private farmers, but their number had declined to 160,125 by the end of 1979. Although profit has become a major indicator of state managerial performance—as well as an incentive for state employees, private farmers, and the self-employed—the leadership remains uncomfortable with private gain, which is criticized when it reaches high levels and harshly repressed when obtained through illegal channels. In spite of some decentralization in decision making, the principle of planner's preference rules unequivocally. Thus, all macroeconomic decisions are centrally made, e.g., the allocation of resources between investment and consumption, the distribution of invest- ment among economic branches, and the division of consumption between collective and individual. The consumer now has more freedom of choice (e.g., through free and parallel markets) than in the 1970s but is still significantly limited by the rationing system, which covers about one-third of consumer goods including the most important foodstuffs and manufactures. The state is the employer of about 94 percent of the labor force and determines all labor conditions including wages. Strikes are prohibited, trade unions are controlled by the state, and the labor movement's major objective is, not to fight for labor's rights and better working conditions, but to cooperate with the state in the fulfillment of production goals.

It is obvious that in Cuba, the state has an economic power that is far superior to that of any other Latin American country. Furthermore, that power is highly concentrated in a relatively small number of leaders, and there are very few channels for effective mass participation and control. On the one hand, this concentration of power has its advantages: It allows the state to unify and mobilize scarce national resources to accomplish priority tasks such as capital accumulation and its investment in key development areas, full employment, expansion of social services, and a more equitable distribution of income. On the other hand, there are disadvantages to such concentration of power: It inevitably curtails economic freedoms, often does not utilize the knowledge and experience of—and prevents crucial feedback from—middle and lower echelons, facilitates radical rather than sufficiently studied and tested changes in economic policy, and increases the risks of large-scale and costly errors. All of these factors involve an ethical dilemma as well: The top leaders are basically protected from the negative effects of their decisions since it is practically impossible to remove them from office and they are unaffected by consumption restrictions. Meanwhile, the majority of the population, which does not actively participate in the decisions, has to endure the consequences. Therefore, a fundamental issue to be analyzed in this chapter is whether the Cuban state has effectively used its enormous economic power to actually accomplish the pursued goals of development. Another question, which can only be touched upon here, is whether other Latin American states, with less economic power than Cuba, have been able to achieve the same goals with fewer hardships for their people.

Economic Performance Under Socialism

Economic Growth

Like other socialist countries, Cuba uses the "material product system." That system's global social product (GSP) excludes the value of nonproductive services (e.g., health care, education, social security, defense, public admin-istration, financing) and, hence, is smaller than GNP. On the other hand, in the calculation of Cuba's GSP, intermediate consumption is often counted twice, which results in considerable duplication and a GSP that is higher than the GNP. Attempts by international and U.S. organizations to accurately convert Cuba's GSP into GNP have failed so far, and the only conversion done by Cuban experts is limited to the year 1974 (for a thorough review and evaluation of all these estimates, see Mesa-Lago and Pérez-López 1985a).

Another problem is that Cuba's method of calculating GSP has been changed at least three times, and the resulting series cannot be connected. The GSP series started in 1962—when a serious recession began—and Cuba has never released GNP data for 1959–1961. Furthermore, until 1982, Cuba's GSP was given only in current prices (except for 1962–1965) and was therefore affected by inflation. Finally, international comparisons are made even more difficult by the fact that the Cuban peso is not freely exchanged in the international market; its value is unilaterally set by the Cuban government,

Table 12.1

ECONOMIC GROWTH RATES (GSP) IN CUBA: 1960-1980
(average annual rates at constant prices)

Periods	Absolute	Per Capita
1960-65	5.2	3.0
1966-70	0.4	-1.3
1971-75	7.5	5.7
1976-80	4.0	3.2
1960-80	4.3	2.6

Sources: 1971-1975 and 1976-1980 from Banco Nacional de
Cuba, Informe económico (August 1982), pp. 17-18; 1960-1965
and 1966-1970 is my disaggregation of the official annual
average growth rate for 1960-1970 (from the same source)
based on growth rates at current prices.

allegedly based on a basket of foreign currencies. In 1981, 1 peso was equal to $1.28.

The figures in Table 12.1 are the first available on GSP growth in constant prices for the whole period 1960–1980. However, such data should be used with caution because they pertain to period averages, the methodology used is not explained, and there are frequent and serious inconsistencies in the figures.[2] In spite of these problems, it can be said with certainty that Cuba's economy badly deteriorated in the second half of the 1960s, during the Mao-Guevarist period, but vigorously recuperated in the first half of the 1970s because of the more pragmatic policy and record sugar prices in the international market. A new deterioration occurred in the second half of the 1970s because of several factors: a decline in sugar prices and increases in the prices of imports, pests that damaged sugar and tobacco plantations, problems in the nickel and fishing industries, difficulties in the implementation of the SDPE, and Cuba's war effort in Africa. Most goals of the first five-year plan (1976–1980) were unfulfilled, e.g., real economic growth was 33 percent below the target, and out of sixteen important output goals, fourteen were not achieved (and by a large margin). The current five-year plan (1981–1985) has set more modest goals, and yet since most of the factors that hampered economic performance under the previous plan are still present, the chances of plan fulfillment are rather low (see Mesa-Lago 1982).[3]

According to the official figures in Table 12.1, Cuba's average economic growth in 1960–1980 was 4.3 percent, but there is a high probability that the actual rate was smaller.[4] Even if the official figure is accepted, it is well below the Latin American average of 5.8 percent in that period.[5] Cuba's per capita economic growth rate in 1960–1980 (2.6 percent) was helped by both heavy emigration (about one-tenth of the population left the island in that period) and declining birthrates since the mid-1960s. The rate of population growth in 1980 was actually negative (−0.6 percent), and in 1981, it was 0.7 percent, the lowest rate in Latin America. Still, Cuba's per capita economic growth rate was below the regional average of 3 percent in 1960–1980. Cuba's growth performance appears even worse when one takes into account the economic power of its state, the enormous aid provided to it by the USSR (to be discussed later), and the restrictions on political and economic freedoms imposed on its people. The head of the Central Planning Board (Junta Central de Planificación, JUCEPLAN) has judged such performance critically: "In the 20 years elapsed [since 1959] we have not reached the average rate of growth needed to step out of underdevelopment and to correct the structural deformation we inherited from capitalism" (Pérez 1978; author's translation).

Inflation

Cuba does not publish data on inflation, and from 1966 to 1982 systematically reported GSP in current prices. The national bank has argued that because all prices (except those for trade and transportation) were frozen between 1965 and 1981, current prices actually approximate constant prices. But not even all rationing prices were actually frozen, and the prices of goods in the parallel market were from three to eight times the rationing prices while prices in the black market and the free-peasant market were even higher. In January 1981, there was a wholesale-price reform that resulted in a price increase of more than 10 percent, and in December of the same year, there was a retail-price reform that increased prices (ranging from 7 to 525 percent) of 1,500 consumer goods plus some services.

Table 12.2 presents inflation estimates based on Cuban official data on annual GSP at current and constant prices for 1963–1966 and 1976–1981 and on average growth rates in current and constant prices for the periods 1966–1970 and 1971–1975. Based on the table data, the annual average inflation rate for 1963–1981 can be calculated at 3.7 percent, showing that indeed there was inflation in Cuba—although the rate was lower than in most Latin American countries. Tables 12.1 and 12.2 indicate that there tends to be a correlation between inflation and economic growth as the highest inflation rates are registered in the periods (years) of greater economic dynamism.

Table 12.2

ESTIMATED INFLATION RATES IN CUBA: 1963-1981

Years	Inflation Rate	Years	Inflation Rate[c]
1963	10.2[a]	1976	0.6
1964	8.5[a]	1977	-1.0
1965	-1.7[a]	1978	3.8
1966	1.7a	1979	0.5
1963-65	5.7[a]	1980	0.8
1966-70	1.3[b]	1981	10.8
1971-75	6.1[b]	1976-81	2.6

[a]1965 prices

[b]Base year unknown

[c]1978 prices

Source: Carmelo Mesa-Lago and Jorge Pérez-Lopez, "Study of Cuba's MPS, its conversion to SNA, and the Estimation of GDP/Capital and Growth Rates," (Washington, D.C.: The World Bank, 1982), 68.

Investment and Capital Efficiency

In view of Cuba's poor economic growth, one should expect a low investment coefficient, and Table 12.3 confirms that assumption. Gross domestic investment sharply declined in the early years of the revolution because of the emphases on consumption and distribution compounded by the process of nationalization, but helped by rationing and other measures to restrict consumption the investment rate slowly increased in 1962-1967 to reach 14 percent. In spite of further restrictions in consumption during the Mao-Guevarist period, and despite official claims, investment then sharply declined, reaching a trough of 9.6 percent in 1970. To compound this problem, capital efficiency was quite low during this period because neither the interest rate nor the Soviet coefficient of relative effectiveness was used to allocate capital. Instead, arbitrary subjective decisions were used. Furthermore, the

Table 12.3

GROSS DOMESTIC INVESTMENT AND EXTERNAL PUBLIC DEBT OF CUBA: 1958-1982
(in U.S. Dollars at Current Prices)

	Domestic Investment		External Debt[a]			
Years	Total (Million $)	% of GSP	Total (Million $)	Per Capita	% of GSP	% of Exports
1958	464	17.3[b]	48	7	1.9[b]	6.5
1965	842	12.4	n.a.	n.a.	n.a.	n.a.
1970	800	9.6	n.a.	n.a.	n.a.	n.a.
1975	2,779	14.6	5,310	564	31.6	149.4
1978	3,489	16.1	5,576	777	35.0	166.8
1981/82[c]	4,104	14.4	12,000	1,230	48.4	194.7

Notes: [a]Includes hard-currency debt and debt with the USSR

[b]Percentage of GDP

[c]1981 for investment, 1982 for debt

Sources: Investment, 1958 from United Nations, Statistical Bulletin (New York, 1964), p. 42; 1965 from Cuba, Direccion General de Estadistica, Boletín estadístico de Cuba 1966 a1971 (Havana, 1971), p. 102; 1970, 1975 and 1981 are from Cuba, CEE, Cuba en Cifras 1981 (Havana, 1981), p. 56; 1978 is based on Central Intelligence Agency, The Cuban Economy: A Statistical Review (Washington, D.C., 1981), pp. 37-39; and 1982 is based on Cuba, Banco Nacional de Cuba, Informe Económico (Havana, 1982), p. 6, and additional data.

central plan was discarded, and a series of special plans were put in operation, all competing for scarce resources without any central coordination. These factors in large measure explain the economic debacle of these turbulent years.

The return to the central plan, the priority given to finish investment projects already initiated, and the partial use of the interest rate induced an increase of the investment coefficient as well as capital efficiency in the 1970s to a peak of 19 percent in 1977. But a new deterioration occurred in the late 1970s because many large projects started during the sugar boom were left unfinished when the crisis hit. Capital efficiency was also affected by excessive centralization of investment combined with very poor coordination, lack of a policy of depreciation, and an inadequate objective evaluation of investment efficiency. In the period 1962-1980, Cuba's annual average investment coefficient was 13.2 percent of GSP, compared with an average of 23.2 percent of GDP for Latin America as a whole. This comparison is not accurate because of the differences between GSP and GDP, but a new series of Cuba's GDP and investment for 1971-1980 show that the Cuban coefficient in this period was below the Latin American ratio in all years except one, and in terms of averages, it was four percentage points below that of the region.[6]

The distribution of state investment has changed significantly throughout the revolution. In the early 1960s, roughly half of the investment went to the productive sphere (e.g., industry, agriculture, transportation), and the other half went to the nonproductive sphere (e.g., education, health, housing). As the state tried to curtail consumption, a larger share of investment was allocated to production, reaching a peak of 86 percent in 1970. The failure of Mao-Guevarism induced an opposite trend, and by 1977, the share invested in production had fallen to less than 62 percent. Thereafter, the allocation of investment to the productive sphere grew again, reaching almost 81 percent in 1979. In 1965, 42 percent of investment went to agriculture and 22 percent to industry; by 1979, those proportions had been reversed.[7] And yet, this capital allocation didn't result in proportional increases in production because the efficiency of investment was not sufficient to assure the path of industrialization required (Rodríguez García 1982).

Economic Diversification

In spite of Cuba's enormous effort to diversify production and industrialize, the fact is that the country basically still has a monoculture economy. Table 12.4 shows that the GSP share of agriculture has shrunk, but the same is true of industry also; the shares of construction and transportation-communication have increased slightly, and the share of trade has expanded greatly. This analysis, however, is distorted by official prices and inflation, e.g., low agricultural prices artificially reduce the agricultural share of GSP but increase that of industry, and inflation mostly affects trade. GSP excludes the value of nonproductive services, but all available information suggests that this branch may be the one to have had the highest growth rate. The distribution of civilian employment, which does include most services (it excludes defense, intelligence, and the private service sector), clearly indicates that the reductions in the employment shares of agriculture and industry have been compensated for by the increase in the share of services. Thus, Cuba is unique among socialist countries in the sense that services, rather than industry, is the most dynamic sector of the economy.

A comparison of the distributions of GSP and employment (Table 12.4) indicates that the productivity of agriculture has badly deteriorated, that of industry has declined (but not as much), the productivity of both construction and transportation-communication is about the same, and that of trade has notably increased.[8] Labor productivity declined sharply in the Mao-Guevarist period, recuperated somewhat in the first half of the 1970s, and declined again during the rest of that decade as the following rates illustrate: 6 percent in 1964, −2 percent in 1966, 7 percent in 1975, and 0.8 percent in 1979. An

Table 12.4

PERCENTAGE DISTRIBUTION OF GSP AND EMPLOYMENT BY ECONOMIC SECTOR IN CUBA: 1962-1980

	GSP[a]					Employment[b]					
	Agric.	Ind.	Const.	Transp. and Com.	Trade	Agric.	Ind.	Const.	Transp. and Com.	Trade	Service
1962	17.8	48.2	7.2	6.5	20.3	27.5	24.6	9.6	6.8	12.2	19.3
1965	16.5	42.5	7.7	5.9	27.4	29.8	21.3	8.0	5.8	15.2	19.9
1970[c]	14.7	47.9	5.2	10.2	22.0	29.0	21.1	6.4	8.4	8.1	27.0
1975	11.5	38.0	9.0	7.8	33.5	28.7	19.7	8.7	7.8	7.5	27.6
1980[d]	11.2	35.6	8.9	8.7	34.0	23.0	20.0	11.5	6.9	11.0	27.3

[a]GSP excludes "nonproductive" services, e.g., finance, public administration, defense, social services

[b]State civilian employment; excludes defense and intelligence as well as private and self-employment in agriculture and services

[c]1971 for employment

[d]Both distributions exclude a small percentage in "other productive activities," employment data are for 1979

Sources: Carmelo Mesa-Lago, The Economy of Socialist Cuba: A Two Decade Appraisal (Albuquerque: University of New Mexico Press, 1981), pp. 56, 115; José Luis Rodríguez García, "La economía Cubana entre 1976 y 1980; resultados y perspectivas," Economía y Desarrollo (Jan.-Feb. 1982), pp. 131, 133; and Cuba, CEE Anuario Estadístico de Cuba 1978-80 (Havana, 1980), p. 57.

Table 12.5

PERCENTAGE DISTRIBUTION OF CUBAN EXPORTS BY PRODUCT: 1959-1980

Years	Sugar	Minerals	Tobacco	Others
1959	75	3	9	13
1960	78	4	10	8
1965	86	6	5	3
1970	77	17	3	3
1975	90	5	2	3
1980	84	5	1	10

Sources: 1959-1960 from Cuba, JUCEPLAN, Comercio Exterior de Cuba: Exportacíon 1962 (Havana, 1963). The rest from Cuba, Dirección Central de Estatistica, Boletin Estatistica de Cuba 1966 a 1971 (Havana, 1971), and Cuba, CEE, Anuario Estatístico de Cuba 1978-80 (Havana, 1980).

evaluation of productivity trends in 1976–1980, conducted by a Cuban economist, concludes that the worst deterioration was registered in the industrial sector (Rodríguez García 1982:121, 137; for an analysis of labor productivity trends in 1962–1976, see Mesa-Lago 1982:132–135).

Export Concentration

Another fundamental indicator of the revolution's failure to diversify is the nation's continued dependency on sugar. The combined industrial/agricultural share of GSP has hovered around one-tenth, with a slight tendency to decline, but the shares in 1962 and 1981 were almost identical: 11.4 and 11.5 percent. According to Table 12.5, sugar and its by-products accounted for 75 percent of Cuba's total exports in 1959, and the figure was 84 percent in 1980. The share of minerals (basically nickel) has increased somewhat, thus partially compensating for the reduction in tobacco exports; the share of other exports has declined. Sugar's average percentage of all exports was 81.4 percent in 1950–1959, 83.3 percent in 1960–1969, 82.2 percent in 1970–1979, and 80 percent in 1980–1982. The value of sugar exports in relation to GDP (new series) was 22.2 percent in 1958 and 23.3 percent in 1980.[9]

Since Cuba sells about one-third of its sugar to market economies, wide fluctuations in the price of sugar in the international market have had a significant impact on the Cuban economy and induced unstable economic growth (although the Soviet Union's paying a higher price for sugar bought from Cuba has somewhat attenuated such negative effects). For instance, sugar prices increased from less than $0.04 per pound in 1970 to almost $0.30 in 1974 ($0.21 in 1975), which largely explains Cuba's economic boom of the first half of the 1970s. But sugar prices declined in the second half of the 1970s, reaching a trough of less than $0.08 in 1978, which provoked a downturn in the Cuban economy in that period. Sugar prices rose again in 1980–1981 to decline once more in 1982 to about $0.08 per pound—the lowest *real* value in fifteen years—with consequent ups and downs in Cuba's economy.[10]

Cuba is the world's major exporter of sugar so there is a close relationship between its domestic production and the world price of sugar. In the first twenty years of the revolution, Cuba's sugar production averaged less than 6 million tons (the same as in 1946–1958), but since 1978, Cuba has been producing 7 million tons, and in 1982, it turned out slightly more than 8 million tons. This rise in output has had a depressing effect on the world sugar price—the jump in 1980–1981 was largely the result of a dramatic fall in Cuba's output provoked by the sugarcane rust pest. The future stability of international sugar prices is threatened by increasing world production (the European Common Market, which was a net importer of sugar, has become a net exporter) and the expanded use of corn sweeteners. And yet, Cuba's current five-year plan's principal goal is to produce 10 million tons of sugar in 1985, and the twenty-year development plan (1980–2000) still relies on sugar as the prime factor in the Cuban economy.[11]

The four Cuban exports that could potentially reduce the country's dependency on sugar are nickel, tobacco, citrus fruits, and fish and seafood. Altogether, they account for about 14 percent of all exports, and substantial increases in their export shares are not probable, at least not until the second half of the 1980s. There is a high probability that nickel output will double by the end of the 1980s, but this industry faces a serious problem of competition in world markets. Cuba's nickel laterite deposits have a low nickel content, which means extracting the mineral requires high-energy consumption, and Cuban leaders have acknowledged that the nickel industry is severely depressed because of its fuel-inefficient technology.[12] It appears that the new nickel plants under construction will use the same obsolete technology as the old plants. Tobacco output reached 58,900 tons in 1963 but then declined sharply. Moreover, in 1980, the whole crop was wiped out by a blue mold epidemic. A vigorous recuperation in 1981—induced by better incentives to private growers—lost momentum in 1982–1983 because of adverse climatic conditions. The fabrication of the famous Havanas has steadily declined from 657 million cigars in 1965 to 166 million in 1980.

The success of the fishing industry climaxed in 1978 with a catch of 211,100 tons, a tenfold increase over 1958. But production declined thereafter, to 164,000 tons in 1981, because the universalization of the 200-mile fishing zone has forced the Cuban fleet to move into less familiar zones, which has resulted in higher fuel costs and a decrease in the catch. Thus fishing exports, which reached 3 percent of total exports in the late 1970s, have fallen since 1980. Citrus production has so far been a success story, having increased almost sevenfold from 1958 to 1981, but citrus exports account for less than 1 percent of total exports, and virtually all go to socialist countries. Attempts to market Cuba's citrus products in the West have failed mainly because Cuba's produce does not meet world market standards.

Cuba has significantly expanded its manufacturing sector under the revolution, but practically all manufactured goods are for internal consumption. Although there have been gains because of import substitution, manufactures account for less than 0.3 percent of total exports. Furthermore, the improvement in manufacturing has been concentrated in selected lines of production. Electricity is the only line showing a steady increase throughout the revolution although a few lines like cement have had steady increases since the early 1970s. The output of manufactures like steel and textiles first increased and then became stagnant in the 1970s; the production of fertilizers peaked in 1969, and that output level was not surpassed until 1980. The output of many nondurable consumer goods (shoes, soap, tires, detergents) has been stagnant throughout the revolution, thus explaining continuous rationing since 1962. Production of a few consumer durables initiated under the revolution (refrigerators, radios, TV sets) has had ups and downs but was mostly stagnant through the 1970s.

Two hard-currency earners for Cuba are tourism and overseas personnel, but the two combined generate earnings similar to those of nickel exports. In 1981, Cuba made an estimated $85 million from tourism, but the probabilities of any significant expansion are hampered due to the deterioration of U.S.-Cuban relations and the 1982 U.S. Treasury Department's ban on both tourist and business trips to Cuba. In 1981, Cuba earned about $100 million as payment for technicians and construction personnel working abroad on projects in countries such as Algeria, Libya, and Iraq. This source of revenue is promising, but still small.

Trade Balance and Foreign Debt

The failure of Cuba to significantly expand and diversify its production and exports, combined with its population growth and ambitious social programs (to be discussed later), has provoked an economic disequilibrium that is clearly manifested in its foreign trade, whose volume in 1975–1981 accounted for an average of 44 percent of GSP. The island buys abroad a very large proportion of what it needs (e.g., machinery, transportation equipment, foodstuffs, fuel, manufactures, chemicals, and raw materials) and pays basically with sugar and, in a small proportion, with nickel, tobacco, fish, citrus fruits, and rum. Table 12.6 shows that the value of Cuban exports stayed about the same from 1958 to 1972, basically because sugar output was also stagnant (the only exception was 1970 when Cuba produced 8.5 million tons of sugar, still the largest harvest of the revolution). On the other hand, imports have steadily increased since 1963, provoking growing trade deficits. Even in the 1970s, when Cuba was able to expand its sugar output (or benefited from high sugar prices), the deficits persisted because imports kept rising at a faster pace than exports (except in 1974, the crest of the sugar boom). The cumulative trade deficit for 1959–1982 reached 7.7 billion pesos; in 1981, the deficit broke all records when it surpassed the $1-billion mark.

After the 1961 imposition of the U.S. economic embargo, Cuba gradually shifted to trading with socialist countries. Thus in 1982, 67 percent of Cuba's foreign trade was with the USSR (compared with 66 percent with the United States prior to the revolution), and an additional 18 percent was with Eastern European and Asian socialist countries (see Table 12.7). Trade with market economies has fluctuated with a peak of 40–41 percent in 1974–1975 at the time sugar prices reached their zenith in the world market. In general, when the international price of sugar rises, allowing Cuba to choose its trade partners, the island buys needed machinery, transportation equipment, chemicals, and manufactured goods from countries with industrialized market economies rather than from the USSR.

From 1962 to 1974, Cuban trade with socialist countries was in the red with the USSR holding about 60 percent of the total trade deficit (see Table 12.7)—in spite of the fact that the USSR bought Cuban sugar at prices usually higher than the world market price and sold oil to the island at prices lower than the international price. In this period, Cuba's trade deficits were covered with Soviet loans to be repaid within twelve years at an interest rate that was below 4 percent. In addition, the USSR granted Cuba development loans with a twenty-five-year repayment period and a rate of interest of 2–2.5 percent. In 1972, as a response to the bad shape of Cuba's economy and the island's move to reintroduce the Soviet model, the USSR postponed the repayment of Cuba's accumulated debt since 1961 for fifteen years and suspended payment of interest during that period. Another important concession was made in 1975 when the value of Soviet exports to Cuba was balanced by the value of the country's Cuban imports, thus eliminating the trade deficit between the two countries (see Table 12.7). This balance meant that Soviet subsidies (nonrepayable grants) were substituted for previous repayable trade loans. But in 1979, the huge trade deficits with the USSR reappeared, being 82 percent of Cuba's total deficit in that year. In 1981, that percentage rose to 93 percent of the country's record $1-billion deficit. Although full infor-

Table 12.6

BALANCE OF TRADE OF CUBA: 1958-1982
(in million pesos at current prices)

Years	Exports (f.o.b.)	Imports (c.i.f.)	Trade Balance
1958	734	771	- 37
1959	636	675	- 39
1960	608	580	+ 28
1961	627	639	- 12
1962	522	759	-237
1963	545	867	-322
1964	714	1,019	-305
1965	691	866	-175
1966	598	926	-328
1967	705	999	-294
1968	651	1,102	-451
1969	667	1,222	-555
1970	1,050	1,311	-261
1971	861	1,387	-526
1972	771	1,190	-419
1973	1,153	1,463	-310
1974	2,236	2,226	+ 10
1975	2,947	3,113	-166
1976	2,692	3,180	-488
1977	2,918	3,461	-543
1978	3,417	3,558	-141
1979	3,500	3,687	-187
1980	3,967	4,509	-542
1981	4,259	5,081	-822
1982[a]	4,839	5,451	-612

[a]Preliminary

Sources: Carmelo Mesa-Lago, The Economy of Socialist Cuba: A Two Decade Appraisal (Albuquerque: University of New Mexico Press, 1981), p. 81; updated and corrected with Anuario Estatistico de Cuba 1978-80 (Havana, 1980), p. 57; Cuba, CEE Cuba in cifras 1981 (Havana, 1981); Cuba, Banco Nacional de Cuba, Preliminary Report on the Economy for 1981 (Havana, 1981); Economic Commission for Latin America, Statistical Yearbook for Latin America 1980 (New York: United Nations, 1981).

Table 12.7

PERCENTAGE DISTRIBUTION OF CUBA'S FOREIGN TRADE AND TRADE
DEFICIT BY TRADE PARTNERS: 1959-1982

	Foreign Trade with:			Trade Deficit with:		
Years	USSR	Other socialist countries	Market economies	USSR	Other socialist countries	Market economies
1959	1	0	99	0	0	100
1965	48	29	23	60	9	31
1970	52	20	28	58	0	42
1975	48	12	40	0	3	97
1980	60	14	26	77	23	0
1981	61	18	21	93	7	0
1982	67	18	15	71	29	0

Sources: Carmelo Mesa-Lago, The Economy of Socialist Cuba: A Two Decade Appraisal
(Albuquerque: University of New Mexico Press, 1981), pp. 93, 96; Carmelo Mesa-Lago,
"The Economy: Caution, Frugality and Resilient Ideology," in Jorge I. Dominguez, ed.,
Cuba: Internal and International Affairs (Beverly Hills: Sage Publications, 1982) p. 121;
Cuba, CEE, Anuario Estatistico de Cuba 1978-80 (Havana, 1980); and Economic Commission
for Latin America, Statistical Yearbook for Latin America 1980 (New York, United Nations,
1981); and Cuba, CEE, Anuario Estatistico de Cuba 1978-80 (Havana, 1980), p. 57.

mation is lacking, it appears that economic pressures on the USSR (both domestically and from client states) induced a return to the previous system of covering the trade deficits with repayable loans and obvious disadvantages for Cuba. Without counting subsidies and grants, the Cuban repayable debt to the USSR was estimated to be about $8.5 billion in 1982.

Cuba's trade with market economies has usually resulted in deficits as well. In 1975-1977, the Cuban leaders went on a buying spree because of their incorrect expectations for continued high sugar prices, and the final outcome was a cumulative deficit of $2.5 billion. The combination of the Soviet Union's trade-balancing concession in those years, declining world sugar prices, and heavy trade with the West shifted the bulk of Cuba's trade deficit to the market economies (see Table 12.7). To finance these trade deficits, Western governments and international banks granted loans to Cuba, first long-term loans but increasingly short-term ones at high interest rates. Cuba's hard-currency foreign debt steadily rose from $462 million in 1970 to $1.4 billion in 1977 to $2.6 billion in 1980 to $3.5 billion in 1982. In 1978, Cuba was faced with payments of half a billion dollars in principal due to servicing of the debt; the principal and interest payments reached a record $1.3 billion in

1982. Because of the payment drainage, the island's hard-currency reserves declined by almost two-thirds in less than eight months: from $414 million at the end of 1981 down to a dangerously low level of $133 million in August 1982. This drop occurred at a time when world sugar prices were at their lowest point in two decades and international credit was extremely tight.

In response to the grave liquidity crisis, Cuba asked its Western creditors for a debt rescheduling in August 1982, including a three-year grace period and a ten-year deferral of $1.2 billion in principal due in 1982–1985 in exchange for continued payment of interest (Cuba, BNC 1982a:55–57). After six months of tough bargaining, an agreement was reached on March 1, 1983, to stretch out principal payments due between September 1982 and the end of 1983. Discussions continued on the rescheduling of the debt, which fell due in 1984 and thereafter. Hence, the debtor got a brief respite, but Cuba's financial situation in the long run is uncertain. So far, neither the USSR nor the Council for Economic Assistance's bank has come to Cuba's rescue. Since the island is not a member of the IMF or of the World Bank, it cannot benefit from their loans. Finally, credit from private banks is tighter than before due to international conditions, higher priorities elsewhere, U.S. pressure to not loan to Cuba, and the shattered image left by the island's financial crisis.

In 1982, Cuba's foreign debt (combining the hard-currency debt and the debt with the Soviets) was about $12 billion, representing almost half of the island's GSP and twice the value of its exports (see Table 12.3). In per capita terms, the Cuban debt was one of the highest in Latin America. About 70 percent of the debt is with the USSR, and although that country provides generous terms, a good part of it will be due in 1986. In its 1982 annual report, the Economic Commission for Latin America stated that Cuba had requested that the USSR postpone both the debt accumulated in "recent years" and the one to come through in 1982–1985. This statement, however, appears to have been an incorrect interpretation of a speech by the president of JUCEPLAN, who actually referred to the hard-currency debt (Pérez 1983). Two scholars who visited Cuba in March and June 1985 were told by high Cuban officials that the debt due in 1986 had been postponed although the details still had to be worked out.

There are several indications that the USSR may have reached its limit with regard to its generous aid to Cuba. To begin with, the Soviet economy is under enormous pressure because of domestic demands, the urgent needs of Eastern European clients, and the international arms race. Second, Cuba's five-year plan revealed a significant slowdown in the rate of growth of Soviet aid, trade, and oil supply expected in 1981–1985. Finally, the USSR did not bail out Cuba from its financial crisis by guaranteeing the island's obligations in hard currency in spite of the assumption previously held by Western bankers.[13]

308   Carmelo Mesa-Lago

In an attempt to attract foreign capital from the West and reversing a long-standing revolutionary rejection of foreign investment, Cuba promulgated a law in early 1982 that encourages joint ventures. According to this law, foreign investors may own as much as 49 percent of the joint enterprise—but in special cases (e.g., tourism) may own the majority. Such a joint enterprise is to be independent of the state and thus have absolute freedom to appoint its board of directors and managerial staff, define the production plan and financial policy, set prices, export and import directly, conduct its operations in freely convertible currency, receive financing conditions from local banks in that currency, and remit abroad its share of the profits with no restrictions. No taxes will be imposed on the enterprise's gross income, the shareholders' dividends, or the executives' personal incomes. A profit tax will be due, but the state can exempt the enterprise from it (as well as custom duties) when the enterprise is involved in international tourism. The Cuban law is quite flexible in comparison with similar existing laws in most socialist countries—Yugoslavia and Hungary have the most flexible (Cuba, Chamber of Commerce 1982)—but the international recession and U.S. pressures have so far resulted in no takers.

Satisfaction of Basic Needs

If Cuba has performed poorly on the basis of most economic indicators, the opposite is true in terms of social indicators such as income distribution, employment, and social services. However, it is important to recall that prior to the revolution, Cuba ranked among the top two or three countries of Latin America on the basis of most social indicators.

Cuba has never published data on income distribution, either before or after the revolution, but the figures in Table 12.8 (rough estimates prepared in the West) show that the most dramatic redistribution of income took place in the early years of the revolution: Between 1953 and 1962, the richest 30 percent of the population lost 17.3 percent of the income (14 percent was lost by the top 5 percent), almost two-thirds of that income lost went to the poorest 40 percent, and the rest went to the middle-income 30 percent. Unfortunately, there are no data for 1970, the end of the Mao-Guevarist period when so much emphasis was put on egalitarianism. The data for 1973 include the early pragmatic years of the 1970s, when egalitarianism began to be deemphasized, and reveal a more modest redistribution: The highest-income 20 percent had lost an additional 6 percent of income, half of which went to the poorest 40 percent and the other half to the middle-income groups. Finally, the data for 1978, when the reintroduction of material incentives had taken place, indicate that the top 10 percent lost a small income share (1.8

Table 12.8

PERCENTAGE DISTRIBUTION OF PERSONAL INCOME IN CUBA: 1953-1978

Decile groups	1953	1962	1973[a]	1978[b]
Poorest	0.6	2.5	2.9	3.4
Second	1.5	3.7	4.9	4.4
Third	1.9	4.8	5.4	5.3
Fourth	2.5	6.2	7.1	7.1
Fifth	4.3	6.8	8.7	9.3
Sixth	6.8	9.5	10.5	10.4
Seventh	10.6	12.0	12.0	12.6
Eighth	13.9	13.1	13.5	14.1
Ninth	19.1	18.4	15.1	15.3
Richest	38.8	23.0	19.9	18.1
(Top 5%)	(26.5)	(12.7)	(9.5)	(9.5)
Total	100.0	100.0	100.0	100.0

[a]Excludes private sector

[b]Includes private sector

Source: Claes Brundenius, Economic Growth, Basic Needs and Income Distribution in Revolutionary Cuba (Lund: University of Lund, 1981), pp. 142, 147, 151.

percent). Most of it went to the middle- and highest-income groups (deciles five through nine), although the poorest 10 percent received a small portion. The remaining low-income groups (deciles two and three) suffered a decrease. In 1953, the ratio between the lowest and the highest income groups was 1:65; in 1978, the ratio had dramatically declined to 1:5. Although available data do not allow for an accurate comparison with the rest of Latin America, it is obvious that no other country in the region has redistributed income so drastically as Cuba has.

Another important achievement of the revolution has been the substantial reduction in open unemployment, from 11.8 percent of the labor force in 1958 to 1.3 percent in 1970 (see Table 12.9). However, this feat was in part accomplished by the expansion of underemployment and

Table 12.9

INDICATORS OF SATISFACTION OF BASIC NEEDS IN CUBA: 1958-1980

| Years | Illiteracy rate[a] | % of population of school age[b] in | | | Mortality Rates[c] | | Daily calories per capita[d] | Construction of dwellings per 1,000 inhabitants[e] | Unemployment rate[f] | Life expectancy (Years)[g] | Durable consumer goods per 1,000 inhabitants | | |
		Elementary	Secondary	Higher	General	Infant					Cars	TVs	Phones
1958	23.6	58	19	6	6.3	33.4	2,740-2,870	n.a.	11.8	61.8	25.0	n.a.	26
1960	n.a.	109	14	3	7.1	41.5	2,410	2.3	11.8		25.6	74	29
1965	n.a.	121	23	3	6.4	37.8	2,452	1.9	6.5	65.1	20.7	n.a.	30
1970	12.9	121	22	4	6.3	38.7	2,567	0.5	1.3	68.5	8.4	68	32
1975	n.a.	124	42	11	5.4	27.3	2,636	2.0	3.1	70.9	8.5	64	32
1980	4.0	112	48/71	19	5.7	19.6	2,866	1.5	5.4	71.8	n.a.	n.a.	n.a.

aThe date for 1958 is actually 1953. The date for 1980 is 1979 and excludes the population above 49 years old, which has a higher illiteracy rate; the overall rate for this year should be from 6 to 7 percent.

bElementary: 6-11 years; secondary: 1960/65 12-17 years, 1970/76 12-18 years, 1977-80 12-17 years; higher 20-24 years. The two figures for secondary in 1980 correspond to two different age groups. Data for 1958 exclude private schools.

cGeneral: annual deaths per 1,000 inhabitants; infant: deaths of infants less than one year old per 1,000 live births.

dData for 1960 are actually for 1962 to show the peak in both rates.
1957-1958, 1961-1963, 1964-1966, 1969-1971, 1974-1976, and 1980.

eThere are no annual figures from 1959 to 1967, hence data for 1960 is the annual average of 1959-1963 and that for 1965, the annual average of 1964-1967.

fThe date for 1980 is actually 1979.

g1955-1960, 1960-1965, 1965-1970, 1970-1975 (projection), and 1975-1980 (projection).

Sources: Carmelo Mesa-Lago, "The Economy: Caution, Frugality and Resilient Ideology," in Jorge I. Dominguez, ed., Cuba: Internal and International Affairs (Beverly Hills: Sage Publications, 1982), pp. 41, 122, 164-165, 173; UNESCO, Statistical Yearbook (various years); United Nations, Economic Commission for Latin America, Statistical Yearbook for Latin America 1980 (New York: United Nations, 1981), pp. 68, 85-88, 90; Cuba, CEE, Cuba en Cifras 1981 (Havana, 1981), pp. 3, 252; Cuba, CEE, Anuario Estadistico de Cuba 1978-80 (Havana, 1980), pp. 28, 38, 317.

disguised unemployment, at the cost of a decline in labor productivity. In the 1970s, unemployment increased again because infants born during the baby boom of 1959–1965 began to enter the labor market at the same time that labor productivity was being emphasized by the reintroduced Soviet economic model. The situation was accentuated in the second half of the decade when the slowdown in economic growth induced a gradual decline in the rate of expansion of state civilian employment: from 6.2 percent in 1977 to 5.5 percent in 1978 to 1.6 percent in 1979 to −1.2 percent in 1980 (Cuba, CEE 1980, 1981b). The government tried to tackle the jobless problem with a reactivation of private employment in personal services, an expansion of the armed forces, and agreements signed with socialist and Third World countries to use part of Cuba's labor surplus. Still, in 1979 the rate of open unemployment was 5.4 percent (more than two-thirds of it women), and an additional 6.7 percent was officially labeled as "potential labor force" (people, mostly women, who wanted to work but could not find a job).[14]

Other advances in social indicators are also summarized in Table 12.9.[15] The illiteracy rate was reduced from 23.6 percent in 1958 to 12.9 percent in 1970 and possibly 6 or 7 percent in 1979 (but certainly not the 3.9 percent claimed in 1961). Enrollment in primary education had become universal by 1980 while enrollment had increased two- or threefold in secondary education and had tripled in higher education. The mortality rate rose in the 1960s but declined in the 1970s to below the prerevolutionary level. Social security coverage in pensions increased from 63 to 95 percent from 1958 to 1980, and health care coverage became universal. Life expectancy steadily grew with a net advance of ten years from 1960 to 1980. At the beginning of the 1980, Cuba ranked among the top of all Latin American countries according to these indicators, but the same was true in the late 1950s.

On the other hand, calories per capita apparently declined during the early years of the revolution and did not regain the prerevolutionary level until 1980. Construction of dwellings decreased sharply, reaching a trough in 1970 and staying well below prerevolutionary levels despite some improvement in 1980.[16] The availability of most durable consumer goods has declined in spite of the government's efforts to domestically produce durable goods such as television sets and refrigerators.

The deterioration of the Cuban economy and the country's debt obligations have forced a tightening of the belt in the 1980s that threatens some of the social advances made earlier. This movement began at the end of 1981 when Fidel Castro described the difficult economic situation, promised to fulfill international financial commitments, and announced the need for more restrictions and sacrifices starting with a dramatic increase in consumer prices.[17] In 1982, investment was cut by 10 percent and fuel consumption by 3.7 percent, Western imports were reduced from 21 to 15 percent of total exports, and state budget allocations to production and social services were cut by 34.5 and 5.4 percent, respectively. The only sector not affected by the squeeze was defense, which actually received an increased share of the budget: 7.5 percent in 1981, 9.4 percent in 1982, and 10.8 percent in 1983.[18] According to the Economic Commission for Latin America, consumption was reduced in Cuba in 1982 by the following percentages: −7.4 in milk and dairy products, −7.1 in vegetables, −5.9 in tubers, −4.2 in eggs, −2.4 in cereals, and −1.7 in sugar (UN ECLA 1984:Table 2).

In 1983, the president of JUCEPLAN declared that Cuba had exhausted all means to cut down hard-currency imports and went on to announce a new reduction from 15 to 13 percent of total exports, one-third less than the "rock bottom needed." Other cutbacks were announced in the supply of clothing and meals served in workers' and students' cafeterias (Pérez 1983). The planned economic growth rate for 1983 was set at 2–2.5 percent, but that depended on a sugar crop of 8.8 million tons. Heavy rains and floods that hit the island during the harvest inflicted a loss of from 1 to 2 million tons of sugar, making the plan's target impossible to achieve.[19] Ironically, the expectation of a bad sugar harvest in Cuba combined with poor harvests in Western Europe prompted an increase in sugar prices in the international market.

The Effects of Trading Off Equity for Growth

As has been seen in the preceding pages, the Cuban state has utilized, with varying success, its great economic power to achieve most social goals such as more equal income distribution, less unemployment, price stability of essential consumer goods (at least until the 1980s), and better social services (with the exception of housing). Conversely, the state has failed to reach most economic goals such as self-sustained and stable economic growth, sufficient capital accumulation and its efficient use, export promotion, and diversification of trade partners. In spite of the enormous power of the state and the colossal Soviet aid, the Cuban leadership has been unable to significantly change the island's economic structure after twenty-five years of socialism.

Frequent and erratic changes in economic policy (resulting in considerable waste) coupled with the excessive emphasis on equity (particularly in the 1960s) largely explain the dismal economic failure. The increase in consumption during the early years of the revolution and the expansion of social services throughout the whole process sharply reduced investment. This reduction, combined in the early years with an ambitious and doomed attempt at industrialization and the temporary neglect of sugar production, provoked the external disequilibrium. The radical collectivization process and idealistic egalitarian policy practiced during the Mao-Guevarist period reduced economic incentives and blocked private initiative, while the state and moral stimuli were unable to manage and motivate the economy. The cost of achieving full employment, partly through artificial job creation, had a negative double effect: Workers ceased to fear unemployment and reduced their labor effort, and the cost of reduced labor productivity was distributed among the whole population. Subsidies for consumer goods aggravated the disequilibrium while rationing, although just and egalitarian, hampered incentives. Continued dependency on sugar has maintained the economic links to international market fluctuations.

The economic embargo and the needs of defense have been additional constraints to growth in certain periods of the revolution, but the current weight of those factors has been exaggerated. Although in the 1960s the U.S. embargo badly hurt Cuba, by the 1970s the island had been able to break away from this limitation and reestablish trade links with and receive credit and loans from Western Europe, Japan, Canada, and Latin America. The crucial impediment to a diversification of trade partners has not been the embargo but Cuba's inability to significantly expand and diversify its exports. The need for defense against the United States was obvious in the first stage of the revolution, but the U.S. threat significantly diminished throughout the 1970s. During both the Ford and Carter administrations, Cuba had a chance to normalize relations with the United States. And yet, in both instances the Cuban leaders chose to become militarily involved in Africa, which interrupted the negotiations and added an extra burden to the island's economy. Under the Reagan administration the specter of U.S. intervention has reappeared, but the situation might have been different today if an accommodation had been reached before. Furthermore, Cuba is not a mere victim of hemispheric tensions but has partly contributed to them through its involvement in Central America.

In any event, it seems that the costs of the embargo and defense have been compensated by the generous Soviet aid, which supersedes, both in magnitude and flexibility, the total amount of U.S. aid granted to all of Latin America during the bountiful years of the Alliance for Progress. The USSR has also apparently supplied Cuba, free of charge or at very low cost, with all the needed military equipment for domestic use and for operations abroad. The Cuban model is impossible to replicate in Latin America without the integral component of substantial Soviet aid. The duplication of that aid is highly questionable since so far, the Soviet Union has failed to extend such assistance to other countries such as

Chile during the Allende years, Peru under Velasco, ana Nicaragua today. The USSR has too many problems already, both internally and with its European clients, to be willing to support several Cubas elsewhere. Instead, it seems that Moscow is attempting, if not to reduce, at least to freeze the aid provided to Havana.

Still, some people could argue that, in spite of everything, Cuba can show an impressive record in social goals, something that is impossible to achieve in the region without its type of model. However, I have proved elsewhere (Mesa Lago and Díaz-Briquets 1985) that in 1960–1980, at least one other Latin American country, Costa Rica, equaled or surpassed many of Cuba's achievements in the social sphere (e.g., decline in infant mortality, increase in life expectancy, enrollment in education, expansion of social security) and, at the same time, exceeded the Cuban record in several economic goals (e.g., in capital accumulation, output and export diversification, better equilibrium in the trade balance). Moreover, at the starting point, Cuba was more advanced than Costa Rica in practically all economic and social indicators, hence the latter had to make a greater effort to close the gap with the former. Finally, Costa Rica was able to accomplish all this with a less powerful state and without sacrificing economic and political freedoms of the people.

Although Cuba introduced a more pragmatic economic policy in the 1970s and 1980s, the island's economy still remains excessively centralized and collectivized. The heavy dependency on sugar should continue at least until the end of the century, and there are few probabilities that Cuba will reduce its dependence on the USSR. The recent deterioration in the island's economy, the enormous foreign debt it faces, and the apparent Soviet reluctance to increase its aid could promote changes in both domestic and international policies. A revitalization of the Cuban economy would require greater decentralization in decision making; more use of market mechanisms; better and more stable economic incentives for managers, workers, and farmers; and increased private initiative, as Hungary has successfully done. But the Cuban leaders still have ideological hangovers that are extremely resilient and a taste for centralization of power that is difficult to relinquish. A rapprochement with the United States has been precluded by the inflexibility of the Reagan administration, the continuation of Cuba's military involvement abroad, and the escalation in the U.S.-Soviet confrontation.

Cuba may weather its financial crisis temporarily, but prospects for the medium range are dim, and a long-term solution will require the policy changes indicated above in order to diversify both the country's economy and its markets. Such diversification is extremely difficult to achieve, otherwise Cuba would not have a history of almost 200 years of sugar monoculture and more than 400 years of economic dependence on a world power.

Notes

Information for this paper was gathered until mid-1983; in one or two cases, new information has been added resulting from comments and criticism of the original version completed in November 1983.

1. For an economic history of Cuba under socialism and an assessment of the country's economic performance in 1959–1978, see Mesa-Lago (1978, 1981). For other viewpoints, see McEwan (1981), Brundenius (1981), and Cuba, CEE (1981a).

2. The National Bank of Cuba (BNC) gives the following divergent annual growth rate averages in BNC (1982a): 2.8 percent for both 1965–1970 and 1960–1970 (pp. 29–30); 10 percent and 7.5 percent for 1970–1975 (pp. 17, 29); and 4 percent and 4.6 percent for 1976–1980 (pp. 17–18).

3. According to official figures, real GSP increased by 12 percent in 1981, by "approximately" 2.5 percent in 1982, and the planned target for 1983 was 2–2.5 percent. The 1981 figure is probably a gross overestimation due to high inflation in that year.

4. A study by Wharton Econometrics Forecasting Associates, which promises to be the most sophisticated done on the subject, estimates Cuba's annual average growth rate at 3.3 percent, 1 percentage point less than the Cuban rate.

5. Comparisons of Cuba with Latin America throughout this chapter, unless specified, are based on United Nations, ECLA (1980) and United Nations, ECLA (n.d.).

6. For comparative figures, see Mesa-Lago and Pérez-López (1985a). Data on Cuban investment are unavailable for 1959–1961, scarce for 1967–1970, and usually inconsistent for the 1970s and early 1980s. For instance, five different figures have been published for 1980: two released by the CCE, two by the BNC, and one by UNCTAD based on Cuban sources.

7. Based on data published in CMEA (1979), Table 47, and CMEA (1980), Table 51, provided by Jorge Pérez-López to the author.

8. Productivity trends described in the text are accentuated if the service sector is deleted from the employment distribution and private employment is added, especially in agriculture.

9. See Mesa-Lago and Pérez-López (1985a:75–78). The very low price of sugar in the world market reduced the value of this export, which created the illusion of a decline in Cuba's dependency on sugar in the late 1960s and early 1970s. This situation led one notable scholar to the wrong conclusion (see LeoGrande 1979).

10. Prices from the IMF's *International Finance Statistics*, 1970–1982, and the *New York Times*, January–December 1982.

11. This analysis is based on Mesa-Lago (1981, 1982), updated with new data from Cuba, CEE (1980), Cuba, CEE (1981b), and *Granma Weekly Review*.

12. A documented article by a Cuban economist asserts that "the rapid increment in oil prices has provoked a significant increase in nickel production costs"; for

each $1 increment in the cost of one barrel of oil, the production cost of a pound of nickel increases as much as $0.07, for a total increase of $1.50 per pound in 1973–1980. Thus—argues the article—Cuba must increase the nickel content of the mineral extracted to compete in world markets (see Cuevas 1981:81, 95).

13. The London-based *Latin American Weekly Report* denied, three months before the crisis, the rumors that Cuba was on the verge of default, basing its evaluation on the international bankers' faith that the USSR would come to the island's rescue.

14. Cuba, CEE (1981b:1, 13). For a detailed study of the survey, see Brundenius (1983).

15. For a detailed analysis of social services under the revolution, see Mesa-Lago (1981:Chapter 7) and Brundenius (1981).

16. In 1970, 36 percent of the rural population lived in *bohíos* (palm-thatched homes), and the number of *bohíos* had increased by 27 percent in 1981, suggesting a deterioration in rural housing in the 1970s compared with a significant advance in the 1960s (see Cuba, Dirección General de Estadística 1970:Table 22 and 1981:xix).

17. Castro (1981) argued that defense had a high priority and although its cost was high, it couldn't be subject to cuts.

18. Pérez (1981, 1983). State budget figures are from *Bohemia* (January 2, 1981:58); *Granma Weekly Review* (December 31, 1981:2); and *Granma Weekly Review* (January 9, 1983:3).

19. See *Latin America Commodities Report* (February 11, March 11, and April 15, 1983).

References

Brundenius, Claes. 1981. *Economic Growth, Basic Needs, and Income Distribution in Revolutionary Cuba*. University of Lund, Research Policy Institute. Lund.

————. 1983. "Some Notes on the Development of the Cuban Labor Force 1970–1980." *Cuban Studies* 13, no. 2 (Summer):65–77.

Castro, Fidel. 1981. "Speech to Close the 2nd Congress of the CDRs." *Granma Weekly Review* (November 1):3–4.

CIA. *See* United States, Central Intelligence Agency.

Council for Mutual Economic Assistance (CMEA). 1979. *Statisticheskii ezhegodnik*. Leningrad.

————. 1980. *Statisticheskii ezhegodnik*. Leningrad.

Cuba, Banco Nacional de Cuba (BNC). 1960. *Memoria del Banco Nacional de Cuba 1958–1959*. Havana.

————. 1982a. *Informe económico*. Havana.

————. 1982b. "Preliminary Report on the Economy for 1981." Havana.

Cuba, Chamber of Commerce. 1982. *Possibility in Joint Ventures in Cuba*. Legislative Decree 50 of February 15.

Cuba, Comité Estatal de Estadísticas (CEE). 1980. *Anuario estadistico de Cuba 1978–1980*. Havana.

_____. 1981a. *Cuba: Desarrollo económico y social durante el período 1958–1980*. Havana.

_____. 1981b. *Cuba en cifras 1981*. Havana.

_____. 1981c. *Principales características laborales de la población de Cuba: Encuesta demográfica nacional 1979–1981*. Havana.

Cuba, Dirección General de Estadística. 1970. *Censo de poblacíon y viviendas de 1970: Resultados provisionales*. Havana.

_____. 1971. *Boletín estadística de Cuba 1966 to 1971*. Havana.

_____. 1981. *Censo de poblacíon y viviendas de 1981: Resultados provisionales*. Havana.

Cuba, Junta Central de Planificación (JUCEPLAN). 1963. *Comercio Exterior de Cuba: Exportación 1962*. Havana.

Cuba, Junta Central de Planificación (JUCEPLAN), Dirección de Estadística, Sección Comercio Exterior. 1981. *Cifras de estadísticas*. Havana.

Cuevas, Nidia. 1981. "Características del mercado del níquel: Situación actual y perspectiva." *Economía y desarrollo*, no. 63 (July-August).

International Monetary Fund (IMF). 1970–1982. *International Financial Statistics*.

LeoGrande, William. 1979. "Cuban Dependency: A Comparison of Pre-Revolutionary and Post-Revolutionary International Relations." *Cuban Studies* 9, no. 2 (July):1–28.

McEwan, Arthur. 1981. *Revolution and Economic Development in Cuba*. New York: St. Martin's Press.

Mesa-Lago, Carmelo. 1978. *Cuba in the 1970s: Pragmatism and Institutionalization*. 2d ed. Albuquerque: University of New Mexico Press.

_____. 1981. *The Economy of Socialist Cuba: A Two-Decade Appraisal*. Albuquerque: University of New Mexico Press.

_____. 1982. "The Economy: Caution, Frugality, and Resilient Ideology." In *Cuba: Internal and International Affairs*, ed. Jorge I. Domínguez. Beverly Hills, Calif.: Sage Publications.

Mesa-Lago, Carmelo, and Díaz-Briquets, Sergio. 1985. "Cuba and Costa Rica." In *Different Strategies, Similar Countries, the Consequences for Growth and Equity*, ed. Gustav Papanek.

Mesa-Lago, Carmelo, and Pérez-López, Jorge. 1985a. "Study of Cuba's Material Product System, Its Conversion to a System of National Accounts, and Estimation of GDP/Capital and Growth Rates." Staff Working Paper no. 770 Washington, D.C.: World Bank.

_____. 1985b. "Imbroglios on the Cuban Economy: A Reply to Brundenius and Zimbalist." *Comparative Economic Studies* 27, no. 1 (Spring):79–80.

Pérez, Humberto. 1978. "Discurso en el acto de clausura del Seminario Nacional Preparatorio para la elaboración de los estudios de estrategia de desarrollo perspectivo económico y social hasta el año 2,000." *Granma Weekly Review* (October 18).

_____. 1981. "Informe ante la Asamblea Nacional acerca del cumplimiento del Plan de la Economía Nacional en 1981 y sobre el Proyecto de Plan para 1982." *Granma Weekly Review* (December 30):2.

———. 1983. "Report to the National Assembly on the Fulfillment of the Plan for 1982 and on the Draft Plan for 1983." *Granma Weekly Review* (January 16):4.

Rodríguez García, José Luis. 1982. "La Economía cubana entre 1976 y 1980: Resultados y perspectivas." *Economía y desarrollo,* no. 66 (January-February):118.

A Study on Cuba. 1965. Miami: University of Miami Press.

United Nations. 1964. *Statistical Bulletin* 1, no. 1:42.

United Nations, Economic Commission for Latin America (ECLA). n.d. "Síntesis estadística de América Latina, 1960–1980."

———. 1980. *Anuario estadístico de América Latina 1980.*

———. 1981. *Statistical Yearbook for Latin America 1980.* New York.

———. 1984. "Cuba." In *Estudio económico de América Latina y el Caribe 1982.*

United Nations, Educational, Scientific, and Cultural Organization (UNESCO). 1978–1980. *Statistical Yearbook.* New York.

United States, Central Intelligence Agency (CIA). 1981. *The Cuban Economy: A Statistical Review.* Washington, D.C.

13

Nicaragua: The Experience of the Mixed Economy

Elizabeth Dore

In July 1979, the new government of Nicaragua announced that its economic strategy would be based on a mixed economy, characterized by the joint participation of the state and the private sector. But mounting economic and political pressures and lack of agreement among the members of the governing junta about the essential nature of the mixed economy prevented the government from defining its economic goals or developing an explicit and detailed economic plan. Fundamental obstacles to the projected mixed economy—the reluctance of the private sector to coop-erate with the new government and the scarcity of resources available to the state—appeared immediately and still persist.

Economic strategy in Nicaragua has developed by confronting im-pending problems on a day-by-day basis rather than through the logical implementation of a coherent and well-defined plan. The Sandinistas initially focused primarily on economic reconstruction. In late 1984, however, Comandante Jaime Wheelock Román, minister of agriculture, noted that as a result of external economic pressures, the hostility of the U.S. government, and the counterrevolutionary war, the Sandinistas were no longer able to even think about an economic strategy. The government was struggling just to keep the economy functioning from week to week.

Three background factors are fundamental to an understanding of the constraints on the Nicaraguan economy in the 1980s. One is the history of U.S. intervention and the nature of the family dynasty that ruled Nicaragua for more than forty years with the support of the United States. Another is the extent of the domestic opposition to the Somoza regime. The third factor is the magnitude of the economic destruction and social dislocation that resulted from the war against Somoza. I will discuss these factors before considering the nature of either the economic problems or the policy alternatives that confronted the government of

319

Nicaragua after 1979. Then I will turn to an analysis of the nature and performance of Nicaragua's mixed economy as the country's leaders sought economic reconstruction (1979–1982) and then as they dealt with war (1983–1985).

U.S. Intervention and the Somoza Dynasty

Although there is general agreement that the political and economic development of the countries of Latin America has been strongly influenced by their relationships with the United States, this influence has been qualitatively more pervasive in Central America and the Caribbean than in South America. Because of the former's particular historical development, proximity to the United States, and perceived strategic importance, the governments of the United States have directly intervened politically, economically, and militarily in this region for a century.

The history of Nicaragua in many respects represents the prototype of this relationship. It is unfortunate that nationalists and leftists have used such terms as "neocolonial" and "puppet ruler" so loosely that they have come to lose their meaning and credibility, because in characterizing the Nicaraguan governments in this century, those terms are the most precise. The first military intervention in Nicaragua from the United States occurred in the 1850s and was led by William Walker. Walker briefly established himself as dictator of Nicaragua and legalized slavery. He was defeated by an army drawn from all of Central America, and the anniversary of that battle is celebrated throughout the region.

The second period of direct U.S. presence in Nicaragua was provoked by the nationalist stance of José Santos Zelaya, president of Nicaragua from 1893 to 1909. In 1894, Zelaya expelled the British from the Atlantic coast of Nicaragua and subsequently refused to concede sovereignty over part of Nicaragua to the United States for the construction of a canal. Zelaya also attempted to unify Central America under his rule, and he took the position that Washington had no right to intervene in the region. The United States could not tolerate this policy and endorsed an internal revolt that forced Zelaya to resign.

Nicaragua was then a de facto U.S. protectorate for twenty years. A special U.S. envoy was sent to supervise the organization of the post-Zelaya government, which reestablished the economic and political concessions to the United States that Zelaya had abrogated. In 1911, the Nicaraguan president formally accepted U.S. protectorate status. This act stimulated considerable internal opposition, and the government requested troops from Washington. For almost twenty years, the U.S. Marines occupied Nicaragua, and North Americans commanded the Nicaraguan army, collected the customs duties, managed the railroads, and directed the national banking system. In 1916, the United States and Nicaragua signed the Bryan-Chamorro Treaty, which gave the United States "perpetual" rights to a canal route through Nicaragua.

The marines withdrew in 1925 to return a year later with an agreement that they would train a permanent force to take their place, a force that became the National Guard. This accord was an anathema to many Nicaraguans, among them a mining engineer named Augusto C. Sandino. From 1928 to 1933, Sandino led a successful war against the U.S. Marines, finally forcing them to withdraw. Sandino then negotiated a settlement of the conflict with the Nicaraguan government. A year later, upon leaving the presidential palace, Sandino and his associates were murdered, apparently at the order of Anastasio Somoza García, whom the U.S. government had chosen to lead the National Guard. The National Guard then proceeded to eliminate Sandino's followers.

Sandino was the quintessential patriot whose ideal was an independent and sovereign Nicaraguan nation. To this end, he fought against direct U.S. intervention. Today's Sandinistas view themselves as carrying on Augusto C. Sandino's struggle. The centerpiece of their ideology is national sovereignty and independence, and they have adopted Sandino's motto of Patria Libre o Morir (Independence or death).

With the defeat of the first Sandinista movement, Anastasio ("Tacho") Somoza became one of the most influential people in Nicaragua. In 1937, he had himself elected president of Nicaragua, and he ruled until assassinated in 1956. He was succeeded first by his oldest son Luis Somoza Debayle (1956–1963), and then by Anastasio ("Tachito") Somoza Debayle, who held power until fleeing before the victorious army headed by the Sandinista National Liberation Front (Frente Sandinista de Liberación Nacional, FSLN). Having attained office with the assistance of the United States, the Somoza family accordingly regarded Washington as its most important constituency. As a consequence, the Somozas believed that they could remain in power with merely the acquiescence of the Nicaraguan population, not its active support. This type of rule gave the economic and political development of the country its particular character (Weeks 1985b:Chapter 7).

Throughout the reign of the Somoza family, the two most important institutions in Nicaragua were the U.S. embassy and the National Guard. The guard served as the domestic power base of the dictatorship, rendering unnecessary any other internal support. Opposition political parties were intermittently permitted to function when this situation coincided with the interests of the Somozas, though the parties' electoral candidates were usually chosen by the dictator. There was little pretense of democracy or of pluralism.

The Somozas' monopoly of political and military power facilitated their increasing control over the Nicaraguan economy. In the first decades of the dynasty, the family wealth was amassed primarily through the state. The Somozas made no distinction between the state's money and their private coffers, and they magnified their wealth by accepting bribes and levying personal fees. They then invested in agriculture and industry. Along with other wealthy families, the Somozas profited from an expanding world market and high international prices in the 1950s and 1960s by investing in the production of agroexport crops (cotton and beef). In the 1960s, the Somozas and other Nicaraguan entrepreneurs took advantage of an increased market for manufactured products, which resulted from the creation of the Central American Common Market.

The effects of these policies hastened the economic transformation of Nicaragua. The 1950s and 1960s were characterized by the concentration of lands into large-scale modern enterprises, which led to the dispossession of a sizable segment of the peasantry, many of whom became rural workers.[1] This same period also witnessed an expansion of the manufacturing sector with a concomitant growth in the size of the urban working class. During the forty-year Somoza dynasty, it is clear that the Nicaraguan economy evolved from being a primarily precapitalist system to an economy in which the major areas of economic growth were based on relatively modern enterprises, agricultural as well as industrial, that employed wage labor.

Despite the transformation of the economy, there was significant continuity in the role of the state. In Nicaragua, the state had been historically one of the major vehicles for enrichment. The Somozas accentuated this national tradition. Although the Nicaraguan state was in the hands of a family dynasty for more than thirty years, the Somozas were forced to tolerate competition from other Nicaraguan entrepreneurs, many of whom were dissatisfied with the Somozas' monopolization of state power. But as long as the business community enjoyed considerable economic freedom and prosperity, facilitated by repression of the peasantry and control of the working class, it resigned itself to the continuation of the dynasty with a few notable individual exceptions. But this modus vivendi abruptly ended after the earthquake of December 1972, which leveled much of Managua. As emergency aid flowed into Nicaragua, Anastasio Somoza and his associates initiated new businesses that accumulated huge profits from the reconstruction effort. They excluded the other sectors of Nicaragua's elite from participating in this reconstruction, which became the primary growth sector of the economy.

The earthquake marked the beginning of the end for Somoza. The exclusion of the business elite from the reconstruction boom was made even more bitter by a slump in other sectors of the economy, caused in part by increased prices of imports, particularly petroleum. This slump coincided with, and perhaps partly caused, a slowdown in growth in manufacturing, a sector that had experienced rapid expansion in the 1960s (Weeks 1985b:Chapter 6). These economic pressures caused many wealthy Nicaraguan families to convert their lack of support for Somoza into active opposition. Believing that Somoza would continue to rule only as long as he had U.S. backing, the business opposition attempted to convince Washington to terminate its support for the dictatorship, with no success. However, in the late 1970s, an alternative means of ending the dictatorship was gaining strength—armed insurrection led by the Sandinista National Liberation Front.

The FSLN was ideologically diverse. Indeed, in the late 1970s the front split into three separate factions, and these factions probably agreed on only three issues: Somoza and his dictatorial apparatus had to be eliminated, armed struggle was necessary to accomplish this goal, and the U.S. domination of Nicaragua must end. Throughout the 1970s, the FSLN's attempts to overthrow the Somoza dictatorship were unsuccessful.

In the late 1970s, the active opposition to Somoza was broadened considerably with the inclusion of large sectors of the middle class, including professionals and the intelligentsia. In 1977 prestigious figures in the private sector (known as *los Doce*—the twelve) endorsed the Sandinistas. Somoza's murder of his most renowned moderate opponent, Pedro Joaquín Chamorro, in January 1978 convinced the business elite that the Sandinistas held out the only hope of overthrowing the dictatorship. But ultimately the urban poor was the decisive force in overthrowing Somoza as it rose in spontaneous insurrection. The factions of the FSLN reunited only four months before the fall of Somoza to coordinate these popular insurrections. The business community hastened Somoza's fall by ordering the cessation of all economic activity on two occasions.

In June 1979, the broad opposition united to form a government in exile in Costa Rica in preparation for the defeat of Somoza. Somoza declared that he would resign when ordered to do so by Washington (Booth 1982:176). The military successes of the FSLN coupled with pressure from other Latin American countries eventually forced the U.S. government to discontinue its support of Somoza. The United States sought to include Somoza's political party, the Liberal Nationalist party (Partido Liberal Nacionalista), in the new government, to maintain the National Guard, and to limit the participation of the FSLN. The broad opposition to Somoza, the hatred of the guard, and the popular support and military strength of the Sandinistas precluded these efforts. However, an agreement was reached that stipulated the inclusion of some less-tainted members of the National Guard in the new army. But after the outgoing regime reneged on its side of the agreement,[2] the incoming provisional government announced that it would not permit the incorporation of ex-National Guardsmen into the new army.

The Legacy of the War Against Somoza

Knowledge of the history of U.S. intervention in Nicaragua and the nature of the Somoza governments is necessary for understanding the contemporary process of social and economic transformation in Nicaragua. Of immediate dramatic consequence is a third factor, the destruction wrought by the war that overthrew Somoza. Human and economic losses were overwhelming. The United Nations Economic Commission for Latin American (ECLA) estimated that 35,000 people died, equal to 1.5 percent of the population. Another 100,000 people were maimed or disabled, and 50,000 children were orphaned. There was further social dislocation as 600,000 people were left homeless as a result of Somoza's bombing of the cities (UN, ECLA 1979:5).

The economic losses due to the war were devastating. The GNP experienced zero growth in real terms from 1977 to 1978 and then fell by 26 percent in 1979 (Table 13.1). The World Bank estimated that the loss of production alone from 1978 to 1980 (excluding damage to equipment, buildings, inventories, raw materials, etc.) was equal to $2 billion (World Bank 1981). This loss, $800 per capita, was approximately equal to the GNP for one year. Despite a growth rate of 10 percent in 1980, GNP in real terms barely exceeded what it had been a decade earlier, and per capita income declined to the level of the early 1960s. ECLA estimated war damage to infrastructure and productive capacity to equal $481 million. The loss of plant and equipment in manufacturing was equal to more than 25 percent of net fixed assets (UN, ECLA 1979:61).

In agriculture, the losses were similarly crippling, particularly with regard to agroexports. By early 1979, many large producers had perceived the inevitability of the collapse of the regime, and uncertainty about the future caused them to refrain from planting or harvesting their crops. This situation was compounded by social dislocation in the countryside as fighting intensified. The value of Nicaragua's principal agricultural exports fell by 30 percent from 1978 to 1980, which reflected a marked decline in the volume of each of Nicaragua's principal exports rather than a decline in prices (Table 13.2).

The two product lines most affected were those traditionally dominated by Somoza and his associates: cotton and beef. Since the 1950s, cotton had been one of Nicaragua's major export products, but in 1980, the volume of cotton exported was only 15 percent of what it had been in

Table 13.1

NICARAGUA: MACRO-ECONOMIC INDICATORS

1979-1984

Growth Rates (%)

	1979	1980	1981	1982	1983	1984
Gross National Product (GNP)	-26.4	10.0	8.5	-1.2	4.0	1.0
Gross Domestic Investment	-143.7	365.5	63.0	-23.1	-17.3	n.a.
Exports of Goods & Services	14.4	-40.6	14.9	-9.8	23.6	n.a.
Imports of Goods & Services	-18.8	81.6	3.8	-25.5	-7.1	n.a.

Sources: Inter-American Development Bank, Economic Report: Nicaragua (Washington, D.C., 1983) and Inter-American Development Bank, Economic and Social Progress in Latin America: Economic Integration (Washington, D.C., 1984). Data for 1984 are from Central America Report (Inforpress) 12:6 (February 15, 1985), p. 45 (nonofficial).

1978. Even more detrimental to the possibilities of a quick recovery of the agroexport sector was the destruction of the cattle industry. By the 1960s, beef had become Nicaragua's third-largest export. The industry was tightly controlled by the Somoza family, which owned most of the livestock as well as nearly all of the slaughterhouses. During the fighting, Somoza and other leading ranchers slaughtered large portions of their herds, including breeding stock, and drove across the borders into Honduras and Costa Rica as much of what remained of their herds as possible. The total number of cattle in Nicaragua declined between 25 percent and 35 percent from 1977 to 1980 (Nicaragua, Ministerio de Comercio Interior 1983:3:I-4). In 1981, the volume of beef exported was 27 percent of the 1978 level (Table 13.2). For at least a decade, it will be virtually impossible for Nicaragua to reassert itself as a major exporter of beef and dairy products.

The decimation of the herds also had a significant impact on domestic consumption. In 1982, per capita beef consumption was just over half of what it had been in 1977 (Nicaragua, Ministerio de Comercio Interior 1983:3:I-5), and Nicaragua now imports large quantities of powdered milk.[3]

Table 13.2

NICARAGUA: MAJOR EXPORTS

1977 - 1982

	1977	1978	1979	1980	1981	1982
Cotton						
Vol.	2.5	2.8	2.4	0.4	1.6	1.4
Value	150.6	140.9	135.7	30.4	121.9	87.2
Price	59.5	50.2	54.9	71.2	75.0	64.5
Coffee						
Vol.	1.1	1.2	1.2	1.0	1.1	1.0
Value	198.8	199.6	158.5	165.7	136.4	123.9
Price	184.7	168.0	131.6	165.7	119.1	122.5
Sugar						
Vol.	2.2	2.1	2.0	1.3	2.1	2.1
Value	27.8	19.6	19.6	20.5	48.7	36.4
Price	12.9	9.2	9.9	15.2	23.4	17.6
Meat						
Vol.	58.1	74.9	78.3	45.0	20.2	32.0
Value	37.3	67.7	93.5	58.6	21.2	34.2
Price	0.64	0.9	1.19	1.3	1.05	1.07

Volume: Millions of quintals except for meat which is millions of pounds
Value: Millions of US$
Price: Dollars per unit

Source: Inter-American Development Bank, Economic Report: Nicaragua (Washington, D.C., 1983), Statistical Appendix, Table 15.

In 1979, Nicaragua had a balance-of-trade surplus of over $200 million, the largest in the country's history. Much of this surplus can be attributed to the fact that many of Nicaragua's largest business people, ranchers, and commercial farmers exported all they could, including machinery, spare parts, and even primary and intermediate materials they had previously imported. However, it is probable that a large portion of these export earnings never entered the Nicaraguan financial system. The Somoza family was extremely successful in secreting money abroad, and in the months before the fall of Somoza, there were massive outflows of foreign exchange. For example, there is no evidence that the $15 million granted to the Nicaraguan government by the IMF in March

1979 as standby credits ever reached the central bank. Similarly, Nicaraguan private banks received foreign loans of $400 million from 1977 to 1979 but disbursed loans of only $120 million. The estimates of net short-run private capital movements out of the country from January–July 1979 vary from $315 million, or 25 percent of GNP, to $650 million, or 40 percent of GNP (Weeks 1985b:Chapter 8). Whatever the precise figures, foreign exchange reserves fell dramatically in 1979.

Although the new government made a commitment to honor the foreign debt, it quickly discovered that it did not have enough foreign exchange to import the inputs, spare parts, and machinery required to reactivate the economy, much less to pay the interest on the debt. In the short term, the situation of near financial bankruptcy proved even more debilitating to the economy than the material losses. The new government had inherited a country racked by social dislocation and an economy in ruin.[4]

Economic Reconstruction: 1979–1982

The government that came to power in 1979 had no predetermined economic model. The Governing Junta of National Reconstruction (Junta de Gobierno de Reconstrucción Nacional, JGRN) represented a wide spectrum of political ideologies, and its various members favored different economic policies. However, there was unanimity on one issue: the confiscation by the state of the properties of Somoza and his closest associates.

Economic data were in such disarray due to the Somocista tradition of falsifying statistics, compounded by the disruption of the economy and the destruction of records as a result of the war, that it was months before the new government could accurately take account of what it owned. It was widely believed that about half of the economy had been in the hands of Somoza and his close associates. Only in mid-1980 did it emerge that Somoza and his associates had owned considerably less than that. In agriculture and manufacturing, only 15 percent and 20 percent, respectively, of production came into government hands. Excluding general government expenditures and public utilities, the state portion of GNP was 25 percent.

Debate over Organization of Economy

The resulting economic form was a "mixed economy," which included participation by the state and the private sector. Although there was general agreement within the new government that there would be significant state participation in the economy, there was no consensus as to what form this participation would assume. Some people advocated an economic strategy similar to that of Western European social democracy while others proposed adopting a Cuban-style model.

Since the triumph of the revolution, a series of economic issues have been at the center of the policy discussions.[5] In the agricultural sector, these have revolved primarily around three issues. The first is whether the medium- and long-term strategy should favor export promotion or whether the production of basic foods should be given priority. The second is what form of ownership structure should be favored in the rural sector: state enterprises, cooperatives, or private holdings, either large or small. The third issue is whether the state should favor large-scale enterprises, because they may be more efficient, or whether the strategy should be to provide incentives for relatively small-scale production, because it may allow for more popular participation.

In the industrial sector, the major discussion has been whether those industries that are based on predominantly imported raw materials and intermediate goods can be viable in the future. Several economic advisers have argued that the past profitability of a large portion of the manufacturing sector was predicated on the irrational economic policies of the Somoza regime. They conclude that these branches of manufacturing should be eliminated.

Another extensively debated issue concerns the policy regarding nationalization of private property. In the first few years after the triumph, the major discussion was whether only the properties of Somoza and his associates should be subject to nationalization or whether properties suffering decapitalization should also be nationalized; secondarily, it was also debated whether the state should provide compensation to the former owners. Although it was decreed that severely decapitalized properties in both the agricultural and the industrial sectors would be subject to nationalization, limitations on the capabilities of the state apparatus precluded the enforcement of this policy. Virtually all large private enterprises in Nicaragua have been decapitalized. Private fixed investment in 1980 was less than 1 percent of what it had been in 1977. In 1981, it increased to 24 percent of its 1977 level, only to decline again in 1982 (Table 13.3). Despite this factor, apart from the properties of Somoza and his associates, only a handful of enterprises had been nationalized by the end of 1982.

The role of the private sector in the Nicaraguan economy has also been the subject of intense discussions. There continue to be divergent viewpoints within the government on this major question, even after the resignation of original junta members Alfonso Robelo and Violetta Barrios de Chamorro, who propounded economic policies that favored the interests of the large agriculturalists and industrialists. The dominant

Table 13.3

NICARAGUA: PRIVATE FIXED INVESTMENT

1977 - 1982

(millions of 1980 cordobas)

1977	3,080.4
1978	1,804.6
1979	547.0
1980	24.8
1981	731.0
1982	473.8

Source: Inter-American Development Bank, Economic Report: Nicaragua (Washington, D.C., 1983), Statistical Appendix, Table 6.

position within the Nicaraguan government has been that the role of the private sector should be carefully delimited and the state should determine the overall direction of the economy. Within this framework, there coexist many currents that can be classified into the two general tendencies of, one, the economics of social democracy or, two, the economics of Cuban-style socialism. In this area, the major debates within the government have been (1) to what extent the government should provide economic incentives to private entrepreneurs in an attempt to induce them to invest, (2) what sectors of the economy should be left to the control of the private sector during the 1980s, and (3) the nature of the policies that govern the relationship between state and private enterprises.

Finally, the last major issue of political economy that conditions the overall orientation of the economic strategy is Nicaragua's role in the international economic system. The majority of voices within the Sandinista government maintain that it is essential that Nicaragua remain nonaligned and that the Nicaraguan government should actively seek to establish economic relationships wherever it can. A small minority of people argue that although nonalignment might be ideal, this is an unattainable goal for a Central American country. They argue that Nicaragua must become allied with either the United States or the USSR.

Since the former is objectionable because of the long history of U.S. domination of Nicaragua, proponents of this position argue that there is no alternative to Nicaragua's establishing political and economic ties with the countries of the Soviet bloc.

Role of the State in the Economy

Initially the planning ministry was designated to develop economic policy. In 1980 and 1981, it designed one-year plans that projected that GNP would grow in the first year at 37 percent and in the second at 18 percent (Nicaragua, Ministerio de Planificación 1980:17, 1981:153). The exaggerated optimism of those plans, which bore little relation to reality, tended to undermine the legitimacy and authority of the policy directives issued by the ministry, which in any case had little authority. Somoza's business empire may have been rational for the purposes of personal profitability; it could not provide a basis for economic planning or centralizing direction of the economy.

After nationalizing the property of the Somoza family and its associates, the state controlled only 15 percent of Nicaragua's cotton production, 12 percent of the coffee production, and 8 percent of the country's livestock. Much of the property that was acquired represented stock ownership in enterprises in which the majority of the assets continued to be privately owned. Throughout the economy, the state enterprises represented one of several competitors among a number of producers in each product line, making economic planning virtually impossible. As Solon Barraclough, a foreign economic adviser, said in late 1981, the government owned one-quarter of the economy and controlled none of it. Furthermore, the enterprises in the state sector had been so decapitalized and had lost so many of their administrative and technical personnel that frequently, their continued operation became highly problematical.

The initial reactivation, while not as rapid as had been predicted by government economists, was nonetheless impressive. The urgent need after the triumph was for foreign exchange to purchase inputs, replenish inventories, and repair machinery as well as to service the foreign debt inherited from Somoza. With amazing rapidity, the short-term foreign exchange problem was solved by loans from the multilateral lending agencies, particularly the World Bank and the Inter-American Development Bank. From July 1979 to July 1981, multilateral loans to Nicaragua totaled $320 million, almost 30 percent of all loans that Nicaragua received in this period (Table 13.4). These loans permitted an initially rapid recovery of the manufacturing sector, whose output rose by over 15 percent in 1980, and an impressive reactivation of construction. In 1980, GNP grew at 10 percent, which seemed to augur well for future economic growth.

Table 13.4

FOREIGN LOAN COMMITMENTS TO THE NICARAGUAN GOVERNMENT

July 1979 - July 1981

(Millions of US$)

Agency	Amount	Percentage
Inter-American Development Bank	$ 193	16.8
World Bank	91	7.9
BCIE[1]	36	3.1
MULTI-LATERAL TOTAL	$ 320	27.8
Latin-American Governments[2]	$ 258	22.4
Eastern European Governments	132	11.5
OPEC Governments	120	10.4
Western European Governments	97	8.4
U.S. Government (USAID)	73	6.3
OFFICIAL BILATERAL TOTAL	$ 680	59.1
Private Banks	$ 150	13.1
TOTAL	$1,150	100

[1]Banco Centroamericano de Integración Económica
[2]Does not include concessionary oil sales by Mexico and Venezuela

Source: John Weeks, The Economies of Central America (New York: Holmes and Meier, 1985).

To stimulate investments in the private sector, the government passed an agrarian reform law, which provides that land productively used will not be confiscated regardless of the size of the holding. Only those properties that are either idle or significantly underutilized are subject to confiscation. In such cases, the law provides that the landlords can retain ownership while forfeiting the right to work the land. A similar law was enacted for the industrial sector, safeguarding private property so long as there is no evidence of decapitalization of the enterprise.[6]

Two important sectors came under state control: banking and foreign trade. In an effort to consolidate the foreign debt, as well as to rationalize the internal credit system, the state nationalized the financial institutions.

One objective of the reorganized banking system was to extend loans to small- and medium-sized producers, who formerly had had little access to credit. This policy was first applied extensively to the agricultural sector, where approximately three times more credit was extended to small- and medium-sized producers of basic grains during the 1980-1981 crop cycle than before the war. However, because a high proportion of the recipients defaulted on their loans, the policy was modified to restrict credit to those producers who could satisfy more-traditional lending requirements.

The purpose of the nationalization of foreign trade was to control foreign exchange in order to keep an eye on its rational allocation and to thwart capital flight. Perhaps more than any other economic policy, this measure antagonized the business people who wanted to control their own foreign exchange and especially to have the freedom to take it out of Nicaragua if they saw fit.

By the end of 1982, approximately 40 percent of total GNP was generated in the public sector (Inter-American Development Bank 1983:ii). However, state participation in the productive sectors—i.e., agriculture, fishing, cattle raising, and manufacturing—did not exceed 30 percent. Given this situation, a successful reactivation of the economy was contingent upon the participation of the private sector, and the government adopted several measures in an effort to promote private investment. The most important of these was the export incentives program, initiated at the beginning of the 1981-1982 crop year. The program established a system of multiple exchange rates designed to encourage the expansion of production for export. The government also passed several regulations providing tax advantages to exporters (Inter-American Development Bank 1983:6 and Annex D). In addition, the foreign investment law enacted during the Somoza regime remained in force, permitting foreign companies to repatriate profits. Perhaps most important, the JGRN appointed several respected members of the business community to high-level positions in the government.

These economic policies, though, had little effect upon the Nicaraguan business community, and investment decisions were conditioned primarily by the overall political situation or business climate (clima). The loss of state power and the continued political uncertainty (including the possibility of regional warfare) led the overwhelming majority of Nicaraguan business people to not invest as they concluded that the clima was highly unfavorable.

Revitalization of the Economy

The revitalization of the economy in 1980 and 1981 was based primarily on the reactivation of installed capacity, financed through external borrowing. By 1982, the possibilities of further expansion based on this dynamic were exhausted. The slight decline in GNP in 1982 (see Table 13.1) was the result of a virtual absence of investment in the private sector and the scarcity of resources at the disposal of the state. Exports declined disastrously in 1980, increased slightly in 1981, only to decline again in 1982. Although the government was committed to stimulating exports to alleviate the balance-of-payments crisis, it was difficult to accomplish this goal in light of the scarcity of public resources and the business community's unwillingness to risk its capital.

In 1980 and 1981, imports in almost every economic category were higher than they had been at their previous peak in 1977 (Table 13.5). In 1981, total imports were 31 percent higher than in 1977. The importation of consumer goods experienced the greatest increase from 1977 to 1981 (34 percent), with consumer nondurables increasing by 77 percent. Much of this latter increase was accounted for by the importation of foodstuffs, which increased by more than 200 percent in this period. The massive importation of basic foodstuffs in 1980 and 1981 was undertaken by the Nicaraguan government in order to allow the population to recover the levels of consumption achieved in 1977, as well as to expand consumption among the urban and rural poor. The government had to import basic foodstuffs because domestic production of staples such as corn, beans, vegetable oil, and meat had declined. In addition, the increase in real income in 1980 and the integration of large sectors of the rural population into the national market resulted in an expansion of demand (Nicaragua, Ministerio de Comercio Interior 1983:1:B1–B10).

Intermediate goods have traditionally accounted for the highest percentage of total imports (approximately 38 percent), and in 1981, imports in this category were 24 percent higher than their previous peak in 1977 (Table 13.5). This higher level of imports relative to the level of total output was necessitated by the destruction of machinery, spare parts, and inventories during the war. Many intermediate and final goods that were produced in Nicaragua prior to 1979 subsequently had to be imported. This destruction would imply the need to import capital goods, yet imports of items in this category in 1980 were just over half of what they had been in 1977. However, in 1981, the importation of capital goods increased markedly, slightly exceeding the 1977 level. Most of this increase was facilitated by a loan from the World Bank to purchase capital equipment for industry. As private entrepreneurs were not investing in such equipment, the state had to commit resources to expand imports for the industrial sector, and imports for industry almost doubled from 1980 to 1981.

Nicaragua has been heavily dependent upon imported crude and refined petroleum products.[7] Although Nicaragua's consumption of energy from

Table 13.5

NICARAGUA: IMPORTS BY ECONOMIC USE
(millions of dollars)

	1977	1978	1979	1980	1981	1982
Merchandise Imports	761.9	593.9	365.9	887.2	999.4	775.5
Consumer Goods	180.9	148.0	101.2	257.8	243.0	160.4
Non-Durable	110.6	98.2	81.8	214.9	195.8	116.6
(Food)	(30.7)	(31.3)	(30.1)	(98.6)	(93.0)	(50.1)
Durable	70.3	49.8	19.4	42.9	47.2	43.8
Intermediate Goods	284.4	243.3	136.7	339.5	352.1	268.7
Agriculture	40.1	36.7	15.6	61.7	55.7	34.9
Industry	212.3	181.0	106.4	248.1	262.5	187.1
Construction Materials	32.0	25.6	14.7	29.7	33.9	46.7
Fuel & Lubricants	103.0	89.0	75.7	174.1	197.3	178.7
Petroleum	78.0	57.8	65.6	148.1	172.9	148.0
Capital Goods	192.8	113.4	46.2	109.7	200.7	166.7
Agriculture	21.9	12.8	4.3	24.0	29.7	24.8
Industry	117.6	75.2	31.4	60.8	120.7	108.8
Transport	53.3	25.4	10.5	24.9	50.3	33.1
Misc.	0.8	0.2	6.1	6.1	6.3	1.0

Source: Inter-American Development Bank, Economic Report: Nicaragua (Washington, D.C., 1983), Statistical Appendix, Table 16.

commercial sources was approximately 8 percent lower in 1981 than at its peak in 1977 (reflecting for the most part the decline in GNP), the value of that decreased energy consumption had increased by 120 percent because the dollar price that Nicaragua had to pay for its petroleum imports had increased by 160 percent (Table 13.6). In 1981, 35 percent of Nicaragua's total export earnings was used to import petroleum products. Mexico, and more recently the Soviet Union and Iran, have supplied petroleum to Nicaragua on highly concessionary terms. Nevertheless, in mid-1982 the government instituted rationing for gasoline, hoping to reduce petroleum consumption by 20 percent.

Although a relatively high level of imports was mandatory to revitalize the Nicaraguan economy and to satisfy the consumption demands of the population, it proved impossible to maintain such a policy. The paucity of foreign exchange forced the government to reduce imports by more than 20 percent across the board in 1982. The category that exhibited the sharpest drop was consumer goods, which fell by 34 percent from 1981 to 1982 (Table 13.5). A 46 percent decline in the imports of foodstuffs, although partially compensated by a growth in domestic output, still had severe repercussions on the living standard of the majority of the population.

The decline in the availability of food occurred concurrently with a decline in social services. In 1980, considerable public expenditures were devoted to health and education (Table 13.7). The funds financed the construction of hospitals, rural health clinics, and schools as well as the salaries and training of medical personnel, teachers, administrators, etc. As a result of these programs, there was a significant improvement in the social welfare of the population. The illiteracy rate was substantially reduced, life expectancy increased, and infant mortality declined.[8] In 1982, a lack of resources required the contraction of many of these programs. The paucity of foreign exchange resulted in an extreme scarcity of essential medicine, hospital and laboratory equipment, books, paper, and pencils. By mid-1981, then, the country's initial optimism had faded as serious economic constraints slowly tightened. Internally, the fundamental difficulties were two: (1) the capacity to export in terms of both production (supply side) and markets (demand side) had fallen by as much as 30 percent from 1978 to 1980, and (2) due to the destruction of industrial plants and equipment, to the decimation of the cattle herds, and to a decline in agricultural production, the import requirement of the economy had risen by as much as 20 percent for a given level of national income (see Weeks 1985b:Chapter 7). This situation implied that short of imposing draconian measures upon the population, it would be impossible to approach an equilibrium in the balance of payments.

Table 13.6

NICARAGUA: IMPORTS OF PETROLEUM PRODUCTS

	1977	1978	1979	1980	1981	1982	1983
Merchandise Imports							
Crude and Partially Refined Products							
Value[1]	78.0	57.8	65.6	148..	172.9	148.0	n.a.
Volume[2]	5.4	3.9	3.1	4.1	4.6	4.3	3.8
Price[3]	14.4	14.71	20.99	33.23	37.6	34.68	n.a.

[1]Millions of dollars

[2]Millions of barrels of 159 liters

[3]Dollars/barrel

Sources: Inter-American Development Bank, Economic Report: Nicaragua (Washington, D.C., 1983) and Inter-American Development Bank, Economic and Social Progress in Latin America: Economic Integration (Washington, D.C., 1984).

Table 13.7

NICARAGUA: INSTITUTIONAL EXPENDITURE FOR
SOCIAL WELFARE

(Millions of cordobas)

	1977	1978	1979	1980	1981
Ministries of Health and Social Welfare	88	111	317	995	967
Ministries of Education and Culture	326	320	428	772	789

Source: Inter-American Development Bank, Economic Report: Nicaragua (Washington, D.C., 1983), Statistical Appendix, Table 11.

Table 13.8

NICARAGUA - BALANCE OF PAYMENTS
(millions of U.S.$)
1977 - 1984

	1977	1978	1979	1980	1981	1982	1983	1984
Trade Balance	-68.0	92.7	227.2	-352.5	-422.6	-315.8	-349.5	-479.0
Merchandise Exports	636.2	646.0	615.9	450.4	499.8	407.7	411.4	461.0
Merchandise Imports	704.2	553.3	388.7	802.9	922.4	723.5	760.9	940.0
Current Account Balance	-182.0	-25.0	180.2	-407.3	-514.3	-469.0	-451.1	n.a.

Sources: Inter-American Development Bank, Economic Report: Nicaragua (Washington, D.C., 1983) and Inter-American Development Bank, Economic and Social Progress in Latin America: Economic Integration (Washington, D.C., 1984). Data for 1984 from Central America Report (Inforpress) 12:8 (February 15, 1985), p. 45 (nonofficial estimates).

In 1980, there was a current account deficit of $407.3 million (see Table 13.8). In 1981, the deficit increased to $514.3 million, approximately 20 percent of GNP (Inter-American Development Bank 1983). Even though exports fell by 19 percent from 1981 to 1982, the strict control on imports resulted in only a 13 percent decline in the deficit on the current account.

The disequilibrium in the balance of payments was the result of many interrelated factors. The volume and value of exports fell because of (1) destruction caused by the war; (2) a decline in the world market prices of several of Nicaragua's traditional exports, which made production relatively unprofitable; and (3) reluctance on the part of the private sector to invest. Concurrent with the drop in export earnings, foreign exchange was increasingly allocated to imports in order to reactivate the economy and to maintain the consumption levels of the population. A deterioration in the terms of trade between exports and imports worsened the balance-of-payments crisis (see Weeks 1985b). This critical situation was rendered even more acute by the immeasurable (but "unmeasurable") capital flight. The deficit on the current account forced the government to seek foreign loans.

External Debt

In July 1979, the new government in Nicaragua inherited an external debt of $1.1 billion, which, according to the Inter-American Development Bank, "had been contracted on extremely onerous conditions as regards cost and term [sic]" (Inter-American Development Bank 1983:15). The government pledged to recognize the entire debt, but by 1982, the foreign debt had grown to approximately $2.6 billion. Despite the fact that in 1980 and 1981 the government had renegotiated the debt on relatively favorable terms, the burden of debt servicing placed severe strains on the economy. In 1982, service payments on the debt ($154.2 million) were equal to approximately 38 percent of total export earnings. Under the terms of the renegotiation, the service payments will increase in the second half of the 1980s.

The effect of the size of the debt on the balance of payments is clearly one of the major problems of the Nicaraguan economy. Yet Nicaragua is only one of many Latin American debtor countries in terms of the relative cost of servicing the debt to total export earnings (Table 13.9). Indeed, the service on the debt for many Latin American countries in 1983 was equal to a much higher percentage of the value of their exports than in Nicaragua.

For Nicaragua, the solution to the debt crisis is a political as well as an economic problem. The multilateral lending institutions and private

Table 13.9

SERVICE PAYMENTS ON THE PUBLIC DEBT AS A PERCENTAGE
OF EXPORT EARNINGS[1] FOR SELECTED LATIN AMERICAN COUNTRIES

Country	1982	1983
Nicaragua	64.3	24.3
Argentina	94.8	92
Brazil	86	51.6
Chile	63.6	47.5
Mexico	41.9	40.7
Peru	40.1	21.6

[1]Debt service as a percentage of exports of goods and non-factor services.

Sources: Inter-American Development Bank, Economic and Social Progress in Latin America: Economic Integration (Washington, D.C., 1984).

commercial banks, for the most part, have denied new loans to Nicaragua. In part, this denial may be a reflection of the crisis of the Nicaraguan economy. However, it probably can be attributed more to the extreme hostility of the administration in Washington toward the government in Managua and the use of the former's influence to veto and discourage loans to the latter.

The War Economy: 1983–1985

Economic conditions were difficult during the first three years after the triumph, and they have deteriorated since 1983. The major economic constraints have been the large trade gap, the debt burden, the fiscal deficit, and most serious of all, the counterrevolutionary war.

That war, financed and directed by the U.S. government, and the economic sanctions imposed by the Reagan administration have strained the extremely fragile economy of Nicaragua. The U.S. Congress allocated a total of almost $100 million through 1985 to finance the contras, forces that are dedicated to overthrowing the Nicaraguan government.[9] The Nicaraguan Democratic Forces (Fuerzas Democráticas Nicaragüenses, FDN) is the largest of these armies with an estimated 15,000 troops, many of whom are former members of Somoza's National Guard. Despite its financial resources, its logistical support from the U.S. and the Honduran armies, and its bevy of U.S. Central Intelligence Agency advisers, the FDN has been remarkably unsuccessful in conventional military confrontations with the Sandinista army. This lack of success has led it to alter its tactics, concentrating on economic sabotage and on terrorizing the civilian population.

In their attempt to disrupt the coffee, tobacco, and cotton harvests, the contras have killed government workers, peasants, rural workers, and students mobilized to harvest the crops. The Nicaraguan government estimates that in 1984 alone, the contras killed 2,500 civilians (Prevost 1985:7). The counterrevolutionary forces have affected Nicaragua's principal export products, destroying infrastructure and crops, and a great deal of land has not been planted or harvested out of fear. Estimating only direct physical damage and lost agricultural revenue, the cost of the war through 1984 was approximately $1.2 billion,[10] more than double Nicaragua's total annual export earnings.

The war has distorted the economy in many other ways as well. Despite the imposition of austerity measures designed to curtail government expenditures, it has been difficult to reduce the large fiscal deficit because approximately 40 percent of the government budget has been allocated to defense (Prevost 1985:10). In addition, the war has diverted scarce human and material resources from civilian uses to the war effort.

It is possible, though, that the discipline, patriotism, and sacrifices engendered by the armed conflict may have contributed to economic growth. Nicaragua's GNP grew at a rate of 4 percent in 1983,[11] the highest growth rate in all of Latin America and Nicaragua was the only country in Central America to experience economic growth in that year (Inter-American Development Bank 1984). Increased resource mobilization and an improvement in the allocation and use of both human and material resources may partially account for this surprising rate of growth (see Weeks 1984).

Agricultural output expanded by 14 percent, with growth occurring primarily in the export sector. In the 1982-1983 crop cycle, cotton production was 26 percent higher than the previous year because of an expansion in the area under cultivation and an increase in yields, due in part to climatic conditions. Technical assistance to small and medium coffee producers and the large-scale mobilization of labor for the harvest resulted in an increase in the output of coffee. Finally, there was an expansion in the production of rice for the domestic market as credit incentives stimulated large private enterprises to increase the area under cultivation. Expansion in agricultural output was complemented by a growth of 8 percent in construction. The government built and repaired roads and storage facilities in order to facilitate the expansion of land under cultivation by providing the means to transport and store the higher volume of output.

Notwithstanding the impressive increase in export production, the trade gap grew in 1983. A deterioration in the world market prices of Nicaragua's traditional exports means that export earnings were only slightly higher than in 1982, and despite the imposition of severe import controls, the growth in export revenues was more than offset by an increase in the value of imports.

The cost of imported petroleum remained one of the most serious economic constraints. In 1983, the government further decreased petroleum consumption by reducing the ration, raising the price of gasoline by 50 percent, shortening the work week, and rationing energy in those industries that do not produce basic necessities. As a result of these measures, petroleum represented 16 percent of the total value of imports in 1983, down from 19 percent in 1982. Still, the value of oil imports represented 30 percent of export earnings in 1983.

The current account balance was a negative $451.1 million in 1983, only slightly lower than in the previous year and higher than total exports (Table 13.8). Since private and multilateral banks effectively cut off their lending to Nicaragua because of pressure and vetoes by the United States, the gap was filled by bilateral loans and aid from the countries of Western Europe and the Soviet bloc, as well as from Iran and Libya. Although this assistance was essential to the Nicaraguan economy because it provided short-term liquidity and necessary resources, it also increased the country's foreign debt to approximately $4 billion in 1985.

The fiscal deficit grew to an increasingly unsustainable 27 percent of GNP in 1983. Government expenditures financed extensive health care and education programs, the expanding defense effort, high interest payments on the debt, and large subsidies on basic foodstuffs and transportation (which alone equaled more than 25 percent of the deficit).

The economic crisis deepened in 1984. The foreign debt with its associated interest payments, the trade gap, and the fiscal deficit all continued to mount even as private sector investment declined further, and external financing slowed down. These macroeconomic imbalances were accentuated by new economic sanctions imposed by the U.S. government and by an intensification in the sabotage carried out by the counterrevolutionary forces. The combination of all of these factors restrained economic growth, and the rate of expansion of the GNP fell to approximately 1 percent. It is surprising that the economy grew at all.

Government economists identified the balance-of-trade deficit and escalating interest payments on the debt as the primary economic problems. Together, these drained the country of resources that were sorely needed for economic reconstruction and made the Nicaraguan economy heavily dependent upon foreign financing. A major restructuring of the economy in order to economize on imports and expand exports was necessary (Weeks 1985a). The government sought to promote expanded production in cotton, sugar, and coffee for export, and the state also provided incentives for the development of nontraditional exports such as tobacco, timber, vegetables, and African palm oil. The export promotion policy resulted in a 12 percent increase in the value of exports, but the government proved unable to stop a growth in imports of 24 percent, and the balance-of-trade deficit grew to $479 million, 37 percent higher than in 1983 (Table 13.8).

Additional problems plagued the economy. Defense spending and high interest payments on the debt made it extremely difficult to reduce the fiscal deficit even though the tax burden was substantially increased and subsidies were reduced by half. Shortages of consumer goods stimulated hoarding and speculation, which contributed to a 60 percent rise in the consumer price index. In addition, the exchange rate on the black market quadrupled, distorting the economy and making planning even more difficult.

Military and economic aggression directed and carried out by the United States aggravated an already critical situation. The U.S. administration cut off Nicaragua's sugar quota by closing it out of the high-priced U.S. market, in which 90 percent of Nicaragua's sugar had been sold. In 1984, Nicaragua was able to find other markets for its sugar but was forced to accept lower prices. Exports were further affected when the contras bombed Corinto, damaging the port facilities. The bombing also destroyed part of the coffee crop, which was stored at the port awaiting transport, as well as millions of dollars worth of food, petroleum, and medical supplies that had recently arrived.

One effect of the war has been the acceleration of the agrarian reform. Although Comandante Jaime Wheelock, minister of agriculture, had announced in 1981 that there would be few additional confiscations, the rising proportion of idle land, combined with the efforts of the counterrevolutionary forces along the Honduran border to recruit the peasants into the army of the FDN, convinced the Sandinistas to modify their previous policy. The government expropriated abandoned lands, gave titles to peasants, and simultaneously organized them into cooperatives. The Sandinistas hoped these measures would solidify their support within the peasantry. By 1984, 37 percent of Nicaragua's agricultural land had been affected by the agrarian reform. Earlier discussions about the ideal form of production unit for Nicaraguan agriculture were effectively resolved due to the scarcity of government resources and the peasants' opposition to state farms. Expropriated lands were turned over to cooperatives, and the government did not create any new state farms. Unfortunately, the great majority of these cooperatives will exist in name only as the government lacks the resources to provide the technical assistance and financial support necessary to develop effectively functioning cooperatives.

The accumulation of economic, political, and military pressures led the Nicaraguan government to modify its economic strategy in early 1985. Government economists persuaded the Sandinistas to accept a reduced level of state regulation of the economy and to adopt a more-traditional capitalist orientation (Weeks 1986). These changes reflected a new realism (or resignation) on the part of the Sandinistas.

One of the primary objectives of the new policy package was to win private sector support. Exporters were allowed to retain a portion of their earnings in dollars, and the cordoba was devalued according to a complicated set of new exchange rates that greatly favored exports by increasing the exporters' cordoba earnings. In addition, the government announced new and higher producer prices for export crops. Other domestic policy changes included a substantial rise in interest rates and a commitment to bringing the black market under control.

Certainly least popular was the decision to eliminate the subsidies on consumer commodities and to raise the official prices of basic foodstuffs by more than 100 percent because policymakers were convinced that the government could no longer sustain the enormous cost of the food subsidies. In addition, the state had proved unable to administer effectively the distribution system or to control hoarding and speculation. The immediate effect of these measures was that the price of many basic foodstuffs such as meat, poultry, rice, and sugar rose between 200 percent and 300 percent.

It is difficult to avoid the conclusion that the Nicaraguan government waited too long to impose these economic austerity measures. It would have been more successful both from an economic as well as from a social standpoint if it had imposed an austerity package in July 1979. Such a policy would not have appeared particularly severe at that time, since the population had just lived through the denials and economic and social upheavals of the revolutionary war. Further, the government would have diminished the external borrowing that was required to finance a large portion of the higher levels of consumption.

As it is, government economists do not expect that the new economic policies will bring about economic growth. They hope these measures will prevent further deterioration, and they may have stimulated private sector support. The head of the Superior Council of Private Enterprise (COSEP), the antigovernment association of business people, characterized the new policies as "capitalist measures of the type recommended by the International Monetary Fund as conditions for its loans" (*Central America Report* 1985b:63). However, so long as the U.S. government continues its active opposition to the Sandinista government, it is unlikely that the Nicaraguan business community will alter its investment boycott.

In May 1985, the embattled economy suffered yet another blow when the Reagan administration announced a trade embargo of Nicaragua. Although commerce with the United States had declined steadily after 1980, that country had remained Nicaragua's leading trading partner. In 1984, the United States had supplied approximately one-fifth of Nicaragua's imports, and about one-sixth of the country's exports had been sold in the United States (Weeks 1986). Although enterprises in Nicaragua are experiencing difficulties in obtaining specialized industrial inputs and spare parts as a result of the trade sanctions, their overall effect appears to be relatively limited. Despite U.S. pressure, none of its allies have joined the embargo.

Given all of these complex and interrelated economic problems, there is little reason to expect that overall economic conditions will improve in Nicaragua in the next few years. Both external and internal constraints are likely to tighten as the population of Nicaragua is forced to endure a war economy, possibly until the end of the 1980s.

Evaluation of the Experience of the Mixed Economy

Although more than six years have passed since the triumph of the Nicaraguan revolution, it is difficult to evaluate the results of the mixed economy. The Nicaraguan economy is in crisis, but the causes of that crisis are largely attributable to variables other than the choice of economic policies or the efficiency with which they have been implemented. In the first half of the 1980s, the international economy was characterized by low prices, reduced demand for primary products, and generally unfavorable terms of trade between industrial and primary goods. These conditions adversely affected the economies of most underdeveloped countries, including Nicaragua. Economic constraints posed by escalating interest payments on the debt, imports in excess of exports, and a fiscal deficit were hardly unique to Nicaragua. Indeed, these conditions became part of a pattern of economic crisis in nearly all Latin American countries. In addition to these familiar economic problems, the collapse of the Central American Common Market (CACM) in the late 1970s had disastrous consequences for Nicaragua as Nicaragua's exports to Central America fell from $146 million in 1978 to $71 million in 1981 (Weeks 1985b:Chapter 8).

Even more significant is the fact that Nicaragua is a country at war. Besides the direct and indirect costs of the defense effort and the U.S. economic boycott, consideration of economic policy does not receive the attention it merits because the highest officials of the government are preoccupied with military affairs.

The gradual elimination of Nicaragua's traditional markets and sources of foreign assistance have compelled the government to establish new international economic ties. The Sandinistas first sought to replace its economic relationship with the United States with ties to Western Europe. When it became clear that the governments of the Western European countries were willing to commit only limited resources to Nicaragua, the Sandinistas turned to the Soviet bloc. For most of the Nicaraguan leaders, this move was seen, not as a desirable alternative, but as a last resort. Initially, this assistance has proved to be of relatively little use. What the Nicaraguan economy needs is free foreign exchange to maintain the existing infrastructure and productive apparatus, as well as to service the foreign debt. For the most part, Eastern European countries have provided modest amounts of "tied" aid, i.e., loans that can be used to purchase commodities only from the country making the loan. Because of the traditional orientation of the Nicaraguan economy to the West, these loans have had only limited usefulness. The first sign of increased economic assistance from the Soviet bloc came in mid-1985, just after the United States declared its trade embargo, when President Daniel Ortega Saavedra announced that the Soviet Union had agreed to supply a large portion of Nicaragua's petroleum imports.

Certainly, the Sandinistas have made a myriad of mistakes in managing the economy. Their lack of experience, combined with a scarcity of trained personnel and material resources, has contributed to a general inefficiency in the handling of the economy. The process of making economic policy, as well as the economy itself, has frequently been in chaos. Nevertheless, it is unlikely that Nicaragua's economic performance would have been considerably improved if a different set of policy alternatives had been implemented. In my view, the economic destruction caused by the war against Somoza; the stagnation in the international economy, which aggravated many of the external economic constraints; and the implacable opposition of the U.S. government primarily determined the economic possibilities for Nicaragua. Policy options open to the Nicaraguan government were further conditioned by the Sandinistas' commitment to placing a high priority on social and economic equity. In fact, Nicaragua's economy appears considerably more robust than one would expect: It is remarkable that its economic growth outstripped that of any other country in Latin America in 1983.

Political Realities

During the first year of the new government, the private sector demonstrated its willingness to compromise in order to retain its influence with the junta. At the same time, the Sandinistas stressed the importance of private sector participation in the mixed economy in an effort to gain the confidence of the business community. On both sides, there were efforts at moderation and coexistence.

But the decidedly hostile attitude of the newly elected administration in Washington made this delicate modus vivendi increasingly untenable. In 1981, the United States suspended delivery of all previously committed U.S. government aid, and late that same year, it became public knowledge that the Central Intelligence Agency was financing groups that were committed to overthrowing the Sandinista government. Public recognition of Washington's active opposition to the new government reduced the pressure on the private sector to compromise, and the political situation rapidly became polarized. The business community did not feel compelled to come to terms with the new government because Washington was providing an attractive alternative: armed counterrevolution with the goal of overthrowing the government of Nicaragua. Well versed in the history of Central America, the private sector felt little need to compromise with a government Washington was working to eliminate.

Nor were the historical precedents lost on the Sandinistas or on their supporters. The statements and actions emanating from Washington served to convince the new government that its future was in danger. In March 1982, in reaction to the bombing of two major bridges in northern Nicaragua by the counterrevolutionaries, the government decreed a state of emergency. Along with sanctions designed to prevent economic sabotage and an expansion of the black market, the government suspended freedom of assembly and imposed censorship on the media. Although justified on grounds of national defense, in my view, the suspension of civil liberties demonstrated that the leadership of the FSLN did not have sufficient confidence in its popular support.

There is considerable evidence that the majority of the population backs the Sandinistas and, in general, approves of government policy. This support was demonstrated most clearly in the November 1984 national elections for president, vice-president, and a legislature. When the electoral campaign began, the government reestablished the civil liberties that had been suspended in 1982, retaining press censorship only on particularly sensitive military matters. Three of the seven parties that participated in the elections were to the right of the FSLN, and their platforms repudiated many of the policies of the Sandinistas. The campaign unleashed an intense debate on the record of the Sandinistas and on future policy alternatives. With more than 80 percent of the population over sixteen years of age voting, the Sandinistas received just over two-thirds of the votes and a slightly lower proportion of the seats in the legislature. Over 100 official delegations from all over the world observed the elections and declared that they were honest and free from fraud (LASA 1984).

It is hardly surprising that the FSLN was the winner. It had waged a long and often heroic struggle against Somoza and had assumed the leadership of the final popular insurrection. In addition, it had an active and a relatively well organized party apparatus throughout the country that was rooted in the lower and middle classes. All except the most ideologically motivated analysts agree that although far from ideal, this election was the most democratic in Nicaragua's history. Indeed, if the public debate on policy issues is allowed to continue, the elections will be recognized as an important first step in the establishment of democratic institutions in Nicaragua.

The fact that the counterrevolutionaries have been unable to hold any Nicaraguan territory also reflects the mass support of the government. Despite their impressive financial backing, their free use of Honduran territory to launch operations and to take sanctuary, and military assistance from the Central Intelligence Agency and the Honduran army, the contras have been remarkably unsuccessful. The Nicaraguan population has consistently repudiated them and is willing to fight to prevent their return. The elections and the lack of success on the part of the counterrevolutionaries provide evidence that the Sandinistas could have allowed considerably more dissent in the early 1980s with little threat to security.

At the same time, had the Reagan administration not made the elimination of the Sandinistas its goal (see Fontaine, Tambs, et al. 1980) and had it not actively pursued this objective, the political situation in Nicaragua would not be as polarized as it is today.[12] Many leading agriculturalists and industrialists in Nicaragua ultimately cooperated with the Sandinistas in the struggle to overthrow Somoza in the hope that their interests would dominate the future Nicaraguan state. The Sandinista government, however, has clearly favored the interests of the traditionally disadvantaged sectors of society: the peasants, the workers, the urban poor, and to a lesser extent, the middle class. The rational response to this situation would naturally be for business people to exercise extreme caution before risking investment and to endeavor to take their capital out of Nicaragua. However, had the private sector not found fervent and well-financed support for its unyielding opposition to the Nicaraguan government, as it did in Washington, it would probably have adopted a somewhat less intransigent position than it currently holds. Had the Nicaraguan business community accepted the fact that the political changes, and the government that brought them about, would endure, it is likely that the leaders of the private sector would have made greater efforts to reach an accommodation with the Sandinistas.

Likewise, if the Sandinistas had not perceived that the survival of their government was threatened, they might have moderated their economic and political positions. Some of the leaders of the FSLN, probably the majority, wanted to maintain the cooperation of the private sector, as well as peaceful relations with Washington. But the extreme hostility of the Reagan administration elicited extreme reactions from the FSLN. The more radical voices, convinced it was not possible to sustain normal diplomatic relations with the United States, gained credibility and influence because their forecasts proved to be correct.

There now appears to be nothing that the Sandinistas can do to placate the Reagan administration. The U.S. government is committed to overthrowing the Sandinistas, as it believes that U.S. policy objectives will be achieved only when the Sandinistas are eliminated. Despite assurances from the Defense Department in May 1985 that defeating the Sandinistas will be "as easy as falling off a log," the reality might well turn out to be quite different. The pursuit of this foreign policy objective would probably involve the United States in direct military intervention in Nicaragua, and possibly in all of Central America, for many years.

Notes

I would like to thank Margaret Crahan, Richard Feinberg, Peter Hakim, and John Weeks for their comments on the first draft of this paper.

1. This expulsion of the peasantry has contributed to Nicaragua's high incidence of landlessness. In the 1970s, Nicaragua had the highest percentage of landless rural families in Central America with almost 35 percent of the rural families having no access to land (see Weeks 1985b:Chapter 5).

2. According to the agreement with the U.S. government, the interim president of Nicaragua, Dr. Francisco Urcuyo M., was to hold the office for only twenty-four hours after the departure of Somoza. He would then turn over the government to the incoming Junta de Gobierno de Reconstrucción Nacional. In a bizarre turn of events, after Somoza fled, Urcuyo announced his intention of completing Somoza's term of office, which would terminate in 1981. His presidential aspirations were quickly thwarted by the combined pressure of the United States, the provisional government, and the troops of the FSLN.

3. For a decade, Nicaragua was an exporter of powdered milk, supplying much of the Central American market. By 1982, there was such a scarcity of milk in Nicaragua that pasteurized milk was produced from two parts imported powdered milk to one part fresh milk (see Nicaragua, Ministerio de Comercio Interior, 1983:3:L-2).

4. Furthermore, many Nicaraguans feel that the greater part of these human and economic losses could have been avoided had the U.S. government abandoned its support of Somoza earlier and followed the lead of the governments of Venezuela, Mexico, and others. The downfall of Somoza was inevitable by June 1979, yet Somoza refused to resign. The war intensified when Somoza ordered the bombing of factories and poor neighborhoods in Managua and other cities. It is estimated that more than 15,000 people died in June and July 1979.

5. These issues have not been discussed in any structured way. They have generated few written materials, and they have not been clarified in the newspapers or in the speeches of government officials. Rather, they are, for the most part, discussed informally by persons involved in economic policymaking, as well as by ranking members of the FSLN.

6. In 1981, the World Bank's assessment of these measures was that "the Government seems to have laid to rest most fears regarding expropriation" (World Bank 1981:11).

7. There are several projects under way to produce hydroelectric and geothermal energy. In addition the government has recently negotiated with Petrobrás of Brazil concerning exploration for oil.

8. Because the data are not reliable, I refrain from including statistics to demonstrate this improvement. Despite the difficulty in quantifying gains, it is indisputable that the Nicaraguan government achieved notable successes in these areas.

9. This figure includes only that aid authorized for direct support of the contras. It does not include other forms of assistance that flowed through a variety of covert channels.

10. Interview with Fr. Xabier Gorostiaga, director of INIES, Managua, Nicaragua, January 15, 1983, cited in Prevost (1985:10).

11. The figure of 4 percent is an official estimate of the Inter-American Development Bank (1984). However, the Economic Commission for Latin America estimates that GNP grew at 5.3 percent in this same year.

12. For a discussion of how the Reagan administration has rejected political concessions made by the Sandinistas and undermined the Contadora process, which is seeking a peaceful solution to the conflicts in Central America, see Feinberg (1984).

References

Booth, John. 1982. *The End and the Beginning: The Nicaraguan Revolution*. Boulder, Colo.: Westview Press.

Central America Report (Inforpress). 1985a. Vol. 12, no. 6 (February 15).

———. 1985b. Vol. 12, no. 8 (March 1).

Feinberg, Richard. 1984. *Analysis of the Report of the National Bi-Partisan Commission on Central America, Chaired by Henry Kissinger.* Testimony before the U.S. Senate Committee on Foreign Relations, February 8. Washington, D.C.: Government Printing Office.

Fontaine, Roger; Tambs, Louis; et al. 1980. "A New Inter-American Policy for the 1980's." Council for Inter-American Security, Inc. Mimeograph.

Inter-American Development Bank. 1983. *Economic Report: Nicaragua.* Washington, D.C.

————. 1984. *Economic and Social Progress in Latin America: Economic Integration.* Washington, D.C.

Latin America Studies Association (LASA). 1984. *The Nicaraguan Elections of November, 1984: Report of the Delegation of the Latin American Studies Association.* Austin, Tex.: Latin American Studies Association.

Nicaragua, Ministerio de Comercio Interior. 1983. *Sistemas de comercialización: Productos básicos de consumo popular.* Managua.

Nicaragua, Ministerio de Planificación. 1980. *Plan de reactivación económica en beneficio del pueblo.* Managua.

————. 1981. *Programa económico de austeridad y eficiencia.* Managua.

Prevost, Gary. 1985. "The War and Its Effect on Nicaragua." Paper prepared for delivery at the International Studies Association Annual Meeting, Washington, D.C., March 5–9.

United Nations, Economic Commission for Latin America (ECLA). 1979. "Nicaragua: Economic Repercussions of Recent Political Events."

Weeks, John. 1984. "External Threats: Stimulus or Obstacle to Development?" Manuscript.

————. 1985a. "The Central American Economies in 1983 and 1984." In Jack Hopkins, ed., *Latin American and Caribbean Current Record,* vol. 3. New York: Holmes and Meier.

————. 1985b. *The Economies of Central America.* New York: Holmes and Meier.

————. 1986 (forthcoming). "The Central American Economies in 1984 and 1985." In Jack Hopkins, ed., *Latin American and Caribbean Current Record,* vol. 4. New York: Holmes and Meier.

World Bank. 1981. "Nicaragua: The Challenge of Reconstruction." Washington, D.C.

Part 3
Commentaries

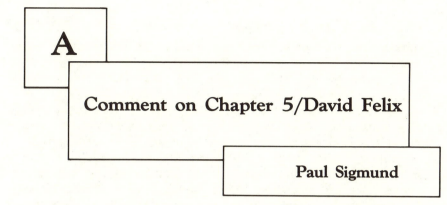

A

Comment on Chapter 5/David Felix

Paul Sigmund

Chapter 5 is very ambitious: It is really two chapters—one on why neoliberalism failed and the other on why "dirigismo" went wrong. (As Professor Felix says, the bureaucratic-authoritarian model doesn't quite apply to either case.) In the case of the analysis of the neoliberal policy, what I found interesting was the way the chapter underlined the blindness of the neoliberals to the world financial market—what Felix calls "the bubble." The world financial market did not fit into the neoliberal model; therefore, for the neoliberals, it did not exist. In fact, it did exist, and it brought them down—or at least it had much to do with bringing them down.

In the analysis of Brazil and Mexico, what I found novel was Felix's argument that the policies of supposedly quasi-authoritarian or authoritarian regimes were in fact heavily consumerist and that consumerism created a part of the problem in both cases: because of indexing in Brazil and because of expanded social expenditures in Mexico. I coedited *The Political Economy of Income Distribution in Mexico* (New York: Holmes and Meier, 1984), and one of the things that comes through very strikingly in several of the chapters in that book is how much of the oil revenues went to social expenditures and price subsidies of various sorts to gain political support. A supposedly quasi-authoritarian regime was playing to its own populist rhetoric by trying to fulfill the populist promises with actual fact. There was a considerable expansion of social security coverage and health care and of the CONASUPO (National Popular Subsistence Corporation) populist stores, the price of kerosene and other petroleum products consumed by the poor was kept down, and so on.

One question that has puzzled me is why the neoliberals had so much trouble bringing interest rates down. In the case I know best, Chile, this difficulty had a lot to do both with the policymakers' insistence on maintaining a fixed exchange rate and with the expansion of private debt. One of the ways the Chileans tried to bring interest rates down was by giving the ordinary person in Chile access to international borrowing. Everybody rushed off to the bank to borrow in dollars because they were available at a 12 percent real rate rather than 36 percent or 40 percent. Why did the domestic rate remain at 40 percent? Why didn't the Chicago model work in bringing domestic interest rates down?

A second question suggested by Felix's chapter is the relation between the internal, intrinsic causes of the failure of the neoliberal model and the external, exogenous ones. Some people place the blame on the scissors effect, but the two parts of the scissors—the international recession and the rise in international interest rates—were both exogenous. One has to try to separate how much was due to the forces of the international economy, over which policymakers had no control, and how much was the result of the ideological implementation of the model. Chilean economists have looked at this problem. The consensus seems to be that it was about one-third external and two-thirds internal. So, a lot of the blame does go to the model.

On the question of income distribution, I get terribly tired of the discussion of deciles. Can't we get beyond that? There is something else behind deciles—things like absolute levels of income. Anyone who has been out in the countryside of Cuba and of Costa Rica (as I have) can see an astounding difference in the two countries. One can say that income distribution is bad in Costa Rica, but the absolute level of the standard of living in the countryside in Costa Rica is much higher than that of the people living in the countryside in Cuba, including literacy rates and health care. One has to look at the question of how to get at basic human needs. I think that is a better focus than just looking at percentiles, as so much of the literature does.

Finally, I would like to inject some political science. At the International Conference on Models of Political and Economic Change in Latin America (Vanderbilt University, November 1983), we talked a little bit about "the pendulum." I have been interested in the political pendulum—authoritarian-democratic—for many years and have argued in print that this is the political pattern that one finds frequently in Latin America. I think we added another pendulum at that meeting—one between economic orthodoxy and statist populism. A kind of consensus seemed to be emerging that there is a third position in economic policy: A country doesn't have to lurch from one extreme to the other. The papers at the conference spelled out some of the details of such a policy: maintenance of the market system, but with government encouragement of exports and agricultural development, and some use of the state to help in achieving certain specific targeted goals, on the basis of a kind of "consensual stabilization" (I think that was the term that Professor Fishlow used).

My question is whether we are not also seeing something like a similar slowing down of the pendulum in politics at this point. In Argentina, for instance, just as there was a series of bad economic experiences with statist populism and economic orthodoxy, there also has been a number of very bad political experiences with military repression and bureaucratic authoritarianism. A number of countries—Spain, Portugal, Venezuela, Colombia—have come out of a politically unpleasant experience with authoritarianism and attempted to develop a kind of consensual democracy, diminishing the intensity of the ideological, factional, and party battle. I think a number of other countries in South America may be at that point. There is the emergence of the "Alianza" in Chile, and we may see the end of the polarization between Peronistas and anti-Peronistas in Argentina. In Peru, the Aprista–anti-Aprista polarization clearly doesn't have the meaning it used to have. Thus, we may be at a point where the political pendulum and the economic pendulum have both slowed down so that one can get—under the pressure, not of *repression*, but of *depression*—some kind of real beginning of political and economic stability on the basis of the fact that human beings can learn from the past.

The slowing down of the two pendulums could become mutually reinforcing. Recognizing that democracy requires sacrifice and that excessive demands cannot be made in a time of financial stringency, groups that previously put pressure on democratic governments for instant solutions that led to confrontation, inflation, and violence will moderate their demands. Elites that previously were attracted by the "magic" of an opening to market forces under authoritarian rule will now recognize that a mixed economy and a considerable state role are inevitable if Latin America is to emerge from its economic crisis. A mixed economy will be linked to a mixed polity in that elected governments are given considerable leeway to deal with the resolution of the crisis and the political opposition is willing to lend at least minimal cooperation to that effort.

Analyses have shown that Latin America can learn from the economic past. My hope is that it can also learn from its political past—and that the two learning processes can work together to promote mixed economies and stable democracies in Latin America.

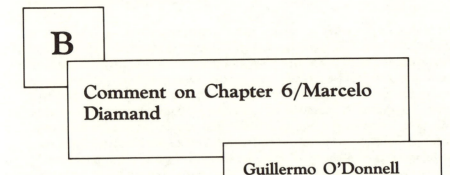

B

Comment on Chapter 6/Marcelo Diamand

Guillermo O'Donnell

I have been an admirer of Marcelo Diamand for many years—of his conceptual clarity, his courage, and the creativity that he has used in pointing to very crucial specificities of Latin American countries, particularly Argentina. At the same time, I regret the degree to which what he has been saying has been, until recently, "preaching in the desert."

The chapter I am commenting on here is a densely packed argument, a synthesis of years of work. It is also an important step forward in some directions, particularly in the discussion of financial mechanisms. Furthermore, this chapter has the merit of being a sort of pulse of the times that Argentina is living in, including the proposed policy measures to try to get the country out of its present quandary.

In commenting on Diamand's chapter, I will restrict myself to a few points. I find very convincing the picture that Diamand presents of the economic mechanisms of the suicidal spirals of Argentine history and also his very fine sense of the interplay between economics, on the one hand, and ideas, ideologies, and perceptions, on the other. On this matter, a real puzzle comes up: Insofar as Marcelo, I think, succeeds in showing to what extent both "populist" and "liberal" policies were quite stupid (it should have been evident long ago that both were leading to disastrous consequences), why was nothing learned? In other words, the question is why have no other policy packages been attempted when it should have been evident—and Diamand has been convincingly arguing this point for years—that the policies referred to above, in the medium and long run, have only exacerbated Argentina's economic and political problems. One hypothesis would be that policymakers and perhaps all of us Argentines are very stupid. Some people may consider this a plausible hypothesis, but allow me to explore some alternative ones.

Maybe, and this possibility entails smuggling a bit of politics into Diamand's argument, another hypothesis would be that a kind of perverse collective learning has been occurring. In other words, every actor assumed that either of these two kinds of policies was doomed to fail, so everyone adjusted his or her behavior in terms of the prediction that resulted from that assumption (for reasons that were clear to Diamand but unclear to others). So everyone acted in terms of those—correct—expectations, generating a typical prisoner's dilemma. When I say "expectations," I introduce a psychological factor that has a lot to do with politics, not only with economics. If, as results from Diamand's persuasive argument, the microrationality of economic actors is unlikely to stop generating the destructive pendulums between populist and liberal policies, the political dimension enters the picture when one asks what other conditions might lead to a reversal of those widely held expectations. There may be a chance that a change—in policies, also, not only in expectations— may be achieved because of the authority a democratic government is endowed with.

This hypothesis leads to further questions, which I would like to see Diamand tackle in his next work, particularly those related to the opportunities that might be generated by finding points of convergence between democratically grounded governmental authority and the kind of fresh ideas that Diamand presents. This possibility of convergence has been absent in Argentina for many years; it is a new factor in the recently emerged situation, and the possibility of actually bringing it about is what a new style of politics would be about.

On the other hand, one of the necessary conditions for policies such as those proposed by Diamand, for which I must feel some pessimism in the short term, is that a very active, as well as a quite skillful and noncorrupt, role of various segments of the state apparatus will be necessary. This contribution is required for the formulation, and even more for the adequate implementation, of policies other than the blunt and gross policies followed until now. I am not saying that this condition is impossible (after all, it does not require that all of the state apparatus be radically transformed), but it is a complicated political and administrative problem to which close attention should be paid. One should not forget the deep degrees of demoralization and depopulation of many skilled personnel of the Argentine public administration that is another of the legacies of the authoritarian regime.

Another point at which I would put some political factors in Diamand's arguments is that there is no solution for Argentina if some progressive tax scheme is not applied to pampean agrarian production. Such schemes have been proposed and have failed quite a few times in Argentina. This kind of taxation has been sternly opposed by pampean landowners as a serious threat not only to their economic position but also to their social, cultural, and political influence in Argentina. Is it possible to gather sufficient urban support for an indirect agrarian reform, which these tax schemes imply, without peasant pressure for access to land—in a country where there are no peasants? Is it possible, as at some points Diamand seems to believe, to gather such support on the basis of good ideas and assume that the enlightened perception of their long-run interests will convince the pampean landowners not to oppose these changes? It might be, but it sounds to me extremely unlikely. Rather, I believe that the question is, in this hopeful democratic period we are beginning, Which social and political forces will accept these ideas and be powerful enough to face and finally break the deadlock that has given the pampean landowners the continuing ability to veto tax reforms that even moderately may affect them? This requires political strategy, alliances, and conflicts.

On another matter—invading the economists' turf—I find Diamand's concept of an "unbalanced productive structure" very useful. Argentina is clearly one case of such a structure, but I am not sure if the concept can be directly applied to other countries, insofar as it includes the idea that these social formations have strong comparative advantages in the agrarian export sector. One can think of quite a few countries that do not have such comparative advantages. In this sense, Diamand's concept is perhaps too Argentine and needs some further elaboration before it can yield its full analytical potential.

In this connection, maybe one could risk a hypothesis that is linked to my previous commentary about the pampean landowners. If Hirschman coined the idea of a "blessing in disguise,"[1] we Argentines might employ the notion of a "curse in disguise," of having an agrarian sector that is *too* competitive internationally so it becomes *too* strong politically—and becomes so indispensable in the short term in terms of the balance of payments that it has sufficient power to veto the kind of modernizing or efficiency-oriented policies that would allow Argentina to break the destructive stalemate that Diamand depicts so well. This idea may or may not be interesting to explore. The point is that more comparative work is needed on Diamand's concept of the unbalanced productive structure. For instance, the persuasive way in which Diamand shows how and why Argentina's heavy foreign indebtedness came after and largely as a consequence of "liberal," recessionary policies does not strictly apply to two cases, Mexico and Brazil, that clearly fit Diamand's concept in most other respects. From a comparative perspective, it might be perceived that the situation in those two countries is more complex and varied, and that this fact might be related to the different characteristics— and relative weights—of the export-oriented agrarian sectors in each country.

However, as a further indication of the analytical power and promise of Diamand's chapter, it is striking that even though the sequences are quite obviously different, the outcome today is so similar in many Latin

American countries. This observation could lead to the fatalistic argument that whatever you do, whenever you try to grow, whenever you try to implement efficient policies, you end up with goblins of foreign debt and other misfortunes. It is obvious that, like myself, Diamand does not agree with such a pessimistic and mechanistic conclusion. But to explore better answers one needs, it seems to me, two intellectual tools. The first is careful comparisons with other countries, such as Colombia, that even though they share many of the characteristics defined by Diamand, have avoided, if not the problem per se, its more negative consequences. The other is the introduction of a specifically political dimension in the analysis, at least with regard to the conditions for the generation of sufficient support for the decision and implementation of more enlightened economic policies and particularly with regard to the opportunities that might be offered by a democratic framework.

I finish by rendering due tribute to Diamand, who in his chapter and preceding works has been deciphering crucial aspects of the Argentine dilemma: Why, with so many favorable "objective" conditions, have we been reproducing—and sharpening—very destructive political and economic crises? Furthermore, as is evident in his chapter, Diamand has never shied away from offering creative, challenging solutions to the economic quandaries that have plagued Argentina. This attitude, in the dark years our country has hopefully ended, took not only intellectual but also personal courage.

Notes

1. Ed. note: See Albert O. Hirschman, A Bias for Hope: Essays on Development and Latin America (New Haven: Yale University Press, 1971), pp. 29-30, 313-318.

C

Comment on Chapter 9/Daniel Schydlowsky

Cynthia McClintock

I would like to begin by repeating Daniel Schydlowsky's opening statement: "For the Peruvian economy, 1983 was the worst year of the century." The severity of Peru's current economic crisis cannot be underestimated. Since the debacle of 1983, when real growth fell by almost 12 percent, the economy has not recovered. In per capita terms, there was no real growth in 1984, and none was expected in 1985. Inflation doubled in 1983 to about 130 percent, remained at this historically very high level in 1984, and was expected to soar to 200 percent in 1985. Peru's economic performance during the early 1980s has been both a historical nadir for the country and one of the weakest in the Latin American region during this period.

The toll on the Peruvian people has been appalling. Whereas in 1975 approximately 53 percent of the nation's economically active population was adequately employed (Panfichi 1984:70), the figure had fallen to only about 35 percent by 1984 (Peru, Presidencia de la República 1984:124). As of mid-1984, average real wages were only approximately 40 percent of their 1973 level. The year 1973 was a peak period, and average wages had been down by almost 50 percent at the end of the military government in 1980, but 1984 wages were yet another 20 percent below 1980 (Dietz 1982; *Andean Report* [April 1984]:70 and [April 1985]:49). For some sectors, the decline in real wages was even more precipitous. State employees, for example, suffered a drop in their real incomes of more than 50 percent between June 1980 and December 1984 (*Resumen semanal* [DESCO] 8, no. 307 [March 9–15, 1985]:5). As of mid-1984, the minimum monthly wage was merely about $45, $20–$50 below figures for neighboring Chile and Ecuador (*Business Latin America*, September 5, 1984:282).

With the fall in income, health and nutrition standards have deteriorated. According to official data, daily per capita calorie intake among lower-class people throughout the country plummeted from 1,934 calories in 1972 to 1,486 in 1979 (Fernández Bacca 1982:89–90). By 1985, calorie intake figures were undoubtedly lower. For example, in 1971, five of every ten children admitted to the Children's Hospital in Lima were malnourished; by 1983, the figure was between eight and nine (Latin American Bureau 1985:98). Tuberculosis, polio, and other diseases that had been relatively controlled during the 1970s are now prevalent.

The key question for us here is, Why has the Peruvian economy performed so poorly? I agree with Daniel Schydlowsky that a major factor has been the selection of inappropriate policy packages by Peruvian regimes. As Schydlowsky emphasizes, it seems ironic and especially tragic that Peruvian governments have chosen certain policy packages after they have already been proved failures in other Latin American nations. This was the case for both the import substitution industrialization model chosen by the Velasco regime and the neoliberal, Chicago school model chosen by the Belaúnde government. In my view, just as in Professor Schydlowsky's, both the Velasco and Belaúnde administrations doggedly persisted in the application of these models well after their flaws were apparent, with fatal consequences for the Peruvian people.

I do not believe, however, that the blame for Peru's economic disaster lies exclusively with the misguided policy packages of the economic teams of the respective governments. The very fact that rather different policies have been tried, and have failed, suggests that the problem may be more intractable. As Schydlowsky emphasizes, there was no lack of technocratic expertise in the economic team of the Belaúnde government. Policy shifts may indicate not only elite disagreement but also elite frustration over successive policy failures. One of the statements that is most frequently made in Peru today is *No hay salida*, or "There is no way out, no solution [to our economic crisis]."

Peru is a small country with limited natural resources. In the early 1970s, the nation hoped to achieve an oil bonanza comparable at least to Ecuador's, but this aspiration was not realized. Although today Peru's top legal export is oil, production is less than half that in Ecuador. Peru's other major traditional exports are minerals—primarily copper, silver, lead, and zinc—but with the exception of the 1979–1980 period, the international prices for these minerals have been low, and they are not expected to improve significantly very soon. Ironically, during the 1980s Peru's only boom export product has been illicit: coca. Although coca is now estimated to be worth as much as $1 billion annually to Peruvians, more than any of the country's legal exports, its production has entailed various serious problems. It is widely believed that drug traffickers' money supports the Shining Path (*Sendero luminoso*) guerrillas. Of course too, the United States opposes the drug trade, and the militant U.S. stance on the issue has complicated U.S.-Peruvian relations.

I agree with Schydlowsky that nontraditional exports should be encouraged, but the barriers to these exports are currently considerable and may increase in the next few years. Textiles constitute about one-third of Peru's nontraditional exports, for example (López de la Piniella 1985:47), but Peruvian textiles have recently been encountering higher trade barriers in the United States. Fish products have also been an important nontraditional export, but the supply of fish has been unstable, varying with climatic conditions. Neither Schydlowsky nor other economists have identified new nontraditional exports that would meet large, receptive markets abroad. With the considerable export subsidies of the late 1970s, nontraditional exports constituted only slightly more than 20 percent of all exports, about what they did again in 1984 (López de la Piniella 1985:46 and *Andean Report* [April 1985]:50).

Nor is Peru a naturally rich country agriculturally. The nation's narrow coastal strip is mostly desert, and the water supply in the dozen or so river valleys in the region has been declining in recent years. In most of Peru, the Andean mountains are higher and more barren than in neighboring Ecuador, Colombia, or Venezuela. Although successive governments have hoped that the lowland slopes and jungles to the east of the Andes could become Peru's breadbasket, the development of the region has proved very difficult for various reasons, perhaps most important of which are the high transportation costs and health hazards.

Yet, as Schydlowsky argues, none of the constraints upon development in Peru absolves the Belaúnde government of its economic policy failures. Whereas Schydlowsky places the blame heavily upon the government's economic team, I believe that this team was to a significant extent the captive of larger political and economic forces beyond its control. In my view, responsibility for the errors of economic policy lies not just with the economic team but with the Belaúnde government as a whole, and even more generally with certain features of the international economic order, or disorder, of the early 1980s.

More specifically, I think that we should perceive the economic team as representing only one faction within the governing Acción Popular party: what was called the "internationalist" faction. It was led, not by the highly trained economists mentioned by Schydlowsky, but by Manuel Ulloa, an extremely successful international investment banker who served as prime minister and minister of economy, finance, and commerce from July 1980 to December 1982. Peruvians tend to perceive Ulloa as dynamic and even brilliant, but unscrupulous. The internationalist faction was pitted against the "nationalist" faction, led by Javier Alva Orlandini, who was second vice-president of Peru and general secretary of Acción Popular. The two factions were intensely competitive, although by 1982 the Alva group was clearly ascendant. Ultimately, Alva won Acción Popular's presidential nomination over Ulloa in 1985, despite the fact that Alva was one of the least charismatic presidential candidates in Peruvian history.

There were significant substantive differences between Ulloa's internationalist faction and Alva's nationalist one (Malloy 1982). As Schydlowsky indicates, the Peruvian economic team espoused the neoliberal, promarket ideologies that are highly favored by the international agencies. In contrast, the Alva group was perceived, essentially, as "big spenders." In this critical respect, the Alva faction enjoyed the support of President Belaúnde. As many observers have reported, including one of his own ministers (Kuczynski 1977), Belaúnde has always been relatively disinterested in economic principles and very interested in the promotion of large-scale public works. An architect by training, Belaúnde hopes that history will describe him as a builder, citing his jungle highway and other infrastructure projects as the ultimate "conquest of Peru by the Peruvians."

How could these factions have worked together for several years? In my view, the Alva faction and President Belaúnde understood that without the orthodox promarket policies favored by the internationalist economic team, international loans to Peru would be scant. The Chicago school policies were only a means to an end, and not a particularly attractive means at that. The Alva faction and the president were apparently unconcerned by the fact that a huge state-run investment program would catapult the public sector deficit to almost 10 percent of GDP and contradict key tenets of neoliberal economics. For their part, as Schydlowsky points out, the internationalist economic team hoped to control public spending and tried to do so, but without success. The team's educational credentials could not be translated into political clout. Most of the economic team had greater professional experience in the United States than in Peru and did not enjoy any real network of support within the country.

Between 1980 and 1985, the Belaúnde government borrowed heavily abroad, and the external debt is now the country's most serious problem. In mid-1981, the government announced an $11.5-billion development program (Andean Report [May 1981]:83–85; Business Latin America, June 3, 1981:174–175). Ultimately, total disbursements to Peru from official and private creditors over the three-year period between 1981 and 1983 totaled slightly over $5 billion; between 1980 and mid-1985, the total external debt increased from about $9.5 billion to $13.7 billion, or by more than 40 percent (Devlin 1985:43; Latin América Weekly Report, May 10, 1985:4). After 1980, the total external debt increased considerably more in Peru than in other Latin American countries (Devlin 1985:43). As of mid-1985, Peru was about $1.8 billion behind in the service of its debt, and it was estimated that the total payments due at the end of the year would be approximately $3.5 billion, or about 10 percent more than expected export revenue for the year (*Latin America Weekly Report,* May 10, 1985:4). Although the new government will be able to change tariff and related policies without great difficulty, the external debt will weigh heavily upon it for a long time.

A crucial question follows: How was all the money spent? Not very well, in the opinion of most Peruvians and international economists. It would seem that public expenditure in Peru during Belaúnde's administration was more a function of politics than of economics. Deposed by the military in 1968, President Belaúnde was determined to complete his second term and apparently reasoned that dollars would be a critical resource. In particular, he wanted to meet the expenditure requests of the military. Accordingly, between 1980 and 1983, about a quarter to a third of total public expenditure was for military projects and weapons (*Latin America Regional Reports,* May 17, 1985:4). The cost of a new naval base at Chimbote has been estimated at about $1 billion and the cost of new Mirage jets, about $500 million.

The Belaúnde government also devoted large sums—probably over $1 billion—to mammoth, capital-intensive irrigation projects that are widely considered, both inside and outside Peru, to be white elephants (*Latin America Regional Reports,* May 17, 1985:4). They are very expensive, risky, and of dubious utility; for example, at least $600 million has been spent on just one such project, Majes, and yet it is still not even near completion. Again, it would seem that the primary rationale is political rather than economic. During the period of military rule, political parties in Peru atrophied; Acción Popular was never a tightly organized party, and Belaúnde and other key party leaders were exiled during the military regime. Belaúnde presumably felt a need to build party loyalty, and for such ends, political leaders everywhere turn to pork-barrel projects. Water projects are a favorite in the United States also.

To explain Peru's economic problems during Belaúnde's administration, I think we must consider also the overall international political and economic climate during the period. Generally, for much of Latin America, this was a time of desperation, of lost confidence in the future of the region and a renewed sense of dependence upon the United States. Most Latin American leaders struggled to cope with an external debt crisis that they judged to be due primarily to international economic developments beyond their control. As many Latin American countries suffered economic decline and widespread violence, national elites became more pessimistic about the future of their own countries, and more determined to assure their personal security in any way possible. Probably especially in the nations where the drug trade flourished, corruption seemed to increase at all levels of society. More and more, elites sought a financial and professional base abroad, most often in the United States. Although it is of course impossible to measure the exact impact of this particular climate upon economic policymaking, I think it has been important. The problem was emphasized often in Peru's 1985 presidential campaign by the victorious candidate, Alan García.

The failures of economic policymaking under the Belaúnde government raise important questions: Was the economic policymaking process democratic? Should the Belaúnde government be considered democratic? In the United States, where the touchstone of democracy is generally considered to be honest, competitive elections, these questions may seem anomalous; of course the Belaúnde government was duly elected. In Peru, however, there is a tendency to answer these questions in the negative, both among opposition political forces and among average citizens. Note that previously in Latin America, the kind of drastic economic liberalization program implemented by the Belaúnde government had been launched only by military regimes.

When campaigning in 1980, Belaúnde gave almost no indication that he would promote markedly neoliberal policies. For example, his party's formal statement on tariffs said they would "be determined according to the political economy and regional agreements"; on imports specifically, "their gradual liberalization would be controlled according to local industry and international commerce" (Universidad del Pacífico 1980:78–79). Nor was Belaúnde's program fully debated in Congress. After the 1980 election, Acción Popular united with the conservative Partido Popular Cristiano (PPC) and achieved a majority in the legislature. Citizens had not expected a governing majority for Belaúnde, and it is doubtful that they desired this outcome. Possessing a majority, the governing executive "railroaded" the 1981 budget through Congress and gained a "special powers" authority for a free hand on most financial legislation for the first six months of 1981 (*Andean Report* [January 1981]:2–3). As there are no mid-term congressional elections in Peru and the governing coalition between Acción Popular and the PPC endured until April 1984, the executive could also disregard popular opposition to the economic program. For example, the popular approval rating of the economic team's leader, Manuel Ulloa, had been below 20 percent for over a year before he finally left his post in December 1982 (*Caretas*, October 15, 1982:16). President Belaúnde named a successor whose essential policy preferences were similar to Ulloa's, despite popular rejection of these orientations.

Under these circumstances, it is less anomalous that the majority of Peruvian citizens do not seem to consider the Belaúnde government democratic. In informal surveys by my research team, interviewing forty individuals from two coastal farm cooperatives in 1983 and fifty individuals from three highland villages in 1984, 67 percent of the respondents agreed with the statement that "the current government was not acting in agreement with the principles of democracy." Asked why, the citizens generally said that the government was acting in the interests of only a small elite rather than the Peruvian people as a whole, or that the government had not fulfilled its promises. Yet, Peruvians retained hope that future democratically elected governments would do better, and in April 1985 they went to the polls in greater numbers than ever before, electing the Aprista candidate, Alan García.

Will the new president be able to ameliorate the nation's economic crisis? Of course, the external debt is an extremely serious problem for the new government, and the available policy alternatives are not attractive. Perhaps, however, there is more consensus than Schydlowsky suggests on certain issues. Alan García has pledged pragmatism, implying that he will not identify one single economic path as "the" salvation for Peru, careening down it blindly and stubbornly as has been the case at times in the past. Alan García has also asserted that agriculture will be the nation's top development priority, and he has affirmed that Peru will be less open to international economic forces. These promises have brought the new president broad support. To keep them will be the challenge— a challenge that has to be met if democracy is truly to be consolidated in Peru.

References

Devlin, Robert. 1985. "La Deuda externa en América Latina." In Eduardo Ferrero Costa, ed., El Perú frente al capital extranjero: Deuda e inversión, pp. 39–78. Lima: CEPEI.

Dietz, Henry A. 1982. "National Recovery vs. Individual Stagnation: Peru's Urban Poor Since 1978." Paper presented at the Forty-fourth International Congress of Americanists, University of Manchester, Manchester, England (September).

Fernández Bacca, Jorge. 1982. "La Producción de alimentos en el Peru." Que Hacer, no. 17 (June).

Kuczynski, Pedro-Pablo. 1977. Peruvian Democracy Under Economic Stress. Princeton: Princeton University Press.

Latin America Bureau. 1985. Peru: Paths to Poverty. London: Russell Press.

López de la Piniella, Julio. 1985. El Nuevo Proteccionismo y las exportaciones no tradicionales peruanas, 1979–1983. Lima: Fundación Friedrich Ebert.

Malloy, James M. 1982. "Peru's Troubled Return to Democratic Government." Universities Field Staff International Report, no. 15.

Panfichi, Aldo. 1984. Población y empleo en el Peru. Lima: Centro de Estudio y Promocion de Desarrollo (DESCO).

Peru, Presidencia de la República. 1984. Peru 1984. Lima.

Universidad del Pacífico. 1980. Peru 1980: Elecciones y planes de gobierno. Lima.

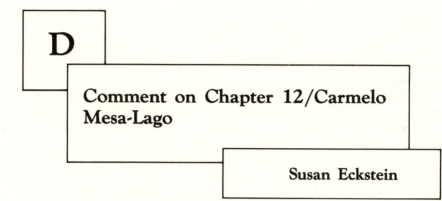

D

Comment on Chapter 12/Carmelo Mesa-Lago

Susan Eckstein

Much of our knowledge and understanding of the Cuban economy under Castro derives from the work of Carmelo Mesa-Lago. However, I will show that his contention that alleged island economic failures derive from the misuse and implicit abuse of extensive power embedded in the state apparatus is only partially correct. To illustrate my points, I will focus on several key aspects of economic performance; namely, economic growth and diversification, trade vulnerability, the foreign debt, and economic equity.

Mesa-Lago correctly notes the methodological problems in assessing Cuba's macroeconomic accomplishments. There are no uniform time series data covering the pre- and postrevolutionary period, and Castro's material product calculations differ from the national product estimates of the economies in the region, making crossnational comparisons cumbersome.

Nonetheless, Mesa-Lago fails to draw upon Claes Brundenius's efforts (1979, 1984) to convert material product into GDP estimates. According to Brundenius's estimates, plus data for other Latin American countries, Cuba's regional national product ranking is the same today as when Fulgencio Batista fell, although its per capita ranking has deteriorated (see Eckstein 1985:474). Brundenius's data therefore suggest that the state-class transformation has not done wonders for the Cuban economy. However, the island has "held its own" vis-à-vis neighboring countries.

In reference to specific economic sectors, Mesa-Lago suggests that the revolution's industrial performance has been unimpressive. However, Brundenius's data indicate that the value of manufacturing production (in constant 1965 prices) increased 193 percent between 1962 and 1976, with the increase of specific sectors ranging from 50–477 percent (Brundenius 1979:6–7).[1] Moreover, the technologically complex metal and machine sector experienced the greatest growth. According to available

367

data, manufacturing output has improved more in Cuba since the revolution than in other leading Latin American industrial countries during the same time period; Cuba's regional ranking in the value of manufacturing output has risen under Castro. Meanwhile, the island's regional ranking on the centrality of technologically complex metal and machine activity in total industrial production has also risen (Eckstein 1985:475).

Mesa-Lago attributes what he considers poor industrial performance in Castro's Cuba primarily to bureaucratic inefficiency, inappropriate policies, and, in the late 1960s, the subordination of rational decision making to ideology. Yet world sugar prices appear to have at least as much bearing, if not more, on industrial performance as specific state policies and bureaucratic constraints. Industrial output and productivity have expanded and contracted over the years with the price of foreign sugar sales: Sugar prices plummeted in the late 1960s (during the Mao-Guevarist period, to borrow Mesa-Lago's terminology), rose dramatically in the first half of the 1970s, and then contracted, and industrial growth followed suit.

In sum, Cuban industry has done well by regional standards. Changes in the class structure and in state priorities, plus the state's greater role in the economy, undoubtedly contributed to the sectoral growth.

Nonetheless, global political-economic forces continue to determine the parameters of the island's production options. The global influences are partly the same as those affecting development options in other countries in the region, and comparable to prerevolutionary Western influences; however, some are distinctive to Cuba, owing to peculiarities of the Council for Mutual Economic Assistance (COMECON), which will become more apparent below.

Mesa-Lago correctly highlights Cuba's continued excessive dependence on a single export, sugar. Yet once again his explanation for the island's failure to diversify is incomplete. Indeed, as of 1980, Cuba was the most monoproduct export country in the region (Eckstein 1985:477). However, Mesa-Lago incorrectly attributes the continued centrality of sugar to faulty policy. Were Cuba able to market whatever it chose in international markets, the emphasis on sugar would surely be a mistake.

Global forces have, however, constricted Cuba's export potential, directly and indirectly. For one, Cuba's current dependence on Soviet technology and marketing networks limits its ability to turn its expanded industrial production into an exportable asset, as other major regional industrial powers have. Soviet industrial technology is not internationally competitive, and most Soviet development aid to the island goes to industry. Moreover, Soviet marketing networks in the West are not well developed. Meanwhile, COMECON countries do not provide Cuba with an alternative manufacturing export market, both because member countries tend to have similar, rather than complementary, industrial structures, owing to the Soviet policy of exporting variants of its own industrial model to satellite countries, and because they prefer, when possible, to buy cheaper, better quality products from the West.

International political dynamics further constrict Cuba's manufacturing export options. The blockade cuts Cuba off from the U.S. import market. Moreover, U.S. regulations prevent banks and multinationals (MNCs) from investing in Cuban industry. Yet U.S.-based MNCs have been a driving force behind LDC industrial export expansion in recent years. The U.S. government has not even modified its stance toward Cuba since the Castro leadership formalized guarantees for foreign investors in its new investment code.

Similar global dynamics restrict Cuba's mineral and nonsugar agricultural export possibilities. Nickel export options remain limited in part because Cuba is unfortunately blessed with laterite deposits with a low nickel content, making the cost of extraction internationally uncompetitive. Independent of cost, Cuba's mineral export market remains limited because the United States refuses to buy not only nickel directly from Cuba but also products from third countries that contain the island mineral. And in agriculture, even more than in industry, Cuba is constrained by Soviet technology. Since Soviet farming is notoriously inefficient, the superpower is not well equipped to help the island diversify its agricultural economy, above all for overseas markets.

Thus, Cuba's continued monoproduct export dependence is largely attributable to factors beyond its control. Although sugar remains the linchpin of the economy, its domestic significance has changed since the revolution. Adverse effects of a sugar-based economy on the domestic populace have been reduced. Under Castro, sugar workers have come to enjoy more social benefits, job security, and higher earnings. They now rank among Cuba's best-paid workers. Moreover, in the 1970s, technological innovations permitted previously labor-intensive sugar tasks to be mechanized, freeing labor for other less back-breaking economic pursuits.

Despite the failure to diversify commodity exports, Cuba has developed one source of export earnings that distinguishes it from most LDCs. It has turned its success in human capital development into a marketable asset. As Mesa-Lago notes, foreign countries pay Cuba in foreign exchange for some of the island's overseas military and civilian projects. In 1979, for example, Cuba generated at least 18 percent of the value of its hard-currency commodity trade in overseas skilled labor contracts. Although the foreign projects have generated needed hard-currency revenue, Cuba is unlikely to be able to expand its overseas ventures in the foreseeable future. Only politically sympathetic and, in the case of teachers, Hispanic-speaking countries with sufficient state resources are likely to contract for human capital assistance from Cuba (cf. Eckstein 1982b). Yet the early 1980s world recession led the "friendly" Ethiopian government to cut back its Cuban aid program, and in early 1984, Cuba considered withdrawing its troops from Angola in part because the impoverished nation had trouble meeting its payments (*Boston Globe*, March 13, 1984:1, 6). However, both African countries had strategic as well as economic reasons for reducing local Cuban involvements. Meanwhile, U.S. pressure also caused Cuba to reduce its overseas programs.

Thus, Cuba remains trade vulnerable, despite its reduced dependence on the United States and the restructuring of its domestic economy. COMECON long-term trade contracts and subsidies have reduced the island's vulnerability to world market vicissitudes, but integration into COMECON has also marginalized the island's ability to compete in international markets. Despite the Cuban state's more pivotal role in the economy, other Latin American countries have been better able to renegotiate trade relations in their favor. In ignoring the impact of such external constraints, Mesa-Lago "blames the victim" for conditions beyond its control.

Mesa-Lago similarly errs in his discussion of Cuba's trade imbalance and foreign debt. Cuba's debt crisis results in no small part from international political and economic conditions beyond its control. To emphasize faulty state policy is again incomplete and therefore misleading.

Because the island receives substantial export and import subsidies from the Soviet Union, Mesa-Lago assumes that the government is responsible for the large trade deficit and foreign debt. Yet he fails to note that the Soviet Union contributes to Cuba's debt problem at the same time that it helps mitigate the problem. For one, Soviet subsidies are a form of "tied aid." Since Cuba is paid in nonconvertible rubles for most exports to the Soviet Union, it must purchase goods from the trade partner with the export revenue. Yet Soviet industrial products are often more costly than comparable Western goods; accordingly, they drive up the island's import bill. Meanwhile, the Soviets purchase only a few island products. Were they, for example, to buy the industrial items that the national leadership would like to market abroad, Cuba's export earnings would be higher and its balance-of-payments deficit, in turn, lower. Similarly, though the Soviet Union offers Cuba concessionary financing, most funding covers Cuba's trade deficit with the superpower (although, as previously noted, most funding earmarked for domestic development has gone to industry). Therefore, Cuba has access to little funding from the Soviets for import substitution projects that would make trade less vital to the economy and for export diversification that would reduce the island's trade imbalance.

Mesa-Lago also implies that the Cuban government is to blame for the island's Western debt. The island went, according to him, on a "buying spree" in the mid-1970s, "because of their incorrect expectations for continued high sugar prices." Yet a comparison of Cuba's and other Latin American countries' Western debt structures reveals that between 1974 and 1980, Cuba's regional ranking in the size of its debt remained around the median even though the debt increased fourfold (see Eckstein 1985:487). In this respect, Mesa-Lago fails to examine the island's debt in the context of global trends that adversely affected Latin America in general: a world commodity recession followed by a dramatic rise in interest rates. Furthermore, Cuba is the only country in which the debt figures represent the total Western debt. Cuba's official debt figures include only state-guaranteed loans, but in all other countries, private borrowers have negotiated foreign loans on their own. Were all foreign borrowing included in the debt estimates, Cuba's regional Western debt ranking undoubtedly would be lower.

Cuba's Western debt, like its Soviet debt, must be understood in the context of global political-economic dynamics, not merely faulty domestic policy. There are peculiarities of Cuba's external relations that exacerbate its Western debt problems. The island's Western debt is partly attributable to the unfavorable terms on which Cuba must export to and borrow money from capitalist countries since the revolution. The island no longer enjoys "most favored nation" status in the West. Consequently, Western countries no longer offer Cuba preferential access to their markets and above-world-market prices for Cuban goods as the United States did before the revolution. Meanwhile, Western banks and government creditors have forced Cuba to pay unusually high interest rates and service fees on the debt that has been rescheduled (New York Times, December 25, 1983:12).

Interestingly, at the same time that Cuba's Western debt situation deteriorated, its continental ranking in the size of its total public debt—to the Soviet Union and to Western creditors—and the size of this debt relative to the value of the national product and to exports actually improved. Cuba's total debt standing has held up comparatively well because the Soviet Union made the political decision to subsidize the island's sugar exports more than ever before, so Cuba's export earnings improved during an international commodity recession. Meanwhile, Cuba successfully shifted a significant portion of its import dependence from the Western bloc to COMECON; Cuba enjoys positive terms of trade with COMECON.

Shifting to equity considerations, Cuba is unquestionably the most egalitarian country in the region: in income and land distribution and in access to education, health care, and consumer goods. Policies initiated in the 1970s have reversed the egalitarian trends of the 1960s somewhat, though not to the same extent or in the same manner as in other Latin American countries at the time. Cuba to date is the only country to provide free health care and universal primary school education, plus retirement pensions, unemployment insurance, and low-rent housing to nearly all citizens. It also continues to regulate access to and prices of basic goods through rationing.[2]

Mesa-Lago suggests that neither the social welfare nor the economic accomplishments of the revolution are impressive when compared to accomplishments in Costa Rica during the same time period. Yet data from the World Bank and other sources consistently rank Cuba equal to or above Costa Rica and all the other countries in Latin America on a variety of social indicators. For example, around 1980 Cuba had the longest life expectancy in Latin America, the lowest infant mortality rate, the largest percentage of secondary school age children enrolled in school, the third-lowest population per physician bed, and the largest share of income going to the bottom 20 percent of the labor force (World Bank, 1984; Brundenius, 1984). These are impressive indicators of an equitable growth strategy.

Aggregate statistics cannot, of course, tell us how different socioeconomic groups in the two countries have fared. Available evidence suggests that income and land are more equitably distributed, and that access to medical care is also more egalitarian, in Castro's Cuba than in Costa Rica. In general, the transformation of the Cuban political economy has enabled the government to reduce inequities and improve the social welfare of low-income groups to an extent that Costa Rican governments have not.

It may, nonetheless, be true, as Mesa-Lago posits, that Cuba has sacrificed some growth for equity. However, comparisons between Cuba and the other countries in the region show that the island has managed to improve its regional ranking on many key dimensions of economic development at the same time that the benefits of the growth have been widely shared. Although the revolution has not ushered in an "economic miracle," it has not ushered in a debacle either. If the revolution is evaluated in a regional context, and not in terms of an ideal construct of socialism, its accomplishments are not meager. Although one might like the economic and social accomplishments to be accompanied by a significant political opening, the political changes under Castro are another chapter of the revolution beyond the scope of Mesa-Lago's paper.

Notes

1. Total industrial production figures include industrial sugar production. However, between 1962 and 1976, the gross value of industrial sugar production, in

relation to the value of total industrial output, dropped from 16 to 10 percent (calculated from Brundenius 1979:6–7).

2. According to Brundenius's data (1984:103), education, health care facilities, and, to a lesser extent, food consumption have improved significantly under Castro, but clothing and housing have barely surpassed prerevolutionary levels.

References

Blasier, Cole. 1979. "COMECON in Cuban Development." In Cole Blasier and Carmelo Mesa-Lago, eds., *Cuba in the World*, pp. 225–256. Pittsburgh: University of Pittsburgh Press.

Brundenius, Claes. 1979. *Measuring Economic Growth and Income Distribution in Revolutionary Cuba*. Research Policy Studies, Lund University Discussion Paper 130. Lund, Sweden: Research Policy Institute.

———. 1984. *Revolutionary Cuba: The Challenge of Economic Growth with Equity*. Boulder, Colo.: Westview Press.

Dirección Central de Estadística (DCE). 1975. *Anuario estadístico de Cuba*. Havana: Junta Central de Planificación.

Eckstein, Susan. 1982a. "The Impact of Revolution on Social Welfare in Latin America." *Theory and Society* 11 (January):43–94.

———. 1982b. "Structural and Ideological Bases of Cuba's Foreign Aid Program." *Politics and Society* 11, no. 1:95–121.

———. 1985. "Revolutions and the Restructuring of National Economies." *Comparative Politics* 17 (July):473–494.

U.S. Congress, Joint Economic Committee (USJEC). 1982. *Cuba Faces the Economic Realities of the 1980s*. Washington, D.C.: U.S. Government Printing Office.

Wilkie, James. 1978. *Statistical Abstract of Latin America 19*. Los Angeles: University of California, Latin American Center.

Wilkie, James, and Haber, Stephen. 1981. *Statistical Abstract of Latin America 21*. Los Angeles: University of California, Latin American Center.

Wilkie, James, and Reich, Peter. 1980. *Statistical Abstract of Latin America 20*. Los Angeles: University of California, Latin American Center.

World Bank. 1978–1984. *World Development Report*. New York: Oxford University Press.

About the Contributors

José Ayala received his degree in economics and his Ph.D. in Latin American studies from the National University of Mexico in 1971, where he has been a professor of economics since 1973. He is the author of *Mexico Hoy* and co-author of *Desarollo en Crisis: La Economia Mexicana*. He is currently the principal investigator of a project studying the state, the economy, and society in the twentieth century.

Marcelo Diamand is an Argentine electrical engineer, manufacturer of electronic components, and economist who lives in Buenos Aires. He is a member of the board of directors of the *Union Industrial*, Argentina's main employers association; a former president of the Chamber of Electronic Industries of that country; and the founder and director of the Center for Studies of Economic and Social Reality (CERES), a "think tank" of Argentine businessmen, persons from various professions, and social scientists. His book, *Doctrinas Economicas, Desarrollo e Independencia* [Economic Doctrines, Development and Independence], published in Buenos Aires in 1973, has met with acclaim in Latin America. He has written numerous articles for economic and business journals and is a frequent contributor of articles for the economic and financial press of Argentina.

Elizabeth Dore is an economic historian who has taught at universities in the United States, Latin America, and Europe. She is author of *The Peruvian Mining Industry: Growth, Stagnation, and Crisis* (Westview, forthcoming) and *Acumulación y crisis en la minería peruana 1900-1977* and is co-author and editor of *Sistemas de comercialización de productos básicos de consumo popular en Nicaragua*. She was the country representative for Chile at the Inter-American Foundation and on the staff of development projects funded by the World Bank and the Inter-American Development Bank.

Clemente Ruiz Durán received his Ph.D. in economics from the University of Pittsburgh in 1975 and has been a professor of economics at the National University of Mexico since 1981. He is the author of *Noventa Dias de Politica Monetaria y Crediticia Independiente* and is currently the chief Mexican researcher on a project financed jointly by the Ford Foundation and the National University entitled "Financial Crisis and International Monetary Reform."

Susan Eckstein is currently a professor of sociology at Boston University. She earned her Ph.D. in sociology at Columbia University in 1972 and is the author of *The Poverty of Revolution: The State and Urban Poor in Mexico* and *The Impact of Revolution: A Comparative Analysis of Bolivia and Mexico*. She has also written numerous articles on the outcomes of revolutions in Latin America and is currently completing a book on the Cuban revolution and editing a book on protest and resistance movements in Latin America.

David Felix, professor of economics at Washington University in St. Louis, received his Ph.D. in economics from the University of California at Berkeley in 1955. His articles on Latin American industrialization, finance, income distribution, and more general topics of economic development and economic history have appeared in leading U.S. and Latin American journals.

Albert Fishlow is currently professor of economics and chairman of the Department of Economics at the University of California at Berkeley. He has previously served as director of the concilium on international studies at Yale and as deputy assistant secretary of state for Latin America. He received his Ph.D. from Harvard in 1963 and has written extensively on Latin American debt problems, import substitution, and the distribution of income.

Manuel Antonio Garretón is a Chilean sociologist and professor and senior researcher at the Latin American Faculty of Social Science (FLACSO) in Santiago. He was director and dean of the Center for Studies of National Reality (CEREN) at Catholic University of Chile until 1973 and has been visiting fellow at Oxford University and Wilson Center in Washington and visiting professor at University of Chicago, UNAM, Catholic University of Peru, and University of California at San Diego. He has published numerous articles on the political process in Chile and Latin America. Among his recent books are *El Proceso Politico Chileno* and *Dictaduras y democratización.*

Jonathan Hartlyn is an assistant professor of political science at Vanderbilt University. He received his Ph.D. from Yale University in 1981 and is particularly interested in problems of democratic regimes in developing countries. Two of his recent publications are "Military Governments and the Transition to Civilian Rule: The Colombian Experience of 1957–58" and "Producer Associations, the Political Regime and Policy Processes in Colombia." He is currently completing a study of democratic politics in the Dominican Republic.

Bolivar Lamounier teaches political science at both the University of São Paulo and the Catholic University of São Paulo. He is also director of IDESP (São Paulo Institute of Economic and Political Studies) and writes a column for *Afinal,* one of Brazil's main weekly magazines. He is currently a member of the commission appointed by President José Sarney to prepare a draft of a new constitution for Brazil.

Cynthia McClintock is associate professor of political science at George Washington University. She is the author of *Peasant Cooperatives and Political Change in Peru* and the co-editor, with Abraham F. Lowenthal, of *The Peruvian Experiment Reconsidered.* Her most recent research was focused on redemocratization in Peru and Ecuador. She earned her Ph.D. in political science from the Massachusetts Institute of Technology.

Carmelo Mesa-Lago is director, Center for Latin American Studies, and Distinguished Professor of Economics, University of Pittsburgh. He has been a regional adviser with ECLA and a visiting professor at Oxford University and has taught or been a researcher at Instituto Guido Di Tella, the University of Miami, and universities in Havana and Madrid. In 1980, he served as the president of the Latin American Studies Association (LASA). He is the author of many books and articles/essays on Cuba, Latin American social security, and comparative economic systems, including *The Economy of Socialist Cuba* (1981) and *Cuba in the 1970s* (1974, 1978). He has been a consultant for the World Bank, USAID, BID, ILO, OAS, PAHO, ILPES, Wharton Econometrics, and the Institut für Market und Plan.

Samuel A. Morley is currently professor of economics at Vanderbilt University. He received his Ph.D. from the University of California at Berkeley in 1965 and specializes in Brazilian economic problems, employment, and macroeconomics. His latest book is *Labor Markets and Inequitable Growth: The Case of Authoritarian Capitalism in Brazil* (1982). He has been an adviser to the World Bank, the United Nations Development Program, and the ILO. He is currently working on stabilization and deficit problems in Latin America.

Alkimar R. Moura, who holds a Ph.D. in applied economics from Stanford University, is professor of economics at the Fundacão Getúlio Vargas in São Paulo and also associated with IDESP. He has authored articles and monographs on the Brazilian economy with particular emphasis on trade, debt, and financial questions.

Guillermo O'Donnell is an Argentine who is currently academic director of the Helen Kellogg Institute of the University of Notre Dame and Helen Kellogg Professor of Government at the same university as well as senior researcher at CEBRAP in São Paulo, Brazil. He received his B.A. from the National University in Buenos Aires and his Ph.D. in political science in 1971 from Yale University. He has been professor at the National University of Buenos Aires and senior researcher at IUPERJ, Rio de Janeiro, Brazil. He was visiting professor at the University of Michigan (Ann Arbor) and the University of California (Berkeley) and fellow at the Institute of Advanced Studies (Princeton). He has done extensive work on issues of authoritarianism and democratization in Latin America, including the books *Modernization and Bureaucratic-Authoritarianism* (1973), *El Estado Burocratico-Autoritario, Argentina 1966–1973* (published in Buenos Aires in 1982), and *Transitions from Authoritarian Rule, Latin America and Southern Europe,* which he co-edited with Philippe Schmitter and Laurence Whitehead (forthcoming).

María José Pérez is senior lecturer of macroeconomics research in the Program on Macroeconomic Analysis and Forecasting at the Center for Economic Development Studies (CEDE) of the Faculty of Economics at Los Andes University, Bogotá, Colombia. She was formerly managing editor of *Desarrollo y Sociedad,* the journal published by that faculty.

Edgar Revéiz is dean of economics at Andes University, Bogotá. He is the author, co-author, or editor of *Poder E Información: El Proceso Decisorio en tres Casos de Política Regional y Urbana en Colombia* (1977), *La Cuestión Cafetera y su Impacto Económico Social y Político, Colombia, Costa Rica y Costa de Marfil* (1980), *Colombia y la crisis energética* (1981), *Controversia sobre el Plan de Integración Nacional* (1981), *La información para el Desarrollo Colombiano* (1984), and *Deuda Externa Latinoamericana y proceso de ajuste* (1985). His articles on economic policy, planning, and urban economics have appeared in English, Spanish, and French publications.

Daniel M. Schydlowsky, a Peruvian, is professor of economics and chairman of the Center for Latin American Development Studies at Boston University. He received his Ph.D. from Harvard in 1964 and specializes in trade policy, development, and the Peruvian economy. He is the author of many books and articles, the most recent of which are: *Anatomia de un Fracaso Economico* (1979) and *La Promocian de Exportaciones no Tradicionales en el Peru* (1983).

Paul Sigmund is professor of politics and director of the Latin American Studies Program at Princeton University. He is the author or editor of twelve books, including *The Overthrow of Allende and the Politics of Chile* (1977), *Multinationals in Latin America: The Politics of Nationalization* (1980), *The Political Economy of Income Distribution in Mexico* (with Pedro Aspe, 1985); and *Poder, Sociedad y Estado en USA* (1985). He is currently writing a book on liberation theology.

Index